14693750

AMERICAN TRADE POLITICS

American Trade Politics:

I. M. DESTLER

System Under Stress

INSTITUTE FOR INTERNATIONAL ECONOMICS
Washington, DC

and

THE TWENTIETH CENTURY FUND
New York, NY
1986

I. M. Destler is a Senior Fellow at the
Institute for International Economics.
He was formerly Senior Associate at the
Carnegie Endowment for International
Peace and The Brookings Institution.
His previous books include *Our Own
Worst Enemy: The Unmaking of American
Foreign Policy* (1984), *Coping with U.S.-
Japanese Economic Conflicts* (1982), and
Making Foreign Economic Policy (1980).

The views expressed in this publication
are those of the author. He wrote this
book under the sponsorship of The
Twentieth Century Fund, as part of the
research program of the Institute. It
does not necessarily reflect the views of
individual members of the Board or the
Advisory Committee of the Institute, or
of the Trustees or staff of The Twentieth
Century Fund.

Library of Congress Cataloging in
Publication Data

Destler, I. M.
    American trade politics

    Includes index.
    1. United States—Commercial policy.
I. Institute for International
Economics (U.S.)   II. Twentieth
Century Fund.   III. Title.
HF1455.D48   1986   380.1'3'0973
86–27168
ISBN 0–88132–057–9 (paper)
ISBN 0–88132–058–7 (cloth)

To My Mother

Katharine Hardesty Destler

Who Got Me Interested in Politics

Contents

Foreword

Trade policy in the United States has been central to the course of the world economy since early in this century. Protectionism in the interwar period, culminating in the infamous Smoot-Hawley tariff, was a major factor in deepening and prolonging the Great Depression. The subsequent American embrace of trade liberalization, and world leadership in promoting it, was instrumental in creating the GATT and underwriting the postwar prosperity. The recent reversion toward restrictions on trade, already apparent in the 1970s but rapidly gathering momentum in the 1980s, has again threatened international economic stability and elicited deep concern both at home and abroad.

This book seeks to analyze the ebb and flow of American trade policy, and where it may be headed, at its roots: the domestic politics of the issue. It assesses the interaction between Congress and the executive branch resulting from congressional delegation of responsibilities for specific trade decisions; the interaction between the domestic and international considerations that determine trade policy; the linkages between trade policy itself and related nontrade issues, such as exchange rates and macroeconomic policies; and the symbiotic ties between trade economics and trade politics. Its aim is to increase understanding of the nature and purposes of American trade politics. It concludes with suggestions for reviving our nation's ability to contribute constructively to economic prosperity and political harmony in both the United States and the world as a whole.

The project was made possible by The Twentieth Century Fund, which in 1983 asked I. M. Destler to undertake a comprehensive study of the topic. Dr. Destler was then a Senior Associate at the Carnegie Endowment for International Peace, but shortly moved to the Institute for International Economics where he did most of the research and writing of his study. The Fund, which sponsored his study, subsequently selected the Institute to publish the manuscript, and the project is thus a truly collaborative venture between our two organizations.

ix

The Institute for International Economics is a private nonprofit research institution for the study and discussion of international economic policy. Its purpose is to analyze important issues in that area and to develop and communicate practical new approaches for dealing with them. The Institute is completely nonpartisan.

The Institute was created in November 1981 through a generous commitment of funds from the German Marshall Fund of the United States. Support is being received from other private foundations and corporations, and the Institute is now broadening and diversifying its financial base.

The Fund, which was founded in 1919 by Edward A. Filene, who made a series of gifts that now constitute the Fund's assets, is a not-for-profit research foundation engaging in policy oriented studies of economic, political, and social issues and institutions.

The Institute's Board of Directors bears overall responsibility for the Institute and gives general guidance and approval to its research program—including identification of topics that are likely to become important to international economic policymakers over the medium run (generally, one to three years) and which thus should be addressed by the Institute. The Director, working closely with the staff and outside Advisory Committee, is responsible for the development of particular projects and makes the final decision to publish an individual study.

Similarly, the Fund's Board of Trustees is responsible for its overall program of supporting and supervising research on public policy issues, suggesting different areas where research is needed and approving individual proposals for book-length studies in those areas. Its Director and program staff supervise each project and its editorial staff readies the resulting manuscript for publication. The Fund encourages its authors to put forward their own views, for which, of course, they assume responsibility.

We are grateful to Mac Destler for his informative and timely study. We think his analysis and recommendations will enlighten and inform the current debate over trade policy.

C. FRED BERGSTEN
Director
Institute for
International Economics

M. J. ROSSANT
Director
The Twentieth Century
Fund

Preface

In the mid-1980s, American foreign trade policies came under unprecedented pressure from embattled domestic industries. The immediate cause was economic. Fueled by the strong dollar, imports of foreign goods—conservatively measured—shot up 24 percent in one year, from $269 billion in 1983 to $332 billion in 1984. By the first half of 1986, they were running at an annual rate of $362 billion. Meanwhile, exports stagnated at just above $200 billion.

Such a trade imbalance had no parallel in modern US history. In 1972, Americans had been shocked when imports topped exports by $6.4 billion; this was only the second time in the century that the nation had run a "negative" trade balance. Thirteen years later, the trade deficit had soared to twelve digits—well over $100 billion—and the *ratio* between imports and exports indicated that Americans were spending more than $3 on foreign goods for every $2 foreigners were spending on ours. The last time this ratio had been so unfavorable was in 1864, in the midst of the War Between the States.

Economic imbalance begets political imbalance, so it is not surprising that the United States Congress found itself under enormous pressure to "do something" about trade. Industries beset by import competition were hurting as never before; exporters were demoralized. So even though the imbalance was not something that trade measures had caused or could cure, it drove laborers and businessmen to seek import relief and legislators to press their cause. The volume of trade-restrictive bills soared, and a number of them made uncommon progress. One bill that would severely curtail textile and shoe imports won strong congressional majorities, eliciting a presidential veto in December 1985. In the summer of 1986, a proposal in the House to override that veto came within eight votes of the required two-thirds majority.

Along with this rise in congressional activity came an increase in ad hoc restrictions arranged by the executive branch. In the first half of the 1980s, new quotas were negotiated for autos and steel, and enforcement of the textile-import regime was tightened. Indeed, even before the peak of congressional concern, the *New York Times* could editorialize that "Industry by industry, the battle to maintain open markets is being lost" (14 January 1985).

The immediate source of America's trade policy crisis was economic: trade politics had become tougher because of a surge in imports and a sag in exports. But there was another important factor. This unprecedented economic pressure was landing upon governmental institutions whose effectiveness, whose capacity to resist protectionism, had long been eroding. The story of this erosion is a political one. Its telling requires a look back over fifty years, at how our trade policy-making institutions were created and how they have been changing. And the effects of this erosion will last beyond the current trade crisis, beyond the time when the decline of the dollar from its 1985 peak will have brought greater balance to American trade accounts.

This book, therefore, seeks not only to shed light on the 1985–86 crisis in the politics of trade but also to place that crisis in its broad historic context. Beginning in the 1930s, Americans developed a rather ingenious "system" for coping with pressures for trade restrictions and limiting their impact on US trade policy. This system made it possible for our economy to enjoy the benefits of growing internationalization, and for our government to exercise global economic leadership. But this system has been subject to considerable erosion, particularly during the past fifteen years. When the full force of the import surge hit in the mid-1980s, our trade policy-making institutions were in a weakened state. So today we must ask: can they survive? Through what process and policy changes might they be reinforced? The concluding chapters address these questions.

This book is, in the end, one man's interpretation of postwar American trade policy experience. It is informed by considerable research, including interviews and discussions with many current and recent trade practitioners. The research became the author's main preoccupation in mid-1983, when this book project began, but it originated more than a decade ago, in an investigation of US-Japanese textile diplomacy. Hard data have been sought wherever available, such as, for example, the best possible count of the flood of unfair trade practice cases brought to the US Department of Commerce since 1980, or a careful search for objective indicators of trends in congressional trade activity. But ultimately, the most important events are *sui generis*, and so their aggregation into larger patterns becomes a qualitative, interpretive enterprise. Other observers might well aggregate them differently. The true test of this effort will be whether it captures the issues of trade politics accurately enough to shed useful light on the difficult policy and procedural choices the United States now faces.

The focus throughout is on the *politics of imports*. With this emphasis, the book neglects or subordinates a variety of other trade issues: the direct promotion of exports; economic sanctions; trade controls aimed at protecting defense-related secrets. This approach has its costs. The prime justification is that pressure for import protection is not only the most persistent and thorny trade problem our government faces, but also that the way we respond to that problem tends to shape the way the US government responds to export interests. It is hoped that the chapters that follow will demonstrate why, to the reader's satisfaction.

In the course of writing such a work, an author accumulates many obligations. My greatest in this case are four. One is to The Twentieth Century Fund, whose financial support and encouragement made it possible for me to undertake this study. Another is to C. Fred Bergsten and the Institute for International Economics, where I have had the pleasure of writing it. I doubt there exists anywhere a more stimulating environment in which to study US trade policy. Third, Diane T. Berliner provided superb research assistance and much more: the appendices listing recent trade cases are her work, and those involving countervailing duties and dumping reflect a fact-gathering and organizing effort far beyond what will be apparent from the tidy result. Deepest of all is my debt to my wife, Harriett Parsons Destler, for her encouragement and support throughout my research and writing career.

This manuscript benefits particularly from the comments of many who took time to read and critique an earlier draft. C. Michael Aho, C. Fred Bergsten, Robert C. Cassidy, Jr., William L. Diebold, Jr., Gary N. Horlick, Gary Clyde Hufbauer, Lawrence B. Krause, Harald B. Malmgren, Gary W. Nickerson, Pietro S. Nivola, Jeffrey J. Schott, Gilbert R. Winham, and Alan Wm. Wolff read the entire original manuscript and provided many helpful suggestions. Barber B. Conable, Claud L. Gingrich, Carl J. Green, C. Randall Henning, John H. Jackson, Stephen Marris, Myer Rashish, William A. Reinsch, Richard R. Rivers, Susan C. Schwab, John Williamson, and Rufus Yerxa offered corrective commentary on specific chapters and draft papers. Julie K. Harris and Cindy R. Ware not only helped in typing and managing the manuscript, but also in bringing the author into the wondrous world of word processing. Kenneth D. Balick assisted in my initial research. Kimberly Ann Elliott and Laura J. Knoy helped in the study's final stages. Tammy Mitchell edited the manuscript for The Twentieth Century Fund; Kathleen A. Lynch did so for the Institute for International Economics, and worked assiduously to bring it to publication. But, as ever, responsibility for the result—and blame for any errors or omissions—rests with the author.

I.M.D.

I Origin

1

Trade Politics: The Root Problem, the Current Crisis

Fifty-one years ago, an assistant professor at Wesleyan University published a book on the politics of trade. Its full-blown title was *Politics, Pressures and the Tariff: A Study of Free Private Enterprise in Pressure Politics, as Shown in the 1929–1930 Revision of the Tariff.* The author sought to explain why, in enacting the now-famous Smoot-Hawley bill, the United States Congress had ignored the warnings of experts and had raised import duties to record levels. The reason, he found, was that the combined power of special interests seeking import protection had dominated the legislative process. The "history of the American tariff," he concluded, "is the story of a dubious economic policy turned into a great political success. . . . The very tendencies that have made the legislation bad have made it politically invincible."[1]

The book became a classic, and its author rose to the pinnacle of his profession. He became president of the American Political Science Association in 1956–57, and, to this day, the E. E. Schattschneider Award is presented biennially by that organization "for the best doctoral dissertation in the field of American government."

As prophecy, Schattschneider's book was a failure. He found "no significant concentration of forces able to reverse the policy and bring about a return to a system of low tariffs or free trade."[2] Yet before his manuscript reached print, Congress had passed a bill, the Reciprocal Trade Agreements Act of 1934, which began a shift of US policy toward lower trade barriers, one that would last for decades. But if the author wrongly concluded that the tariff was "politically invincible," he was right on target in his depiction of the root political problem that advocates of international trade would have to overcome. "Although . . . theoretically the interests supporting and

---

1. E. E. Schattschneider, *Politics, Pressures and the Tariff* (New York, NY: Prentice-Hall, 1935), p. 283.
2. Ibid.

opposed to [tariff] legislation are . . . approximately equal," he wrote, "the pressures upon Congress are extremely unbalanced. That is to say, the pressures supporting the tariff are made overwhelming by the fact that the opposition is negligible."[3]

□ □ □

Most people benefit from international trade, for the same general reasons that most people benefit from the division of labor within nations and within localities. By participating in a broader community within which individuals and groups sell what they can produce with the greatest (comparative) efficiency, people can secure a far greater quantity and variety of goods than each individual could possibly obtain if he had to produce every one himself. There are, of course, many instances when blocking or limiting trade can bring advantages to particular groups at the expense of the broader society. But the more these groups succeed in enforcing such restrictions, the lower the standard of living and the slower the economic growth for the community as a whole.[4]

As with communities, so too with nations. Specific interests can gain from import restrictions, and economic theory even recognizes a few cases in which a trade barrier might leave an entire nation better off, albeit at the expense of other nations. In most circumstances, however, open trade—by maximizing economic efficiency—enhances the welfare and the standard of living of the nation and of the wider world.

But the costs of international trade are concentrated. They bear particularly on those firms and workers whose home markets will be diminished by foreign competition. Trade policy must respond to their concerns as well, and some form of action constraining some imports will inevitably be part of that response. Free-trade purists deplore this, seeing a "slippery slope" on which protection for one industry leads to protection for others. But free trade, however attractive it may be as a goal, is unreachable as practical policy.

A more attainable aim is not to avoid all import restrictions but to keep those who seek them from dominating the decision process. Through most of American history, these special interests did dominate: trade policy responded to their concerns all too well. The reason for this was highlighted in Schattschneider's book: there is a chronic political imbalance between the beneficiaries of trade protection and those who pay the costs.

---

3. Ibid., p. 285.
4. For an arresting development of this argument, see Mancur Olson, *The Rise and Decline of Nations: Economic Growth, Stagflation, and Social Rigidities* (New Haven, Conn.: Yale University Press, 1982).

It is an imbalance in *intensity* of interest and, as a result, in political *organization*. Producers and workers threatened by imports tend to be concentrated, organized, ready and able to press their interests in the political arena. Those who benefit from trade are diffuse, and their stake in any particular trade matter is usually small.

It is also an imbalance between clear, *present* benefits and possible *future* benefits. Exporters who would profit if increased US imports allowed foreigners to buy more from us are unlikely to expend the same effort to achieve a conjectural gain as their adversaries will to preserve a current market.

Finally, it is an imbalance between *those who are doing well* and *those who are facing trouble*. Firms with expanding markets and ample profits tend to concentrate on business; their worry is that government may get in their way, by placing constraints on their flexibility and their profits. It is the embattled losers in trade who go into politics to seek trade protection.

Under our Constitution, the United States Congress has primary responsibility for regulating "commerce with foreign nations." Congress is a decentralized, undisciplined institution, particularly susceptible to pressure from organized interests. So if it "does what comes naturally," if the politics of benefit seeking and logrolling goes unimpeded, the result will be a high level of trade barriers, to the benefit of certain groups and the detriment of the nation as a whole.

For a politician who must respond to concentrated interests, a vote for lowering trade barriers is therefore, as one former executive official put it, an "unnatural act."[5] If he is to vote this way—and if Congress, more generally, is to divert or turn back the pressures for trade protection, counterweights have to be built into our policy-making system. These counterweights can be ideas, such as the view of Cordell Hull, Franklin D. Roosevelt's Secretary of State, that liberal trade promotes peace among nations. They can be processes: means of setting tariffs that insulate Congress from direct responsibility. They can be institutions: an executive branch agency that measures its success in terms of how well it copes with trade-restrictive pressures and thus allows international commerce to flourish.

The main story in the politics of American trade during the years since Schattschneider's classic statement of the problem has been the development of just such antiprotectionist counterweights, devices for diverting and managing trade-restrictive pressures. Such devices, taken together, have

---

5. "Outline for Remarks by William R. Pearce, before the Committee on Foreign Relations" (Des Moines, Iowa, 11 December 1974; processed), p. 6. Pearce was Deputy Special Representative for Trade Negotiations in 1972–73.

constituted an American "system" for trade policy making that not only has opened up the US market and fueled our postwar prosperity, but has served also as a pillar of our global economic leadership. The fact that during this period the United States was pursuing, credibly and persistently if not always consistently, policies that aimed to reduce its own import barriers, made it possible for this country to take the lead internationally, and to press others to do likewise. Thus, our domestic trade policy-making system was a necessary foundation for building an international regime of relatively open trade under the auspices of the General Agreement on Tariffs and Trade (GATT), negotiated in the late 1940s and implemented in the decades thereafter. This international trade-negotiating process was, in turn, useful in American domestic politics as an argument against trade restrictions.

Postwar trade liberalization did not institute "free trade," or anything that resembles it. Visible and invisible national barriers to imports remained widespread. But it did bring *freer* trade, contributing to an explosion in the volume of international commerce and an era of unprecedented global prosperity and growth.

The regime of freer trade had strong domestic support. For the American trade policy-making system benefited from the rise of international economic liberalism among the emerging government and business elite. During the early New Deal, liberalism was simply one contending viewpoint on trade. But in the decades that followed it became the dominant viewpoint. As the world slid into war in the 1930s, and as the war was fought and won thereafter, a powerful consensus formed among the American internationalists who took the lead in postwar reconstruction. It was, in important part, Wilsonian: a world open for commerce would be a world at peace. Hull espoused this view explicitly. So did the talented new leadership generation that came to Washington during and after World War II.

In this consensus, the Smoot-Hawley Act of 1930 played the same role for economic affairs that Munich played for military. Just as Neville Chamberlain's sincere search for "peace in our time" had only strengthened those who made war, so too had congressional use of trade barriers to aid depression-hit American producers backfired, postwar leaders believed. Other nations had retaliated, exports had plummeted even more than imports, and the world economic catastrophe helped to spawn Adolf Hitler's Nazi regime in Germany and aggressive militarism in Japan. Only by building a more open world could we prevent the sort of mutually destructive, beggar-thy-neighbor competition that had produced national economic disaster and international bloodshed. This meant reducing barriers to trade, as well as to cross-border economic transactions in general. And in the first two postwar decades, as Judith Goldstein has written, success confirmed the liberal ideology, just as the Great Depression had discredited protectionism.[6]

Public opinion polls underscored this elite support. When the Gallup organization, in June 1953, asked "a cross-section of people listed in *Who's Who in America*" whether they would "favor lowering tariffs from their present level," 67 percent said "yes" and only 11 percent expressed opposition. There were still prominent people in Washington in the 1940s and 1950s who called themselves "protectionists," just as there were still "isolationists." But they were on the defensive, politically and ideologically.

"Free trade" was never especially popular among the mass public. When the Gallup poll asked citizens in the 1940s and 1950s whether they favored higher or lower tariffs, a plurality did back the latter.[7] But when a 1953 Roper poll inquired, "Would you rather see this country import *more* goods from foreign countries than we do, or put *more restrictions* on goods imported into this country from abroad," 37 percent opted for restrictions, and only 26 percent for the goods.[8] What really mattered, however, was that trade was not high on the list of public concerns. So governmental leaders had the leeway to press the policies they felt were needed.

Liberal trade policies were further buttressed by a concern that *was* at the top of almost everyone's list: countering the threat of communism. Military alliances with Western Europe and Japan became the prime US instrument for containing the Soviet Union and the People's Republic of China.

Both the internal stability and the external alignment of our allies were dependent, in important part, on their economic recovery and prosperity. The United States provided massive aid to facilitate this recovery, permitting recipients to buy needed capital goods in the American market. But our allies' return to self-sufficiency also depended on their ability to sell in our market. To make this possible, the United States not only granted market access, following the general nondiscriminatory trade rules of the newly established GATT regime, but we also acquiesced in substantial de facto discrimination against ourselves—in the maintenance of import and ex-

---

6. Judith L. Goldstein, "A Domestic Explanation for Regime Formation and Maintenance: Liberal Trade Policy in the U.S." (paper prepared for delivery at Annual Meeting of American Political Science Association, Washington, 30 August–2 September 1984). Goldstein's full argument is presented in "A Re-examination of American Trade Policy: An Inquiry into the Causes of Protectionism" (Ph.D. dissertation, University of California at Los Angeles, 1983).

7. *The Gallup Poll,* passim.

8. Raymond A. Bauer, Ithiel de Sola Pool, and Lewis Anthony Dexter, *American Business and Public Policy: The Politics of Foreign Trade* (Chicago: Aldine-Atherton, Inc., 1972), p. 85.

change controls while these countries recovered, and thereafter in the formation of a common market in Western Europe.

Such one-sided concessions were relatively painless for the United States for, in the fifteen years following World War II, the American economy dominated the world as never before or since. We were competitive in all major industrial sectors. We were prosperous, as the anticipated postwar depression never arrived. We were relatively insulated, with our merchandise imports totaling, prior to 1960, only about 3 percent of our gross national product. And finally, exchange rate stability avoided one source of trade risk that would become important in later years.

All of these factors—the "lesson" of Smoot-Hawley, the Cold War imperative, US economic predominance, and prosperity—contributed to one crucial underpinning of the American trade policy-making system: the fact that trade barriers were not a major source of conflict between the Republican and Democratic parties during the postwar period.

This was emphatically *not* the case in earlier decades. Before 1932, Republicans had used their support of the tariff to help build the broad business backing that had made them the dominant party. In the early Roosevelt administration, almost all Republicans opposed trade-liberalizing legislation, while the great majority of Democrats voted in favor. But by the end of World War II, partisan trade divisions were waning. In the quarter century thereafter, neither party, while out of office, singled out trade policy as a primary point of difference with the administration in power.

This meant there could be continuity across administrations. Presidents, regardless of party, could champion liberal trade, for both foreign and domestic policy reasons. This White House support was a key to making the system work.

Such was the broad political and policy context within which American trade-policy institutions developed and evolved. But if the early postwar years were ones of creation, the more recent period has been one of erosion, of system weakening, which began in the 1970s and accelerated in the 1980s.

One cause was the opening up of American political institutions. As the United States Congress, for example, became more democratized, more responsive to the initiatives of individual members, it became harder for it to resist the demands of special interests. Prominent among these interests, as ever, were businessmen and laborers seeking protection from "foreign imports."

Also contributing to pressures on the system was the internationalization of the American economy, as trade doubled as a share of total US output of goods. This exposed more and more firms and workers to foreign competition, increasing the number of "trade losers" to whom officials would have to respond.

American anxiety about foreign competition grew as the relative position of the United States declined. The striking success of nations like Japan sowed seeds of doubt about liberal doctrine. Here was a nation which seemed committed to a "mercantilist" trade strategy, pushing exports and discouraging imports, and doing very well indeed. Other rising East Asian competitors—Korea, Taiwan, Hong Kong—appeared to be following Japan's example. Might they know something we didn't?

Concern was also growing about the direct support that foreign governments gave to chosen industries. Subsidizing steel was the rule, not the exception, in both Old World Europe and newly industrializing countries (NICs). Official trade agencies "targeted" growth sectors like semiconductors and computers. It was hard to determine how substantial such foreign industrial subsidies were; available data suggested that in the strongest trading nations they were not particularly large. Still, US businessmen were alarmed: "We can compete against foreign countries," they would say, "but not against national treasuries."

In this atmosphere of broad trade frustration, many became deeply skeptical about the liberal image of a world growing more and more open, governed increasingly by common rules of nondiscrimination in trade. What they came to see was an "unfair" world where other nations played loose with the rules and "nice guys" were likely to finish last. They were willing to compete, but they demanded a "level playing field," not one tilted against the United States.

Compounding these problems in the early and middle 1980s was the remarkable and unanticipated rise in the value of the dollar. It went up 70 percent within five years, to 40 percent above the level where US firms were broadly competitive, before beginning its decline in 1985. The strong dollar might be good for Americans traveling abroad, but for producers it was equivalent to a 40 percent tax on exports and a 40 percent subsidy to competing imports. Foreign goods poured in as never before, and the United States suddenly faced a trade imbalance without parallel in its modern history. Its trade policy-making system was not in good shape to cope. Imports rose more than 50 percent above exports, and the US trade deficit swelled beyond $100 billion and kept growing. Restrictions on imports increased, their legitimacy grew, and protectionist proposals proliferated.

The weakening of our capacity to pursue liberal trade policies poses a severe threat to the world standing of the United States. Internationally, relatively open trade relations remain a central element in the network of economic, political, and security relations among advanced industrial nations, a network which is, in turn, critical to America's position in the world. Domestically, the problems posed by imports, fair or unfair, pale before those which large-scale import restriction would bring. For protection would, in the preponderance of cases, mean greater stagnation. It would reinforce the inefficient, and thus bring further deterioration of our relative position in the world economy.

The need then is to combat the erosion of our trade policy-making institutions. The question is how. One route to insight is to examine in detail how our trade policy-making system used to work, exactly how it has deteriorated, and how it might be repaired or—if necessary—replaced. Can the system of the past be restored, in reasonably close approximation? Or must we move on to other means of dealing with protectionism?

This book opens its analysis of these questions by setting forth the main features of the American system for managing trade pressures as it evolved in the decades since 1934. Subsequent chapters focus on changes in the primary institutions that deal with the politics of trade—Congress, the executive branch, the quasi-judicial procedures—and on changes in the broader economic and political environment. At the end, the author considers what all this means and what might be done about it.

2

The Old System: Protection for Congress

Fifty-six years ago, the United States Congress took final action on the most famous trade law in American history. The Tariff Act of 1930, better known as "Smoot-Hawley," amended "specific tariff schedules for over twenty thousand items, almost all of them increases."[1] It established "the highest general tariff rate structure that the United States [had] ever experienced," with duties actually collected reaching, by one estimate, 60 percent of the value of dutiable imports.[2]

What followed is well known. The law quickly "occasioned," as one contemporary critic put it, "more comment, more controversy, more vituperation in the national as well as in the international sphere than any other tariff measure in history."[3] Country after country raised its tariff barriers in retaliation. World trade stagnated: for the United States, imports dropped $4.399 billion in 1929 to 1.45 billion in 1933, and exports plunged even more: from $5.157 billion to $1.647 billion.[4] The Great Depression—already well under way in 1930—deepened and became truly global. World War II followed less than a decade later.

Not as well remembered today is the fact that Smoot-Hawley was the last general tariff law ever enacted by the United States Congress. From the

---

1. Robert A. Pastor, *Congress and the Politics of US Foreign Economic Policy, 1929–1976* (Berkeley: University of California Press, 1980), pp. 77–78.

2. John M. Dobson, *Two Centuries of Tariffs: The Background and Emergence of the United States International Trade Commission* (Washington: USITC, December 1976), p. 34.

3. Joseph M. Jones, Jr., *Tariff Retaliation: Repercussions of the Hawley-Smoot Bill* (Philadelphia: University of Pennsylvania Press, 1934), p. 1.

4. US Department of Commerce, Bureau of the Census, *Historical Statistics of the United States: Colonial Times to 1970*, part 2, Washington, 1975, p. 884. Much of this fall, of course, reflected the depression's sharp price and output decreases. But even after adjustment for these changes, exports fell, as a share of total US goods production, by more than 20 percent between 1929 and 1933.

"Tariff of Abominations" denounced by Andrew Jackson and John C. Calhoun in 1828 through the McKinley Tariff of 1890 and the Fordney-McCumber Act of 1922, such comprehensive tariff bills had been prime congressional business and the level of US import barriers one of the hottest issues between the Republican and Democratic parties. The tariff, "more than any other single topic, had engrossed [congressional] energies for more than a hundred years."[5] And high rates of duty had been the rule, not the exception.

But barely four years after Smoot-Hawley, our national legislature enacted an entirely different sort of trade law. The Reciprocal Trade Agreements Act of 1934 began a movement of tariffs in the opposite—downward—direction, by authorizing the President to negotiate and implement pacts with other nations in which each agreed to cut tariffs on items of interest to the other. With this authority, he could reduce any US tariff by up to 50 percent without further recourse to Congress. And the authority was renewed in 1937, 1940, and 1943.

Secretary of State Cordell Hull lost no time in exploiting this authority. By 1945, the United States had entered 32 such bilateral trade agreements with 27 countries, granting tariff concessions on 64 percent of all dutiable imports and reducing rates by an average of 44 percent.[6]

In the immediate postwar period, trade negotiations went multilateral. The reciprocal negotiating authority was updated in 1945 to allow further reductions of up to 50 percent from that year's rates. Under American leadership, the General Agreement on Tariffs and Trade (GATT) was negotiated. Its articles provided guidelines for national trade policies, a framework within which the United States and its major (primarily European) trading partners could enter a series of global negotiating "rounds" resulting in further tariff cuts.

This approach began to flag in the 1950s: item-by-item tariff negotiations produced diminishing returns; protectionist pressures regained strength in the United States, and the European Common Market, created in 1957, posed a new challenge. Congress responded in 1962, on the President's recommendation, by authorizing negotiations to cut tariffs across the board. The resulting "Kennedy Round," completed in 1967, produced further cuts in US protective duties averaging 35 percent.[7]

---

5. James L. Sundquist, *The Decline and Resurgence of Congress* (Washington: Brookings Institution, 1981), p. 99.

6. John H. Jackson, et al., *Implementing the Tokyo Round: National Constitutions and International Economic Relations* (Ann Arbor: University of Michigan Press, 1984), p. 141; and John W. Evans, *The Kennedy Round in American Trade Policy: The Twilight of the GATT?* (Cambridge, Mass.: Harvard University Press, 1971), p. 7.

7. Evans, p. 283

When, in the early 1970s, it became clear that impediments other than tariffs were becoming the prime barriers to international trade, Congress authorized the executive branch to bargain yet again—by entering a broad multilateral trade negotiation (MTN) to work out "codes" to regulate government practices that affect trade in such areas as product standards, government procurement, and government subsidies. The result was the MTN agreements of 1979.

Smoot-Hawley, the Tariff Act of 1930, remained on the books, in form still the basic US trade law. But because of negotiations authorized by subsequent Congresses, its average tariff level on dutiable imports had been reduced from 60 percent in 1931 to 5.5 percent in 1985.[8]

Total US exports did not return to their predepression level until 1942. But thereafter they grew rapidly: to $10.2 billion in 1950, $20.4 billion in 1960, $42.6 billion in 1970, and $216.7 billion in 1980.[9] The parallel figures for imports were $8.9 billion in 1950, $14.7 billion in 1960, $40 billion in 1970, and $244.9 billion in 1980.

These numbers reflected, of course, the unprecedented postwar rise in overall national production, compounded by inflation. But they reflected more: between 1933 and 1980, for example, "real" (price-deflated) exports more than doubled as a share of US goods production.

The increase in global commerce was even greater. This unprecedented trade explosion was a prime contributor to a remarkable era of world prosperity. And it also contributed to something the twentieth century had not previously seen: four decades of peace on the European continent.

How was it possible, politically, for the United States to reduce its own trade barriers and persuade the world to do likewise? As noted in the opening chapter, E. E. Schattschneider had demonstrated how politics must drive Congress to respond to producer pressures and raise levels of protection. By what political magic had "Schattschneider's law" been repealed?

The short answer is that Congress legislated itself out of the business of making product-specific trade law. There were exceptions, of course. But, as a general rule, Congress as a collective body was as assiduous in avoiding specific trade barriers after 1934 as it had been in determining them the century before.

A new system for trade policy making came into being. Like any ongoing set of policy processes, it was not created by any one actor at any single

---

8. Dobson, *Two Centuries of Tariffs*, p. 34; US Department of Commerce, "Highlights of US Export and Import Trade," FT 990, December 1985, p. C-99.

9. Bureau of the Census, *Historical Statistics of the United States*, p. 884, and US Department of Commerce, *Statistical Abstract of the United States, 1984*, p. 831. These data differ slightly from the Commerce Department data employed later in this study in discussions of contemporary US trade flows.

time. It evolved, not only because of creative leadership from men like Cordell Hull, but also because it served the political interests of those Senators and Representatives most responsible for trade policy.

Protecting Congress from Trade Pressures

Article I of the United States Constitution grants Congess sole power "to regulate commerce with foreign nations." It also provides Congress authority "to lay and collect . . . duties," and the tariff supplied about half of federal revenues as recently as 1910.[10] The Constitution grants the President no trade-specific authority whatsoever. Thus, in no sphere of government policy can the primacy of the legislative branch be clearer. Congress reigns supreme on trade, unless and until it decides otherwise.

Beginning in the mid-1930s, Congress did decide otherwise, changing the way it handled trade issues. No longer did it give priority to protecting American industry. Instead, its members would give priority to protecting themselves: from the direct, one-sided pressure from producer interests that had led them to make bad trade law. They would channel that pressure elsewhere, pushing product-specific trade decisions out of the committees of Congress and off the House and Senate floors to other governmental institutions.

The instruments for accomplishing this goal developed and changed with time, and political protection was never, of course, the sole congressional motive. What moved some legislators was a conviction that trade regulation had become too complicated and too detailed for Congress to be handling its specifics. For Secretary of State Cordell Hull and some of his fellow Democrats—historically the lower tariff political party—the aim was to reduce trade barriers in any way that was practical. As a Tennessee Congressman during World War I, the Secretary himself had become convinced that "unhampered trade dovetailed with peace; high tariffs, trade barriers, and unfair economic competition, with war."[11] And without the combination of his determination and an economic crisis that produced lopsided Democratic majorities in Congress, the historic shift of 1934 would not have come about—at least not then. Twenty years later, a landmark trade policy-making study could report that protectionists "shared in the consensus that somebody outside Congress should set tariff rates or impose

---

10. Dobson, p.31. In fiscal year 1984, by contrast, customs duties comprised just 1.7 percent of total federal budget receipts.

11. *The Memoirs of Cordell Hull*, vol. 1 (New York, NY: Macmillan, 1948), p. 81.

and remove quotas."[12] But no such bipartisan consensus existed in the 1930s.

The shift did not mean that legislators abdicated all responsibility for trade. They continued to set the guidelines, regulating how much tariff levels could be changed, by what procedures, and with what exceptions. Individual members also remained free to make ample protectionist noise, to declaim loudly on behalf of producer interests that were strong in their states or districts. In fact, they could do so more freely than ever, secure in the knowledge that most actual decisions would be made elsewhere.

Nineteen hundred thirty-four was not the first year Congress had delegated specific trade authority to the President. The US Tariff Commission (USTC) had been created in 1916 as a nonpartisan, fact-finding agency. And the "flexible tariff" position of the Fordney-McCumber Act of 1922 empowered the President, at the Commission's recommendation, to raise or lower any tariff by up to 50 percent in order to equalize the production costs of domestic firms and foreign competitors. (If fully applied, which it never was, this provision would have eliminated "comparative advantage," the primary economic reason for trade, since it is such differences in production costs that make trade profitable!)[13]

But as long as Congress was expected to pass comprehensive bills adjusting tariffs every few years, such measures could never keep protectionist wolves from the Capitol's doors. For those affected knew that Congress would shortly be acting on their specific products, in a process that gave priority to their interests. This could only encourage them to press all the harder, for greater and greater protection. As Hull put the matter, "it would have been folly to go to Congress and ask that the Smoot-Hawley Act be repealed or its rates reduced by Congress. This [approach had], with the exception of the Underwood Act in 1913 . . . always resulted in higher tariffs because the special interests enriched by high tariffs went to their respective Congressmen and insisted on higher rates."[14] What was required was a system that would make the buck stop somewhere else. In the 1930s, the legislative and executive branches began to construct such a system.

The central need was obvious: *to delegate specific tariff setting.* But meeting this need required answers to two basic questions. First, how could Congress rationalize giving up such a major power? And second, would not whoever was delegated this power be subject to the same unbalanced set of pressures, with similar policy results?

---

12. Raymond A. Bauer, Ithiel de Sola Pool, and Lewis Anthony Dexter, *American Business and Public Policy: The Politics of Foreign Trade* (Chicago: Aldine-Atherton, Inc., 1972), p. 39.

13. Dobson, pp. 87–95.

14. *Memoirs,* p. 358.

The need for a rationale for the delegation of congressional power was answered by linking tariff setting to international negotiations, a clear executive branch prerogative. To borrow the phrase of Joseph M. Jones, Jr., a strong advocate of this approach, the United States moved decisively from an inflexible, statutory tariff to a "bargaining tariff."[15] The President could reduce rates by up to 50 percent, but only after negotiating bilateral agreements in which the United States "got" as well as "gave."[16]

Another way that Congress rationalized the delegation of authority was by making it temporary. As Dean Acheson noted many years later, "unlike almost all of the New Deal economic legislation once regarded as radical, the executive power to negotiate trade agreements has not been permanently incorporated in American legislation, but only extended from time to time for short periods with alternating contractions and expansions of scope."[17]

By its answer to the first question—the rationale for delegating power— the Reciprocal Trade Agreements Act of 1934 also addressed the second: how to avoid unbalanced trade pressures. In the process of trade negotiation, "getting" and "giving" were defined in terms of producers, not consumers. But the "bargaining tariff" shifted the balance of trade politics by engaging the interests of export producers, since tariff reductions could now be defended as direct means of winning new markets for American products overseas. Export interests had long been an influence on US trade policy, but usually they were no match for producers threatened by imports. The bargaining tariff strengthened the exporters' stakes and their policy influence, creating something of a political counterweight on the liberal trade side.

Thus, partly as a genuine objective (we *did* want other countries to lower their trade barriers), and partly as a political device, the "bargaining tariff" was an essential ingredient in the emerging American trade policy-making system. And since the United States, from the 1920s onward, regularly

---

15. *Tariff Retaliation,* pp. 303ff.

16. The delegation of tariff-setting authority to encourage "reciprocal" concessions was not unprecedented. As David A. Lake has noted, the barrier-raising McKinley Tariff Act of 1890 gave the president authority to adjust tariffs of sugar and other specified commodities according to the "reciprocity" shown American exports by particular Latin American countries. But such authority was not continued in the succeeding tariff law. See "The State as Conduit: The International Sources of National Political Action" (paper prepared for delivery at Annual Meeting of American Political Science Association, Washington, 30 August–2 September 1984), pp.25–28.

17. Dean Acheson, *Present at the Creation: My Years at the State Department* (New York, NY: W. W. Norton, 1969), p. 10.

extended bilaterally negotiated tariff cuts to its other trading partners (under the unconditional "most favored nation" [MFN] principle), country-by-country deals were an effective means of reducing trade barriers across the board.

In 1934, legislators could grant the new authority tentatively, experimentally. Hull had wanted it to be unbounded in time, but Congress limited it to an initial three years. (However, the agreements negotiated during this period would remain in effect indefinitely.) Hull also would have liked to bargain multilaterally, but he settled for "the next best method," bilateral negotiations, because "it was manifest that public opinion in no country, especially our own, would at that time support a worth-while multilateral undertaking."[18] Yet in one crucial respect the executive authority to negotiate trade agreements was unconstrained by the traditional limits—Congress did not insist on approving the specific agreements that were negotiated.

In subsequent decades, presidents would employ tariff-negotiating authority more ambitiously—to negotiate multilaterally (after World War II) or to bargain on general tariff levels rather than item by item (the Kennedy Round). And in the Trade Act of 1974, Congress would grant new authority to negotiate agreements on nontariff trade distortions, though these would require subsequent congressional approval. Always there were limits in time and in the range of negotiation. Nevertheless, Congress continued, through the 1970s, to respond to new trade policy demands by shifting the basic pressure and responsibility onto the president.

The "Bicycle Theory" and "Export Politics"

One political effect of trade negotiations was to divert some trade policy-making attention from the problems of the American market to the benefits of opening up markets overseas. In fact, the very existence of ongoing negotiations proved a potent rationale for deferring protectionist claims. It gave negotiators (and their congressional allies) a strong situational argument: to impose or tighten an import barrier now, they could assert, would undercut talks aimed at broader American trade advantages. Conversely, the unavailability of this argument in periods between major trade negotiations strengthened the hand of those seeking protection. Trade specialists came to label this phenomenon the "bicycle theory": the trade system needed to move forward, liberalize further, or else it would fall down, into new import restrictions. It could not stand still.

---

18. *Memoirs*, p. 356.

Even in the absence of major negotiations, trade officials sought ways to shift from "import politics" to "export politics." Since the late 1960s, for example, every US administration has had to cope with severe pressures generated by rising sales from Japan. Although interest-group pressures would tend to skew the balance heavily toward curbing imports, officials have regularly, with congressional cooperation, shifted the focus to exports, to opening up the Japanese market. Responding to arguments that other countries were unfair, US trade negotiators did not have to defend them or point to the motes in our own eyes. Instead, they could demonstrate their toughness by demanding market-opening concessions from our trading partners.

But to delegate power over specific trade barriers with reasonable confidence, Congress needed more than an international negotiating process. It also needed two sorts of executive agents: *brokers* who would be responsive to legislators' concerns domestically even as they pushed for bargains internationally, and regulators who would technocratically apply statutory import relief rules to a set of exceptional cases.

The Executive Broker

In preparing Smoot-Hawley, the House Ways and Means Committee "accumulated 11,000 pages of testimony and briefs in forty-three days and five nights," but no one came to speak for the executive branch.[19] At hearings for the 1934 Act, by contrast, 7 of 17 witnesses represented the Roosevelt administration.[20] Congress would not have adopted such a law without executive branch leadership. And if the new American trade policy-making system were to work, Congress needed a focal point for trade policy management within the executive branch, an official who could balance foreign and domestic concerns.

For the first decade, the position of trusted executive agent was admirably occupied by a man from Capitol Hill, Cordell Hull. While he tilted trade policy in the market-expanding direction as much as was politically feasible, the Secretary of State retained his sensitivity to congressional concerns. He moved immediately and aggressively to exploit the new bargaining authority. At the same time, he never forgot that the hand that had granted this authority could also take it away.

Hull resigned in 1944, leaving a gap on the trade scene which would not

---

19. E. E. Schattschneider, *Politics, Pressures and the Tariff* (New York, NY: Prentice-Hall, 1935), p. 36.

20. Pastor, p. 88.

be filled in any durable way for nearly twenty years. In the immediate postwar years it did not really matter. Europe and Japan were devastated. Triumphant and economically dominant, the United States was in a position to sell abroad far more than the world could sell us in return. Thus, it was logical—and politically feasible—for trade policy to be subordinate to the broader American foreign policy of constructing a free world coalition founded on a liberal world economic order. And it was logical for the State Department, staffed by such talents as Under Secretary Will L. Clayton, to continue to play the lead trade-negotiating role.

But in the 1950s, as resurgent international competition once again began to threaten American industries, attacks on State stewardship increased. The department was charged with favoring foreign interests over American interests, with bargaining away US commercial advantages in the interest of good political relations or other diplomatic goals. For a time, State managed to keep the primary negotiating responsibility, and it could play this role aggressively when its senior economic official was someone like Under Secretary C. Douglas Dillon. However, in 1953, President Dwight D. Eisenhower found it necessary to join Congress in setting up a commission chaired by Clarence B. Randall to develop recommendations for his overall trade policy. Randall was then brought into the White House as a special trade adviser to implement the commission's report. And the Kennedy administration developed its major trade expansion program in the White House, under a temporary staff headed by Howard C. Petersen.

So when, to meet the challenge of the new European Economic Community (EEC), that administration went to Congress seeking broad new authority to reduce tariff rates across the board (not item by item), it was not suprising that House Ways and Means Chairman Wilbur D. Mills (D-Ark.) raised the question of whether State could be trusted with this new authority. Should it not be given instead to a negotiator responsive at least equally to domestic clients? No existing agency was a good candidate. The Commerce Department was, in Mills' view, incompetent. Moreover, Mills and another well-placed critic of State, Senate Finance Committee Chairman Harry F. Byrd, Sr. (D-Va.), thought Commerce insufficiently responsive to agricultural interests. So perhaps there should be a new presidential negotiator who could balance domestic and foreign concerns.

Mills proposed, therefore, that the President designate a Special Representative for Trade Negotiations (STR). An important figure in developing and brokering this idea was Myer N. Rashish, a Mills aide in the late 1950s, who was serving as Petersen's White House deputy in preparing the Trade Expansion Act. Rashish suggested that the Petersen office itself was an appropriate model. He believed that conflicting bureaucratic interests made it impossible for the administration to initiate such a reorganization proposal;

however, if Mills proposed it, the President would consider reorganization an acceptable price to pay for the broad new negotiating authority he was seeking. And Kennedy did accept it, but reluctantly; like most presidents, he resisted efforts to establish special-purpose offices in "his" Executive Office.

Congress not only created its own agent in 1962; it protected and strengthened the Special Representative a decade later. When the Nixon administration proposed to place the STR under its Council on International Economic Policy (CIEP) staff, Ways and Means responded by voting to make the office of the STR (not just the Representative) statutory, in an amendment to what became the Trade Act of 1974. By the time the Senate finished its work, the office had been placed formally in the Executive Office of the President, and (on the proposal of Finance Committee Chairman Russell B. Long [D-La.]) its head was given cabinet rank. Long underscored legislators' sense that they owned a piece of this White House trade operation when he suggested, during the confirmation hearings of Jimmy Carter's STR, Robert S. Strauss, that "it might be a good idea for us to ask" the Secretaries of State and Treasury to meet with his committee "so that there can be no misunderstanding" about which official was to have trade primacy.[21]

Organizationally, STR was an anomaly. Though housed in the Executive Office of the President, few of its heads had close personal contact with the chief executive. (Strauss was in fact the prime exception.) For presidents were politicians who, like members of Congress, wanted to limit their direct responsibility for decisions that went against important trade constituencies. Neither was trade negotiating the normal type of White House activity. In fact, it was the sort of day-to-day operating function usually housed in a cabinet department. But no appropriate department existed.

The White House location offered flexibility, balance, and (sometimes) power. During the Kennedy Round, STR Christian A. Herter and his deputies, W. Michael Blumenthal and William M. Roth, enhanced their leverage by initiating close working relationships with State—which then retained authority for most trade negotiations outside the Kennedy Round—and with the international economic component of the National Security Council staff. In the early 1970s, when influence in such matters shifted to the economic side of the White House, STR William D. Eberle and his deputies William R. Pearce and Harald B. Malmgren made their presidential connection through George P. Shultz, Secretary of the Treasury and "economic czar" of the Nixon administration. But whatever the specific rela-

---

21. US Congress, Senate, Committee on Finance, *Hearing on Nominations,* 95th Cong., 1st Sess., 23 March 1977, p. 4.

tionships of the STR, the White House location—combined with special status and separation from the White House political staff—offered him flexibility in working with legislators across as well as along party lines, drawing in some interests to balance others, and keeping the trade policy game as open as possible.

The office of STR allowed executive branch trade officials to do what Hull had done three decades before: to employ their leeway to tilt trade policy in the liberal, market-expanding direction. Sensitive to the political winds, they could lean at least moderately against them, recognizing that Congressmen who bucked interest group demands to them did not always require their full satisfaction. The STR-led executive branch certainly advocated US interests in international negotiations—it had to do so to retain credibility at home. But the role of such negotiations in US trade politics was to keep the game open, to limit protection, and to respond to the trade problems of specific industries with market-expanding solutions.

Domestically, American trade policymakers were noninterventionist. Unlike their counterparts in Japan's Ministry of International Trade and Industry (MITI), for example, they did not aspire to nurture those industries at home that promised future competitiveness abroad. But when it came to international trade barriers, they were definitely not policy neutral. They wanted to limit such barriers insofar as was possible. This made them trade policy activists, for when they feared being trapped by one-sided pressure for protection, they would look for countervailing interests and encourage them to weigh in on the other side. This approach created frequent tension with legislators championing particular industries. But most congressional trade leaders, most of the time, sympathized with the broad objective of liberal trade and, free of direct responsibility themselves, often connived with their executive counterparts to steer the political game in the direction of trade expansion.

"The Rules"

As legislators worked with executive branch leaders in constructing a system to protect themselves from trade pressures, they also needed a different sort of administrative institution, one modeled on quasi-judicial regulatory procedures. For there remained broad agreement that, under certain exceptional circumstances, American industries ought to have recourse to trade protection. Unless "objective" procedures could be devised to provide such protection, these industries would demand specific statutory action. Thus, US law and practice maintained a set of "trade remedies" designed to offer recourse to interests seriously injured by imports, and to those up against what were considered "unfair" foreign practices.

The major legal trade remedies originated well before the Reciprocal Trade Agreements Act of 1934. A law that originated in 1897 required the Secretary of the Treasury to impose a special, offsetting duty if he found that foreign governments were subsidizing exports with a "bounty or grant." The Anti-Dumping Act of 1921 called for similar measures if foreign sellers were determined to be unloading goods in our market at prices below their home market price. (After World War II, GATT Article VI authorized and regulated national antidumping and countervailing duty [CVD] measures.)

There remained the problem of industries injured by import competition they did not, or could not, claim to be "unfair." If, for example, a US tariff reduction led to an unexpectedly large surge in imports, should not competing domestic producers have the right to seek at least temporary trade relief? Congressional trade specialists generally thought so; they were worried about the uncertainty inherent in the international negotiations they had authorized, and they wanted some form of insurance for domestic interests. In the 1943 agreement with Mexico, the United States, drawing on pre-1934 precedents, included an "escape clause" allowing an affected industry to appeal for temporary import relief if it could prove injury from the results of US trade concessions. This approach was incorporated in Article XIX of GATT.[22]

Seeking to retain executive discretion, State officials proposed to include such a clause in all future US trade agreements, and President Harry S Truman issued an executive order in 1947 setting forth procedures by which injured firms could seek relief. This deferred statutory action for a while, but by 1951 Congress had found this insufficient, so legislators incorporated a general "escape clause" provision in an act extending presidential trade-negotiating authority.

By making protection the "exceptional" recourse in the "normal" process of trade-barrier reduction, the escape clause kept the quasi-judicial form of the old flexible tariff but turned the substance on its head. Protection-minded legislators sought to counter this with so-called "peril point" requirements that were incorporated in the 1948 law and intermittently thereafter. These required the Tariff Commission to estimate the point beyond which tariffs could not be reduced without "peril" to specific industries and had the aim of pressuring the executive not to negotiate rates below that level.

If regularly followed, the peril point principle would have made protection

---

22. For background on American and GATT law, together with case examples, see John H. Jackson, *Legal Problems of International Economic Relations: Cases, Materials and Text*, American Casebook Series (St. Paul, Minn.: West Publishing Co., 1977), pp. 617–64.

the norm and trade liberalization the exception. And in fact, with this and other devices, Congress in the 1950s slowed the momentum of trade liberalization to a crawl: by grudging, sometimes single-year extensions of presidential negotiating authority; by escape clause criteria that made it fairly easy for industries to qualify for relief; by a 1958 provision allowing Congress, with a two-thirds vote in both houses, to compel the President to implement a Tariff Commission escape clause recommendation; and by limiting the range of future tariff reduction. In the "Dillon Round" negotiation of 1960, for example, authority for tariff cuts was limited to 20 percent. In fact, only a 10 percent reduction was achieved.

The Trade Expansion Act of 1962 brought major revision and codification of the escape clause. An interest seeking relief had to demonstrate serious injury, the major cause of which was an increase in imports due to US tariff concessions. If the Tariff Commission found that a particular interest met this rather tough test, the President had a choice of whether to accept the Commission's recommendations for tariff or quota relief. If he did not, Congress could override his negative decision by a majority vote in both houses. But while the administration had to swallow this "legislative veto" provision, it was able to beat back a Senate floor amendment adding a "peril point" requirement. (And in fact, the veto would never be exercised.)

During congressional debate, President John F. Kennedy illustrated the political utility of the escape clause by implementing a Tariff Commission recommendation to increase tariffs on Belgian carpets and sheet glass. When the European Community retaliated, Kennedy stuck to his decision, adding that if his bill were already law, he "could have them offered an alternate package [of compensating tariff reductions] which . . . would have prevented retaliation."[23] He was thus able to simultaneously demonstrate his readiness to help injured industries and to argue that trade-liberalizing legislation offered a better way to do it.

The 1962 Act also added an innovative approach to injury from imports—"trade adjustment assistance" (TAA). The idea was originally suggested, it appears, in a Council on Foreign Relations planning paper prepared during World War II, and it was given broad public exposure when proposed to Eisenhower's Randall Commission by David J. McDonald of the United Steelworkers Union in 1953. The TAA idea offered an alternative, or a supplement, to tariff relief. Workers or firms hurt by imports could apply for government financial, technical, and retraining assistance—including relocation allowances—which would help the firms to become more competitive and the workers to move to other lines of endeavor. The political

---

23. Pastor, p. 114.

aim was to weaken support for trade restrictions by offering a constructive alternative to those hurt by imports.

The Randall Commission had rejected the idea, by a 16-to-1 vote. But it was picked up by several senators including one John F. Kennedy. When he became President, he favored its adoption on both substantive and political grounds, since it was something to offer AFL-CIO leaders to help secure labor support of his Trade Expansion Act. TAA was, moreover, consistent with his administration's emphasis on worker retraining as a response to unemployment.

By the 1960s, therefore, a number of administrative remedies were available to companies and workers injured by increased import competition. Substantively, their goal was equity—an established set of procedures, available to all, offering *insurance* against damage from trade liberalization or *offsets* for trade-distorting foreign practices like subsidies. Politically, the administrative remedies were another means by which Congress could divert trade pressures elsewhere. Legislators could say to those seeking statutory remedies, "Have you looked into the escape clause?" or "It sounds like a dumping case to me—can I make an appointment for you at Treasury so you can learn the procedure for relief on that?" Rather than trying to arbitrate the many trade claims, legislators could point to "the rules" under which firms and workers were entitled to relief. And officials of the executive branch could do likewise.

But in practice, the administrative remedies could not satisfy the largest trade-impacted industries. These industries wanted greater assurance of relief, and their political power gave them reason to believe they could do better by applying direct pressure at both ends of Pennsylvania Avenue.

Deals for "Special Cases"

International negotiations brought executive branch officials and export interests more effectively into trade politics; remedy procedures offered the injured a recourse other than going to Congress for new legislation. There remained the "special cases": those large, import-impacted interests that saw in open trade more threat than promise, and which were powerful enough not to settle for such relief as the regular rules might afford. The trade policy-making system also needed means to cope with them, or they might join together in a protectionist coalition and overthrow the liberal order. And even if that were beyond their immediate reach, they could certainly do much to impede an administration's trade-expanding initiatives.

In the postwar period, the most important "special case" was textiles (including apparel), followed by certain agricultural products[24] and steel. Oil imports were a prime issue until a 1955 statutory compromise authorized the President to restrict imports in cases in which they threatened to impair the national security, and President Eisenhower imposed oil import quotas four years later. The auto industry remained committed to open trade until the late 1970s. But the textile-apparel coalition, with its two-and-a-half million workers and firms located in every state of the Union, had sufficient concern about trade and sufficient political power to threaten the general trade policy-making system unless its specific interests were accommodated.

For the first nine postwar years, the industry was relatively inactive. It shared in the benefits of the artificial economic dominance the war had provided the United States. So confident were its leaders that in 1946, they endorsed and cooperated in a mission to Japan—a fierce prewar trade competitor—to aid in reconstructing that country's textile industry during the American occupation. But in 1955, suffering a depressed market at home and resurgent sales from across the Pacific, seeing in the debate over reciprocal trade renewal an opportunity to make the industry's weight felt:

Textiles entered the [legislative] battle in full force. Letters poured in on the congressmen from the textile districts. The Georgia and Alabama delegations, long-time mainstays of Southern free-trade sentiment, went over to the protectionist side.[25]

At that time, US cotton textile exports exceeded imports, and the latter were less than 2 percent of domestic production. But if the industry's substantive case for relief was a bit overstated, its power was taken very seriously. In the House of Representatives, it took an enormous personal effort by House Speaker Sam Rayburn to beat back efforts to open the trade authority bill of 1955 up to protectionist amendments. A year later, a proposal for rigid textile quotas failed by just two votes in the Senate. The

---

24. Agricultural interests sometimes won specific statutory protection for products like meat and sugar, through legislation that moved through the House and Senate agriculture committees (which never fully joined in the tradition of congressional self-denial on trade). At other times they won import relief through executive action under legal authorities like Section 22 of the Agricultural Adjustment Act of 1933, which authorized the President, on the recommendation of the Tariff Commission and the Secretary of Agriculture, to impose quotas or fees to the extent that imports were interfering with a domestic commodity program designed to buttress prices and limit production.

For a comprehensive survey of "special protection," see Gary Clyde Hufbauer, Diane T. Berliner, and Kimberly Ann Elliott, *Trade Protection in the United States: 31 Case Studies* (Washington: Institute for International Economics, 1986).

25. Bauer, Pool, and Dexter, p. 60.

Eisenhower administration got the message, and Japan was pressured to limit its cotton textile exports. When the US textile industry found this "voluntary" Japanese restraint insufficient, Congress added Section 204 to the Agricultural Act of 1956, authorizing the President to negotiate bilateral export limitation agreements with foreign governments on "textiles or textile products." The Eisenhower administration moved promptly to exercise this authority.[26]

What was clear to Eisenhower was clearer still to John F. Kennedy. As senator from a declining textile state, he knew both the industry's power and its interests. As presidential candidate, he had promised action to control textile imports from Hong Kong and elsewhere, which—now that Japanese sales were limited—were growing in volume. As President, he wanted to deliver on this promise. He recognized also that unless this key industry were appeased, Congress was unlikely to approve general trade-expanding legislation.

The result was a special multilateral deal for the industry, known officially as the Long-Term Arrangement Regarding International Trade in Cotton Textiles (LTA). This pact was completed in 1962 under GATT auspices, although it constituted a massive exception to normal GATT rules. The LTA set guidelines within which importing nations could negotiate detailed, product-by-product quota agreements with exporters. And once negotiations for the LTA were well under way, the American Cotton Manufacturers Institute returned Kennedy's favor by endorsing his trade legislation: "We believe that the authority to deal with foreign nations proposed by the President will be wisely exercised and should be granted."[27]

This pattern was repeated eight years later, albeit at considerably greater international cost. At industry insistence, the Nixon administration embarked on a fractious, three-year negotiation with Japan, eventually threatening use of the "Trading with the Enemy Act" to force that nation to broaden its export restraints to include textiles of wool and man-made fibers. Then, in 1973, this too was multilateralized in a Multi-Fiber Arrangement (MFA) which succeeded the LTA. Not entirely by coincidence, Congress completed action on Nixon's trade expansion proposal the following year.

And in the late 1960s, with the steel industry feeling growing import pressure, the State Department shepherded an arrangement among Japanese, European, and American producers to limit the volume of the major foreign sales to the US market. This arrangement was abandoned in the 1970s, in

---

26. For an extended treatment of textile policy making, especially vis-à-vis Japan, see I. M. Destler, Haruhiro Fukui, and Hideo Sato, *The Textile Wrangle: Conflict in Japanese-American Relations, 1969–1971* (Ithaca, NY: Cornell University Press, 1979).

27. Bauer, Pool, and Dexter, p. 79.

part due to uncertainty about its legality under American antitrust law, and in part because dollar devaluation (plus an economic boom) brought a temporary easing of US steel-trade problems. But in 1977, the Carter administration would respond to renewed pressure from the steel industry with a new form of ad hoc import limit, the "trigger price mechanism" (TPM).[28]

These special deals circumvented both national and international rules. Typically, they involved pressuring foreign governments—primarily Japan in the 1950s and 1960s—to enforce "voluntary" export restraints (VERs). This device got around the domestic rules for proving injury and limiting the duration of protection. For the United States, VERs had the international benefit that, unlike measures taken directly against imports, they were not subject to the GATT proviso allowing other nations to impose equivalent trade restrictions unless the United States offered "compensation" in the form of offsetting tariff reductions. In both of these ways, they undercut the American trade policy-making system, for they showed how easily its rules could be avoided by those with power to do so.

Yet at the same time, special deals reinforced the protection for Congress which was that system's political foundation. They kept industry-specific protection out of our trade statutes. They gave executive officials significant leeway to cooperate with exporting countries in working out the form that protection would take, thus limiting the risk of retaliation. They let congressmen play the role they preferred: that of making noise, lobbying the executive branch for action but refraining from final action themselves. (And for foreign firms they had one major benefit that tariffs or US import quotas did not have—they allowed them to raise their prices, thus pocketing the "scarcity rents" available because they were selling less than the market wished to buy. This was the real "compensation" provided, and it was one that directly benefited the industry hurt by the restraint.)[29]

Strong Congressional Committees

Last but not least, Congress needed internal safeguards. For the various means of diverting trade pressures shared one fundamental weakness:

---

28. See Hideo Sato and Michael Hodin, "The U.S.-Japanese Steel Issue of 1977," in *Coping with U.S.-Japanese Economic Conflicts,* edited by I. M. Destler and Hideo Sato (Lexington, Mass.: D. C. Heath & Co., 1982), pp. 56–70.

29. The special deals also exempted foreign firms from US antitrust laws, allowing them to enforce cartel arrangements restraining their trade with the United States. For a general analysis, see C. Fred Bergsten, "On the Non-Equivalence of Import Quotas and 'Voluntary' Export Restraints," in *Toward a New World Trade Policy: The Maidenhead Papers,* edited by C. Fred Bergsten (Lexington, Mass.: Lexington Books, 1975).

Congress could always override them by enacting a trade-restrictive statute, since it did not, and could not, yield up that fundamental power to make any law "to regulate commerce with foreign nations." Thus, since the political interests of an individual senator or representative continued to be tilted in the direction of supporting the claimant for protection, there was always the danger that, if forced to an up-or-down vote, legislators would impose statutory trade restrictions.

So there was a need for internal procedures and institutions that would keep this from happening. Insofar as was possible, product-specific bills and amendments had to be kept off the House and Senate floors.

This required strong committees. Fortunately trade policy had long been the province of two of the most powerful congressional panels: Senate Finance and House Ways and Means. They were the tax committees, and their jurisdiction over foreign commerce derived originally from the tariff's revenue function. From the 1930s onward, their power was enhanced by jurisdiction over social security. As tax committees, they had broad authority, close links to domestic interests, and the reputation for being hard-nosed, realistic, and slightly conservative. Unlike Senate Foreign Relations or House Foreign Affairs, they were unlikely to be disparaged by their colleagues as soft on foreign interests. Because they had other major legislative fish to fry, they were content with a system that delegated trade details, satisfied with considering major trade authority bills just once every few years.

Particularly pivotal was House Ways and Means. In comparison with the House of Representatives, the Senate was smaller, more informal and personality-dependent in its mode of operation. It had always allowed individual members more sway—more opportunity to delay action with unlimited debate, more leeway to propose amendments to legislation being considered on the floor. Once an influx of liberal activists broke down the informal dominance of Southern seniors in the 1960s, the Senate became a very open place, where leaders reigned but did not rule. Senate rules did not require an amendment to be "germane" to the pending legislation. So if a trade-restrictive amendment was suddenly sprung, proposed on the floor for attachment to a semirelated bill, the Finance Committee Chairman often lacked the ability to block it.

But the Ways and Means Chairman could. Because of its size, the House was inevitably more dependent than the Senate on formal institutions, rules, and procedures. And after the power of the House leadership had been limited by the revolt against Speaker Joe Cannon in 1910, committee chairmen—chosen by seniority—rose to dominance. In fact, "the zenith of committee government occurred betweeen the years 1937 and 1971,"[30]

---

30. Roger H. Davidson, "Subcommittee Government: New Channels for Policy Making," in *The New Congress,* edited by Thomas E. Mann and Norman J. Ornstein (Washington: American Enterprise Institute, 1981), p. 103.

precisely the period in which the American trade policy-making system flourished. A strong and skillful Ways and Means leader could virtually ensure that the full House considered only those trade proposals that his committee wished to place before it. He could also place a strong personal imprint on whatever his committee recommended.

The most artful practitioner of this power was Wilbur D. Mills (D.-Ark.), Ways and Means Chairman from 1958 to 1974. He kept his committee relatively small for the House—25 members—and resisted the formation of subcommittees. Working closely with these members, he dominated his panel not by arbitrary action—although he valued and used the chair's prerogative—but by his superior grasp of both substance and politics. He was always listening: to committee members, to lobbyists, to administration leaders and staff experts. In his committee, he knew how to put together bills that had consensus support. And he was determined not to take the slightest risk that a Ways and Means bill would lose on the House floor, or would be subject to an amendment the committee could not abide.

On trade, this meant playing the game of protecting his colleagues: blocking floor votes, diverting pressure elsewhere, pushing an administration to work out special deals when the heat got too strong. And while Mills was a free-trader by personal conviction, he was clever enough not to seem insensitive to import-affected petitioners. He would listen to them sympathetically, and make sure that they had access to the proper procedures. Simultaneously, he would maneuver to avert statutory protection of any sort for specific products.

A classic example of how Mills made the system work was his response to mounting textile industry pressure in the years following the Kennedy round. In 1968, a junior South Carolina Senator, Ernest Hollings, proposed, as an amendment to the Johnson Administration's pending tax bill, that statutory quotas be established for textile and apparel products. The full Senate approved the amendment, and the vote was not close. Mills, in alliance with the White House and the State Department, refused to accept it when the bill went to the Senate-House conference committee; he insisted, as a matter of constitutional propriety, that such provisions should originate in the House. (Trade was tariffs; tariffs were revenue measures.) Senate conferees receded, as they did normally in such cases in those days. So the quota proposal died without House members ever having to vote on it.

But Mills did not rest here. Realizing that the rise of then-uncontrolled imports of man-made fiber textiles meant that the industry was very likely to win some form of protection, Mills began to advocate it—in the nonstatutory form of restraints negotiated with Japan and the other major East Asian suppliers. And while his goal was to prevent direct congressional action, he buttressed the Nixon administration's bargaining position by introducing his own quota bill. If "voluntary" restraints were not achieved, Mills declared repeatedly, Congress would be forced to act.

Mills was playing a game familiar to trade practitioners: hyping the "protectionist threat" from Congress so as to create pressure on foreign governments to come to terms and to render legislative action unnecessary. The administration, in turn, was supposed to talk about the threat of legislation but stop short of supporting it. However, Richard Nixon broke this unwritten rule in June 1970 when, frustrated by Japan's failure to carry through on high-level promises to come to terms, he "reluctantly" endorsed the statutory quota bill Mills had introduced.

The Chairman was now in a bind. He had no choice but to move forward with a "Mills bill" he did not really want enacted. But it somehow took until late November for the House to complete floor action, and although supporters rushed the bill to the Senate floor in December, they were unable to force a vote. Finance Chairman Russell Long played his part by attaching to the bill a controverisal social security-welfare reform package, so it was subject to twin filibusters: by liberal traders, and by welfare reform critics. The bill died when the Ninety-first Congress adjourned.

Then in early 1971, in order to avoid having to travel the same road again, Mills encouraged the Japanese textile industry to develop its own unilateral plan to restrain exports. It did so, and though the limits were far less stringent than those the administration had been seeking, Mills endorsed the plan immediately upon its announcement.

In the end, this Japanese industry plan did not resolve the US-Japan textile dispute. But it did achieve both of Mills' objectives: removing the threat of legislation and providing some relief to the US industry.[31] Thus Mills protected the Congress. He also protected the nation's capacity to pursue generally liberal trade policies.

The fact that it regularly diverted proposals for statutory protection of specific industries did not mean that Congress never employed its independent legislative authority in matters of trade. When, every few years, presidents proposed major trade-negotiating legislation, Ways and Means and Finance were anything but administration rubber stamps. They held lengthy hearings; they reworked executive branch drafts from beginning to end. But the most thorough academic study of the House panel pointed out that in the typically closed Ways and Means "markup" sessions, "executive department representatives not only attend . . . but are an integral, active part of the discussion."[32] And markups focused on adjusting the details of the system of delegation—setting the range and limits of negotiating

---

31. See Destler, Fukui, and Sato, *The Textile Wrangle*, esp. ch. 11.

32. John F. Manley, *The Politics of Finance: The House Committee on Ways and Means* (Boston, Mass.: Little, Brown and Co., 1970), p. 348.

authority and refining the rules for trade remedies. With rare exceptions, general trade bills did not include product-specific protection.

Trade as a Non-Party Issue

As it operated in the decades following the 1934 legislation, therefore, the American trade policy system provided protection for Congress with a range of devices: the bargaining tariff, the executive broker, the quasi-judicial "trade remedies," the "special deals," and the strong congressional committees that worked with liberal-leaning executive branch leaders to make the system work. It also benefited enormously from the fact that trade was not a primary focus of partisan political competition.

This had not been true for most of American history. Schattschneider went so far as to argue that "the dominant position of the Republican party before 1932 can be attributed largely to the successful exploitation of the tariff by this party as a means of attaching to itself a formidable array of interests dependent on the protective system and intent upon continuing it."[33] In the early Roosevelt administration, the great majority of Democrats had supported the reciprocal trade legislation, and virtually all Republicans had opposed it. (In 1934, 1937, and 1940, no more than five Republican votes were cast in favor of reciprocal trade in either house.)

But beginning with the wartime extension of 1943, and increasingly in the late 1940s and 1950s, Republicans began to support final passage of liberal trade legislation, although they often backed restrictive amendments.[34] And by the early 1970s, members of the GOP were increasingly aligned in favor of liberal trade, as was logically consistent with their skepticism about intervention in the domestic economy.

By this time, the Democrats had begun to move in the opposite direction. Policy logic might have inclined them toward protectionism in the 1930s, since in the New Deal they were the party that became committed to aggressive intervention in the US economy. Instead, throughout the 1940s and 1950s they maintained their low-tariff tradition as exemplified by Cordell Hull (who had fought New Deal interventionists seeking to restrict trade), even though textile industry pressure created a shift among representatives from the South, historically the strongest free trade area. And after President Kennedy had appeased that industry, members of his party voted overwhelmingly in support of his Trade Expansion Act of 1962. Only

---

33. Schattschneider, p. 283.

34. For the main votes through 1958, see Pastor, p. 97.

when organized labor left the liberal trade camp in the late 1960s did substantial numbers of northern Democrats begin to defect.

Thus, in the quarter-century after World War II, neither party, while out of office, singled out trade policy as a primary point of difference with the administration in power. This contributed to cooperation on Capitol Hill: Ways and Means, characterized by sharp party division on taxes, handled trade in a bipartisan, consensus manner as the issue "lost its partisan character nationally."[35] Presidential candidates would, of course, target appeals to particular interests—Kennedy sought votes from textile states with industry-specific promises in 1960, and Nixon, bested in that encounter, emulated him eight years later. But the basic open-market orientation of overall policy was not challenged. "Protectionism" remained a discredited concept, and while a politician who advocated it might win gratitude from specific interests, he would lose respect in the broader public eye.

This meant that presidents of both parties could tilt in favor of open trade, as they had to for the system to work. There were variations in their degrees of personal commitment: on balance, Gerald Ford's was greater than Richard Nixon's and Lyndon B. Johnson and Jimmy Carter were more devoted free-traders than John F. Kennedy. But all proved willing to play the role of tilting policy in the liberal direction—in the decisions they made themselves and in the appointments they made to key trade positions. And all proved *able* to play this role, for they knew that they were not thereby subjecting themselves to broad, partisan assault. So they could take some of the interest group heat. This continuing presidential commitment made it possible for the Congress to buck responsibility, and for the "brokers" in the bureaucracy to do their trade-expanding work.

The System's Advantages and Limits

Operating within the broader context just described, the American trade policy-making system had enormous advantages—not just for trade, but also for the major governmental participants. The President could generally treat trade policy as a component of US international leadership. Yet, he could occasionally respond to specific industry constituencies, and he could avoid making very many decisions *against* particular producers, except those taken in broader negotiations that brought compensating benefits to other producers.

If presidents could pick and choose among trade issues while tilting

---

35. Richard F. Fenno, Jr., *Congressmen in Committees* (Boston, Mass.: Little, Brown and Company, 1973), p. 207.

generally in the liberal direction, members of Congress had even greater leeway. The majority were free to make noise, to give "protectionist" speeches or introduce bills favored by particular constituencies, secure in the knowledge that nothing statutory was likely to result. Or they could respond sympathetically to constituents and point to all the possibilities for help available elsewhere, sending them "downtown" to the Tariff Commission or the STR. Members of the trade committees could use their potential influence over trade legislation to press the executive branch to do something for particular constituencies, on either the export or the import side. All could avoid final responsibility for product-by-product trade action, and thus avoid the choice between what they felt to be good politics and what they believed to be good policy.

For the senior trade officials of the executive branch agencies, the system was cumbersome, inefficient, and frustrating in a day-to-day sense. There were always interest groups to respond to, or interagency battles to fight, or technical problems to thrash out with foreign officials who had their own full agendas of political and operational problems. But over the longer term the system "worked"; maneuvering within it, trade officials could manage issues and negotiations so as to limit trade restrictions. They could give priority to bargaining about *foreign* trade barriers. They could bring in countervailing interests if a US industry's campaign for protection threatened to overwhelm them. And by timely domestic brokering, they could prevent the formation of a protectionist coaliton seeking broad, Smoot-Hawley–type restrictions. Thus they could avoid negative actions that might reverse the continuing growth of trade that was bringing profit to producers worldwide.

Finally, the American trade policy system benefited from the "checks and balances" built into our governing charter. Since the prime need was to prevent restrictive action, it proved helpful that much in our Constitution is designed to inhibit rash governmental action of any kind. Division of power between branches and within the Congress meant that bad proposals might be stopped at several points. A President could resist or veto legislation. A strong House Committee Chairman might kill it. The two houses might not agree on details. This Constitutional bias was particularly important in those relatively rare instances—like that of textiles in 1969–71—when a President became so committed to achieving a particular trade restriction that his support for the overall liberal system was compromised. For it meant that an adroit legislator—like Congressman Wilbur Mills—could come to the rescue.

The system had, of course, important limits. It never provided "free trade," nor did its proponents seriously claim it did. What they sought and achieved was *relative* openness, but the exceptions could prove significant and expandable. On textiles, for example, what began as "voluntary"

Japanese restraints on sales of cotton products grew, by stages, into an elaborate network of bilateral agreements that subjected sales of any textile or apparel item from any substantial developing country to tight quota limits.

The system was weak also in the area of agricultural trade. Here the controlling legislation went through the House and Senate agriculture committees, and the farm legislators did not always play by the same rules. Despite an increasingly favorable overall trade balance in agricultural products, the United States imposed quotas on imports of products such as sugar, cheese, and beef. In fact, to reconcile such restrictions (and broader US crop production programs) with GATT rules against quotas, the United States sought and obtained in 1955 a waiver exempting such measures from GATT coverage. Today, when heavy subsidies and quota restrictions deny American farmers substantial markets in Europe and Japan, they have cause to rue this precedent, which is regularly cited by EC trade negotiators defending *their* agricultural trade barriers.

Another limitation was that nationally and internationally, the system dealt primarily with direct trade measures such as tariffs and quotas, tending to neglect broader national policies that had an important trade impact. There had been one major effort to go further, by creating an International Trade Organization (ITO). The "Havana Charter," signed in March 1948, provided for an organization that would not be limited to regulating trade barriers, but would also address such matters as international commodity agreements and domestic full-employment policies. But when the charter came up for legislative ratification, its broad scope alienated not only congressional protectionists but pro-trade "perfectionists" who feared it would encourage government actions that inhibited business enterprise. The ITO charter was never ratified.[36] So these issues had to be addressed ad hoc, under the auspices of a GATT originally conceived as a temporary arrangement.[37]

The system also depended, to a considerable degree, on favorable economic conditions for the nation as a whole and for specific industries. Textile protection began in a decade—the 1950s—when that industry faced stagnant domestic and international demand. Increased demand for trade restrictions

---

36. William Diebold, Jr., "The End of the ITO," *Essays in International Finance*, no. 16 (Princeton, NJ: Princeton University Press, October 1952), esp. pp. 11–24.

37. In fact, trade bills in the 1950s regularly included a clause reading as follows: "The enactment of this Act shall not be construed to determine or indicate the approval or disapproval by the Congress of the Executive Agreement known as the General Agreement on Tariffs and Trade." See Jackson, *Legal Problems of International Economic Relations*, pp. 408–410.

tended to rise with the level of unemployment and the overvaluation of the dollar.

And the system could be shaken if a key player departed from the script. When Richard Nixon "reluctantly" supported statutory quotas for the textile industry Congress nearly enacted them in 1970.

The Contradictions of the System

More important than these particular kinds of limits, which no system could have avoided, were some deeper contradictions. In several respects, the American trade policy-making system would become the victim of its success, as its accomplishments weakened the instruments that had made success possible.

The "Bargaining Tariff" as Vanishing Asset

As long as the primary trade policy business involved the traditional barriers—tariffs and quotas—international negotiations could focus on limiting and reducing them. This made for efficient international negotiations, as national delegations had clear and measurable things to trade off against one another. They could point to concrete results and monitor implementation without great difficulty. And the prospect of barrier reduction abroad served as a brake on pressures at home—protection for an industry could be denied or limited on the grounds that it would undercut the chance to gain export benefits for other industries.

Tariff negotiations also facilitated the delegation of congressional power. Legislation could specify in advance the range of permitted reductions, and the executive branch could negotiate and the President proclaim them without Congress' having to ratify their specifics. And to the degree that trade policy was tariffs, the jurisdiction of the "tax" committees, Finance and Ways and Means, was hard for Hill competitors to contest.

However, the more trade negotiators accomplished, the lower the tariffs that remained. Attention shifted to nontariff trade distortions, which were harder to define and more fractious to negotiate internationally; it was hard to point to clear, measurable results.

Domestically, there were two major complications. First, Congress could not simply authorize a negotiation and let an administration take it from there, since legislation could not fully anticipate, in advance, the sorts of changes in US law that would be required to implement an agreement. So Congress would have to enact trade legislation at both ends of the process. Second, to the degree that trade negotiations explicitly involved many other things besides tariffs, the control of the trade committees would be weakened. They would be under pressure to share jurisdiction. For subjects like product standards and government procurement regulations were the province of other, competing committees.

International Openness vs Domestic Intervention

The demise of tariffs as *the* key trade issue exacerbated another contradiction built into the postwar GATT regime—between the drive to lower economic barriers *among* nations and the increasing governmental intervention *within* them.[38] For if one lesson of the Great Depression had been the folly of protectionism, an even more powerful one was that national economies, left to themselves, would not necessarily provide full employment, much less assure equitable income distribution and personal economic security. So almost all "capitalist" governments entered the postwar period determined to conduct activist, interventionist economic policies at home. Their electorates expected them to do so and held them accountable for the results.

As long as trade policy involved tariffs—a distinct, separable instrument—nations could reconcile barrier reductions with activist policies at home. They could be "liberal" on cross-border transactions and interventionist within the home market. But their "domestic" economic actions had considerable impact on trade, and the lowering of tariffs made this impact more visible. Inevitably, American producers began to focus less on tariffs and more on other nations' domestic steps: the subsidies benefiting Europe's state-owned steel companies, or the buy-Japanese policies of the government telecommunications agency in Tokyo.

The many asymmetries in what various governments were doing made it hard to put together packages of "reciprocal" national concessions on nontariff trade issues. Pressures on nations to change their domestic subsidy, regulation, and procurement policies struck at the *policy tolerance* which had been a central, if largely implicit element of the international consensus that created and maintained GATT. Negotiating about many nontariff barriers (NTBs), like product standards or systems of taxation, raised sensitive questions of national sovereignty.

Within the United States, attention to nontariff barriers fueled charges of "unfairness," the political Achilles' heel of the liberal trade consensus at home. From the numerous specific cases in which foreign governments

---

38. See John Gerard Ruggie, "International Regimes, Transactions, and Change: Embedded Liberalism in the Postwar Economic Order," *International Organization* (Spring 1982), pp. 379–415.

intervened in trade to the disadvantage of particular American producers, it was easy to construct a broad general argument that Uncle Sam had become "Uncle Sucker"—that our competitors were taking away with oft-invisible domestic policies the trade opportunities they apparently granted in tariff negotiations.

Success as Multiplier of Trade Pressures

To the degree that the postwar regime brought about expanded trade, it created another problem for the policy-making system. For it increased the number of "losers," producer interests adversely affected by foreign competition and driven to seek help. It was one thing when the major trade-impacted industries were few and predictable: textiles, steel, shoes. But when imports rose from less than 5 percent of GNP to more than 10 percent, the ranks of the "injured" multiplied. Large industries previously ranked among America's finest—consumer electronics, automobiles, machine tools, even semiconductors—began coming to Washington with their problems. The system, accustomed to facing only a handful of specific pressures, now had to cope with a basketful.

There were also, of course, an increased number of American producers who were profiting from the export side of international trade, not to mention importers and retailers with a stake in foreign products. But for all the traditional reasons, they did not so readily join the political arena. If trade "losers" go regularly into politics to seek relief, trade "winners" generally stick to business. Trade officials and politicians could work to involve them, and they regularly did so, but this only increased their leadership burden.

The Dilemma of the Rules

A final contradiction was one built into the trade-remedy procedures. These procedures were, in principle, an important escape valve, diverting pressures at least temporarily away from Congress (and the executive branch). Yet to remain credible, they had to result—reasonably often—in actual trade relief.

Viewed from overseas, actions granting such relief were viewed as departures from liberal trade policy, signs that the United States was "going protectionist." The fact that our foreign competitors were imposing their own (often less visible) trade restrictions did not seem to lessen their propensity to express alarm about ours. Moreover, if the trade-remedy procedures regularly resulted in restraining trade they would in fact have a protectionist result. Thus, relief procedures that were credible domestically weakened US trade leadership internationally.

In the 1960s, this dilemma was resolved by rules that made escape clause relief hard to obtain, and by lax administration of the countervailing duty and antidumping laws. In the short run, this facilitated international trade leadership, but it brought petitioners back to congressional doorsteps. And the new Trade Adjustment Assistance program, which might have absorbed some of the pressure, proved as hard to qualify for as relief under the escape clause. So in the 1970s legislators, seeking continued protection for themselves, responded by rewriting the trade-remedy laws so that relief would be easier to obtain.

This meant that more escape clause petitions came to the President with USITC recommendations for favorable action. This forced the dilemma onto him personally. He had to choose between credibility for the trade procedures at home and international leadership abroad. To the degree that he tilted toward the latter, he undercut the rules further, creating pressures to reduce presidential discretion and moves toward "special case" treatment for more industries.

It also meant more cases in which US petitioners alleged unfair foreign trade practices. These were particularly sensitive abroad, because they challenged national sovereignty over economic policy, and because they combined "moral" claims (allegations of foreign "unfairness") with what foreigners saw as rules and procedures weighted against them. At home, these cases reduced the leeway of trade policy managers, because the countervailing duty and antidumping statutes granted them less discretion to balance industry-specific with broader concerns.

□ □ □

From the 1930s through the 1960s, the main story of American trade policymaking was the story of the construction and elaboration of a pressure-diverting policy management system. No one planned this system in its entirety. It evolved from a mix of strong executive and congressional leadership and ad hoc responses to particular pressures. It gave the American body politic not only an unaccustomed capacity to resist new trade restrictions, but remarkable success in reducing old ones, as evidenced by a series of negotiations that culminated in the Kennedy Round agreements of 1967.

This chapter has sought to describe the "old system"—how we got it and how it worked. The body of this book, however, is concerned with how this system has been shaken in the 1970s and 1980s, not only by pressures and contradictions such as those described above, but also by more turbulent economic times—for the United States, its major competitors, and the international trading system. The next chapter treats the global changes to which trade policy has been forced to respond. Thereafter, the book looks at how specific institutions and processes—Congress, the executive branch, the rules—have actually responded to this new world.

II Erosion

3

A Tougher World: Changes in the Context of Trade Policy

The 1970s and 1980s brought far-reaching changes to the world economy. US firms and workers became much more exposed to foreign competition in both home and overseas markets. The relative position of the United States declined, as European rivals were joined by Asian ones—first Japan, then rapidly industrializing countries like Korea. The rules of the international trading regime, the General Agreement on Tariffs and Trade (GATT), grew less effective. The advanced industrial economies, buffeted by two "oil shocks," entered a period of stagflation, combining rapid price increases with sluggish growth. Fixed exchange rates among currencies could not hold, and so the world moved to a floating rate regime, featuring massive financial flows and increasingly severe and protracted misalignments.

August 15 as Prologue

The new era was punctuated by a United States policy action both dramatic and unexpected. On 15 August 1971, at the urging of Treasury Secretary John B. Connally, President Richard M. Nixon took several related steps aimed at reducing the value of the dollar. He suspended the US commitment to support its currency by selling gold reserves on demand; he called upon other major nations to raise the value of their currencies against the dollar; and, to get everybody's attention, he imposed a temporary 10 percent "additional tax" on imports. The aim, Nixon declared, was to ensure "that American products will not be at a disadvantage because of unfair exchange rates. When the unfair treatment is ended, the import tax will end as well."[1]

---

1. This action was aimed importantly at getting the US economy moving before the 1972 election, without worsening inflation. It also included, therefore, domestic economic stimulus measures and wage and price controls.

The financial context of the August 15 actions was the increased vulnerability of the dollar in foreign-exchange markets. Since the late 1950s, the United States had been running regular deficits in its international balance of payments, and these deficits had generated intermittent concern, in Washington as well as overseas, about the dollar's long-term strength. Because, under the Bretton Woods system, the dollar was the unit against which other nations defined their currency values, concern about the dollar was synonymous with concern about the viability of that broader international monetary system. Until 1971, the dollar's value had been sustained by a variety of cooperative efforts among US, European, and Japanese central banks. The speculative pressure that summer, however, was of an entirely new order of magnitude.[2]

The trade context of August 15 was a shift in the overall US export-import balance. Merchandise trade surpluses had been a constant feature of the postwar American economic landscape, averaging more than $5 billion annually in the early 1960s. In 1968 and 1969, however, our surplus dropped below $1 billion, and critics like Senate Finance Committee Chairman Russell B. Long argued that our *commercial* trade was actually in deficit, since export statistics included more than $2 billion financed by foreign aid.

An increasing number of economists saw the trade shift as evidence that the dollar had become overvalued. Its exchange rate with other currencies reflected a postwar preeminence that no longer existed. American industry and labor were experiencing greater foreign competition as a result, and official Washington was under new pressure for trade restrictions. Hardly was the ink dry on the Kennedy Round tariff-cutting agreement when a range of industries began pushing for new protection. These included textile and apparel manufacturers, alarmed by the growing imports of man-made

---

For an account of the decision in historical perspective, see Robert Solomon, *The International Monetary System 1945–1976: An Insider's View* (New York, NY: Harper and Row, 1977), chs. 11 and 12. For comprehensive analyses of the forces behind this major policy change, see John S. Odell, *U.S. International Monetary Policy: Markets, Power, and Ideas as Sources of Change* (Princeton, NJ: Princeton University Press, 1982), ch. 4; and Joanne Gowa, *Closing the Gold Window: Domestic Politics and the End of Bretton Woods* (Ithaca, NY: Cornell University Press, 1983). For a thorough analysis of American policy interests during this period, see C. Fred Bergsten, *The Dilemmas of the Dollar: The Economics and Politics of United States International Monetary Policy* (New York, NY: New York University Press [for the Council on Foreign Relations], 1975), esp. part 2.

2. "In the first nine months of 1971 . . . US liabilities to foreign monetary authorities increased by more than $21 billion." Solomon, *International Monetary System,* p. 184. These authorities' increased dollar holdings reflected the movement of other holders out of dollars into other currencies. The average annual increase in such foreign official dollar holdings in the late 1960s, by contrast, was only $637 million. *Economic Report of the President,* Washington, February 1974, table C-88.

fiber products, and steel firms and workers concerned about competition from resurgent European and Japanese competitors. Organized labor, which had endorsed the Kennedy Round, was arguing by 1970 that a new competitive situation had "made old 'free trade' concepts and their 'protectionist' opposites increasingly obsolete." Labor now called for policies aimed at "*orderly* expansion of world trade."[3] As recounted in chapter 2, these pressures, combined with the Nixon administration's mismanagement of the textile issue, led the House of Representatives to pass a restrictive import quota bill in November 1970.

The overvalued dollar put the United States in an economic policy bind. Through the 1960s, devaluation was considered impractical—even unthinkable, because it would undercut the entire exchange rate system on which postwar financial transactions across national borders were based. John F. Kennedy told his advisers he did not want the subject mentioned outside of his office; for JFK, devaluation "would call into doubt the good faith and stability of this nation and the competence of its President."[4] The traditional medicine for righting one's trade balance without devaluation was to depress overall demand. This would, however, drive up unemployment and generate increased pressures for trade restrictions. (And in fact, the Johnson administration did the opposite in the late 1960s. Its inflationary policies—increasing spending for the Vietnam war years before new taxes were enacted to finance it—made the trade balance worse.)

The United States could also support the dollar with measures that would limit capital outflows and discourage other activities requiring its conversion to foreign currencies. The Kennedy and Johnson administrations had employed a variety of devices to this end: an interest equalization tax, limits on direct foreign investment, reduction of the value of duty-free goods that traveling Americans could purchase overseas, even a "balance of payments" program to cut official US overseas staffing. But these palliatives had no durable impact.

Richard Nixon and John Connally broke the United States free from this bind in a way that was deeply disruptive to the postwar economic system. Not only was the content of their actions unsettling; their rhetoric generated strong doubts in foreign capitals about whether the United States could still be counted on to support the international monetary and trade regimes its leaders had fostered. Connally actively provoked such anxieties, in part to increase US leverage: Europeans and Japanese might yield more if they saw

---

3. Statement of AFL-CIO economic policy council, as reported in *New York Times*, 22 February 1970. Emphasis added.

4. Theodore G. Sorensen, *Kennedy* (New York, NY: Harper and Row, 1965), p. 408.

their concessions as the only way to bring a suddenly rogue America back onto the international economic reservation.

Within four months and three days, however, agreement was reached on a new set of exchange rates that effectively devalued the dollar by about 10 percent against other major currencies. Within two years, the dollar went down substantially further, and the major trading nations were forced to abandon the system of fixed exchange rates altogether. By the mid-1970s, in fact, it seemed that the net effect of the "Nixon shocks" had been not to bury international economic cooperation but to give it new life. Realignment of exchange rates restored the US capacity to pursue open trade policies and press others to do likewise. The US trade balance began to improve in early 1973, just as legislation to authorize the new Tokyo Round made its way through the House of Representatives. With their competitiveness thus buttressed, firms and workers were less disposed to press for protection against foreign products and more conscious of the opportunities a new trade round might bring. When the oil crisis hit later that year, the floating rate regime made it easier for the world to make the wrenching adjustments forced by the fourfold increase in the price of that critical commodity.

Nonetheless, from the perspective of the mid-1980s, the world Americans faced after 15 August 1971 was clearly one of greater economic insecurity and turmoil. Six intertwined features of this world stand out: the increased exposure of our economy to trade; the relative decline of the United States, real and perceived; the rise of new (particularly East Asian) competitors; the erosion of the GATT international trade regime; the worsening of "stagflation," with the United States and its European trading partners facing a combination of slow economic growth, high unemployment, and rapid price increases; and the move to floating, and oft-misaligned, exchange rates. All of these developments put new strains on an American trade policy-making system shaped in more insular economic times.

The Trade Explosion

In 1960, US exports to the rest of the world totaled $19.7 billion. In 1985, exports totaled $214.0 billion. During this same period, our global merchandise imports shot up from $14.8 to $338.3 billion.[5] The numbers are in

---

5. Commerce Department data, as reported in the 1986 *Economic Report of the President*, table B-99, and Joint Economic Committee, *Economic Indicators*, March 1986, p. 36. Implicit price deflators obtained through Data Resources, Inc., were used to convert dollar to "real" increases in trade flows.

current prices and ballooned by inflation, but they reflect substantial *real* increases: more than a tripling of exports and a sixfold rise in imports. Perhaps the most important indicator, however, was the growth of trade in proportion to our economy. In 1950, we exported just 6.3 percent of our total production of goods. This percentage rose modestly for two decades— to 7.7 percent in 1960 and 9.2 percent in 1970. Then it shot up to 19.7 percent percent in 1980. The corresponding figures for imports were 5.6, 5.8, 8.7, and 21.9 percent.[6]

The expansion of trade with our primary overseas trading partner was even more dramatic. In 1960, we sold $1.4 billion in goods to Japan, and bought $1.1 billion. By 1985, we were exporting $22.6 billion and importing $68.8 billion.[7] When adjusted for price increases, this amounted to a fivefold increase in US exports to Japan over this period and an eighteenfold increase in imports.

The causes of the trade explosion were many: reduced international transportation and communication costs; reductions in tariff barriers; the broader internationalization of the US economy; the ballooning cost of oil imports, which required an expansion of foreign sales to pay for them. A thorough examination of these causes goes beyond the scope of this book. But the effects of the trade explosion are an important part of our story, and they were substantial.

First and perhaps most significant, the expanded inflow of foreign products brought an inevitable political response. Measured by any standard, US firms were facing significantly more import competition in the 1980s than they had during the trade crisis year of 1970. Of course, exports also rose during this period. But the interests that benefited from exports were by no means comparably aggressive in the political arena.

Furthermore, there was great disparity in the impact of the trade explosion on various industries and regions. Producers of farm and high-technology products reaped great benefits in the 1970s. Overall, "in high-technology

---

6. Percentages obtained by dividing total merchandise exports (or imports) by total production of goods, as reported in the 1985 *Economic Report of the President*, tables B-98 and B-6.

These numbers, which measure trade in current dollars, exaggerate the impact of expanded trade on the US economy during the 1970s, since during this period both export and import prices rose more rapidly than the overall cost of living. But if one employs price-deflated figures for production, exports, and imports, the increase in the trade share of US goods production between 1970 and 1980 is still significant: from 9.3 percent to 13.9 percent for exports, and from 9.3 percent to 11.2 for imports. (Implicit price deflators for merchandise exports and imports were obtained through Data Resources, Inc.; other data are drawn from the 1985 *Economic Report of the President*.)

7. US Department of Commerce. Exports are f.a.s. value; imports are customs value.

industries in which U.S. comparative advantage continue[d] to increase," the US trade surplus "grew from $15 billion in 1973 to $52 billion in 1980."[8]

But those who made standard producer and consumer goods suffered, whether their business was steel or autos or television sets. And the suffering was regional as well as sectoral. In the United States as a whole, employment in manufacturing stayed roughly the same between 1973 and 1980. But in the "rust belt" states from New York to Michigan, it declined 10 percent to 15 percent. Within the highly unionized basic industries concentrated within this region, laid-off workers faced, on the average, substantial drops in their income levels even after they found new jobs outside those industries. As William H. Branson has noted, this meant that the greatest adjustment was being forced upon those very "workers and companies . . . in the best position to bring pressure on trade policy."[9] With their plight as concrete evidence, they could claim that a major American achievement of the earlier twentieth century, the bringing of industrial workers into the middle class, was now being threatened by foreign competition.[10]

The "Decline" of the United States

The nation that was suddenly more exposed to world trade was also comparatively less well off. As late as 1960, the incomes per capita of our major "trilateral" competitors, the European Community (EC) nations and Japan, ranged from 30 percent to 68 percent of our own. By 1979, the per capita incomes of these competitors had risen to between 52 percent and 86 percent of ours.[11]

---

8. Robert Z. Lawrence, *Can America Compete?* (Washington: Brookings Institution, 1984), p. 95. Between 1980 and 1985, as spelled out later in this chapter, all US product sectors, including agriculture and high-tech industries, were hurt by the rise in the dollar.

9. William H. Branson, "The Changing Structure of U.S. Trade: Implications for Research and Policy" (paper prepared for Washington Conference of the National Bureau of Economic Research, 9 March 1984; processed), p. 9.

10. Defining a middle-class income as within 30 percent of the median for the economy, Lawrence finds that, according to census data, the proportion of manufacturing workers earning such incomes declined from 44.6 percent in 1969 to 39.3 percent in 1979. But this drop was not, apparently, a product of a shift of jobs from traditional to high-tech industries, as some have hypothesized, for in both years the proportion of high-tech workers earning middle-class incomes was slightly higher than the overall manufacturing average: 47 percent in 1969 and 41.8 percent in 1979. *Can America Compete?*, p. 80.

11. Irving B. Kravis, Alan Heston, and Robert Summers, *World Product and Income: International Comparisons of Real Gross Product* (Baltimore, Md.: Johns Hopkins University

Our share of world trade had also declined, albeit less dramatically, and in the context of rapidly growing absolute trade flows. In 1950, United States international commerce accounted for fully one-third of the trilateral total. This portion dropped to 27 percent in 1960, 23.5 percent in 1970, and 22.1 percent in 1980.[12] Or to take another approximate measure, the US share of total *world* trade dropped from 13 percent in 1965 to 12 percent in 1975 and 11.6 percent in 1980.[13]

As some of these statistics suggest, most of the decline in the US share of world production and trade took place before the 1970s. Moreover, a major goal of postwar US foreign policy had been to restore our European and Japanese allies to economic health. Since 1970, broad indicators suggest that the United States has been holding its own economically vis-à-vis Western Europe; for example, American and EC industrial production in 1983–84 were each a bit more than 50 percent above the level of 1967. And while Japanese industrial production had grown by *150* percent during the same period, the difference between the real annual economic growth rates of the United States and Japan was only about 2 percent a year in the 1970s and 1980s—compared to an average difference of 7 percent in the 1960s.[14]

But if the US "decline" came mainly in the 1950s and 1960s (an inevitable correction of the abnormal and unsustainable preeminence created by World War II), its full impact began to be felt only in the 1970s. And it was reinforced by a separate phenomenon that was frequently, albeit oversimply, interpreted as showing a *continuing* American decline. This was the onset of regular merchandise trade deficits.

Every year from 1894 through 1970, the value of the goods the United States sold on world markets exceeded the value of those that Americans bought. The inflow of funds from these merchandise trade surpluses was offset, in important part, by an outflow of funds for investment overseas. But beginning in 1971, the year of Nixon's policy bombshell, the pattern changed: the United States ran a merchandise trade deficit that year, and in all but 2 of the 14 years thereafter. And the numbers looked increasingly alarming. The negative balance of $2.3 billion in 1971 was succeeded by

---

Press [for the World Bank and the United Nations Statistical Office], 1982), p. 15. Figures are for "gross domestic product per capita."

12. Calculated by Robert O. Keohane from *UN Yearbook of International Trade Statistics, 1981.* See his *After Hegemony: Cooperation and Discord in the World Political Economy* (Princeton, NJ: Princeton University Press, 1984), p. 199.

13. These percentages are computed from table B-105 of the 1985 *Economic Report of the President,* by dividing total US exports plus imports by world exports plus imports.

14. These data are taken from tables B-107 and B-109 of the 1985 *Economic Report of the President,* p. 43.

records of $6.4 billion in 1972, $34.0 billion in 1978, and $36.5 billion in 1982 (even before the soaring dollar helped to bring the deficit to new heights thereafter).[15] Bilateral deficits with our most-watched trading partner, Japan, grew apace; with records of $4 billion in 1972, $11.6 billion in 1978, and $16.8 billion in 1982.[16]

In economic terms, a strong argument could be made that the single most important source of these negative trade figures was something that, on balance, benefited the citizens of the United States. The overseas investments that had offset our earlier trade surpluses were now yielding very substantial returns. It was natural for Americans to use the funds earned from these investments to buy more foreign products, just as an individual with a substantial investment portfolio can spend more than his job earnings would allow. This also brought benefits to the world in the form of stronger US demand for the products of other nations. Once the United States stopped running consistent net deficits on capital account (i.e., ceased being a consistent net capital exporter), simple mathematics dictated that modest "structural" trade deficits (amounting to less than 10 percent of total US trade) would be our normal condition, to offset our net returns on overseas investment. No one, of course, "decided" that the United States should do this, and we could have made our future returns even greater by continuing to send capital overseas. Yet the pattern that evolved was not particularly alarming, for, until 1982, the United States was, on the average, running an approximate balance in its "current account." Our trade deficits were no larger than what our overseas earnings could finance. So we were not going into debt to pay for imports.

However, this was hardly the way the deficit was characterized in US politics. At the level of specific interests, of course, it reflected a definite problem for those firms and workers most vulnerable to international competition. More foreign products were being sold in *their* markets! And the chronic trade deficit gave them a general argument that could be very potent in American trade politics. For it *looked* like clear evidence that the United States was losing out in the world marketplace.

This was certainly how the matter was viewed by Russell Long, Chairman of the Senate Finance Committee throughout the 1970s. Long argued persistently, in fact, that the standard Commerce Department method of valuing imports in the 1970s—"customs value," or f.a.s.—led to understatement of the real US trade deficit, because it excluded the cost of shipping

---

15. 1985 *Economic Report of the President*, table B-98.

16. Japan Economic Institute of America, *Yearbook of U.S.–Japan Economic Relations in 1982* (Washington: JEI, 1983), p. 129.

imports. To get people to use what he considered the "right" numbers, Long attached to the major trade legislation of 1979 a provision requiring that import statistics be reported on the c.i.f. (cost, insurance, freight) basis "no later than 48 hours before the release of any other government statistics" on imports or the balance of trade.[17] He expected the numbers released first to the press to become the ones most used—and his expectation was borne out.

The emphasis on the negative American trade balance had several related and constraining effects on executive branch policymakers and on the broader political environment.

First of all, it undercut the argument—already very weak in American politics by 1970—that the United States should absorb costs to its specific trade interests in order to help maintain the broader international trading system (and our alliances that were intertwined with that system). The belief that "we could no longer afford" such generosity was hardly limited to Richard Nixon's demanding Secretary of the Treasury, John Connally; in the 1970s and 1980s, it became nearly universal.

Second, merchandise trade deficits increased political receptivity for claims that American firms and workers were facing "unfair" foreign competition, broadly defined. In many instances, foreign governments subsidized products destined for export and restricted imports more than the United States did for comparable products. One plausible—albeit analytically incorrect—explanation for trade deficits was that foreign markets were less open than our own.[18] Once we equated negative trade balance figures with a decline of the United States, it was more comfortable to blame this on foreign nefariousness than on domestic inadequacies.

Third, deficits placed American trade negotiators on the defensive because they suggested a negative market judgement on prior US trade bargaining: we had not been tough enough with foreign governments and were being battered in trade as a result.

All of these constraints forced our negotiators to assume a more demanding international trade posture, by pushing for more concessions overseas and offering fewer in return, at a time when our power in the world was less. This seemed, at minimum, a recipe for increased trade conflict, assuming that our leaders continued to engage in "export politics," bargaining over access to foreign markets as a way of countering pressures for import restrictions at home.

---

17. Trade Agreements Act of 1979, sec. 1108 (a).

18. For the full argument on why, in a floating-exchange rate regime, the US trade balance is not, fundamentally, a function of market openness here or overseas, see chapter 9.

The Rise of New Competitors

The relative decline of the United States meant, by definition, the rise of other nations. Foremost among them was Japan. That story is well known, and it is underscored by the dramatic rise in US-Japan trade that was noted earlier in this chapter. But a few other numbers are worth recalling as well.

In 1960, *after* recovery from World War II, per capita income in Japan stood at just 30 percent of the US level—about equal that of Mexico, a bit below that of Spain. Nineteen years later, it had grown to 70 percent of ours, placing Japan squarely in the middle of the more prosperous Western European nations—ahead of Italy and Britain, if still behind France and Germany.[19] Between 1960 and 1980, Japan's share of total world GNP increased from 3 to 10 percent.[20]

Japan achieved this rise through phenomenal annual increases in national production and trade. Between 1960 and 1970, its real gross national product rose an average of more than 10 percent a year.[21] Its merchandise exports grew even faster: by 17.2 percent annually in the 1960s, and by 8.5 percent (from a much larger base) between 1970 and 1982.[22] Japan's share of world exports rose from 4.5 percent in 1965 to an estimated 8.4 percent in 1984.[23] No other major nation had growth rates anything like these.

Any large country rising so rapidly was bound to cause problems for the world trading system. In fact, Japan had been perceived as a special trade problem, and its products subjected to a range of discriminatory barriers, well before its era of double-digit growth began.[24] But there were other problems in absorbing Japan as one of the preeminent players in the world trading system. As the first non-Western nation to achieve industrial success, Japan was different culturally. This traditionally "closed" and close-knit society had maintained substantial formal barriers to imports throughout the 1960s. The dismantling of these barriers always lagged behind the pace that Japanese export success would have allowed; the de facto opening of Japan's markets seemed to lag even further. Moreover, in contrast to the

---

19. Kravis et al., *World Product and Income*, p. 15.

20. Keizai Koho Center, *Japan 1984: An International Comparison* (Tokyo: Japan Institute for Social and Economic Affairs, 1 September 1984), p. 9.

21. Ibid.

22. World Bank, *World Development Report 1984*, Washington, p. 235.

23. Computed from the 1985 *Economic Report of the President*, table B-105.

24. Gardner Patterson devoted an entire chapter to the various ways that other major trading nations discriminated against Japan in *Discrimination in International Trade: The Policy Issues* (Princeton, NJ: Princeton University Press, 1965).

aggressive business behavior of Japanese firms, the standard style of the Tokyo government in trade diplomacy was not to take the initiative but to await foreign pressure for trade liberalization and to open up markets, bit by bit, in response to this pressure.[25]

Hence, there was a widespread perception of Japan as a "free rider" on the international trading system, exploiting market opportunities abroad while making only grudging changes at home. It also seemed clear that Japanese producers benefited from some special form of government-business cooperation, although experts differed sharply over its precise nature and impact. So, in the 1970s and 1980s, when American firms complained about what they perceived to be unfair trade practices—whether producers dumping television sets or governments promoting development of future export industries—Japan was most often their target. They could compete against companies, US businessmen argued, but not against the government of a major economic power. Making matters more sensitive was the fact that Japan was the first nation, since the rise of mass-production manufacturing processes, to challenge the United States for industrial preeminence across a wide range of industries.

Trade concerns triggered by Japan were magnified by the rise of "new Japans": nations that were following Japan's rapid-growth, export-expanding path. The most impressive single example, perhaps, was the Republic of Korea, whose exports increased annually by 35 percent in the 1960s and 20 percent in the 1970s, and whose growth in income paralleled Japan's, albeit at lower levels.[26] Taken together, the share of the newly industrializing countries (NICs)—including Korea, Taiwan, Singapore, Brazil, and Mexico—in world exports rose from 6 percent in 1970 to 9.3 percent in 1980 and 11.4 percent in 1983.[27] Thus, from the 1970s onward, American firms faced a trading world very different from the bipolar (US-EC) one of the Kennedy Round.

---

25. American trade negotiators, by contrast, were prone to take the initiative, in part to channel trade pressures in the export-expanding, rather than import-restricting direction. Hence, "officials in both governments" have recurrently employed "intense, highly visible United States pressure as a catalyst for Japanese policy change." *Report of the Japan–United States Economic Relations Group* (prepared for the President of the United States and the Prime Minister of Japan, Tokyo and Washington, January 1981), p. 101. See also *Coping With U.S.–Japanese Economic Conflicts*, edited by I. M. Destler and Hideo Sato (Lexington, Mass.: Lexington Books, 1982), esp. pp. 279–81.

26. By the estimates of Kravis et al., gross domestic income per capita for Korea rose from 8.15 percent of the US level in 1960 to 24.8 percent in 1979. *World Product and Income*, p. 15. Korean export statistics are drawn from *World Development Report 1984*, p. 235.

27. IMF statistics, taken from Ernest H. Preeg, "Overview" (paper prepared for Overseas Development Council conference on US Trade Policy and Developing Countries, Washington, 28–29 September 1984), pp. 7, 10.

The Erosion of the GATT

Even as these new competitors were emerging, the system of rules for regulating international trade was weakening. In the first two postwar decades, the General Agreement on Tariffs and Trade (GATT) had provided a surprisingly effective framework for negotiating trade liberalization and disciplining import restrictions. But its impact diminished thereafter.[28]

One reason for its erosion was the identity of the new competitors. GATT had originated as a North American–European enterprise, shaped by leaders who drew common lessons from the prewar (and wartime) experience. Nations from these two continents continued to provide its primary political leadership through the 1970s, but the rise of other nations meant that the lead trading states now formed a less homogeneous community, making it harder to maintain agreement on trade policy norms. And since the new competitors were slow to assert leadership in multilateral trade negotiations, there was a growing divergence between the loci of trade-political activism and trade-economic power.

A second reason for GATT's weakening was, ironically, the enormous success of what it did best: multilateral tariff-cutting negotiations (MTN). As noted in chapter 2, the remarkable postwar reductions in customs duties forced international trade relations onto the harder ground of nontariff trade barriers: harder to measure and negotiate, more intertwined with issues of domestic policy and national sovereignty, and not well defined by the original GATT rules. The Tokyo Round, or MTN, of the 1970s resulted in agreement on a number of "codes" addressing such subjects as subsidies, dumping, product standards, and government procurement. But not all GATT members accepted the obligations of these codes, and enforcement procedures in the early 1980s proved slow and cumbersome.

A more general problem for the GATT was the erosion of its bedrock principle of nondiscrimination, the core notion that each national government would grant equal treatment to the products of all others adhering to the GATT system. The European Community was one enormous exception; by definition, its members agreed to grant one another more favorable (i.e., duty-free) market access than they granted to outsiders. Tariff preferences for less developed countries were another exception.

Governments discriminated among nations in restricting imports as well as in admitting them. Under the GATT escape clause, Article XIX, members

---

28. For a good summary of the original GATT system and its evolution, see Miriam Camps and William Diebold, Jr., "The Old Multilateralism and What Became of It," *The New Multilateralism: Can the World Trading System Be Saved?* (New York, NY: Council on Foreign Relations, 1983), ch. 1.

were allowed to impose temporary import barriers for the products of trade-injured industries. But they were supposed to do this on a nondiscriminatory basis. In practice, Article XIX was increasingly circumvented by "voluntary" export restraints (VERs) or orderly marketing agreements (OMAs), in which specific exporting nations agreed to limit their sales. Such arrangements became the norm for trade in textiles and apparel; they spread to steel and automobiles; and, in particular, they were employed to limit the sales of such rapidly rising competitors as Japan and the NICs.

For American trade policymakers, the erosion of the GATT weakened one important postwar source of leverage in domestic trade bargaining: the argument that a particular restrictive action would undercut the international trading system from which we derived great benefits. For the more the international trade regime was viewed as ineffective and riddled with exceptions, the less credible was any claim that US interests were served by following the rules that remained.

Stagflation

GATT also faced growing strain because, during the 1970s, the United States and its advanced industrial trading partners were beset with what became labeled as "stagflation": slow growth and high unemployment coexisting with high inflation. The United States sowed the seeds of the stagflation era when, for several years, Lyndon B. Johnson refused to seek a tax hike to finance the Vietnam War. Richard Nixon made matters worse with his overstimulation of the American economy in the election year of 1972. In both cases, the United States pursued fiscal and monetary policies that increased overall demand at a time our production was at or near capacity. The immediate result was price rises, which proved contagious. By early 1973, inflation in the United States was running at double-digit levels.

Then came the October War in the Middle East. Seizing the opportunity presented by tight supply conditions, members of the Organization of Petroleum Exporting Countries (OPEC) quadrupled the price at which they offered their crude oil on world markets. This generated enormous new inflationary pressure, driving up costs for productive enterprises and gasoline-dependent consumers. At the same time, the "oil shock" depressed demand in all the advanced industrial countries, since paying for needed oil imports at the new prices forced a massive shift of funds from consumer to producer countries. The world plunged from a 1973 boom to a 1974 recession—the deepest of the postwar era. Then in 1979, revolution in Iran led to the second "oil shock," a near-tripling of the OPEC export price. Again, inflation rates rose and the world economy plunged into recession.

Once under way, "stagflation" proved endemic. The higher our rate of inflation became, the greater the level of unemployment that was needed to wring expectations of future inflation out of the economy. Hence, in 1979, the Federal Reserve Board under Paul A. Volcker began to pursue consistently tight money policies, even as growth flagged and the number of jobless increased. What economists and journalists came to label the "misery index," the sum of the unemployment and inflation rates, rose to new heights.

Statistics once viewed with alarm came to be seen as normal, even encouraging. In the United States in 1957, a 3.6 percent rise in the consumer price index (CPI) had alarmed the Eisenhower administration; for more than a decade thereafter, the country did not again see a year-to-year increase above 3 percent. But the 1970s and 1980s brought us four years of double-digit price inflation, and Ronald Reagan could claim victory when the 1983 CPI was "only" 3.2 percent above that of 1982.[29] Prior to 1975, the highest annual postwar rates of civilian unemployment were 6.8 percent in 1958 and 6.7 percent in 1961. By 1982, unemployment reached 9.7 percent. Our expectations were so reduced that in a year when unemployment averaged 7.5 percent, Reagan could be credited with an impressive economic recovery and ride to a landslide reelection victory.[30]

The trade problems of key industries were exacerbated by their failure to adjust to this less congenial environment. Management and labor continued to negotiate hefty wage increases, notwithstanding slower domestic growth and stiffer international competition: "In 1970 hourly compensation for auto and steel workers was about 30 percent higher than the average compensation in manufacturing. By 1981 the difference had grown to 70 percent for steel workers and 50 percent for auto workers."[31] Only after both industries faced massive layoffs were significant wage and benefit concessions forthcoming.

The twin perils of stagflation and high wages spurred a decline in the rate of economic growth. Not only did the United States experience five negative growth years between 1970 and 1982 (there were none from 1959 to 1969), but its average GNP growth also fell by a percentage point despite an exceptional increase in the labor force.[32] Nor were such changes affecting

---

29. 1985 *Economic Report of the President*, tables B-54 and B-55.

30. Ibid., table B-29. By the end of 1985, Reagan (and the US economy) were beginning also to benefit from an oil *glut*, precipitating a sharp decline in oil prices and undermining the always tenuous OPEC effort to buttress them through national production quotas.

31. 1984 *Economic Report of the President*, p. 92.

32. Average US GNP growth was 3.95 percent in 1961–70, 3.03 percent in 1971–84. Yet the labor force grew by 29 percent in 1971–80, much more than in either previous postwar decade. See 1985 *Economic Report of the President*, tables B-2, B-109, and B-29.

the United States alone. All advanced industrial nations found the going harder after the early 1970s. Average Japanese growth of 4.8 percent in 1971–80 might look good to Americans and Europeans, but it was a big drop from the 10.6 percent of the decade preceding.[33] The worsening in our unemployment looked bad until the much steeper proportionate rises were considered in Germany, France, Canada, and above all, Britain, whose jobless rate leaped from 3 percent in 1970 to 13 percent in 1984![34]

All this meant that the United States was not alone in feeling beset with economic difficulties. Thus, with the partial exception of Japan, other nations would not be very receptive to American demands that they give us more in international trade talks than they were likely to get in return.

Floating Exchange Rates and Dollar "Misalignment"

Last but certainly not least, the monetary regime within which we faced these new difficulties was no longer the Bretton Woods system of fixed exchange rates pegged to the dollar, but one in which the dollar's relative price—the single most important determinant of our producers' trade competitiveness—was being set and reset, day after day, in foreign-exchange markets.

As noted at the outset of this chapter, the end of Bretton Woods initially made life easier for US trade policymakers. The "Nixon shock" of 15 August 1971 had begun the process, and devaluations of roughly 10 percent followed in December 1971 and February 1973. Renewed currency speculation forced the major trading nations to move to a floating-rate regime a month later, in March 1973. After that, the markets generally kept the real (inflation-adjusted) value of the dollar at or below the March 1973 level through the Nixon, Ford, and Carter administrations.[35] American exports benefited; import competition eased somewhat; the management of trade-restrictive pressures was somewhat less of a burden. And it was at a time of dollar weakness, with US exports expanding rapidly, that the world completed, and Congress approved, the Tokyo Round agreements aimed at reducing nontariff barriers to trade.

However, in the first half of the 1980s, this exchange rate situation reversed itself with a vengeance. From its trough in 1980 to its peak in late February

---

33. Ibid., table B-109.

34. Ibid., table B-108.

35. In fact, the markets brought the dollar sharply down in the early Carter administration, necessitating a "dollar defense" initiative on 1 November 1978 to reverse this fall.

1985, the trade-weighted value of the dollar rose an incredible 70.2 percent.[36] At this point, the dollar was roughly 40 percent above the level that would have brought balance to the US current account. This meant that American producers of internationally traded goods faced a 40 percent cost disadvantage in relation to foreign rivals in the US and overseas markets. In terms of trade competitiveness, this was a severe and protracted currency "misalignment" that had been unseen—and unforeseen—by postwar economists, businessmen, and politicians.[37]

Beginning in March 1985, the dollar began to decline. Given a major push by a joint declaration of the Group of Five finance ministers in September, its trade-weighted value dropped 29 percent from its Februrary 1985 peak to September 1986, to a level that seemed likely to bring some improvement to the US trade balance in 1977 and 1978. But for that balance to approach zero, the dollar would likely need to fall still further.[38]

How could the exchange rate shift so much? How could the dollar not merely reach a level that was rendering many American products uncompetitive, as it had by mid-1982, but keep rising for years thereafter despite burgeoning US trade deficits? A critical underlying source of such persistent currency misalignment was a revolution in world capital markets.

Many international economists had favored a floating exchange rate system well before the world was forced to accept one. Generally, they expected that trade transactions would dominate foreign currency markets. Since the trade competitiveness of major countries was generally slow in changing, this would mean that relationships among the strong currencies would be

---

36. Calculations by Institute for International Economics, released 18 December 1985 upon publication of Stephen Marris, *Deficits and the Dollar: The World Economy at Risk*, POLICY ANALYSES IN INTERNATIONAL ECONOMICS 14 (Washington: Institute for International Economics).

37. For a definition of currency "misalignments" and some proposals for reducing them, see John Williamson, *The Exchange Rate System*, POLICY ANALYSES IN INTERNATIONAL ECONOMICS 5 (Washington: Institute for International Economics, September 1983, rev. June 1985), p. 12. On the curious early 1985 psychology by which movement of virtually any economic indicator in any direction seemed to be read, in foreign-exchange markets, as bullish for the dollar, see C. Fred Bergsten, "The Second Debt Crisis Is Coming," *Challenge* (May–June 1985), esp. p. 17.

38. As of 25 September 1986, the dollar had declined 29 percent from its 25 February 1985 value (MERM index), and 20 percent from the 22 September 1985 meeting of the Group of Five. Against the Japanese yen, it had fallen considerably further—from 262 and 239 to the dollar, respectively, in February and September 1985 to around 154 in September 1986. Still, according to projections by the Institute for International Economics, even this major drop would only bring the US trade deficit a bit below $100 billion by 1988. (Marris, preface to the French edition of *Deficits and the Dollar*.) For more on the "Group of Five" initiative of September 1985, see chapter 9.

rather stable.[39] Shifts would be gradual, and a function primarily of shifts in trade flows.

What no one anticipated was the impact of the dramatic increase in the magnitude and international mobility of investment capital, particularly "short-term" funds seeking the most rewarding current situation. As one informed observer characterized matters in early 1985:

The flow of money was now dwarfing the growth of world trade. In 1984, for example, world trade in goods and services was on the order of $2 trillion, while global capital transfers reached $20-30 trillion.[40]

This meant that exchange rates were increasingly driven not by trade transactions, but by whatever might cause those who controlled capital to shift funds from one currency to another. Portfolio managers, responsible for large pools of investment money, became critical participants in the world economy. And while no school of economics could model their behavior with much confidence, they seemed to be motivated primarily by two factors: differences in real interest-rate returns between countries and anticipation as to where, in the near term, a currency's value was likely to move. (An additional factor was the safe haven phenomenon, the preference for placing funds in a country in whose political strength and stability investors had confidence.)

When a major country like the United States pursued policies the markets perceived as inflationary—likely to reduce the currency's value and hence the "real" returns on dollar assets—that currency's value plummeted. The swing was exacerbated by the herd instinct of money managers, whose rewards come from calling *today's* market correctly. Thus the dollar sank in 1977 and 1978.

When, conversely, the United States moved in 1981 to a mix of economic policies that raised real interest rates, funds poured into dollar assets. The United States now needed foreign funds to finance its suddenly mammoth budget deficits. Money flowed in, enticed by favorable returns, and drove the dollar skyward. Reinforcing this flow of money were increased market optimism about future American economic and political prospects, and increased pessimism about those of Europe. Thus, by the end of 1984, a dollar would buy more than twice as many French francs, British pounds,

---

39. This would not, of course, apply to the currencies of countries experiencing very high inflation.

40. Jeffrey E. Garten, "Gunboat Economics," *Foreign Affairs,* vol. 63, no. 3 (America and the World, 1984), p. 453. As Garten's broad range suggests, estimates of the magnitude of capital flows were necessarily imprecise.

and German marks as it had in October 1978. The dollar could even buy about 40 percent more Japanese yen.

The strong dollar brought some major short-term benefits to the American economy. It made imports cheaper, thus dampening inflation. And the same capital flow that strengthened our currency made it possible for us to finance our huge budget deficit *and* the increases in private investment that was important to the Reagan recovery.

But US producers of traded goods found their competitive position demolished, as the currency misalignment made foreign goods far cheaper for Americans to buy and American products very dear for purchasers overseas. The overall US trade deficit ballooned to $67 billion in 1983, $114 billion in 1984, and $124 billion in 1985.

The strong dollar was not the sole cause of the enormous shift.[41] But Secretary of State George P. Shultz stated the consensus view when he blamed it for "over half . . . of the deterioration in the US trade account."[42] From the perspective of producers of traded goods, the strong dollar of the mid-1980s was a devastating source of competitive disadvantage. It was something about which they, as individual economic agents, could do absolutely nothing. And it was something against which traditional inter-governmental trade bargaining was impotent as well.

A Tougher World

As these six changes were intertwined, so too were their political effects. Explosion in the volume of trade meant greater import competition for American producers, and hence greater pressure for trade restrictions, even in the 1970s when the dollar was comparatively weak. The dollar misalignment of the 1980s compounded the political problem. It increased the volume of imports and consequent protectionist reaction, while demoralizing export interests because it curtailed their gains from open trade.[43]

The diminished relative position of the United States joined with stagflation to cast a shadow on future American economic prospects. It thus

---

41. The other major sources were the developing-country debt crisis, which sharply curtailed exports to Latin America, and the fact that the US economy grew more rapidly, in 1983 and 1984, than those of its major trading partners.

42. "National Policies and Global Prosperity" (address at the Woodrow Wilson School, Princeton University, Princeton, NJ, 11 April 1985; processed).

43. As 1986 began, relief was beginning to be felt as the declining dollar eased the pressure on trade-impacted industries. But for reasons elaborated on in chapter 9, the full effect would be more than a year in coming.

discredited, to a degree, arguments for continuing commitment to open trade. More generally, as successive presidents found themselves embattled with economic woes, they had less leeway to press market-opening measures at home, and felt more pressure to restrict trade in specific products.

Stagflation and American "decline" were accompanied by the growing visibility of unfair foreign trade practices, and unequal market access in specific product areas. Thus, there was an understandable tendency to blame at least some of the "decline" on these foreign trade practices. The weakening of the GATT made it harder to achieve effective remedies for unfair practices within the multilateral system; therefore, pressure for unilateral responses increased. Reinforcing such pressure was the threatening nature of our new competitors—Japan, the NICs—whose trade was growing at historically unprecedented rates, who clearly benefited from some form of government-business cooperation, and whose aggressiveness in exports preceded and exceeded their willingness to open their markets to imports.

Changes of this magnitude would have posed severe problems for the American trade policy-making system even if it had retained its basic postwar character and strength. But it too was changing. This was due in part to the new international economic realities, but in part to developments that were specific to US politics.

We turn now to these domestic system changes—the primary focus of this book. And we begin with the United States Congress, that central Constitutional authority whose interest in protecting itself from trade pressures was the key element in the effectiveness of the old trade order.

A Less Protected Congress

For most of the postwar period, the United States Congress was remarkably restrained in the exercise of its constitutional authority to "regulate commerce with foreign nations." Individual senators and representatives engaged in a great deal of trade rhetoric; they gave their names to hundreds of bills proposing trade restrictions for industries that were strong within their constituencies. Congress periodically passed general trade laws to extend, expand, and limit presidential negotiating authority: the reciprocal trade act renewals in the 1950s, as well as larger authorization acts like those of 1962 and 1974. There were also times when Congress failed to deliver on important executive commitments: to the International Trade Organization charter of 1948, for example, or to the Kennedy Round antidumping agreement signed almost twenty years later.

But product-specific legislative output was sparse. Senators and representatives consistently referred particular cases elsewhere: to the Tariff Commission for assessing injury to petitioning industries, for example, or to the executive for negotiating tariff cuts or arranging limits on the inflow of particularly sensitive commodities. Bills proposing statutory protection for textiles or shoes or steel typically died in committee, often without so much as a hearing. With the exception of a few agricultural quotas, Congress almost never *legislated* specific import protection.

As outlined in chapter 2, such "voluntary restraint" by the Congress was the central domestic political prerequisite for US international trade leadership. By delegating responsibility to the executive and by helping fashion a system that protected legislators from one-sided restrictive pressures, Congress made it possible for successive presidents to maintain and expand the liberal trade order.

Congressional trade restraint had depended, in important part, on the capacity of legislative leaders to control the action by preventing floor votes on product-specific restrictions. In the words of one prescient analyst in

1974, the House Ways and Means Committee and its Chairman were "in effect . . . hired to put a damper on particularism in tax and tariff matters."[1]

However, during the postwar period, Congress was changing. Power was spreading out among the 535 individual members; thus the legislative calendar and output were less subject to leaders' control. This change accelerated in the 1970s, particularly in the House of Representatives. At the same time, trade was becoming more important to the American economy.

By the mid-1980s, the old internal barriers to congressional trade action had significantly weakened. This put more pressure than ever on the executive branch, making open US trade policies more dependent than ever on its policy commitment and leadership skill.

□ □ □

The tragedy of one man came to symbolize the demise of the old order. In October 1974, even as the Senate Finance Committee was quietly marking up the authorizing legislation for the Tokyo Round, the Chairman of its House counterpart became involved in a scandal that would force his resignation. For years, Wilbur D. Mills (D-Ark.) had been the consummate insider. The central congressional figure on trade and tax policy, he was perhaps the most powerful member of his chamber, yet he was little known to the general public. In a parliamentary regime, he might well have become Prime Minister. But in the United States, his one quest for national recognition was in a belated campaign for the 1972 Democratic presidential nomination. This campaign had peaked with a 4 percent vote in the New Hampshire primary, and Mills won a total of 33.8 delegate votes at the convention the following August.

Now his name would become a household word, because of a bizarre incident which exposed his heavy drinking and involvement with a woman not his wife.[2] It came at a time when Mills' influence was already in decline. Suffering from a back ailment, he had missed most of the House Ways and Means markups of the Tokyo Round authorization bill the year before. Now his career and reputation would publicly disintegrate. He won reelection in November, but the sudden scandal reduced his usually overwhelming majority to 59 percent. By December, he had declared himself an alcoholic, and announced that he would not continue as Ways and Means Chairman in the next Congress. Two years later, he retired from public office.

---

1. David R. Mayhew, *Congress: The Electoral Connection* (New Haven, Conn.: Yale University Press, 1974), p. 154.

2. A car in which Mills was riding was stopped (for speeding, without lights) by a National Park Service police cruiser, at which point the woman ran from the car and leaped into the nearby Washington Tidal Basin. The episode got extensive press coverage, particularly in the *Washington Post*, as the "full story" was gradually revealed.

Mills was succeeded as Chairman by Al Ullman (D-Ore.). He was replaced by no one. His talented Senate counterpart of the 1970s, Finance Chairman Russell B. Long (D-La.), would develop a formidable personal reputation, as would Long's successor, Robert J. Dole (R-Kan.). But, from the 1960s onward, the Senate was too free-wheeling and democratic to permit the sort of personal policy dominance that Mills had attained. In the 1970s the House would become so as well.

Congressional Reform and the Weakening of Ways and Means

Even before the Arkansan's public fall from grace, the "excessive power" of Ways and Means had been "a major target of reorganization."[3] This was part of a broader challenge to the power of committee chairmen by congressional reformers.

American politics was opening up, and more and more legislators owed their election not to party machines but to personal entrepreneurship. They did not want to run the turtle's race between seniority and senility, by serving quietly as apprentices for the twenty to thirty years it might take to move up the ranks to chair a major committee.

By the end of 1974, it was clear that new House members no longer had to wait. They could aspire to policy influence almost immediately. The Watergate election brought no fewer than 75 new Democrats into the House. Adding to them the newly elected Republicans, and the turnover in the 1972 election, this meant that more than one-third of the House members in January 1975 had not been there three years before.

The freshmen joined the veteran reformers to activate the long-moribund Democratic caucus. Exploiting a recently adopted requirement for caucus votes on all House committee chairs, they ousted three and threatened others. The caucus took particular steps to cut the powers of Ways and Means. Its Democratic members were stripped of one special source of power over their colleagues: the role of "committee on committees," deciding who would fill vacancies on all House panels. Ways and Means was also expanded from 25 members to 37 members, making close management in the Mills mode harder for a successor to accomplish.

Not all reform ideas were adopted. One major internal review group, the "Bolling Committee," proposed in 1974 to take away substantial chunks of jurisdiction, moving authority over trade and tariffs, for example, to House Foreign Affairs. This proposal was set aside, and Ways and Means' substantive sphere remained largely intact.

Nevertheless, like other committees, it was forced to form legislative

3. Roger H. Davidson and Walter J. Oleszek, *Congress Against Itself* (Bloomington: Indiana University Press, 1977), p. 179.

subcommittees with separate staffs. This meant that, in the future, its main trade responsibility would rest with the chairman of the Trade Subcommittee. On the one hand, this was sometimes helpful in delaying product-restrictive proposals, since initial responsibility was buried one layer deeper: a bill had to make it through the subcommittee before it got to the full Ways and Means panel. But a subcommittee Chairman typically lacked the stature and broader chamber leadership role of the full committee head. So it was harder for him personally to block or delay a protectionist bill that had strong backing. And because the Ways and Means Chairman had now delegated day-to-day trade responsibility, it was hard for him to do so either. The committee was also subject to new House rules making markups of bills generally open to the public. Bills were subject to procedural changes that made "open rules"—allowing floor amendments—the norm, so that on-the-record, roll-call votes on such amendments were now far easier for their proponents to obtain.

In both its sources and its goals, the congressional reform movement was unrelated to trade. But the reformers' twin objectives—*decentralization* of power and *openness* of procedures—nonetheless struck at the heart of the old American trade policy-making system. Open US trade policy had been founded, in part, on closed politics, on a variety of devices that shielded legislators from one-sided restrictive pressures. It had prospered under congressional barons—Mills above all—who had enough leverage to manipulate issues and to protect their colleagues from those up-or-down votes that forced a choice between conviction and constituency. As noted in chapter 2, the system did not protect Congress all of the time; for example, agriculture was partly outside its domain. In addition, as illustrated by the "Mills bill" episode of 1970 (see chapter 2), an unfavorable sequence of events could overcome barriers to congressional action. Still, the old system had succeeded in keeping the great bulk of product-specific protectionist proposals from coming to roll-call votes on the House floor.

This was the very sort of thing that reformers wanted to change. Although they were not thinking specifically of trade, their overall goal was to force policy choices out in the open, by publicizing House actions and members' stands. Believing that "special interests" benefited from the closed system, they reasoned that if Congress were democratized and its operations exposed to the "sunshine," then the larger public interest would prevail.

There was both truth and oversimplification in this critique of the cozy old system. Closed procedures could indeed benefit special interests. But they also could offer insulation to members who wanted to resist such interests but were reluctant to do so under the watchful eyes of their lobbyists. For while anyone *could* attend open meetings, it was typically the lobbyists who *did*. They came, they saw, and they reported back on what members were doing for (or against) their particular causes. More open floor procedures also offered new opportunities for special interests to press their proposals.[4]

Two textile episodes, 10 years apart, illustrate how more open House processes offered advantages to those seeking protection. In the spring of 1968, to buttress his candidacy for his first full Senate term, Senator Ernest F. Hollings (D-SC) won adoption of a stringent proposal for statutory textile quotas cosponsored by no fewer than 67 colleagues, attaching it to major Johnson administration tax legislation. However, as noted in chapter 2, this proposal stopped at the House door, for Mills, supported by the administration, refused to accept it in conference. The Senate Finance Committee cooperated; indeed, it generally counted on its House counterpart to kill such initiatives. (And Johnson, according to one who served in his White House, added a personal flourish, making Hollings "an offer he couldn't refuse." He told the junior senator that if he pushed for another Senate floor vote the administration would defeat him and then spread the word around South Carolina that Hollings had bungled the textile industry's case.)

In 1978, Hollings won Senate adoption of another extreme industry proposal, one that would require an eleventh-hour withdrawal of all the textile tariff reductions offered by the United States in the nearly completed Tokyo Round. Senate Trade Subcommittee Chairman Abraham A. Ribicoff (D-Conn.) declared this could "ensure the failure of the negotiation." Again the vehicle was a bill that the administration needed, one that renewed the lending authority of the Export–Import Bank.

The industry was hardly in dire straits. The system of negotiated quota agreements had been broadened in the early 1970s from cotton products to those of all major fibers, and this had helped keep the total volume of textile imports in 1976–78 at about 6 percent below its peak in 1971–73.

But now a weaker Ways and Means Committee, in a decentralized House, could not prevent a floor vote. So a much more elaborate procedural shuffle had to be devised to sidetrack the proposal. The Export–Import Bank measure was formally abandoned, its provisions attached to another bill at 4 A.M. on the last day of the Ninety-fifth Congress. The textile-tariff proposal was brought to the House floor and adopted overwhelmingly, but as an amendment to a bill Carter could afford to veto—one authorizing the sale of Carson City silver dollars. By design or coincidence, this bill was one of the last two of the session to be formally "enrolled" and sent to the White

---

4. John F. Witte draws a similar connection between congressional reform and special-interest *tax* provisions. See his "The Income Tax Mess: Deviant Process or Institutional Failure?" (Paper prepared for delivery at the 1985 Annual Meeting of the American Political Science Association, New Orleans, 1 September 1985).

House. Thus the presidential veto could be delayed until after the mid-term election. (The other straggler, also vetoed, provided for meat import quotas.)

This 1978 textile-industry campaign contributed to the failure of the administration to win enactment that same fall of legislation needed to complete the MTN: extension of authority to waive enforcement of countervailing duties.[5] The Chairman and ranking Republican of the Ways and Means Trade Subcommittee then conceded defeat, declaring in a public letter to Special Trade Representative Robert S. Strauss that the countervailing duty waiver could not be passed in the next Congress unless the textile exclusion was attached. To prevent this, the administration was forced to buy off that industry with policy concessions in early 1979.

If congressional reform thus weakened the key committees, so also did changes in the content of trade policy. Senate Finance and House Ways and Means were, first and foremost, revenue committees. By historical precedent and recurrent argument, their trade authority was derived from tariffs, the main means of raising revenue during most of the republic's existence. Tariffs' declining importance in trade policy, therefore, undercut this jurisdictional rationale. The rise of nontariff trade issues in the 1970s—such as government procurement, product standards, subsidies—inevitably brought other committees into the substance of trade policy.

How then could Congress play its role in the trade system at all? On one major type of business, authorization and implementation of major trade agreements, it showed considerable creativity: developing new rules for expedited action that led to the overwhelming 1979 vote in favor of the MTN. On product-specific issues, however, Congress seemed increasingly under siege.

Renewing the Delegation of Power: The "Fast-Track" Procedures

From the Reciprocal Trade Agreements Act of 1934 through the Trade Expansion Act of 1962, the means by which Congress delegated authority for trade negotiations remained basically the same. Successive statutes authorized executive officials to negotiate (within specified numerical limits) reductions in US tariffs, in exchange for reductions by our trading partners.

---

5. Europeans had insisted from the start that they would not negotiate under threat of such duties being imposed under the old, pre-GATT US law which did not require that petitioning industries prove injury from imports, at the same time as they were working out a new subsidy-countervail–code agreement under which the United States would impose such a test. But though the Trade Act of 1974 had granted a five-year authorization for the Tokyo Round, it only provided a four-year authority for waiving countervailing duties. This expired on 3 January 1979, just as the negotiations were reaching their climax.

When a deal was finally struck, it could be implemented by presidential proclamation, without further recourse to Capitol Hill.

For American trade negotiators, this arrangement had enormous advantages. It gave them maximum credibility abroad, since their power to deliver on their commitments was not in doubt. It also increased their leverage with affected industries at home. Those fearing the effects of particular tariff cuts could and did appeal for congressional backing, but since no formal ratification of the final trade agreement was required, the ultimate decision rested at the northwest end of Pennsylvania Avenue. In theory, of course, lobbyists could prevail on Congress to vote an exception for their product— as the textile industry had sought to do in 1978. But this was very much an uphill fight, for it went against the whole system of delegating power and protecting legislators.

When a nontariff trade barrier (NTB) was at issue, however, there was no comparable system of advance authorization, and therefore no assurance that what US representatives negotiated abroad would become US law at home. This weakness of the trade system was revealed rather dramatically in the final stages of the Kennedy Round. In exchange for related foreign concessions, the Johnson administration made two important nontariff commitments in 1967: to participate in a new GATT antidumping code, and to eliminate a system of customs appraisals called the American Selling Price (ASP). Long resented by Europeans, ASP served to inflate the duties of certain categories of imports ranging from benzenoid chemicals to wool-knit gloves. Congress had authorized neither of these agreements; in fact, the Senate passed a "sense of Congress" resolution in 1966 opposing their negotiation. And Congress implemented neither of them. In fact, it rendered US adherence to the antidumping code meaningless by insisting that whenever it conflicted with our domestic law, the latter would prevail.[6]

These precedents were hardly encouraging. For with tariffs now at a fraction of Smoot-Hawley levels, future trade "rounds" would focus increasingly on NTBs. How could our negotiators be credible internationally? And how could Congress be insulated from pressure to reject or rework what the executive branch had wrought?

The Nixon administration confronted this problem in early 1973 when it sought legislation to authorize a trade round giving priority to nontariff distortions. Not surprisingly, it proposed a procedure nearly identical to that for tariffs. Congress would authorize talks to bargain down NTBs; the President would implement agreements reached by proclaiming the nec-

---

6. For detail and documentation on this episode, see Michael J. Glennon, Thomas M. Franck, and Robert C. Cassidy, Jr., *United States Foreign Relations Law: Documents and Sources*, vol. 4, International Economic Regulation (London: Oceana Publications, Inc., 1984), pp. 1–38.

essary changes in US domestic statutes. In some cases, like that of ASP, the law would authorize a specific negotiating goal in advance. But for most issues, the advance NTB authorization could not be as clearly delimited as that for tariffs, so that administration bill provided that, for agreements on these issues, either house of Congress could veto an executive implementing action within 90 days. The process was similar to that inaugurated in the New Deal for executive branch reorganization: the President could put forward "reorganization plans" which became law unless the House or the Senate objected. But in substance, the administration was now asking for a considerable expansion of its delegated authority, since the statutory changes required to implement an NTB agreement could reach into areas well beyond trade policy.

The House accepted this legislative veto proposal; the Senate did not. It was, argued senior Finance Democrat Herman E. Talmadge of Georgia, "not the way we make laws." This procedure might be all right for government organization, but, for substantive policy, he was convinced that such an open-ended delegation of power to amend statutes was unconstitutional. Talmadge saw no alternative to affirmative congressional action, after the fact, on all specific, nontariff changes in American law resulting from trade negotiations. And his Finance Committee colleagues agreed.

This seemed to render negotiations impossible: how could foreign governments deal seriously with us if Congress might reject or amend the outcome or never take definitive action at all? Fortunately, negotiations among STR leaders, Talmadge, and Finance Committee staff yielded an alternative the Senator found acceptable. This was a statutory commitment to an up-or-down vote, within a specified period of time, on any legislation implementing an NTB agreement submitted by the President.

As finally enacted, the Trade Act included an elaborate procedural timetable aimed at assuring expeditious legislative action. After consulting with the relevant congressional committees, the president would give notice of intent at least 90 days before entering into any NTB agreement. Once he did so, Congress would act within 60 days of his submitting the implementing bill, under rules barring committee or floor amendments.[7]

This was not a perfect solution for executive negotiators, for they could not assure their foreign counterparts that Congress would deliver. But they could promise a clear answer within 90 days.

---

7. For details, see I.M. Destler, *Making Foreign Economic Policy* (Washington: Brookings Institution, 1980), pp. 177–78; Matthew J. Marks and Harald B. Malmgren, "Negotiating Nontariff Distortions to Trade," *Law and Policy in International Business,* vol. 7, no. 2 (1975), pp. 338–41; and Glennon, Franck, and Cassidy, *Foreign Relations Law,* esp. pp. 41–65. The maximum time period for action on an "implementing revenue bill" was slightly longer: 90 days.

These new procedures were adopted to facilitate negotiations abroad. Yet, although no one fully realized it at the time, they would also reshape the policy process at home. Specifically, on new trade agreements, the new procedures allowed the new, "open" Congress to replicate its closed predecessor. With the legislative process limited in scope and time, the stance of the trade committees, Finance and Ways and Means, was once again likely to prove decisive. To be confident of favorable floor actions the Special Trade Representative's office needed the committees' overwhelming support of the agreements negotiated. This meant paying attention to committee members and aides, whom the legislation made official observers and advisers at the negotiations.

In practice, the Hill's substantive contribution was limited for most of the MTN. But as the end of the talks approached in the spring of 1978, the senior trade expert on the Finance Committee staff, Robert C. Cassidy, Jr., posed a procedural challenge. He began pressing for a major congressional role in the drafting of the nonamendable MTN implementing legislation that the President was to propose. Politically, he argued, enactment of such legislation would require a joint commitment by STR and the trade committees. Operationally, this could best be accomplished if they developed that legislation together.

Insofar as was possible, Cassidy proposed, they would replicate the normal legislative process. In sessions with Strauss and other executive branch representatives that became labeled "nonmarkups," Finance and Ways and Means would advise separately on the implementing bill's substance. They would then reconcile their differences in a "nonconference." Finally, the drafting of the actual statutory language would be an interbranch process, with congressional legal aides working with counterparts in executive agencies much as they did on normal trade legislation. Only then would the President send the formal, nonamendable implementing bill to Capitol Hill.

There was some initial skepticism in STR: Did they really want to give Capitol Hill that strong a role in drafting the President's bill? But ties between the trade office and the Finance staff were strong—STR General Counsel Richard R. Rivers having worked for that committee prior to 1977—and so the Trade Representative's office acquiesced. But "unofficially," by one authoritative report, "they said they still hoped to carry on the bill drafting process without too much congressional interference."[8] So Finance senators summoned their man in the administration, Special Trade Representative Robert Strauss, and won his personal assent to this procedure,

8. Glennon, Franck, and Cassidy, *Foreign Relations Law*, p. 161.

which was quickly confirmed in an exchange of letters. House Ways and Means, never a formal party to the arrangement, followed it in practice.[9]

In return for this considerable concession on procedure, the executive branch won near-total congressional approval of the substance of the MTN agreements it negotiated, which were implemented through a single legislative package, the Trade Agreements Act of 1979. In only one case did its congressional consultations force the administration to alter a previously negotiated accord: The House Small Business Committee protested the proposal to open up to international bidding US government contracts reserved for minority-owned enterprises. Strauss responded by substituting other opportunities for foreign firms to sell to US agencies. On the most sensitive issue—how tough an injury test would be applied in US countervailing duty cases—the code commitment to a "material injury" test survived a strong industry challenge. So strong was Strauss's credibility by this time that he reportedly clinched his argument by declaring that "the French want it" this way. "I don't know why and [Deputy STR Alan Wm.] Wolff doesn't know why and Rivers doesn't know why, but I need you to go along!"[10]

Congressional action was expeditious as well. On 4 January 1979, Carter gave the required 90-day notice of intent to conclude the MTN. By 6 March, the Senate Finance Committee had begun its series of nine "nonmarkups," and by 16 May, the House Ways and Means Subcommittee on Trade concluded its fifteenth such session. Representatives of the two then joined in a "nonconference" on 21 through 23 May.

All these meetings were closed to the public, one rationale being that they had begun when the content of the MTN was technically confidential. (The agreements would not be signed and made public until April 12.) But the closure had a broader purpose: to limit the number of legislators and lobbyists who could influence the outcome. The process was not completely closed, however. Hearings were held in both committees and press releases reported major committee decisions as they were made.

---

9. See Robert C. Cassidy, Jr., "Negotiating About Negotiations," in *The Tethered Presidency*, edited by Thomas M. Franck (New York, NY: New York University Press, 1981), pp. 264–82; I.M. Destler and Thomas R. Graham, "United States Congress and the Tokyo Round: Lessons of a Success Story," *World Economy* (June 1980), pp. 53–70; Destler, "Trade Consensus; SALT Stalemate: Congress and Foreign Policy in the Seventies," in *The New Congress*, edited by Thomas E. Mann and Norman J. Ornstein (American Enterprise Institute, 1981), pp. 333–40; and documents in Glennon, Franck, and Cassidy, *Foreign Relations Law*, pp. 153–99.

10. One interesting example of a substantial change in US policies resulting from the MTN was the wine-gallon concession, in which American negotiators agreed to thoroughgoing revision of a method of computing excise taxes on distilled spirits which dated from the mid-ninteenth century, and which had the effect, not originally intended, of penalizing imports. For a full description, see Gilbert R. Winham, *International Trade and the Tokyo Round Negotiation* (Princeton, NJ: Princeton University Press, 1986), ch. 7.

Most interesting perhaps was the fact that this quasi-legislative process cut the full Senate and House out of the main action. When finally a 373-page "committee print" containing proposed statutory language was circulated on June 1, all the major decisions had been made. With a few changes, these same words were what the President proposed to Congress in his nonamendable bill 18 days later. Both chambers passed the bill in July, by votes of 395 to 7 and 90 to 4. Of the 11 opponents, 5 were from Wisconsin, reflecting dairy-industry unhappiness with a modest adjustment in cheese import quotas. Another who voted "nay," reformist Congressman A. Toby Moffett (D-Conn.), gave testimony to how effectively the broad membership had been excluded when he protested that "the speed with which we were expected to get on with this bill did not provide ample opportunity for full analysis." He expressed his puzzlement "that Congress had locked itself into such a method on such a critical piece of legislation."[11]

The Carter administration, with STR Robert Strauss in the lead, had constructed a carefully balanced MTN package that responded to all major US trade interests. Some observers actually felt that Strauss had been too responsive, and cited the overwhelming approval margins as evidence. Ranking Ways and Means Republican Barber B. Conable (R-NY) recalls warning him, "You're buying a landslide," giving away too much. In terms of congressional process, however, the key was that the "fast-track" provisions protected the bulk of legislators from product-specific pressure in 1979 just as effectively as the bargaining tariff, and the closed rule barring House floor amendments, had done in the 45 years before. The administration, in alliance with the primary trade committees, shouldered the main political burden for the members at large. And the main congressional trade players clearly were pleased with the process, for they included in the implementing act a provision that extended this procedure for negotiating and implementing NTB agreements through 3 January 1988.

Still, there were important differences between the new NTB process and the old one on tariffs, and these differences had policy consequences. One was the fact that now Congress had to pass legislation at both ends of a negotiation. For the Kennedy Round tariff agreements, the Trade Expansion Act of 1962 had sufficed. The Tokyo Round required the Trade Act of 1974 to get it going and the Trade Agreements Act of 1979 to conclude it successfully.

This meant that during the talks, US negotiators had to worry about the danger that unhappy industries might join together and mobilize a congressional majority that could block the implementing bill. In fact, negotiators felt they had to prevent even the formation of such a coalition, since once

---

11. *Congressional Record,* Daily Edition, 13 July 1979, p. E3582.

one came together there was no telling how widely it might spread. So in addition to mobilizing maximum support from export interests that stood to gain from a successful MTN, STR had to show particular sensitivity to the demands of the more powerful among the potential losers, the import-affected industries.

So pressure for special deals increased. Textiles, which had already gotten its Multi-Fiber Arrangement during the run-up to the 1974 Act, won a tightening of its implementation vis-à-vis the major East Asian exporters and mainland China. The steel industry won adoption of the trigger price mechanism (TPM), through which the US government pledged to initiate antidumping action if foreign products were sold at prices below certain specified minimum levels. Of course, the Carter administration might have done these things anyway; it was not Strauss who developed the TPM, but Under Secretary of the Treasury Anthony M. Solomon, deputy to Strauss's main Cabinet rival, W. Michael Blumenthal. But the upcoming MTN vote on Capitol Hill provided a powerful incentive to stay on speaking terms with the industries that could cause the most trouble.

Further policy concessions were included in the 1979 law itself. Though consistent with the MTN codes, its drafting was much more than a pro forma implementation exercise. In fact, it grew to exceed the 1974 law in its length, and the key committees used their leeway to press purposes well beyond those the MTN required. As will be recounted in chapter 5, Senate Finance held up final action until President Jimmy Carter submitted a proposal to reorganize the trade bureaucracy. Even more important for trade policy, steel industry ally John Heinz (R-Pa.) joined with trade law reformer John C. Danforth (R-Mo.) to bring about a comprehensive rewriting of the countervailing duty and the antidumping laws, with effects to be set forth in chapter 6. And this new statutory language filled twice as many pages as the major unfair trade practices amendments enacted five years before.

Finally, the content of the codes meant that Finance and Ways and Means had to acknowledge more explicitly than ever that trade regulation reached into the jurisdictions of numerous competing committees. The 1974 Act foreshadowed this recognition, for the fast-track procedures provided only that an implementing bill be referred to "the appropriate committee" in each chamber. So had separate bills been submitted to implement US code commitments on government procurement and product standards, for example, the "appropriate" House committees would very probably have been, respectively, Government Operations and Interstate and Foreign Commerce.

The decision to go with a single implementation vehicle meant that Ways and Means kept its primacy on MTN legislation, and in practice it even proved possible to get the other committees to waive their claim to joint referral. But in return, Trade Subcommittee Chairman Charles A. Vanik (D-

Ohio) invited members of the relevant committees to participate in non-markups affecting their jurisdictions. Senate Finance went even farther, passing entire titles on to sister committees and adopting their recommendations as its own. The committee even incorporated in its report the supplemental views of Governmental Affairs member William S. Cohen (R-Me.), who advocated a tougher approach to Japan on government procurement.[12]

But most important was the fact that the fast-track procedures solved only half of the "Congress problem" insofar as trade was concerned. They established a new mechanism for authorizing and implementing major international, trade-expanding agreements. Thus, they extended the possibility of US leadership in negotiating such agreements into the post-tariff trade world.

But they did not address the need to divert the many *other* product-specific restrictive proposals that individual members had always put forward and always would. As Congressman Conable phrased it a few months before his retirement at the end of 1984, "Congress has become a participatory democracy. So you can't stop bad proposals as easily as you used to."[13]

Industry-Specific Proposals: The Automobile Case

The Hollings textile rider of 1978 was one case illustrating Conable's point. Few congressional trade leaders believed that that industry needed *further* protection at the time, but they lacked both the authority and the mechanisms to sidetrack it.

This did not mean, of course, that Congress had become eager to pass statutory restrictions. In most instances, the aim of particular quota bills was still not to get them enacted into law. Rather, it was to demonstrate the sponsor's allegiance to a particular industry, or to pressure the executive branch, the appropriate foreign government, or both. Congress was still acting as a lobby to influence decisions made outside its halls.

In the early 1980s, the most dramatic and visible example of this phenomenon was the struggle over trade in automobiles. The second oil shock of 1979 caused a doubling of the price of motor fuel, as well as gasoline lines and the prospect of future fuel shortages. As a result, demand for new cars shifted dramatically in the direction of small, high-mileage

---

12. US Congress, Senate Committee on Finance, *The Trade Agreements Act of 1979*, 96th Cong., 1st Sess., 17 July 1979, S. Rept. 96–249, pp. 147–48.

13. Personal interview, 31 July 1984.

models. American carmakers were unprepared for this shift: their sales fell off sharply, as imports, three-fourths of which now came from Japan, expanded to meet the new demand.[14] Ford and General Motors suffered record losses, and the Chrysler Corporation needed a governmental rescue to avert bankruptcy. Most important of all for trade politics, US auto unemployment exceeded 300,000, out of a total of almost one million directly employed in the industry.[15] This hardship was heavily concentrated in one geographic area, that of Michigan and other midwestern states.

Here was an industry long a symbol of US economic supremacy, a prime engine of twentieth-century American prosperity—and suddenly it was in very dire straits. The congressional response to its plight went through three distinct stages. The first, extending through most of 1980, was one of spotlighting the problem and hoping that established remedy procedures would produce a solution. Vanik's Trade Subcommittee held hearings, sending a clear signal that some form of protective action might have to be taken, even though the industry was divided and the Carter administration reluctant. At the same time, legislators supported the United Auto Workers (UAW) in its campaign to get Japanese automakers to build plants in the United States, to "put some of their money where their market is."

The submission of an escape clause petition in June, by the UAW and the Ford Motor Company, offered the hope that "the rules" could provide the needed relief. Since the USITC decision would not come until mid-November, this also put the issue safely beyond the election. Carter did urge, unsuccessfully, that the USITC expedite its decision, and he encouraged provision of generous adjustment assistance for laid-off workers. Meanwhile, his rival, Ronald Reagan, promised in September to "try to convince the Japanese that . . . the deluge of their cars into the United States must be slowed."[16]

But the USITC decided, by a 3 to 2 vote, that it could not recommend relief because the major causes of the industry's woes were other than imports. Congress then moved quickly into the second stage, that of pressing

---

14. In absolute numbers, the growth of imports was moderate, from 2 million in 1978 to 2.4 million in 1980. But their market share shot up from 17.7 percent to 26.7 percent, as sales of American-made vehicles plummeted during the same two years from 9.3 million to 6.6 million, the lowest figure since 1961. See Gilbert R. Winham and Ikuo Kabashima, "The Politics of U.S.-Japanese Auto Trade," in *Coping With U.S.-Japanese Economic Conflicts*, edited by I.M. Destler and Hideo Sato (Lexington, Mass.: Lexington Books, 1982), p. 76.

15. "The U.S. Automobile Industry, 1980," Report to the President from the Secretary of Transportation, January 1981, pp. 83–85.

16. For details on the politics of autos, see Winham and Kabashima, "Politics of U.S.-Japan Auto Trade," and Stephen D. Cohen and Ronald I. Metzger, *United States International Economic Policy in Action* (New York, NY: Praeger, 1982), ch. 3.

for the issue to be treated as a "special case." Vanik, who had frequently urged that import issues be handled by "economic law," not politics, now found the outcome of economic law inadequate. So he rushed to schedule hearings and moved quickly with a special resolution authorizing the President to negotiate an orderly auto-marketing agreement with Japan. This proposal passed the House in early December, but Senate consideration was blocked by Senator Adlai E. Stevenson (D-Ill.), an opponent of trade restrictions.

In the new Ninety-seventh Congress, however, the initiative shifted to the Senate. Vanik, a pragmatist frequently sympathetic to trade-impacted industries, had retired and was succeeded by liberal trade champion Sam M. Gibbons (D-Fla.). On the other side of the Hill, the surprise Republican capture of the Senate made John Danforth Chairman of the Finance Subcommittee on International Trade. Automobiles were an important industry in his home state of Missouri, and he lost no time in promising "to commence hearings" prior to Reagan's inauguration.[17] A month after these hearings, Danforth introduced a bill that would impose statutory quotas on Japanese automobile imports for three years.

The aim was not to pass the bill but to pressure the Japanese, and to ensure that Reagan's general campaign promise won out over the liberal trade views of his senior economic advisers. Tokyo was, in fact, willing, but the Ministry of International Trade and Industry needed strong American pressure as leverage against its auto industry. The smaller companies, in particular, saw the US market as their primary growth opportunity in improving their position vis-à-vis the "big two," Toyota and Nissan. Yet the administration wanted to minimize its own formal responsibility for any restrictive outcome. The result was a "look-no-hands" approach that confused Tokyo and increased the need for congressional threats. Thus Finance Chairman Robert Dole (R-Kan.) indicated that he could count two-thirds of the Senate in support of the quota bill, enough to override a presidential veto. Meanwhile, Danforth held hearings on his specific bill in March, and announced a markup for 12 May unless Japanese action resolved the matter before then.

All of this positioning had the intended result. On 1 May, with US Trade Representative William E. Brock in Tokyo (ostensibly not to negotiate but to advise on the US political situation), the Japanese government announced a unilateral commitment to limit exports for two to three years. This met the Finance Committee's demand for a "multi-year effort,"[18] and in fact the restraints have continued—in modified form—through 1986. It also enabled

---

17. *Congressional Record*, Daily Edition, 12 December 1980, p. S16354.
18. Finance Committee Press Release 81–9, 29 April 1981.

Brock to satisfy the Japanese political need, by assuring them that, in the light of the plan, there was now no prospect of the quota legislation's passing Congress. Back in Washington, Danforth could express grudging satisfaction. Although he would have preferred greater restraint, the plan was "an important step in the right direction," so his bill could be set aside.

So the second phase produced modest protection for autos, and this solution lasted, politically, for about a year. But the recession deepened, helping move the auto issue into the third phase, in which politics now spilled over outside the trade committees' control. Before 1982 was over, the full House would pass, over Ways and Means opposition, a "domestic content" bill for autos. Had it become law, this bill would have slashed future imports of autos and auto parts to a fraction of current levels.

The impetus came from the United Auto Workers, a union long committed to open trade. As late as 1979, commenting on the MTN, UAW President Douglas A. Fraser was pledging his qualified allegiance to "the benefits of liberal trade," and his only comment on domestic content rules was the need to get other countries to "curb" theirs.[19] By the next spring, beset with growing unemployment and frustrated by the slow response by Toyota and Nissan to his campaign for Japanese investment in the United States, Fraser was suggesting "local content legislation" as a long-term solution. Pointing to Volkswagen's move to US-based production as a model, he suggested a requirement that companies selling large numbers of cars here should derive up to 75 percent of their content from US sources. This would, he argued, trigger auto investment, production, and employment in the United States, while retaining healthy competition between American and foreign firms.[20]

The real push for a domestic content law came two years later. The continuing recession had caused US auto sales to plunge even further. So despite the slightly lower sales forced by export restraints, the Japanese share of our market edged further upward. The UAW responded with HR 5133, introduced by Representative Richard L. Ottinger, (D-NY), which provided a rigid domestic content formula: the larger the number of cars a company sold here, the greater the portion of their total value would have to come from the United States, up to a maximum of 90 percent. Brock called it "the worst piece of economic legislation since the 1930's," and Danforth exaggerated very little in declaring that "the overwhelming ma-

---

19. Fraser to Vanik, 2 May 1979, in US Congress, House, Committee on Ways and Means, Subcommittee on Trade, *Hearings on Multilateral Trade Negotiations*, 96th Cong., 1st Sess., 23–17 April 1979, Serial 96–13, pp. 655–58.

20. Statement in US Congress, House, Committee on Ways and Means, Subcommittee on Trade, *Hearings on World Auto Trade: Current Trends and Structural Problems*, 96th Cong., 2d Sess., 7 and 18 March 1980, Serial 96–78, pp. 65–77.

jority" of members saw it as "perfectly ridiculous."[21] By making the bill a "litmus test" of the allegiance of labor Democrats, however, the UAW was able to win a victory in the House of Representatives. The House adopted a modified form of the domestic content bill by 215 to 188 votes in December 1982. In November 1983, a House with 26 more Democrats passed a somewhat stronger bill by a slightly smaller margin, 219 to 199 votes. On both occasions, northeastern and midwestern Democrats voted almost unanimously in favor. The bill never reached the Senate floor, however, and the issue gradually faded from the trade scene as the US auto industry regained sales and strength.

Committee Competition and Policy Entrepreneurship

As important as the progress of domestic content was the process by which it was achieved. By drafting the legislation as a measure to regulate domestic production, its proponents managed to get it referred to the sympathetic Committee on Energy and Commerce. Ways and Means, the panel with established trade jurisdiction, was limited to sponsoring parallel hearings and urging its rejection. The bill did not have comparable success in the Republican Senate, but the fact that it got as far as it did suggested further erosion of the procedural checks on industry-specific trade legislation.

It also illustrated the impact of generational change on the power and dynamism of House committees. Energy and Commerce (successor to Interstate and Foreign Commerce) was chaired by an aggressive old-timer, John D. Dingell (D-Mich.), who had come to the House in 1955. But by 1982, its next eight ranking members, in terms of seniority, were members of the class of 1975. Among them were Ottinger (with three terms of prior service), Henry A. Waxman (D-Calif.), Timothy E. Wirth (D-Col.), Philip R. Sharp (D-Ind.), James J. Florio (D-NJ), and Toby Moffett (D-Conn). They were, for the most part, policy activists in the Democratic party mainstream. They had joined the committee as freshmen and given it most of their legislative attention since then. Now, with energy fading as a national concern, trade policy was a natural focus for their talents.

Ways and Means had also expanded in 1975, as noted at the outset of this chapter. But competition for seats on that committee was much keener, so among those who filled its 12 Democratic vacancies only four were freshmen that year—including two with prior service. By 1982, three of the four freshmen had departed, although several others in their class had joined the committee's middle rank. But the most senior of the 1975 arrivals, Andrew Jacobs, Jr. (D-Ind.), remained number seven on the committee. (Gibbons, who chaired the Trade Subcommittee, had come to the House in

---

21. *Congressional Quarterly Almanac,* 1982, p. 56.

1963.) And the energies of several of the more aggressive mid-level members—James R. Jones (D-Okla. [sixth in seniority]), Richard A. Gephardt (D-Mo. [twelfth]) and Thomas J. Downey (D-NY [thirteenth])—were divided between Ways and Means and the Budget Committee.

The net result in the early 1980s was a certain imbalance of initiative and energy. Dingell and his committee were aggressive and policy-active. Ways and Means continued in the more passive gatekeeper role, but without the power and procedural tools it had possessed a decade before.

Dingell's committee was far from seizing control of trade policy. In fact, when Dan Rostenkowski (D-Ill.) became Ways and Means Chairman in 1981, Dingell faced an adversary whose political skills and concern for "turf" were equal to his own. But Energy and Commerce was an active contestant. In some cases—domestic content, for example—its new role helped proponents of restrictive legislation. In other cases, it slowed down House trade actions as the two competing committees targeted one another's bills. Or it gave the Gibbons Trade Subcommittee strong reason to take initiatives about which some senior members were ambivalent, like toughening the trade remedy laws to demonstrate seriousness about the trade problems of important constituencies.[22] In 1985, Chairman Rostenkowski himself would seize the initiative by cosponsoring a trade-restrictive bill targeted at Japan and other nations running large surpluses with the United States. And in 1986, under strong pressure from House Speaker Thomas P. (Tip) O'Neill, he would keep the initiative by moving through the House an omnibus trade bill the Reagan White House denounced as "pure protectionism," a bill responsive to the restrictive Energy and Commerce approach on several specific issues.

Activism in competing committees was also consistent with another congressional trend. Trade issues were becoming, to a greater extent, entrepreneurial issues. Members were now choosing trade policy as a subject worthy of investment of their discretionary time.

Through most of the postwar period, this was emphatically not the case. Since the 1950s, there had been a sharp rise in policy entrepreneurship on Capitol Hill, particularly among liberals. Senators and representatives would adopt particular issues as their own, seeking both to improve government policy and to enhance their personal reputations. But through the mid-1970s, it is striking how seldom they seized upon the substance of international trade as a vehicle for their ambitions. It was seen as a dull, "no-win" issue. Free trade was hardly a priority with the mass public; protectionism was anathema to the policy community. So neither broad

22. As an aide to a relatively protectionist senator put it, "We always figured that the way to get Gibbons to do something was to get Dingell to do something." The trade remedies bill and its politics are treated in chapter 6.

stand was attractive for presentation to a general national or party audience. Of course legislators and presidential candidates made more specifically targeted noises, responding to constituency interests. But broader trade advocacy was left to idiosyncratic legislators like Senator Vance Hartke, cosponsor of the Burke-Hartke quota bill of 1971. Its fate did not inspire emulation. Nor did the fate of Hartke himself, who was beaten decisively in his 1976 reelection contest.

Even on a central question like trade with Japan, activism was late in coming. It was not until 1977, for example, that a Congressman—Jim Jones of Oklahoma—moved to concentrate his energies on this broad subject, forming a Ways and Means Task Force on US-Japan Trade to push for expanded sales of US products. And one apparent reason why Senator Lloyd Bentsen spoke out strongly and critically on the same subject in early 1979, even suggesting an import surcharge against Japanese imports, was that despite the enormous rise in that country's sales to our market, the Senator's staff judged that none of Bentsen's 99 colleagues had yet made Japan "his" issue.

This could not, of course, continue. As detailed in chapter 3, trade was simply becoming too important to the American economy. So congressional debates reflected increasing trade advocacy: between 1975 and 1980, by one measure, the frequency of House and Senate floor references to trade went up by 70 percent.[23] And a comprehensive count, based on computerized bill summaries supplied by the Congressional Research Service, indicates a gradual increase in the number of trade-restrictive bills introduced in the House of Representatives: from 127 in the Ninety-sixth Congress (1979–80) to 137 in the Ninety-seventh, and 144 in the Ninety-eighth.[24] These

---

23. This figure was arrived at by comparing the number of columns under "Foreign Trade" in the *Congressional Record Index,* adjusted for the *Index's* overall length.

24. This computation draws on the computerized CRS bill digest file. If one counts only those bills whose primary purpose was to restrict trade, and whose primary apparent motivation was to benefit US producers (for example, excluding bills to bar purchases of Iranian crude oil, Ugandan coffee, etc.), this modest trend disappears: the numbers drop to 62, 56, and 57, respectively. There was a clear upsurge in 1985, however. In the first nine months of that year, 49 such bills were introduced, compared to just 30 in the same period two years earlier.

Since this analysis was completed, Raymond J. Ahearn of CRS has published a count more comprehensive in its coverage, and more detailed for 1985. Using a broader definition of "trade," this computer search found 1,089 trade bills introduced in the Ninety-sixth Congress, 1,150 in the Ninety-seventh, 1,401 in the Ninety-eighth, and 879 in 1985, the first year of the Ninety-ninth. Bill-by-bill inspection of the 1985 group to eliminate nongermane legislation reduced the total to 634, of which 99 were significantly and directly protectionist in purpose and effect. There were also 51 routine bills adjusting tariffs upward, 77 "potentially protectionist" bills that would make it easier to obtain quasi-judicial trade relief, and 109 bills to "restrict trade to achieve nonprotectionist objectives." See Raymond J. Ahearn, "Protectionist Legislation in 1985," Congressional Research Service, 31 March 1986, processed.

included proposals to impose steel quotas or link wine-import restrictions to wine export opportunities and even, in one case, a proposal to establish a dollar ceiling for the bilateral US-Japan trade imbalance.

Many proposals have been in the "export politics" tradition of seeking to solve problems through trade expansion, opening foreign markets. But even here, several of the most prominent, in the words of two expert analysts, "break sharply with traditional US trade policy."[25] The Senate has been a sympathetic home to "reciprocity" bills sponsored by Danforth and Heinz. In their original form, these bills sought to require restrictions on access to US markets in sectors where major trading partners denied our products comparable market opportunities. More generally, as Raymond J. Ahearn and Alfred Reifman noted:

Instead of seeking solutions through enforcement or negotiation of reciprocal agreements, nondiscrimination, and, more generally, the rules of the General Agreement on Tariffs and Trade (GATT), the most common congressional approaches are based on unilateral standards of reciprocity, discrimination, and the threat of retaliation. Successive administrations have opposed similar approaches on the grounds they violate US international obligations, undermine US global leadership, and are economically counterproductive.[26]

1982–83: Pressure Building

More than once in the early 1980s, this explosion of specific initiatives signaled to many who followed trade that Congress was at last going to reclaim direct, detailed control over "commerce with foreign nations." For example, at the end of 1982, domestic content for autos had just passed the House after one critic forced a record vote on an amendment to rename it "The Smoot-Hawley Trade Barriers Act." There was record unemployment, which always fuels protectionism, and an overvalued dollar that was sucking in imports and weakening exports. There was disillusionment with our major trading partners: frustration about seemingly endless market access negotiations with the Japanese, and bitterness about European agricultural protectionism. The latter had boiled over at a fractious GATT Ministerial

25. Raymond J. Ahearn and Alfred Reifman, "U.S. Trade Policy: Congress Sends a Message," in *NBER Conference Report: Current U.S. Trade Policy: Analysis, Agenda, and Administration,* edited by Robert E. Baldwin and J. David Richardson (Cambridge, Mass.: National Bureau of Economic Research, 1986), p. 104.

26. Ibid. See also William R. Cline, *"Reciprocity": A New Approach to World Trade Policy?* POLICY ANALYSES IN INTERNATIONAL ECONOMICS 2 (Washington: Institute for International Economics, September 1982).

Conference in November. Trade issues were more prominent in the mid-term congressional elections than they had been in many years. *Congressional Quarterly*, a good mirror of legislators' concerns, featured Toyotas on the docks on its 27 November cover and a boldface heading that read "Getting Tough With Japan." While a strong reaction from liberal trade organizations like the Business Roundtable had persuaded Danforth to modify his "reciprocity" bill,[27] congressional attraction to mandatory, unilateral approaches remained very strong.

Looking at these trends, and at the number of trade-related bills on the near-term legislative schedule, Finance Chairman Robert Dole predicted that 1983 would be "the year of trade" on Capitol Hill. The *National Journal* rang in that year with a headline, "The Protectionist Congress—Is This The Year That the Trade Barriers Go Up?" "The 98th Congress," it reported, "may be dominated by legislators angered by what they view as unfair European and Japanese trade practices and eager to retaliate in kind."[28] Coupled with these specific frustrations was a broader view that the United States needed to recognize that the liberal trade ideal was impractical and outmoded and adopt a more sophisticated, interventionist approach to international trade, comparable to that of its trading partners. Intellectual staff aides put forward appealing alternate conceptions: We should no longer pretend that we or anybody else could make market openness the touchstone of commercial relations. Rather, we should determine the shape of the future economy we want and use trade policy as one tool to bring it about.[29]

In fact, that "year of trade" fizzled. Congress did very little on the subject in 1983. The long-delayed US economic recovery began, taking some of the bite out of the drive for statutory restrictions (including the support for domestic content for autos).

Once again, legislators were willing to channel pressure elsewhere. Even when, in 1984, 201 Representatives signed onto a steel quota bill, the predominant view was that it would serve the traditional function, pressuring the executive branch, rather than find its way into the statute books. And this is in fact what happened. President Ronald W. Reagan, responding to

---

27. The Roundtable warned that "an improper use of reciprocity could worsen, instead of improve, our economic vitality. If misapplied, the concept has the potential for further undermining an already vulnerable multilateral trading system by triggering retaliation." "Statement of the Business Roundtable Task Force on International Trade and Investment on Reciprocity in Trade," 19 March 1982; processed, p. 2.

28. 1 January 1983, p. 18.

29. See, for example, House Energy and Commerce Committee, "The United States in a Changing World Economy: The Case for an Integrated Domestic and International Commercial Policy," Staff Report, September 1983.

multiple pressures and facing a late-September deadline to act on a US International Trade Commission recommendation to provide import relief for most carbon steel products, ordered his trade representative, William Brock, to negotiate export restraint agreements with major foreign suppliers.

The summer and fall of 1984, however, brought a surge of congressional activity, capped by enactment of a broad bill that was relatively balanced between trade-expanding and trade-restrictive provisions. And 1985 and 1986 were truly "years of trade," with the subject leaping to a place near the top of congressional preoccupations. By September 1985, House Speaker Thomas P. O'Neill could declare: "Based on what I hear from members in the cloak room, trade is the number one issue."[30] By May 1986, his leadership would help drive a new, much more restrictive trade bill to one-sided endorsement on the House floor.

The Trade and Tariff Act of 1984: Pressure Contained

The closing months of the Ninety-eighth Congress saw the policy context worsen.[31] The US trade deficit was ballooning to unheard of levels, fueled by the federal budget deficit and the soaring dollar. By summer, most experts had come around to C. Fred Bergsten's projection that it could top $100 billion in 1984. This put advocates of open trade very much on the defensive and made the prospects look bleak for the several relatively specialized trade bills on the legislative agenda.

These included one "must" item for the liberal trade community, trade preferences for developing countries (GSP). In the Trade Act of 1974, the United States had, pursuant to an international agreement, granted these countries duty-free access to our market for a range of their products for a 10-year period ending on 3 January 1985. GSP had precious little support among American economic interests, even though only 3 percent of total US imports were affected—due to exclusion of sensitive articles (for example, textiles, shoes) and ceilings on benefits available to any one country for a specific product. Organized labor opposed the program, particularly for the "big three" NICs—Korea, Taiwan, and Hong Kong—whose products are generally competitive in the United States without special treatment. But Third World nations attached great symbolic importance to GSP. Its abandonment would make it very hard for the United States to negotiate with

---

30. Quoted in *Washington Post*, 19 September 1985.

31. The following pages draw substantially on confidential interviews with persons involved in the enactment of the Trade and Tariff Act of 1984. See appendix A for a more detailed description of its enactment.

these countries on matters that *were* important to interests here—copyright protection and access to *their* markets.

The prospects for passing GSP extension on its own were dim. So unpopular was the GSP renewal proposal that the administration was unable, in 1983, to find a single House member to sponsor it. There was on the table, however, a trade proposal that was much more popular in both Congress (it had *163* House sponsors) and the Reagan White House: a bill authorizing negotiation of a bilateral free-trade agreement with Israel. On 31 July 1984, the Senate Finance Committee voted to combine the two, add a number of other proposals (including Danforth's modified reciprocity bill), and attach the whole package to a minor tariff-adjustment bill (HR 3398) that had already been passed by the other chamber.[32]

US Trade Representative Bill Brock welcomed this development. With the House stymied on GSP, this offered the best opportunity for forward movement. Trade Subcommittee Chairman Danforth favored it for this reason, and another: it was the best vehicle for enactment of his reciprocity proposal. But Majority Leader Howard H. Baker, Jr. (R-Tenn.), was reluctant to allot Senate floor time to the bill. Danforth had not been able to negotiate a "unanimous consent" agreement limiting time for debate or amendments that might be proposed. The leader feared, therefore, that the bill would be tied up procedurally on the floor, loaded with protectionist baubles for a wide range of industries, or both.

But due to a House-Senate-administration impasse on budget legislation, there was floor time available in mid-September. So Baker gave Danforth his chance. The tacit understanding was that if he lost control, the bill would be pulled off the floor, never to return.

In one sense, Baker's fears were borne out. Danforth never lost control, but to keep it—as debate extended from the anticipated two days to three, then four—he had to accept 6 floor amendments on Monday, 14 on Tuesday, 12 on Wednesday, and 11 on Thursday. The pattern, faintly reminiscent of Smoot-Hawley, was to bargain down but then accept industry-specific protection proposals, and among the successful floor amendments were those favoring producers of copper, bromine, wine, footwear, ferroalloys, and dairy products. When, on the second day of debate, the President made his decision to negotiate voluntary restraint agreements with steel-exporting countries, an amendment was added giving the administration legal authority to enforce such restraints.

But for three factors, the damage would have been even greater. First, on

---

32. This legerdemain was necessary because of the constitutional requirement that "all bills for raising revenue," and hence bills affecting tariffs, "originate in the House of Representatives" (Article I, Sec. 6).

the second day, the Senate did signal that there were limits by rejecting a particularly egregious proposal to reverse a USITC decision and raise the tariff on water-packed tuna. Second, during the final two days, Danforth was supported by the personal presence of Brock, who employed his floor privileges as a former senator to involve himself aggressively in the brokering process. (For example, he provided nonstatutory assurances to the textile industry concerning the impact of the Israel free-trade agreement.) Third, organized labor did essentially nothing. The AFL-CIO had been successful in keeping trade bills off the floor for most of the session and reacted very slowly when the legislation was suddenly taken up. Neither domestic content nor anything else for autos was even proposed. Nor did any senator advance a labor amendment curbing GSP, which might either have passed or forced the extended debate that would have been fatal to the legislation.

So the bill survived, passing the Senate late Thursday by a vote of 96 to 0. The margin reflected the number of interests that had been temporarily "bought off" in the bill itself or through agreements negotiated on the side. An alarmed *Washington Post* lambasted the result in an editorial entitled "The Anti-Trade Bill":

The losers in every major trade case of the past year have managed to insert language to try to win in Congress what they lost in litigation. . . . If the bill gets to President Reagan, he will have a clear and urgent responsibility to let it go no farther.[33]

But the Congress was now moving. Senate passage broke the Ways and Means logjam, and a week later that committee reported out four separate trade bills: GSP renewal, US-Israel free trade, "steel import stabilization," and "wine equity." Chairman Rostenkowski secured floor time for each under "modified closed rules" that limited amendments. Six days later, on Wednesday, 3 October, the House passed each of the four separately, defeating in the process, by a surprisingly wide 233 to 174 margin, a labor-backed Gephardt amendment that would have eliminated preferences for the big three NICs. It then attached the four bills as amendments to the Senate-passed HR 3398. The House also attached several previously enacted bills, the most important being the "Trade Remedies Reform Act" developed by Trade Subcommittee Chairman Sam Gibbons, so that they would go to conference as well. Interestingly, the domestic content bill was not among them.

By this point, time for compromising House-Senate differences had grown very short: the target for sine die adjournment of the Ninety-eighth Congress

---

33. *Washington Post,* 28 September 1984.

was the coming weekend. One question was whether the product-specific amendments in the Senate bill (and to some degree the House bill also) could be deleted, rendering the bill acceptable to President Reagan. Another was whether the House conferees could be persuaded to yield on most other issues where the two bills differed—preferences, procedures for approving the US-Israeli agreement, trade remedies. If they did not, Brock and the administration could not accept the bill. But what could House representatives get in return?

The answer, it soon became clear, was in the provisions Rostenkowski was personally most identified with, those on steel. He had pushed through a bill which, in the name of implementing Reagan's just-announced "national policy for the steel industry," incorporated two proposals advocated by presidential challenger Walter F. Mondale and other Democratic critics of the President's action: a market-share target of 17 percent for steel imports; and an "adjustment" condition for steel firms, which were, as a price for continued protection, required to reinvest all net cash flow in steel operations and allocate 1 percent of earnings to worker retraining. Brock was not certain the administration could agree. But Rostenkowski insisted, and was granted most of his demands. One by one the other issues were worked out, in a frenetic 26-hour conference punctuated by both policy and personal tensions. By the conclusion of the Senate-House deliberations Friday afternoon, Congress had abandoned its weekend adjournment target, and the compromise bill, labeled the Trade and Tariff Act of 1984, was adopted by both houses the following Tuesday. Somehow, observed the *Post* in a follow-up editorial, "most of the bad stuff got thrown out (in conference) and all of the good stuff stayed." Singled out for special praise was "William E. Brock, who worked mightily and, as it turned out, highly effectively to change the thrust of this bill."[34]

Somewhat surprisingly, it had proved possible for Congress to pass a general trade bill that extended an unpopular program (GSP), while omitting or gutting more protectionist provisions than it incorporated. Language designed to benefit copper, ferroalloys, shoes, and dairy products was deleted or rendered harmless. On preferences, in fact, the bill represented a move in the liberal-internationalist direction, in comparison with the 1974 law that it replaced. It encouraged the administration to negotiate with the NICs for market access and intellectual property rights, and offered the NICs inducements as well as penalties.

Most remarkable, perhaps, was the fact that the bill and the debate surrounding it scarcely even mentioned Japan, usually the number one target of congressional trade ire.

---

34. "On Trade, a Happy Ending," *Washington Post,* 12 October 1984.

But the bill had restrictive provisions as well. It included a watered-down but still objectionable precedent on wine, allowing producers of grapes to challenge wine imports and thus threatening a serious confrontation with the European Community. It also included technical changes in the trade-remedy laws, with such obscure labels as "cumulation," which tilted them in favor of domestic claimants. Most serious, however, was the protectionist provision that originated in the administration—the new steel policy. The White House had suggested that it would seek to limit total steel imports to a certain level, in a way that the industry read as a promise. So the way was cleared for the bill to incorporate a global import target, something even the textile industry had been unable to achieve. It was written as a bipartisan compromise—between 17 (Mondale) and 20.2 percent (the Reagan target)—reflecting only the "sense of Congress." But it was to become the standard by which the administration's negotiating efforts were judged. And the bill included a future threat, of "such legislative actions concerning steel and iron ore products as may be necesary," if the Reagan program did not "produce satisfactory results within a reasonable period of time."[35]

The entire steel title was enacted hastily, without hearings or serious review of the language in either body. It was pushed by Rostenkowski and embraced by Senate conferees because it was something to give the House, to make the whole bill go.

The legislation seemed to "clear the decks" insofar as congressional trade action was concerned. Aside from the adjustment assistance program that was due to expire in September 1985 (whose extension in the House bill was not agreed to by the conference), there was now nothing that Congress *had* to do on trade until the NTB negotiating authority expired in January 1988. So as the Ninety-eighth Congress completed its work, there was a widespread expectation that its successor would focus on other issues.

However, this was not to be. The year 1985 would prove, by almost any measure, the postwar year of greatest congressional trade *intensity*. After the late-January release of figures showing a $123 billion[36] trade deficit for the calendar year 1984, both House and Senate were seized with trade proposals, many of them highly protectionist. That fall, Congress would pass a highly restrictive textile quota bill, forcing a presidential veto. The next spring, the House would endorse an omnibus trade bill tilted strongly in the protectionist direction.

---

35. Trade and Tariff Act of 1984, Sec. 803.

36. Commerce reported trade figures first on a c.i.f. basis, with imports including the cost of freight, as required by the Trade Agreements Act of 1979. The "customs value" deficit figure, preferred by economists, was $107 billion, later adjusted to $114 billion. This study generally uses customs value trade statistics, to facilitate historical comparison.

1985–86: Congress Seizes the Initiative

The initial target in 1985 was Japan, the nation whose trade surplus with the United States was the largest. As recounted at greater length in chapter 9, Danforth and his Senate Finance colleagues felt frustrated on a number of fronts. The bilateral imbalance, conservatively measured, had shot up from $19.3 to $33.6 billion, making it far higher than any the United States had ever run with any country. At the same time, American negotiators seeking to open Japanese markets felt continuing frustration, even regarding products like telecommunications, which had a long negotiating history and a strong commitment to progress by Prime Minister Yasuhiro Nakasone. And the Reagan administration was declaring itself ready to end voluntary auto restraints. Before March was out, the Senate had passed, without opposition, a strongly worded Danforth resolution denouncing "unfair Japanese trade practices" and calling for retaliation unless Japan opened its markets to American products sufficiently to offset its anticipated increases in auto sales. The House followed with a parallel resolution, which, although it was directed more at the overall US trade imbalance and its macroeconomic causes, still singled out Japan for priority attention.

The concerns of Danforth and his Republican colleagues involved politics as well as policy. If Republicans did not find a way to get out front on trade, the issue might really threaten them in the midterm elections a year from November. This fear gained substance in August 1985, when a Democrat, blaming imports for lost jobs, won a close race for an open congressional seat, taking particular advantage of his opponent's unthinking rejoinder questioning "what trade had to do with East Texas."

By that summer, three prominent, centrist Democrats on the trade committees—Bentsen of Senate Finance, Rostenkowski and Gephardt of House Ways and Means—had cosponsored a bill imposing a surcharge on countries running heavy trade surpluses with the United States. Japan, Korea, Taiwan, and Brazil were the countries potentially affected.

More traditional protectionism flourished as well. The highly restrictive textile quota bill, sponsored by Representative Ed Jenkins (D-Ga.), was originally introduced to stiffen the administration's position in the negotiations on renewal of the Multi-Fiber Arrangement (MFA), which regulates imports from developing nations and Japan. But the bill literally took off, with a majority of senators and nearly three hundred representatives signing on as cosponsors. Its proponents got it through Ways and Means essentially as proposed, with Gibbons reduced to declaring victory when the House passed it by "only" 262 to 159, less than the number required to override a veto.

Unable to get the Finance Committee to take up the measure, Senate sponsors Hollings and Strom Thurmond (R-SC) went around it, attaching the legislation to bill after bill on the floor until Majority Leader Robert Dole was forced to take it up. And in the version passed by the Senate, quotas for shoes were added, as well as a provision calling for voluntary trade restraint on copper. Ronald Reagan vetoed the measure in December, but industry supporters won postponement of an override vote until the following summer. Their minimum aim was to toughen the administration's stance in the MFA talks. In this they were, in the main, successful. They also managed, in the August 1986 veto override vote, to increase their House margin to 276 to 149, although this was still 8 votes short of the two-thirds required.

Legislative initiative continued also on other trade fronts. Danforth's proposal to enforce "reciprocity" on telecommunications products was reported out by Finance. A similar bill was approved by the House Energy and Commerce Committee, which challenged Ways and Means by also drafting its own trade-remedy legislation. The House Democratic caucus formed working groups that made their own proposals, and Senate Democrats did likewise.

In all, by the most comprehensive count, senators and representatives introduced 634 trade bills in 1985. Of these, 99 were directly and seriously protectionist, and 77 more were potentially so, in that they would make quasi-judicial trade relief easier to obtain.[37]

There was also strong movement in both houses to devote 1986 to passing *another* omnibus trade bill. In November 1985, Danforth introduced S. 1860, a new, relatively moderate, 10-title bipartisan proposal with 33 cosponsors, 13 of them from Finance. Early in 1986, the House Democratic leadership launched a more partisan campaign to make trade one of its top priorities. Ways and Means now *had* to move lest it lose its authority, and by early May it had reported out legislation that curbed presidential discretion in trade-remedy cases, mandated retaliation when other nations did not open their markets (with a separate, specific chapter for telecommunications products), and provided for quotas in cases of countries—Japan, Taiwan, West Germany—running large bilateral surpluses with the United States. After being combined with bills reported out of other committees, the omnibus measure passed the House later that same month by 295 to 115.

The White House denounced the bill as "pure protectionism," a "rankly political" action that would be "trade-destroying, not trade-creating."[38] This was technically misleading on its substance, but all too accurate about its

---

37. See fn. 24.
38. Statement by White House Deputy Press Secretary Larry M. Speakes, 22 May 1986.

likely results. Unlike the Jenkins bill or Smoot-Hawley, the omnibus measure did not restrict imports directly. But it revised section after section of general US trade laws to make it easier for firms to qualify for import relief, and harder for presidents to deny it to them. It also represented a giant step toward unilateralism, establishing new, "made in USA" standards for fair and unfair trade that were not sanctioned by GATT rules or established international practice. It therefore merited the label of "process protectionism." The likely outcome, were it to become law, would be a significant rise in *de facto* US import restrictions, even though this was not necessarily the intent of all members who voted for the omnibus legislation.

Senate Republicans did not share President Reagan's unhappiness with the bill. Indeed, many of its provisions had counterparts in S. 1860, although that bill was more moderate, taken as a whole. Members of the Committee on Finance would have liked to move their own trade measure, but they were preoccupied through the spring and summer with major tax-reform legislation: first getting committee agreement, then bringing it to the Senate floor, then working out differences in a conference with the House which lasted until the August recess. Thus, while trade hearings were held as schedule permitted, Finance senators could not get to the actual trade bill-drafting stage until September, a month before adjournment time. With the administration preferring no action in 1986, it proved impossible to achieve consensus among committee members on the omnibus legislation's substance and priority. So it died in committee. But trade was bound to be on the agenda of the One-hundredth Congress which would convene in January 1987.

1984 and Thereafter: The Leadership Difference

In 1984, Congress passed a modest, balanced trade law. Why? Legislative success that year was the product of a confluence of particular personalities: Brock, Danforth, and Rostenkowski. Each, in a different way, wanted the omnibus bill to pass and each was skilled in moving it forward. Each was willing to limit rewards to special interests. Each proved indispensable to its success.

But the way that it moved through the Congress underscored the weakness of the old institutional checks, particularly in the House. With Ways and Means deadlocked, the Senate had to go first, something Wilbur Mills would never have allowed. This exposed the bill to the vagaries of that free-wheeling chamber and guaranteed that there would be an enormous amount of clean-up work to do in conference, with little time to do it. On wine, an assiduous lobby had lined up hundreds of House cosponsors and a relentless

Senate exponent in Pete Wilson (R-Calif.). Trapped, the conferees had to accept a bad, GATT-illegal trade precedent, although they managed to dilute it somewhat.

The erosion of congressional power centers increases the burden on executive branch trade leaders, who must immerse themselves more than ever in the politics of Capitol Hill. The combination of increased protectionist pressure and reduced congressional capacity to handle it makes the trade policy-making system even more dependent on the liberal trade commitment and the political skill of the senior officials at the other end of Pennsylvania Avenue. It becomes necessary for administration people to delve deeply into the legislative game, arguing and resisting and bargaining with protection-seekers.

Brock and his staff performed this service in 1984, helping to protect Congress from itself. In 1985, however, White House attention was elsewhere for most of the year. The administration lost the initiative in trade politics, and despite important September policy changes, proved unable to regain it that year or the next. For the story of how and why, we turn to the subject of the next chapter, the executive branch.

5

An Embattled Executive

From the 1930s onward, the key activator of liberal American trade policies has been the executive branch of the government. Whether negotiating abroad or facing pressure at home, US officials responsible for international economic relations have leaned consistently in the direction of reducing barriers and expanding trade. Presidents, while only occasionally involved in day-to-day decisions, have supported governmental experts in this liberal tendency and lent their names and their weight, periodically, to the major steps forward. Hence, the 1960s negotiations were dubbed the Kennedy Round. The successor talks might well have been remembered as the "Nixon Round" had not Watergate rendered that label unappealing.

Successive congresses not only endorsed executive branch trade leadership, but sought to centralize it in an institution that would balance domestic and international concerns. The Trade Expansion Act of 1962 created the position of President's Special Representative for Trade Negotiations (STR). After two Nixon administration efforts to weaken or abolish it, the Trade Act of 1974 made STR a statutory unit in the Executive Office of the President. Five years later, Congress forced the Carter administration to carry out a trade reorganization that increased the office's size and power and renamed it USTR (for Office of the United States Trade Representative). And in 1983, strong resistance from Senator John C. Danforth (R-Mo.), chairman of the Finance Subcommittee on Trade, helped block an administration-backed proposal to subsume USTR in a new Department of International Trade and Industry.

The White House trade office proved an effective policy leadership institution. It brought the US government successfully through our two most ambitious multilateral trade negotiations. Its leaders got major trade bills enacted by Congress in 1974 and 1979, and salvaged the Trade and Tariff Act of 1984. The demands of trade leadership drove the office into close relationship with the key trade committees and into an interest-balancing, coping mode with private groups. The office showed greater sensitivity to protection-seeking forces than did, say, the State Department or the Council of Economic Advisers. Nevertheless, its aim was not to bury liberal US trade policy but to keep it alive.

Presidents of both parties have lent continued support to liberal trade policies. But they have not given consistent backing to the White House trade representative as a person or to his office as an institution. Just as Kennedy was reluctant to have Congress structuring "his" executive office, his successors have been ambivalent, more often than not, about a high-profile White House trade office with which they had limited day-to-day contact. Presidential political aides have been wary as well. In the first Reagan term, the Secretary of Commerce was able to use his White House ties, and the added trade powers given his department in 1980, to pose a strong challenge to USTR William E. Brock. And in the second Reagan term, Brock's successor, Clayton K. Yeutter, had his hands full trying to establish himself as the administration's senior trade broker.

In the 1980s this presidential ambivalence toward USTR was joined by a rise in piecemeal protectionism, in steps taken to shield specific industries without offsetting measures on the market-expanding side. President Ronald W. Reagan, as committed in principle to free trade as any postwar incumbent, seemed in practice to be granting as many exceptions as any since Herbert Hoover. And when the record trade imbalance of 1984 and 1985 triggered a political storm on Capitol Hill, his divided, disorganized administration wasted most of a year before fashioning a serious response.

□ □ □

From the 1930s through the 1950s, there was little statutory control of the structure and process of executive branch trade policymaking—who should lead in international trade negotiations, for example, or how complementary domestic negotiations should be conducted. Inevitably, then as now, a range of departments and agencies were involved, especially Agriculture and Commerce within their substantive spheres, and interagency committees were the typical means of handling complex policy and operational issues. Yet as late as 1960, Under Secretary of State C. Douglas Dillon could be so dominant—domestically and internationally—that an important negotiation under the General Agreement on Tariffs on Trade (GATT) was given his name.[1]

But the Dillon Round was the State Department's last hurrah in multilateral trade leadership. When John F. Kennedy moved to break a political stalemate by going after sweeping new barrier-reducing authority—including a man-

---

1. Until 1979, moreover, it was the Secretary of the *Treasury* who had authority over countervailing duty and antidumping cases.

date to negotiate across-the-board (as opposed to item-by-item) reductions—Congress, not surprisingly, extracted quid pro quos that included constraints on executive branch structure and process. Most visible was the creation of an "executive broker," the STR, to oversee US participation in the talks.[2]

STR's Early Ups and Downs

Section 241 of the Trade Expansion Act of 1962 established two roles for this new trade official: the STR was to be "the chief representative of the United States" during the authorized negotiations, and also chairman of the "interagency trade organization" that was to manage them for the President. It said nothing about his staff or its location, however. Kennedy had insisted on having leeway to define these himself, which he did in Executive Order 11075 of 15 January 1963, placing the new unit within the Executive Office of the President. The new negotiator and his aides were clearly intended to play the "executive broker" role required by the American trade policy-making system—between domestic interests and foreign governments, between the executive branch and the Congress, and among the concerned government agencies.

During the Kennedy Round, STR played this role with a small staff, about 25 professionals, and substantial sharing of specific analytic and negotiating tasks with State and, to a lesser degree, Commerce and Agriculture.[3] President Kennedy filled the post with a prominent Republican, former Secretary of State (and Massachusetts Governor) Christian A. Herter. Herter had one deputy for Washington management, William M. Roth, and one for Geneva bargaining, W. Michael Blumenthal. When Herter died from a heart attack in December 1966, President Lyndon B. Johnson designated Roth as his replacement. Neither trade executive spent much time with either president; for example, to prepare for his decision in the crucial climactic stages of the talks in the spring of 1967, LBJ worked mainly with and through his Deputy Special Assistant for National Security Affairs,

---

2. Also significant, at least as harbinger for the future, was a provision making two senators and two representatives accredited members of the US negotiating team for the first time. The STR was also required to seek advice and information from industry, agriculture, and labor representatives. As in previous talks, the administration had to give public notice and hold hearings before agreeing to reduce tariffs for a particular industry. And the Tariff Commission was to advise on the probable impact of such reductions on particular sectors.

3. On STR's early years, see Anne H. Rightor-Thornton, "An Analysis of the Office of the Special Representative for Trade Negotiations: The Evolving Role, 1962–1974," in *Commission on the Organization of the Government for the Conduct of Foreign Policy,* appendices, vol. 3, appendix H, June 1975, pp. 88–104.

Francis M. Bator. Yet with his ultimate acceptance of the final Kennedy Round package, Johnson gave his strong endorsement to what the STR-led team had wrought.

From that point until late 1971, however, STR went into eclipse. The big trade negotiation was over, and the role of the office in bilateral and product-specific talks was not well established in either law or practice. In early 1969 Richard M. Nixon's Secretary of Commerce, Maurice H. Stans, made a strong push to have trade coordinating responsibilities transferred to him. Congressional and interest-group opposition blocked this; agricultural groups, in particular, feared they would get short shrift. But Stans won two substantial concessions: the right to control who was appointed STR and the lead role in the major trade action of the early Nixon administration, the "textile wrangle" with Japan. STR became a bureaucratic backwater, weakly led and devoid of presidential support.

There followed a trade policy disaster. Stans bungled the textile negotiation, as his aggressive, insensitive style provoked fierce Japanese resistance. This led to a blunder with Congress: Stans got Nixon to endorse statutory import quotas for textiles. As discussed in chapter 2, this drove Ways and Means Chairman Wilbur D. Mills to push a protectionist bill he privately abhorred. The bill passed the House and got as far as the Senate floor before time ran out in December 1970.[4]

The need to restore central trade policy leadership was now evident, and in 1971 the White House began remedial action by naming a new STR, Idaho lawyer and businessman William D. Eberle. Eberle quickly recruited two strong deputies: William R. Pearce to handle the development of legislation, and Harald B. Malmgren to manage the international negotiations to prepare a new trade round.

But STR was still not secure in the Nixon administration, for the President also established in 1971 a Council for International Economic Policy (CIEP), whose staff was headed by an Assistant to the President for International Economic Affairs—first Peter G. Peterson, then (in 1972) Peter M. Flanigan. And Flanigan moved, with Nixon's apparent endorsement, to have STR formally incorporated in CIEP under his direction.

Many legislators feared that the nonpartisan, "trade expert" character of STR would be destroyed if it were brought into a more "political" (partisan) White House operation. And they had twice seen the Nixon administration ready to sacrifice the trade representative. So House Ways and Means responded in 1973 by adding to the pending bill authorizing a new trade round a section making STR a statutory *office*, something Kennedy had

---

4. For detail on these events, see I.M. Destler, Haruhiro Fukui, and Hideo Sato, *The Textile Wrangle* (Ithaca, NY: Cornell University Press, 1979), chs. 3–10.

resisted. The Senate bill went two steps farther: placing STR in the Executive Office of the President by law, and giving cabinet rank and salary to its chief. As signed by President Gerald R. Ford, the Trade Act of 1974 included all of these provisions.

Even as these steps were being taken, STR was asserting de facto leadership, first in drafting the administration's legislative proposals, then in lobbying the Trade Act through the House and the Senate in 1973 and 1974.[5] In the midst of this campaign, the office enhanced its Capitol Hill standing by what was seen as a tough, successful negotiation of concessions from the European Community to offset the trade-diverting effects of British entry. By the time the MTN bill was enacted, STR had become a congressional as well as a presidential agent. In 1975 and 1976, STR entered another in-between period, as the trade negotiations it was leading moved slowly at Geneva. But this time its position in the executive branch was stronger and more secure. And the stage was set for the ultimate trade brokering success story—the completion of the MTN in 1979 under the leadership of President Jimmy Carter's Special Trade Representative, Robert S. Strauss.

Strauss and the MTN: STR's Days of Glory

Almost alone among senior Carter administration international economic officials, Robert Strauss had no prior experience with trade policy. As former treasurer and then chairman of the Democratic National Committee, his forte had been partisan politics. In the latter post he had begun with a party bitterly divided by its 1972 debacle, and ended with Democrats surprisingly united behind the Carter candidacy. Some of the credit for this outcome was almost universally given to Strauss for his ornery, persistent, inclusive style of interpersonal diplomacy. And along the way he established close relationships with a number of senior senators, including Senate Finance Committee Chairman Russell B. Long.

With his flair for the public spotlight, Strauss brought celebrity to the STR job. Skilled at political maneuvering, he led in reenergizing the MTN negotiations abroad and selling them at home. As STR aides he brought in trade or management specialists, not partisan politicos: Geneva Deputy (later to be Carter White House operations chief) Alonzo L. McDonald; Washington Deputy (and former STR general counsel) Alan Wm. Wolff;

---

5. For a detailed account, see I.M. Destler, *Making Foreign Economic Policy* (Washington: Brookings Institution, 1980), chs. 10, 11.

General Counsel (and former Finance Committee aide) Richard R. Rivers. And Strauss promptly demonstrated his ability to act as a broker in sensitive trade issues by negotiating orderly marketing agreements with Korea and Taiwan on shoes, and with Japan on color television sets. He also led in bilateral, market-expanding negotiations with Tokyo.

His handling of Japanese market issues in later 1977 and early 1978 illustrated Strauss' unique blend of verbal hyperbole and political adroitness. Until that fall, other administration officials had been more active than he on US-Japanese economic issues, voicing special concern about Tokyo's growing world trade and current account surplus. Strauss seized the initiative by exaggerating the danger. He declared—with little if any supporting evidence—that US-Japan relations were near the "bursting point," and that Congress would likely go protectionist when it reconvened in January 1978, unless Japan made significant market-opening commitments. Turning aside an initiative from Senate staff aides to hold Finance Committee hearings on US-Japan issues—that might raise the political temperature too much, he thought—he nevertheless urged senators to be very demanding in their private conversations with Japanese trade officials.

When a newly designated Japanese Minister for International Economic Policy flew to Washington in December, Strauss got Finance Committee senators to host a very tough private luncheon. And Strauss himself immediately and "very candidly" declared the minister's offer of tariff and quota adjustments to be "insufficient," falling "considerably short" of what was necessary. This made it possible for Strauss to find an anticipated further concession "promising," and to imply that US toughness was beginning to bear fruit. He traveled to Japan the following month to complete a revised Japanese trade agreement, and, by threatening to fly home without signing, he won further concessions on its language.

When he then reported the deal to senators at a Finance Committee hearing, the first thing Strauss did was to give *them* the credit. He thanked them, "on behalf of the entire nation," for "the strong bipartisan support" they had given to US negotiators. He described the broad result in expansive terms: Japanese Prime Minister Takeo Fukuda had "crossed the political Rubicon," and the specific Japanese commitments in the agreement represented "an entire change of direction and change of philosophy of trade" on Tokyo's part. But he cautioned that implementation was "just beginning."

When Senator William V. Roth, Jr., (R-Del., no relation to the former STR) suggested hearings every six months to monitor progress with Japan, Strauss responded that that was not often enough. "I think I should report to you on a more frequent basis, if you have the time in the Senate to do it." He wanted the Japanese and the Germans and the European Community (EC) "to feel some of the pressure from the Congress that I feel. You know, you are breathing down my neck every day," he told Senator William D.

Hathaway (D-Me.). "I would like to turn that red hot breath toward the people we are trading with."[6]

The performance was vintage Strauss—part substance, part charade—as his more savvy Senate interlocutors fully realized. But his game was their game too: he was giving them credit for toughness greater than they had actually displayed, and greater credit than they deserved for such negotiating results as were achieved. Yet while deferring to them in rhetoric, he kept the action initiative for himself—just as they wanted him to do. For he was absorbing the political heat, diverting pressure from them. With the Japanese also, Strauss was adroit, for although his strong words ruffled their sensitivities, they also gave Tokyo bureaucrats and politicians a credible rationale for making trade concessions. In both cases, Strauss was the consummate activist broker—keeping the game going, getting results that at least defused the immediate crisis, and spreading credit around in a way that enhanced his own central role, instead of diminishing it.

Strauss was also playing another old game in trade politics, that of "export politics." The main domestic pressures concerning Japan were coming from import-competing industries like producers of color TVs and steel, and the Carter administration accommodated these pressures with moderate trade-restraining arrangements. But it preferred to push trade-*expanding* issues. Thus, it encouraged agricultural export interests and then employed these interests as pressure in winning limited, grudging Japanese expansion of beef and citrus quotas. The overall gain was small—no more than $50 million set against a bilateral trade deficit with Japan that would reach $12 billion in 1978. But to the degree that discontent with Tokyo on trade was generalized in nature, such tactics channeled this discontent into pressure for expanding exports, not restricting imports. (The Carter administration also pressed Tokyo to stimulate its economy and allow the yen to appreciate, in order to reduce Japan's growing trade surplus.)

"Export politics" also was prominent in early 1979 when the United States, in order to broaden the coverage of the MTN government procurement code, pressed Tokyo to internationalize the purchases of its government telecommunications agency, Nippon Telephone and Telegraph (NTT).[7] In

---

6. US Congress, Senate, Committee on Finance, Subcommittee on International Trade, *Hearing on United States/Japanese Trade Relations and the Status of the Multilateral Trade Negotiations*, 95th Cong., 2d Sess., 1 February 1978, pp. 9, 12, 13, 22. For a fuller discussion of those negotiations, see I. M. Destler, "United States–Japanese Relations and the American Trade Initiative of 1977: Was this 'Trip' Necessary?" in *Japan and the United States: Challenge and Opportunity,* edited by William J. Barnds (New York, NY: New York University Press [for the Council on Foreign Relations], 1979), pp. 190–230.

7. See Timothy J. Curran, "Politics and High Technology: The NTT Case," in *Coping with U.S.-Japanese Economic Conflicts,* edited by I.M. Destler and Hideo Sato, (Lexington, Mass.: Lexington Books, 1982), pp. 185–241.

that case again, US officials, with Strauss in the lead, sought to reinforce domestic interests in export expansion and to counter and limit the influence of those seeking import restriction.

A more comprehensive and structured form of brokering took place within the private-sector advisory committees that were established under the Trade Act to work with US negotiators in setting and implementing MTN goals. In response to complaints from some in the business community about their limited and ad hoc role in the Kennedy Round, Congress had added a detailed section to the 1974 law, setting forth requirements and guidelines to institutionalize "advice from the private sector." Working with Commerce, Labor, and Agriculture, STR was required to organize general and sectoral committees that would, "so far as practicable, be representative of all industry, labor, or agricultural interests. . . ."[8]

Initially, some officials feared that the requirement for such elaborate private-sector consultation would prove a strait-jacket, for the law even provided that the Special Trade Representative must inform the advisory committees—and give reasons—when he did not accept their counsel! In practice, however, the advisory network proved a great boon. Membership on the committees gave producers a forum for pressing specific concerns; film manufacturers could argue that a reduction on Japanese tariffs would increase their sales, for example. And committee members knew that trade negotiators would listen and try to respond, since each committee would report independently to the Congress on how it viewed the final MTN agreements. The advisory committee system gave Congress what its members particularly favored: a place away from Capitol Hill where they could refer petitioning interests and assure them that they would get a hearing. Each committee was broad enough (for example, "Industrial Chemicals and Fertilizers," "Nonferrous Metals") to encompass a range of firms and interests. Their exposure to one another gave committee members a broader perspective, and it gave executive officials useful leeway on whose advice they finally took. And because the advisers felt they were taken seriously— and came to understand the constraints faced by their governmental counterparts—they developed sympathy for the larger enterprise and modest personal identification with its success.

As noted by Gilbert R. Winham, broader lessons can be drawn from this experience:

In delegating the task of constituency relations to the executive, Congress took advantage of the capacity of governmental bureaucracy to take the initiative in dealing with constituents. . . . The same [advisory group] system that organized the sectoral interests and gave them influence in govern-

---

8. Trade Act of 1974, Sec. 135.

ment also structured the task of the executive in dealing with those interests. In the words of one government official, "The SAC system gave STR a series of targets to shoot at." . . . [It also] meant that communications with constituency groups generally occurred in an environment defined by trade bureaucracies and not by the constituents themselves. . . .

To sum up, the Tokyo Round experience demonstrated that channels of access could be two-way streets: access to the executive by the private sector could also mean access to the private sector by the executive. In comparison to Congress, which is the normal arena of interest-group activity, the executive was better able to confront constituency groups with a coordinated plan of its own for trade policy. . . . It is customary in classic thinking about government to assume that bureaucracy inhibits initiative, but in fact, because of its superior capacity to gather, organize and analyze information, bureaucracy is the instrument of the initiative in contemporary large-scale government.[9]

At the final stage of the MTN, Strauss's political skills were tested by a crisis that was partially of his own making. Europeans had participated in the MTN on condition that the United States not impose countervailing duties on EC exports before the subsidies code was negotiated. Congress had reluctantly granted the Secretary of the Treasury the authority to waive countervailing duties for four years, until 3 January 1979. But when it became clear that the MTN would not be quite completed by then, and Strauss and his Hill allies failed to get the waiver extended before Congress adjourned for the year in October 1978, Europeans refused to continue. An intricate rescue was required. At home, the United States deferred collection of the duties, while Strauss bargained with Congress to extend the waiver retroactively.[10] In the meantime, the Europeans agreed to resume talking, but not to sign anything until the waiver extension became law, which it did in March 1979.

In the end, everything came together in one of the Carter administration's major policy successes. Nontariff barrier codes were completed to regulate government behavior on subsidies, government procurement, product standards, etc. The United States granted long-sought concessions—abandonment of the American Selling Price system of customs valuation,[11] and an injury

---

9. Gilbert R. Winham, *International Trade and the Tokyo Round Negotiation* (Princeton, NJ: Princeton University Press, 1986), pp. 315, 316, 317. Another useful discussion of the advisory group experience appears in Joan E. Twiggs, *The Tokyo Round of Multilateral Trade Negotiations: A Case Study*" (Washington: Institute for the Study of Diplomacy, Georgetown University School of Foreign Service, 1984), ch. 4.

10. As described in chapter 4, this required increased protection for the textile industry.

11. This was a provision of US customs law, long offensive to America's trading partners, which required that duties on certain products (benzenoid chemicals, rubber footwear, etc.) be calculated by multiplying the tariff rate not by the price of the import, the normal procedure, but by the higher selling price of the competing US product. This inflated actual duties considerably.

test for the imposition of countervailing duties—in exchange for commitments on a range of trade-distorting foreign practices. Of the 38 private-sector advisory committees, 27 made positive reports to Congress, with 5 neutral and just 6 tilted toward the critical side. As recounted in chapter 4, STR collaborated with its congressional counterparts in drafting the implementing bill, which passed overwhelmingly. A triumphant Strauss moved on to other pursuits, as did all of his senior STR colleagues.

The Executive Broker and Its Critics

Strauss was *sui generis*, but the way he handled trade policy was broadly consistent with the tradition of the postwar system. He aimed to balance pressures, build coalitions, give a little here, get a little there—but above all to keep the overall American and global trade regime moving in a trade-expanding direction. For the ultimate goal of postwar US trade leaders was not maximum US advantage but openness in general, a trade world where American products and firms could compete as freely as possible with others. It was assumed that the United States as a whole would do well in such a world; others would gain, but so would we, and we would remain in the front economic rank. Trade was a positive-sum game, and liberal policies would make everyone better off, ourselves included.

Of course, no US trade official could argue openly for brokering as the primary function. If US trade negotiators were to keep their mandate from Congress and product interests, they had to appear tough in advancing and defending US commercial interests. And if aggressiveness simply meant assertive trade bargaining and going after those foreign trade barriers that blocked promising US trade opportunities, this was fully consistent with the postwar brokering tradition. Successive administration leaders *did* pursue market openness abroad even as they did so at home. This was the path to expanding the volume of trade. And "export politics" demanded it. Only by convincing industries and firms that there was money to be earned overseas could officials engage them in policy struggles, balancing the ever-active forces that sought import restrictions.

There were political risks, of course. A tough, critical, visible market-expanding campaign—like those of successive administrations toward Japan—might buttress executive credibility, but it would also fuel anti-Japanese sentiment. For in practice the best "leading indicator" of congressional activism on Japan in the 1970s and early 1980s was executive branch activism. Noisy, visible negotiations got congressional attention and drew members and their staffs into the policy game of pressing their demands. And "Japan-bashing" by the executive branch legitimized Japan-bashing on Capitol Hill, though up to a point, this too could be useful to executive brokers, as Strauss demonstrated.

For Strauss and for his less famous predecessors, the flexibility of the STR arrangement was useful, as was its White House location. These features made it easier not just to engage important business interests but to bring into the balance departments like Treasury or State, which were dependably antiprotectionist for economic or diplomatic reasons. But when compared to other units within the Executive Office of the President (EOP), STR was an organizational anomaly. First, unlike the coordinating staffs for broad subjects like national security or domestic policy, STR was a special-purpose operating unit, typically distant from daily presidential business. Second, it was staffed by "professional" trade specialists, in contrast to the more partisan recruitment pattern that became the norm at the National Security Council and its domestic counterpart. Yet STR did have rapid staff turnover, and hence it was not a career bureaucracy with an institutional memory like, say, the old Bureau of the Budget.

These organizational features made STR a natural target of reorganizers. So did frustration about trade policy. As set forth in chapter 3, the relative position of the United States was, by most measures, declining. Throughout the postwar period, other advanced industrial nations had grown faster, closing the gap in per capita income and individual well-being. Our merchandise trade balance, consistently in surplus through 1970, was almost always in deficit thereafter. Major industries were losing international market share—and not just textiles or shoes, but steel, automobiles, and consumer electronics as well. It was easy to draw from this evidence a broader diagnosis of American industrial decline and to view "trade wars" as a prime contributor to this decline.

Thus, there developed an alternative view of US trade policy which held that priority had to be given to halting and reversing this decline. Uncle Sam had to stop being the world's nice guy. As Russell Long put it in 1974, the United States could no longer afford to be the world's "least favored nation," exposing our markets while the rest of the world employed "practices which effectively bar our products."[12] Others were taking advantage—Japan in particular—and America had to fight back. Our policy should thus give priority to the relative position of the United States, particularly in the industries of the future. There was also a general belief among congressional trade specialists that the US Treasury Department had not, in

---

12. US Congress, Senate, Committee on Finance, *Hearings on the Trade Reform Act of 1973*, 93d Cong., 2d Sess., 4 and 5 March 1974, part 1, p.2. Challenges to the general trade-expanding and brokering tradition in postwar US trade policy are discussed further in chapter 7.

practice, been carrying out its responsibility to enforce laws aimed at penalizing foreign dumping and subsidies.

These factors combined to generate dissatisfaction with the executive-branch trade structure even as Strauss was moving to his triumphant congressional votes. To some, there was a link between the disappointing market results and the dispersion of various trade functions within the executive branch. The Senate Finance Committee summarized these concerns:

Trade is not given a very high priority in terms of commitment of resources and the attention to top governmental policy officials on a regular basis, other than the STR. Additionally, major trade functions are spread throughout the Executive branch making formulation of trade policy and implementation of trade policy haphazard and in some cases contradictory. No single agency exists which clearly predominates in the formulation of trade policy to the extent that people with a trade issue know where in the Executive branch they can turn to find a person who will give their particular problem attention and whom they and the rest of the government can hold accountable. Another problem that has been noted often is that the present organization of the Executive branch with respect to trade has failed to result in retaining experienced trade personnel, so that often the United States is faced with the prospect of entering trade negotiations with other countries who have a tough, seasoned corps of trade negotiators. Further, the lack of coordination and lack of attention to trade issues has often resulted in failure to aggressively enforce US unfair trade practice statutes and to insist on US rights under international trade agreements.[13]

STR had established a clear lead role for major multilateral negotiations and an important one in bilateral and product-specific issues. Yet other trade responsibilities were spread about: Commerce promoted exports, Treasury handled unfair trade practice cases, Agriculture dealt with grain sales, and most major departments influenced presidential decisions on escape clause cases.

One proposal for clarifying matters was to consolidate most of these functions within a new Department of Trade. This idea got its first prominent exposure when the author of a study on US international economic policymaking showed a draft proposal to a staff aide of Senator Roth; the aide liked it and so did his boss, who introduced it as a bill and won the cosponsorship of the Chairman of the Finance Trade Subcommittee, Abraham A. Ribicoff (D-Conn.).[14] So when Finance began meeting on the draft MTN results, it voted initially to recommend that the implementing legislation include a provision extablishing a trade department.

---

13. US Congress, Senate, Committee on Finance, *Trade Agreements Act of 1979*, 96th Cong., 1st Sess., 17 July 1979, S. Rept. 96–249, pp. 268–69.

14. For the story as told by a participant, see Stephen D. Cohen, *The Making of United States International Economic Policy*, 2nd edition (New York, NY: Praeger, 1981), ch. 8.

But the Finance senators' commitment to the idea was less than it seemed: Ribicoff was of two minds, and Russell Long preferred to retain the White House office. Moreover, House Ways and Means members did not favor the departmental approach. So, in the end, a compromise was adopted. The draft trade legislation required the President to *consider* establishing a trade department (along with other options), and to submit a specific trade reorganization proposal to Congress by 10 July 1979. When that date instead found Carter on his famous retreat to Camp David, soliciting insights from a range of national leaders about what had gone wrong with his presidency, Ribicoff held up final Senate action on the MTN package. This had the intended impact. On 19 July, Carter sent forth to Congress a reorganization proposal which, after further consultation and resubmission, became effective in January 1980.

The Carter Reorganization

The Carter reforms created, in essence, a two-tiered executive branch structure. On top was an enlarged and renamed Office of the *United States Trade Representative* (USTR). It was assigned "international trade policy development, coordination and negotiation functions," and it included responsibilities previously handled by State regarding the General Agreement on Tariffs on Trade (GATT), bilateral, commodity, and East-West trade matters, as well as policy responsibility for overseeing trade-remedy cases.

At the level of trade administration, Commerce was to become "the focus of nonagricultural operational trade responsibilities." It was therefore given Treasury's authority over countervailing duty and antidumping cases, as well as State's jurisdiction over commercial attachés. The trade committees had, in fact, insisted on the former step, judging Treasury to be insufficiently aggressive in enforcing the unfair trade statutes. And the adjective "non-agricultural" signaled a bow to political reality: farm interests would never accept the transfer of responsibility and expertise for their products from the US Department of Agriculture.

The USTR half of the Carter reorganization reflected the sensible principle that in restructuring government one should start with organizations and processes that work. The Trade Representative's office had completed the MTN with success and with a reputation for effectiveness, and it was better to build on that than to start anew. There was some risk of making its staff too large.[15] This could incline USTR toward too much in-house detail work,

---

15. The Carter administration, under substantial congressional pressure, increased the number of permanent USTR staff slots to 131, compared to 59 in STR.

at the expense of reaching out and mobilizing the resources of all agencies. And assigning it difficult tasks outside the GATT-MTN mainstream, such as East-West trade policy coordination, did not necessarily bring added strength. Still, a timely, visible reinforcement of STR's mandate helped offset the tendency for trade policy power to disperse whenever a multilateral round was completed.

The reasons for strengthening Commerce were more ad hoc. It was there. It already handled certain operational trade functions, such as industry information and export promotion. So it seemed a logical home for other trade tasks whose current management generated dissatisfaction. Moreover, Carter did not want the White House trade office to grow too much, since this would undo his earlier reorganization, which had *reduced* the total number of Executive Office personnel. So those functions that required an expanded, specialized staff—enforcement of unfair trade laws, for example— were placed in Commerce.

The overall package was rationalized by an old and largely discredited public administration dichotomy—the separation of policy from operations, with the corollary that the former could control the latter.[16] USTR, with policy leadership responsibility, would be in charge; Commerce would carry the policy out. This *could* work, but only if both organizations and their leaders accepted these roles and worked closely and cooperatively, with Commerce deferring to USTR direction.

Under Carter, the system performed adequately; at least there was no major conflict between Commerce and USTR. Both had to adjust to new leaders. Commerce busied itself with filling a range of new positions, including an Under Secretary for trade who would oversee the department's renamed and expanded International Trade Administration, which now had no fewer than 17 officials at or above the deputy assistant secretary level. The new USTR was former Florida governor Reubin O'D. Askew, who lacked Strauss's political mastery and close presidential ties; however, no single competitor rose to challenge his leadership on trade issues.

Reagan I: Commerce vs USTR

Askew's successor, William E. Brock, was not so lucky. Like Strauss four years earlier, Brock in 1981 had just completed a successful term as his

---

16. For a more general discussion of the persistence and limits of this approach to foreign policy management see I.M. Destler, *Presidents, Bureaucrats, and Foreign Policy: The Politics of Organizational Reform* (Princeton, NJ: Princeton University Press, 1972), pp. 18–22.

party's national chairman. And once in the trade job, he would demonstrate comparable talents on Capitol Hill.

Yet a month before Brock was named to the USTR position, President-elect Ronald Reagan chose as Secretary of Commerce a capable, ambitious Connecticut businessman named Malcolm Baldrige. In discussions surrounding the appointment, it became public knowledge that influential Reagan counselor Edwin Meese favored abolishing USTR and giving Baldrige the primary trade responsibility. Again, the fact that the trade representative's office was an organizational oddity, a "line" unit (possessing specific policy responsibility) within the President's Executive Office staff, rendered it vulnerable to reformers who sought to streamline structure before they understood substance. Brock, one of the last Cabinet-level appointees announced by Reagan, had therefore to respond in his confirmation hearings to claims by the incoming Commerce Secretary that he, not Brock, would be the central trade policy figure.

Brock replied by reiterating the "indispensible" USTR function: it "must continue to be, for the President and the Congress, the government's principal architect and exponent of trade policy to insure that we act and speak as one." Three successive laws had made the Trade Representative Chairman of the statutory interagency trade committee, so that matter was settled; moreover, he had had "fairly extended conversations with the Secretary of Commerce" and they had "a very healthy and solid commitment to the same goal": an "aggressive" trade and export policy. He was sure they would "work very effectively together."[17] Nevertheless, when the Reagan administration, under Meese's leadership, created its own (nonstatutory) network of coordinating committees, it was Baldrige who chaired the Cabinet Council on Commerce and Trade.

In practice, neither man was able to establish clear predominance in the first Reagan administration. Brock was supported by the precedent of successful leadership by previous STRs. He also had strong policy and political skills and close ties to senators and congressmen, having served (like Cordell Hull) in both chambers. Indeed, when the new Cabinet Council on Commerce and Trade held its first meeting under Baldrige's chairmanship, both the Finance and Ways and Means chairmen reportedly phoned the President and informed him that this was against the law! Yet the Commerce Secretary had political resources also: a stronger relationship with Reagan (and with Meese), the new authorities given Commerce in the Carter reorganization, and the talents of an aggressive Under Secretary, Lionel H. Olmer. So while Brock handled auto imports from Japan and headed the

---

17. US Congress, Senate, Committee on Finance, *Hearing on the Nomination of William E. Brock, III,* 97th Cong., 1st Sess., 19 January 1981, pp. 3, 10, 12, 13.

US delegation at the unsuccessful GATT ministerial talks of November 1982, it was Baldrige who brokered between American steel companies and European governments to work out a voluntary export restraint agreement earlier that same year.

The Commerce Secretary built up his trade staff in 1982 by adding four deputy assistant secretaries with regional portfolios. Beginning in 1980, Commerce also established the first credible enforcement operation for the unfair trade laws. (The consequences are addressed in chapter 6.)

And Baldrige continued also in his quest for government-wide trade dominance. His persistence was hardly surprising, for trade was by far the most prominent of his department's substantive responsibilities, and it naturally attracted any aggressive Secretary with decent White House connections. And if Maurice Stans had failed egregiously in 1969–71, Baldrige did a bit better 12 years later. In the spring of 1983, despite the opposition of Brock and almost all other senior presidential advisers, President Reagan accepted a Baldrige-Meese recommendation that the administration endorse Senator Roth's proposal for a Department of International Trade and Industry, with USTR incorporated therein. The Commerce Secretary spent much of the rest of Reagan's first term lobbying to win industry support for that reorganization.

The reemergence of the trade department proposal raised anew the question of whether the brokering function was adequate for trade leadership. Roth's Governmental Affairs Committee argued the negative in its report recommending approval of the legislation: "Trade needs a champion in government. The new Department Secretary will be this champion. The USTR was created as a broker, not an advocate." Or to quote the views of three Democrats:

USTR was established basically to pull together our position for multilateral negotiations at a time when our major trade problem was coordinating and balancing our own diverse interests, and we had no significant industrial problems. We now have a host of other problems, and most of the negotiating action has shifted into the bilateral arena. We need a more focused effort to deal coherently with trade, industry, and competitiveness questions.[18]

Nonetheless, the trade department idea did not move very far on Capitol Hill. To win bipartisan endorsement by his committee, Roth had to accept organizational add-ons that compromised the "lean, mean" department he

---

18. US Congress, Senate, Committee on Governmental Affairs, *Trade Reorganization Act of 1983*, 98th Cong., 2d Sess., 3 April 1984, S. Rept. 98–374, pp. 8, 128. The three Democrats were Thomas F. Eagleton of Missouri, Carl Levin of Michigan, and Jeff Bingaman of New Mexico.

favored. Most important was an industrial policy mechanism pushed by Democrats: for any trade-threatened sector of national significance, the Secretary was to convene an "industry sector competitiveness council" representing business, labor, and government to recommend an action program. This was but a watered-down version of a proposal for a permanent Council on Industrial Strategy, but it nonetheless served to reduce the Reagan administration's enthusiasm for the venture. Pungent opposition by Finance Trade Subcommittee Chairman John C. Danforth (R-Mo.) delayed, and ultimately prevented, the bill from reaching the Senate floor in 1984. In the House, it never reached the markup stage.

Still, the fact that the President was proposing to eliminate his organization could only damage Brock's standing and the credibility of USTR generally. Brock was further frustrated by the failure of the 1982 GATT ministerial talks and the difficulty of winning endorsement, at home and abroad, for a new round of trade negotiations.

In part because of the struggle between Brock and Baldrige, the first Reagan administration developed a pattern of endorsing liberal trade in principle but tightening protection in practice. The auto quotas initiated in 1981 were understandable, and probably unavoidable, given the industry's sudden crisis. However, they were followed in December 1983 by toughening of restrictions on textile imports, after Baldrige persuaded the president to overturn an 11 to 1 Cabinet committee vote against such a step. Brock's reputation rebounded the following September, as USTR took the lead in explaining and implementing yet another protectionist step—perhaps Reagan's most significant to date—his decision to negotiate sales-limiting agreements with all major steel exporters. On the other hand, Brock also gained by blocking or neutralizing several industry-specific protectionist provisions in his adroit brokering of the Trade and Tariff Act of 1984 (see chapter 4).

Too often, the Reagan administration of 1981–84 failed to take the initiative in the early stages of an industry's trade-relief campaign. Rather than bringing in other interests in order to balance the political equation—using, for example, the industry advisory committees Strauss's STR had employed during the MTN—Reagan's trade leaders tended to wait until a powerful industry like textiles or steel or autos had defined the issue. The question then became one not of whether to protect them, but of how much additional protection to provide.

There were, however, mitigating circumstances. The executive branch trade coordinators lacked the advantage of a central trade negotiation to strengthen their hand within government and vis-à-vis private interests. This also made it harder to establish a credible role for private-sector advisory committees: they lacked the leverage that came from an upcoming report to a Congress poised for decision, so they were taken less seriously by both the firms that sent representatives and the officials who made trade policy.[19] Even more important, the trade deficit was ballooning to levels previously unknown. Prominent Democrats were pushing for more protection, not less, and it looked for a while as if trade would become a central issue in the President's reelection campaign. Reagan was hardly the first incumbent to buy some insurance with sympathetic responses to politically potent industries like textiles or steel.

The trade policy performance of the first Reagan administration was therefore understandable, if not exactly ideal. But its behavior in the first eight months of 1985 can only be described as bizarre. As the trade pressure mounted and mounted, the administration did nothing, and seemed not even to recognize that there was any problem to address.

Reagan II: An Eight-Month Vacuum

First, the President agreed to a 1985 New Year's meeting with Japanese Prime Minister Yasuhiro Nakasone. But despite the urgings of his trade advisers, and despite the fact that the politically sensitive bilateral deficit was rising to an unheard-of $33.6 billion for the calendar year 1984, he decided not to press trade matters with his counterpart. It was only when Nakasone brought up the subject that a bilateral negotiating agenda was established.

In March 1985, with trade-oriented businesses feeling the squeeze of yet another rise in the dollar and with Congress alarmed at a global trade deficit that had topped $100 billion and was climbing, the White House acknowledged political reality by declaring it would not push the trade department proposal further "at this time." But this was followed, two days later, by the announced transfer of the presumed winner in that decision. Now that he had finally established himself as the administration's most respected and politically astute trade man, William Brock was to become Secretary of *Labor!* What would this do to trade policy making? There is no evidence that Reagan or his new Chief of Staff, Donald T. Regan, even asked this question. As *Washington Post* columnist Hobart Rowen put it at the time, "The reality is that the White House seemed to have only one thing on its mind: the need to build new relationships with the labor movement. . . ."[20]

---

19. However, in one case where the advisory committee process might have functioned effectively, the 1984 free trade agreement with Israel, it was not seriously employed.

20. "Filling Bill Brock's Shoes," *Washington Post,* 28 March 1985.

It took more than three months for Brock's successor, Clayton Yeutter, to be named, cleared by the administration, and confirmed by the Senate; it took almost three more months, until late September 1985, for the White House to put forward a visible trade program. As late as August of that year, Reagan had said "no" to the escape clause petition of the shoe industry, a case championed by Danforth. He did this without any apparent recognition that denying relief through established channels to an industry that was clearly damaged by imports was bound to increase pressure for statutory solutions. In that same summer, the administration was slow in producing a letter to Capitol Hill opposing the broadly supported, egregiously protectionist textile quota bill that would later win strong House and Senate majorities. The form of the letter finally sent—cosigned by several cabinet members—allowed the bill's proponents to claim that the President might still sign it.

The administration was no more helpful to trade-embattled industries on what most considered the prime source of their problems, the sky-high dollar. Through the summer, the President and his Chief of Staff tended to speak of this as a good thing, yet another sign that "America was back." Business leaders who talked to the White House (outside USTR) about the havoc this was wreaking in their markets found themselves rebuffed; some were told, in essence, that they were cry-babies and should stop asking for government help against the workings of the marketplace. This made them angry and frustrated. They felt, like many others, that the prime cause of dollar strength was government policy, and specifically the Reagan budget deficits. It was hard for these companies, through their own efforts, to offset an exchange rate estimated to give foreign competitors a 30 to 40 percent cost advantage! Lacking a hearing downtown, they descended with double strength on Capitol Hill.

In 1985 Congress needed more executive branch help than ever, because of its own decentralization, and above all, because of the enormous trade deficit. It was getting just about none. In fact, the administration was doing the opposite of protecting Congress. It was diverting trade-restrictive pressures to Capitol Hill! Little wonder that the number of trade bills increased, as did their prominence and their progress through committees and onto the House and Senate floors. Not only were legislators genuinely concerned about the trade problem; not only did some of them see partisan advantage (or fear partisan disadvantage) in the issue; but the administration was abdicating its central function in the trade-political system at a time when it was needed more than ever. It was not taking the heat and thereby protecting the Congress!

Indeed, one purpose of the congressional activity was to shock the administration into resuming this function. As one aide to a Senate

Republican involved in the spring's Japan-bashing put it this way: "You don't understand. The target isn't the Japanese; it's the White House!" It was also in the interest of executive branch trade staffs to encourage such congressional action, up to a point, since they too were trying to get presidential attention.

Finally, in late September 1985, the administration did put forward a trade strategy. On Sunday the twenty-second, Treasury Secretary James A. Baker III joined with the finance ministers of France, Germany, Japan, and the United Kingdom in a joint declaration calling for a weaker dollar (more precisely, for the "further orderly appreciation of the major nondollar currencies against the dollar"). The Group of Five indicated their intention to intervene in foreign-exchange markets to help bring this about. The dollar responded by falling, particularly in Tokyo, where the Bank of Japan was a heavy buyer of yen. And on Monday the twenty-third, President Reagan gave a "fair trade" speech at the White House, sounding his determination to fight for the rights of American producers in foreign markets, and announcing an intent to press several unfair trade practice cases against Japan, the European Community, Korea, and Brazil.

Both actions were responses to the protectionist threat from Capitol Hill. But the hour was late. During the eight-month leadership vacuum, many legislators had gotten deeper into trade questions, invested their time and reputations in them, and moved Congress toward trade action. The momentum brought the House of Representatives to develop and pass, by 295 to 115 votes, a restrictive trade bill in May 1986.

In 1979 and 1984, Strauss and Brock had developed the requisite combination of influence downtown and standing on Capitol Hill to make themselves major players in the development of trade legislation. The trade representative needed to be if the American trade policy-making system was to function effectively. But in 1986, Reagan's new USTR, Clayton Yeutter, could not play this role fully because the administration had lost credibility on trade, and because its leaders decided that the best strategy at this point was to disassociate itself from the bill-drafting process and denounce the result as "pure protectionism."

The most important of these leaders, in 1985 and 1986, was Secretary of the Treasury James Baker. He had orchestrated the policy change on the dollar, and the interagency Economic Policy Council which he chaired had become the central administration forum on trade issues. In one respect, this limited Yeutter's role, since it made him visibly subordinate to another Cabinet official. But this arrangement brought him advantages as well. There was a clearer locus of decision power, and USTR used the process to get the go-ahead to push more unfair trade cases with foreign governments. Competition with Commerce was also muted. With Baker in overall charge and Edwin Meese, Baldrige's former White House ally, now at the Department of Justice, Yeutter did not face the sort of leadership challenge that Brock had confronted from *that* cabinet Secretary.

In fact, in the September 1986 GATT ministerial talks at Punta del Este which inaugurated the new "Uruguay Round," Yeutter headed a US delegation which included both Baldrige and Secretary of Agriculture Richard E. Lyng. Working together, they won agreement that the new round's agenda would include trade in agricultural products and services, subjects of particular American interest. In so doing, they demonstrated how the USTR leadership role can and should work within the executive branch.

By the fall of 1986, therefore, the Reagan administration had improved significantly both the substance of its foreign economic policies and its processes for making them. But the question remains: why did it take so long? Why did that administration, genuinely committed in principle to open trade, allow the situation to deteriorate so seriously in the months and years before? Part of the explanation lies in policy, above all in the inconsistency between Reagan's tax and spending goals, which produced record fiscal deficits and a super-strong dollar. Part of it lies in personalities: a "big-picture" President and a new, somewhat doctrinaire, and politically insensitive Chief of Staff. But Reagan's neglect of trade policy and the trade office had ample precedent. For as House Trade Subcommittee Chairman Sam Gibbons (D-Fla.) has phrased it, with only modest exaggeration, "Every President that comes in wants to throw the USTR Office out of the White House."[21]

USTR and Presidential Ambivalence

Why was John F. Kennedy reluctant to create a trade representative in the Executive Office of the President (EOP)? Why were Richard M. Nixon and Ronald W. Reagan ready to reorganize the (U)STR out of existence? There were, of course, answers specific to each president's situation. But broader explanations are discernible as well.

One is that presidents have, traditionally and understandably, resisted establishing units to serve other people's purposes in "their" White House. Presidency scholar Richard E. Neustadt, in his role as transition adviser, warned Kennedy against such proposals. Citing Franklin D. Roosevelt's

---

21. US Congress, House, Committee on Ways and Means, Subcommittee on Trade, *Hearings on Options to Improve the Trade Remedy Laws,* 98th Cong., 1st Sess., 16 and 17 March and 13 and 14 April 1983, Serial 98–14, part 1, p. 389.

staffing practices, he urged that JFK start by filling only jobs "for which the President-elect, himself, feels an *immediate and continuing need."* Neustadt inveighed thereafter against "proliferating advisory staffs in your Executive Office."[22] Kennedy generally followed such advice. And 16 years later, Jimmy Carter's Executive Office reorganization similarly aimed at "limiting EOP, wherever possible, to functions which bear a close relationship to the work of the President."[23]

Kennedy did, of course, accede to STR's creation. Carter retained it and, under congressional pressure, broadened its functions and enlarged its staff. Yet the staff has never had the sort of connection to broad *presidential* policy business possessed by, say, the National Security Council or the Office of Management and Budget. It is too specialized, too focused on a specific slice of policy substance and ongoing operations.

Had Congress not wanted (U)STR, it is unlikely that any postwar President would have created such an EOP office on his own. Trade policy just has not loomed large enough, and presidents have seen it as, for the most part, second-order, technical business. When it does become first-order, it is usually because it bears upon their nontrade concerns, like foreign relations or partisan politics. Generally, presidents want protection from trade issues for the same reasons that legislators do: they don't like to say "no" to important interests or to choose among them when choice can be avoided.

This limited presidential interest has limited the capacity of the trade representative to build personal ties with the man in the Oval Office. Only Robert Strauss attained the status of a close presidential adviser, and he kept his access because he was useful to Carter on a broader range of issues.[24] Trade alone would not have given Strauss enough to talk about with the President and his key aides; however, the universal belief around Washington that Strauss was talking regularly with the President was central to his credibility on trade, not only with business and on Capitol Hill, but in foreign capitals as well.

Conversely, those who, like Brock, could not build such strong presidential ties, were vulnerable to challenge from executive branch rivals. Some managed to build a presidential base indirectly: Herter and Roth through

22. "Memorandum on Organizing the Transition," 15 September 1960, p. 7 (emphasis added), and "Memorandum on the Council of Economic Advisers: First Steps," 19 December 1960, p. 2. Copies obtained from Neustadt: both are available in John F. Kennedy Library, Boston, Massachusetts.

23. US Congress, "Reorganization Plan No. 1 of 1977," *Message from the President of the United States,* 95th Cong., 1st Sess., 15 July 1977, H. Doc. 95–185.

24. The index of Jimmy Carter's *Keeping Faith* (New York: Bantam Books, 1982) has seven references to Strauss. Only two refer to his trade job, and none to this substance of trade policy.

the national security staff; Eberle and his deputies through Nixon's "economic czar," George P. Shultz. Indeed, one advantage of the (U)STR's Executive Office location is that it makes such relationships easier for its head to develop than they would be for the head of a separate executive department.

On the other hand, a high-profile USTR, of the sort needed to manage major international trade talks or domestic trade crises, may be hard for a White House Chief of Staff to swallow. The USTR combines independence in day-to-day actions *and* the White House label. He must swear allegiance to Congress as well as the president. This creates obvious difficulties for a Donald Regan seeking to run a tight, hierarchical White House ship. But it has its risks for more flexible political aides as well.

Thus this chapter must end with a political and organizational dilemma. The USTR role is a critical one for trade policy management, never more crucial than it is today. Yet USTR's power base in the executive branch has been difficult to maintain, particularly in the absence of an ongoing major trade negotiation. Any effort to buttress the American trade policy-making system must speak to this dilemma.

But for a fuller picture of the problems faced by USTR and the broader trade policy system, we must turn first to other changes—in "the rules" under which trade-injured industries seek relief, and in the altered, more open national political circumstances within which trade policymakers now operate. The next chapter, therefore, aims to explain how the rules have been transformed from a device used by Congress and the executive to divert trade pressure, to a means employed by protection-seeking interests to intensify it.

6

Changing the Rules: The Limits of Administrative Trade Remedies

Administrative remedy procedures—"the rules"—played a significant role in concept, and a modest role in practice, in the postwar American trade policy-making system.

Consistent with the "escape clause," Article XIX of the General Agreement on Tariffs and Trade (GATT), our trade laws offered recourse to firms and workers injured by import competition. If they met the statutory criteria, the Tariff Commission could recommend and the President order temporary relief, including tariffs, quotas, or other import restraints.

In addition to such *insurance,* the rules also provided *offsets* to "unfair" advantages of foreign competitors, with the sanction of GATT Article VI. In accordance with a statute dating from 1897, if another government gave a "bounty or grant" to a particular industry or firm, our government, on the petition of the American interests affected, was supposed to impose a countervailing duty (CVD) equivalent to the size of the foreign subsidy. It could impose a similar penalty on imports found to be "dumped," or sold in the US market at prices insufficient to cover a foreign firm's production costs plus normal profits.

Finally, there was a program to facilitate *adjustment.* Under the Trade Expansion Act of 1962, if firms were injured or workers lost jobs due to import competition, they were eligible for "trade adjustment assistance" (TAA), financial aid and retraining above and beyond normal unemployment benefits, designed to help them move into new, competitive lines of work.

Up through the early 1970s, however, firms found it difficult to win relief under these statutes. Eligibility criteria for the escape clause and TAA were tightly drawn, and enforcement of the CVD law was at best a sometime thing. So import-competing interests lobbied successfully for changes in the rules that would broaden eligibility and tighten enforcement. By the early 1980s, industries were submitting many more petitions aimed at gaining administrative import relief. And increasingly, they were winning their cases.

Champions of these quasi-judicial procedures defended them as a way to "depoliticize" trade issues, to "run trade on economic law."[1] They would keep trade decisions "out of politics," and petitioners off of legislators' backs, by establishing objective import relief rules that governed the strong and the weak alike. When the rules did not work that way, their response was to refine them further to reduce executive discretion and catch elusive foreign practices.

But as major industries—steel, textiles—moved increasingly to take advantage of these statutes, the effect—and often the intent—was not to lower the political temperature but to raise it. In the large cases, "the rules" changed from a means of diverting political pressure to a means of asserting it. Typically, the policy result was not the remedy specified in law but new "special case" protection for the claimants.

□ □ □

The trade policy justification for the various quasi-judicial procedures was that they provided options for those damaged by the operation of the open system. The political rationale was that they offered an escape valve, a place for congressmen and executive branch leaders to refer complaints, thus easing the pressure to take immediate trade-restrictive action. There was also the promise of equity. Like other government regulatory procedures, the trade "rules" were supposed to take certain tariff and quota decisions out of the political arena, where benefits went to those with the greatest clout, and entrust them to institutions that would act "objectively," relating the rules to the facts of particular cases.

There was only one problem. In concept, such procedures appeared to give advantages to import-injured petitioners.[2] In practice, however, through most of the postwar period, those who played by these rules tended to come out losers.

Through the Early 1970s: Little Relief

Under the escape clause, the Tariff Commission investigated 113 claims between 1948 and 1962 and recommended relief in 41 cases, but the

---

1. Chairman Charles Vanik, at the House Ways and Means Trade Subcommittee Hearings, "Trade With Japan," 18 September 1980, p. 140.

2. J. Michael Finger and his associates note that the "technical track" favors petitioners because it excludes from the review process those economic interests "who want access to foreign sources of supply." But they conclude that "this bias" toward protectionism "is not large": in 1975–79, "only 2.2 percent of US manufactured imports have been granted relief under the [countervailing duty and antidumping] statutes, and only 3.8 percent under the escape clause." J. M. Finger, H. Keith Hall, and Douglas R. Nelson, "The Political Economy of Administered Protection," *American Economic Review* 72, no. 3 (June 1982), pp. 454, 466.

President provided it in only 15.[3] Things grew worse for affected industries after the Trade Expansion Act of 1962 tightened relief requirements. The Tariff Commission considered 30 cases in the 12 years ended in 1974. It found injury justifying import relief in only four.[4]

Petitioners did not find the countervailing duty law much more helpful. In form, it required relief, as the Supreme Court had declared in 1919:

A word of broader significance than "grant" could not have been used. . . . And if [a grant] be conferred by a country "upon the exportation of any article or merchandise" a countervailing duty is *required*. . . .[5]

But the practice proved very different. The law triggered 191 investigations between 1934 and 1968, but only 30 resulted in the imposition of CVDs. In 1968, just 13 CVD orders were in effect, with only 4 of them imposed in the 1960s: on canned tomato paste from France and on transmission towers, canned tomatoes, and wire mesh from Italy.[6] There were three more affirmative findings in 1969, and just eight more between 1971 and 1974.[7]

Trade relief was similarly elusive on antidumping cases. Out of 371 processed from 1955 through 1968, only 12 resulted in findings of dumping, although 89 more were concluded by revision in the price or termination of sales.[8]

Finally, not a single petition for trade adjustment assistance for workers won favorable action in that program's first seven years, through fiscal 1969, even though TAA had been widely supported by liberal trade advocates as a constructive alternative to protection. The volume of petitions went up sharply in the early 1970s, but out of 110,640 workers seeking benefits by the end of 1974, only 48,314 received them.[9]

So in the first thirty postwar years, import-affected industries that played the trade policy game by the legal rules generally lost out.

The immediate effect was to make US markets more open than they otherwise would have been. The failure of these laws to grant meaningful import relief meant that less trade was being restricted. More important

---

3. Herbert G. Grubel, *International Economics* (Homewood, Ill.: Richard D. Irwin, Inc., 1981), p. 174.

4. Tariff Commission, *Annual Report*, Washington, various years.

5. As quoted in Shannon Stock Shuman and Charles Owen Verrill, Jr., "Recent Developments in Countervailing Duty Law and Practice, *NBER Conference Report* (Cambridge, Mass: National Bureau of Economic Research, 1984), p. 105.

6. "Report of the Secretary of the Treasury," *Annual Report of the Department of the Treasury*, Washington, 1968, p. 416.

7. Ibid., Statistical Appendices.

8. Ibid., p. 416.

9. US Department of Labor, "Labor Issues of American International Trade and Investment" (prepared for the National Manpower Administration Policy Task Force), *Policy Studies in Employment and Welfare*, no. 24, 1976, p. 52.

was the longer term impact. Predominantly negative outcomes for petitioners discredited the trade-remedy procedures, discouraging their use and encouraging affected interests to seek direct help from Congress or the administration. This was, of course, exactly what "the rules" were intended to avoid.

As the Kennedy Round drew to a conclusion in 1967, executive branch trade leaders recognized that to restore the credibility of these statutes, they needed to have them amended so that the criteria were less forbidding. Legislators were even more committed to this goal. If our trade policy-making system was to continue to provide "protection for Congress," other channels had to offer real relief alternatives. Otherwise, pressure on Congress to provide direct, product-specific protection could only increase. Indeed, such pressure built up rapidly in the late 1960s and early 1970s, as evidenced by the House vote in favor of general import quota legislation in 1970 and the introduction of the more restrictive, labor-endorsed Burke-Hartke quota bill the following year.

Twice during the decade of the 1970s, Congress responded to this pressure as one would have predicted. It changed the rules to make administrative trade relief easier for import-affected industries to obtain. It did so in 1974, as part of the Trade Act authorizing US participation in the Tokyo Round trade negotiations. It did so again in 1979, in the Trade Agreements Act that approved the Round's results.

The Trade Act of 1974

The simplest and most straightforward action in 1974 was that governing the escape clause. The Trade Expansion Act of 1962 had toughened the earlier criterion for relief, by requiring that an industry prove that it had suffered serious injury, the "major cause" of which was imports due to US tariff concessions. ("Major cause" meant greater than all other factors combined, a hard standard to meet.) Section 201 of the Trade Act of 1974 lowered that threshold, requiring that imports be only a "substantial cause of serious injury, or the threat thereof." (This was defined as "not less than any other cause.") Section 201 also removed the proviso that such injury had to result from specific US tariff concessions.

Congress also sought to encourage favorable findings by increasing the independence of the Tariff Commission, which ruled on industry petitions. The terms of its members were lengthened from six to nine years, and it was renamed the United States International Trade Commission (USITC) "because tariffs are no longer the major impediments to trade."[10] Moreover,

---

10. US Congress, Senate, Committee on Finance, *Trade Reform Act of 1974*, 93d. Cong., 2d Sess., 26 November 1974, S. Rept. 93–1208, p. 25.

in cases where the USITC recommended relief, the President was required to act on that recommendation within 60 days. If he did not grant the relief, Congress could override him and enforce the USITC recommendation by majority vote of both houses.[11]

As the 1974 legislation moved toward enactment, there was pressure on the Ford administration to commit itself, in advance, to grant escape clause relief in cases found deserving. To head off pressures from shoe interests for direct statutory benefits in December, Special Trade Representative William D. Eberle wrote a letter to Senator Thomas J. McIntyre (D-Me.) declaring that "the escape clause provisions" of the pending Trade Act were "ideally suited for use by the American non-rubber footwear industry" and promising that "if the procedures suggested" that relief was needed, "you can be assured that the Administration would move expeditiously to provide it."[12]

On adjustment assistance, Congress insisted that the program be expanded and made easier to qualify for, notwithstanding organized labor's disillusionment with it and the Nixon administration's skepticism about the appropriateness of a special program for workers displaced by trade. One reason few workers had previously been eligible was that the criteria were essentially the same as those for tariffs or quotas: imports had to be the "major cause" of unemployment or underemployment. House Ways and Means Committee members thought trade adjustment assistance should be the easiest form of relief to obtain. So the law was changed to open it to workers whose jobs were lost if "increases of imports . . . contributed importantly." The magnitude and duration of benefits were also increased.

But the primary focus of efforts to "change the rules" in the early 1970s was the alleged foreign abuses covered by the CVD and antidumping statutes, addressed in a rather lengthy Trade Act title labeled "Relief from *Unfair* Trade Practices" (emphasis added).

This was a natural, even inevitable, emphasis, for the Kennedy Round's success in reducing industrial tariff levels had focused attention on nontariff barriers (NTBs) and other trade-distorting governmental practices. Among those thought to require regulation or discipline, subsidies were at the top of the list for American trade specialists. To some, in Gary Clyde Hufbauer's metaphor, subsidies were a "rising reef," increasingly resorted to in order

---

11. In *Immigration and Naturalization Service vs. Chadha,* the US Supreme Court declared a similar legislative veto provision unconstitutional, on grounds that it did not provide for "presentment to the President," as in the normal legislative process. Congress responded, in the Trade and Tariff Act of 1984, by providing for a *joint resolution* congressional veto for presidential decisions under Section 201. Such a resolution is presented to the chief executive for his signature; should the *President* veto it, a two-thirds majority of both houses would be required to override.

12. Eberle to McIntyre, *Congressional Record,* 13 December 1974, p. 39813.

to buttress favored industries and influence trade flows. Others concluded, more modestly, that it was the "falling water level" of reduced tariffs that had made the NTB reef more important, and certainly more visible.[13]

Joined with increased complaints about foreign subsidies was the sense that the United States was not doing much to combat them. Concerning the primary statute designed to counter such subsidies, the Senate Finance Committee expressed unhappiness "that the Treasury Department has used the absence of time limits to stretch out or even shelve countervailing duty investigations for reasons which have nothing to do with the clear and mandatory nature of the countervailing duty law."[14] This charge was not ungrounded, for at the administration end of Pennsylvania Avenue, particularly in the Treasury, there was a fairly widespread view that the law was archaic, with its old-fashioned language ("bounty or grant") and nineteenth-century origins.

The increased attention to nontariff trade distortions, and above all to subsidies, reinforced the widespread Washington perception that other countries were taking advantage of the United States, that in trade policy we were, in the words of Nixon White House aide Peter M. Flanigan, "more sinned against than sinning."[15] There was—and is currently—evidence to support this view. One study of overall Organization for Economic Cooperation and Development (OECD) data concludes that, among the seven major advanced industrial countries, "the United States has persistently exhibited the lowest ration of subsidies to GDP and, unlike [that of] other countries, the US ratio has declined since the late 1960s."[16] Moreover, the opaqueness of governments' nontariff policies affecting trade—the difficulty in seeing and measuring them and determining their extent—made it hard to resist those who argued that such foreign practices were endemic and the United States needed to respond forcefully.[17] The record on CVDs and dumping suggested that we had not been doing so.

One way Congress addressed this problem was by making clear that subsidies should be given priority in the upcoming Tokyo Round, in which nontariff trade distortions were to be the central focus. The other way was to tighten the remedy procedures. On countervailing duties, the 1974 Act

---

13. Gary Clyde Hufbauer and Joanna Shelton Erb, *Subsidies in International Trade* (Washington: Institute for International Economics, 1984), p. 2.

14. Committee on Finance, *Trade Reform Act of 1974*, p. 183.

15. Quoted in *National Journal*, 13 January 1973, p. 45.

16. Hufbauer and Shelton Erb, *Subsidies in International Trade*, p. 2.

17. For a perceptive discussion of how the opaqueness of nontax trade policy nourishes perceptions of foreign "unfairness," see J. David Richardson, "Currents and Cross-Currents in the Flow of U.S. Trade Policy," *NBER Conference Report* (1984), pp. 2–3.

added a requirement that final action be taken within a year of receipt of a petition, and made provision for judicial review of decisions that denied relief. Such review was also provided for negative antidumping decisions. One technical provision required the Treasury Department to disregard certain low-cost home-market sales in determining the price against which export sales were compared to ascertain whether dumping existed. This had the effect of favoring petitioners, and could even lead to findings of dumping in cases in which the average home and export prices were the same!

Also new, and of enormous potential importance, was the authority granted the President, in Section 301, to take any of a broad range of retaliatory actions against a country that "maintains unjustifiable or unreasonable tariff or other import restrictions," or provide "subsidies . . . on its exports . . . which have the effect of substantially reducing sales of the competitive United States product. . . ."[18]

The Result: Again, Little Relief

The immediate response to the changing of the rules in 1974 was for firms to file many more cases and for the government to move more expeditiously in handling them. Petitions for escape clause relief, for example, rose from 2 in 1973 (and none in 1974) to 13 in 1975. The number of CVD investigations initiated shot up from 1 in 1973 (and 5 in 1974) to 38 in 1975, both because new claims were being submitted and because the Treasury was moving faster on old ones under the new timetable.[19] And between January 1975 and July 1979, 18 Section 301 petitions were filed alleging subsidies or other "unjustifiable or unreasonable" trade actions by foreign governments.[20]

But in terms of actual relief granted, industry petitioners were again to be disappointed.

The new escape clause criteria established by Section 201 were affecting the US International Trade Commission, which was now finding regularly in petitioners' favor. Between 1975 and 1985, the Commission conducted 59 investigations, which resulted in 30 affirmative determinations.[21] This

---

18. Section 252 of the Trade Expansion Act of 1962 provided the President a more limited authority to act against "unjustifiable" or "unreasonable" foreign import restrictions.

19. *International Economic Report of the President*, Washington, March 1976, p. 45.

20. Hufbauer and Shelton Erb, *Subsidies in International Trade*, 115.

21. USITC *Annual Report*, Washington, various years, updated by adding the seven Section 201 cases of 1984 and the four cases of 1985. See also testimony of USITC Chairman Alfred E. Eckes in US Congress, House, Committee on Ways and Means, Subcommittee on Trade, *Options to Improve the Trade Remedy Laws*, 98th Cong., 1st Sess., 16 March 1983, Serial 98–15, part 1, pp. 16–17.

51 percent success rate for those who sought relief contrasted sharply with the 13 percent rate (4 of 30) under the previous law. And the escape clause cases included important import-affected industries: carbon and specialty steel, shoes, color televisions, and, grandest of all, automobiles.

In the 1974 Act, however, Congress had reluctantly retained the President's discretion to modify or reject a USITC relief recommendation, provided he determined that "provision of such relief is not in the national economic interest of the United States." This was a broader criterion than the industry-specific rules that governed the decisions of the Commission. Applying this more comprehensive standard, presidents repeatedly rejected or modified the Commission's escape clause recommendations.

In the 30 cases in which the USITC recommended import relief between 1975 and 1985, the President ordered tariffs or quotas in only 10 and denied all relief in 12. On 5, he provided only adjustment assistance, and on the remaining 3 he initiated negotiations leading to orderly marketing agreements (OMAs) with the exporting nations to limit their sales.[22] Congress complained that the law was not being implemented, but it never actually voted to override the president.

As it did prior to the 1974 Trade Act, this situation again yielded present gains for the liberal trade order.[23] But it piled up future costs. The effect was to discredit the process, perhaps more than previously. Before, almost nobody got relief, but at least the rules were being followed. Now, industries were playing by the rules and winning in the USITC, only to have those decisions reversed by the President, who asserted his prerogative in an opaque White House decision-making process in which they had no established role. The footwear case of 1976 was a good example. The Ford administration's trade representative had promised favorable consideration of such a case when the Trade Act was before the Senate. But it reached the President for decision one month after he had granted relief to the specialty steel industry, and Ford was worried about the international repercussions of restricting trade twice in a row. So he rejected import relief, granting only adjustment assistance.[24]

The shoe case was in fact reconsidered, and the Carter administration negotiated export restraint agreements with Korea and Taiwan a year later.

---

22. USITC and USTR *Annual Report*, various years, and USTR Trade Action Monitoring System, *Pending Investigation Report* (Springfield, VA.: National Technical Information Service), various issues. See appendix B-1 for a full listing.

23. For a detailed analysis welcoming this result, see Walter Adams and Joel B. Dirlam, "Import Competition and the Trade Act of 1974: A Case Study of Section 201 and its Interpretation by the International Trade Commission," *Indiana Law Journal* 52, no. 3 (Spring 1977), pp. 535–99.

24. See Roger Porter, *Presidential Decision Making: The Economic Policy Board* (Cambridge: Cambridge University Press, 1980), ch. 6.

Nor was this unique. The producers of "bolts, nuts, and large screws," to cite another example of the latter 1970s, were denied relief by President Carter in 1978, only to be granted it the next year after strong congressional pressure led to reconsideration of their case.

These and other cases illustrated how, by easing the criteria but retaining presidential discretion, Congress had turned the political process on its head. The aim had been to take trade "out of politics." But once the USITC began regularly finding in petitioners' favor, product cases were thrown squarely into the political arena and resolved in a process governed by different "rules" entirely. The President had to weigh the demands of an injured industry, of trade politics, and sometimes of electoral support against the interest of the larger economy, the need to combat inflation, the demands of international economic leadership, etc. Industries had reason to fear that their legitimate cases would get lost in this larger shuffle.

The escape clause procedure received a further blow in the automobile case of 1980, the most important and visible import issue it had ever addressed. The American industry and its workers were suffering a severe drop in their production and sales, which was clearly exacerbated by record Japanese imports. Yet a 3 to 2 majority of USITC members found that the industry failed to meet the "substantial cause" criterion: factors other than imports were more important causes of the industry's plight—above all, the shift in market demand toward smaller cars brought about by the oil price increase of 1979. Thus, the USITC was unable to recommend relief.

The decision was defensible in terms of the law, and while the USITC might have found "threat of injury" from imports, the case for such a determination was not made effectively by the petitioners. Nonetheless, the result was to further discredit Section 201. The US political system found the negative outcome impossible to live with. House Trade Subcommittee Chairman Charles A. Vanik (D-Ohio) had argued repeatedly for running trade according to the rules, "depoliticizing" it. Yet when the "economic law" produced a negative outcome on autos, he was quick to call hearings to explore the need for alternative trade action.

In response to congressional pressure, and to a Reagan campaign commitment, the new administration ended up pressing—successfully—for Japanese voluntary restraint. As a result, the escape clause procedure was further discredited. In the three years after 1980, the USITC received only four escape clause petitions.

On countervailing duties—unlike the escape clause—there is no general presidential authority to override the procedure in the name of broader American interests. The basic law is mandatory: if a subsidy is found, a duty "shall be imposed." However, a special waiver authority was added for the multilateral trade negotiations of the 1970s, in which a primary United States negotiating goal was to discipline trade distorting subsidies.

Our government had something to give on this issue. Contrary to GATT rules, as Europeans had long complained, United States law did not require that injury be found from dutiable imports before a CVD was imposed. Europeans were not about to negotiate if the United States simultaneously began enforcing a tough antisubsidy statute. So Congress reluctantly granted the Secretary of the Treasury the authority to waive imposition of CVDs for four years if the foreign government was taking steps to reduce a subsidy's effect, and if the Secretary found that imposition of a duty would "seriously jeopardize" completion of the MTN, including the desired subsidies code.

In practice, this waiver authority took away from affected industries much of the gain that the 1974 act provided. From 1976 through 1978, for example, the Treasury made a total of 35 affirmative CVD decisions, a marked increase from previous years. But the Secretary then exercised the waiver in 19 of the cases. More than half of the time, then, "successful" petitioners were denied the full remedy that the law, in principle, provided.[25]

By contrast, the number of antidumping cases during this period remained at about the level of previous years. However, the filing of a large number of such cases by the steel industry in 1977 led the Carter administration to establish a price floor on imports with the trigger price mechanism, which was enforced under the antidumping law.[26]

Finally, cases under the new Section 301 governing "unjustifiable" or "unreasonable" foreign trade practices led to frequent consultations, within and outside GATT. A few of these brought significant changes in foreign behavior. On others, GATT review dragged on for years. And on *none* of the 18 petitions filed between January 1975 and July 1979 did the United States take the retaliatory action that the law authorized.[27]

In summary, in the years after 1974, industries were getting only slightly more relief from administrative procedures than they had before—Trade Act changes notwithstanding. So unhappiness built up again about the remedy procedures. The House Ways and Means Committee reflected this in 1979, declaring that "both the countervailing duty and antidumping duty laws have been inadequately enforced in the past, including the lack of resources devoted to this important area of law."[28]

---

25. US Department of the Treasury *Annual Report*, Washington, various issues, House, and US Congress, Committee on Ways and Means, *Temporary Extension of Countervailing Duty Waiver Authority*, 96th Cong., 1st Sess., 22 February 1979, H. Rept. 96–15. The latter describes the 19 waivers and their status as of the report date.

26. See Hideo Sato and Michael W. Hodin, "The U.S.-Japanese Steel Issue of 1977," in *Coping With U.S.-Japanese Trade Conflicts*, edited by I. M. Destler and Hideo Sato (Lexington, Mass.: Lexington Books, 1982), pp. 27–72.

27. Hufbauer and Shelton Erb, *Subsidies in International Trade*, p. 115; and USTR, *Trade Action Monitoring System's Pending Investigation Report*, July 1983.

28. US Congress, House, Committee on Ways and Means, *Trade Agreements Act of 1979*, 96th Cong., 1st Sess., 3 July 1979, H. Rept. no. 96–317.

The Trade Agreements Act of 1979

The required approval of the MTN in 1979 gave Congress a new opportunity to act. The minimum need was legislation to implement the nontariff barrier codes completed early that year. Since the principal countries were unable to resolve their differences on escape clause issues, the intended safeguards code was not completed. So Section 201, the US law governing escape clause relief, was left unchanged.

The codes on subsidies-countervailing measures and antidumping, however, were the MTN's centerpieces. The negotiation of the former had been fueled by a widely shared conviction, in the words of one leading authority, that "the current rules on subsidies and countervailing duties" were "woefully inadequate to cope with the pressures put upon importing economies by a myriad of subtle (and sometimes not so subtle) governmental aids to exports."[29] Now that the code was completed, legislation was necessary to make US law conform. We had to incorporate in our statutes the requirement that "material injury" be proven before countervailing duties were imposed on imports from countries adhering to the code. But nothing barred more extensive statutory changes as long as they were consistent with the codes and other US international obligations. So revision of these statutes became part of the bargaining process for MTN ratification.

In the 1974 Act, Congress had committed itself to an expeditious, up-or-down vote on whatever implementing legislation the President submitted (see chapter 4). To ensure congressional support for this legislation, Special Trade Representative Robert S. Strauss, who led the Carter administration's negotiating enterprise at home as well as abroad, accepted the proposal of the Senate Finance Committee to have the bill designed and drafted on Capitol Hill, as a collaborative effort of the two branches. Key industries like steel, and concerned senators like John Heinz (R-Pa.), made it clear that their priority was the trade-remedy laws. They wanted to insure, this time, that they would provide petitioners effective and timely relief. And Strauss saw this as a tolerable price for their support.

The most important single change—a "material injury" test for all CVDs on products of countries adhering to the new code—had the formal effect of tightening the criteria relief-seeking firms had to meet. Here, the administration and the House Ways and Means Committee prevailed over a Senate Finance Committee proposal to soften the requirement to the single word, "injury." Lobbyists for the European Community (EC) actively supported the tougher standard. Still, "material injury" was defined as "harm which

---

29. John H. Jackson, "The Crumbling Institutions of the Liberal Trade System," *Journal of World Trade Law* (March–April) 1978, p. 95.

is not inconsequential, immaterial or unimportant"; this is significantly less demanding than the escape clause test that imports be "a substantial cause of serious injury." More important, perhaps, by bringing US law into conformity with GATT and international practice, the injury standard legitimized use of CVDs in future cases.

If the new injury test affected the criteria for obtaining relief, the Trade Agreements Act of 1979 employed a different means to aid petitioners—reforming the law's procedures and administration. Tighter time limits were mandated not just for CVD cases taken as a whole, but for their specific stages; for example, an investigation had to be initiated within 20 days, and only "clearly frivolous" petitions, or those lacking key information reasonably available to petitioners, were to be dismissed without any formal investigation. The overall timetable from initiation to final determination was compressed, in normal cases, from a year to seven months. This tended to favor petitioners, since foreign governments and firms had less time to develop the complicated counter-cases that were needed to rebut the data of those seeking relief. Moreover, if there was a preliminary finding of subsidy (and injury), importers would now have to post a deposit just three months (instead of a year) after a petition was submitted. Thus effective trade restraint could be obtained much sooner.

There were also a number of changes aimed at greater procedural openness. Administrative protective orders gave opposing counsel access to confidential business information supplied to the government in support of one side in a case, so the other could contest it. Limits were imposed on private ex parte meetings between government officials and one party to a case; the substance of these meetings now had to be made public. Rights to public hearings and judicial review were also expanded. For example, labor unions and trade associations which had not initiated a case could now appeal, and intermediate as well as final government determinations could be contested. Parallel steps were taken on antidumping case procedures to shorten time limits, advance the time when exporting firms had to pay or advance penalty duties, and promote openness and judicial review.

Similar changes were made in Section 301, the authority granted Presidents in 1974 to retaliate against "unjustifiable or unreasonable" foreign trade actions. Time limits were established for each step of the procedure, and special emphasis was given to use of this authority to enforce US rights under the MTN codes.

But the most important single change was *organizational,* the shift of administrative responsibility for the unfair trade remedies laws. This, although not an explicit provision of the Trade Agreements Act of 1979, was a not-so-subtle condition of its approval, as the Senate Finance Committee declined to bring that act to the floor until the President had submitted a comprehensive trade reorganization plan. In this plan, the power to enforce the rewritten CVD and antidumping laws was delegated not to the Secretary of the Treasury—the responsible official under the law since 1897—but to the Secretary of Commerce.

Into the 1980s: More Relief, More Political Heat

How have the administrative trade remedies—"the rules" as amended—played out in practice since 1979? The most dramatic development, as shown in figures 6.1 and 6.2, has been the contrast between the declining use of Section 201 and the blizzard of new petitions alleging unfair foreign trade practices.

The escape clause was used above all during the Reagan reelection campaign. The International Trade Commission ruled on just one case in 1981, one case in 1982, and two cases in 1983. January 1984, however, saw the carbon steel, shoe, copper, and table flatware industries all submitting petitions, in order to pressure the Reagan White House for sympathetic action at a time of maximum political vulnerability.[30] By March, the USITC suddenly found itself investigating no fewer than five escape clause cases. Section 201 had been transformed from a means of diverting political pressure to a device for asserting it. In two prominent cases—steel and copper—the USITC recommended protection, forcing presidential decisions in September, within two months of the general election.[31]

What has happened with countervailing and antidumping procedures is more complicated. Accurate data on recent experience are remarkably hard to obtain; for example, the 1,248 printed pages of the general trade-remedy hearings of the House Ways and Means Trade Subcommittee contain no comprehensive count of cases and outcomes, reportedly because the Commerce Department, inundated with specific business, was unable to put

---

30. In 1980, the UAW—in what was widely seen as a political blunder—did not submit its auto escape clause petition until June; as a result, the USITC did not reach its finding until after the November election.

31. The President denied relief to the copper industry but ordered negotiation of export restraint agreements for steel, as spelled out later in this chapter. On shoes, the USITC made a unanimous negative finding on injury: although foreign products were well over 50 percent of consumption, profits were high and manufacturers had adjusted well (in part through the marketing of imports).

The shoe case was reconsidered in 1985, after political pressure from industry champions, modest legislative changes in Section 201, and a worsening of the industry's condition. The USITC now recommended stringent quotas. President Reagan rejected this proposal and denied all import relief to the footwear industry in August of that year.

Figure 6.1   Escape clause investigations, 1975–85

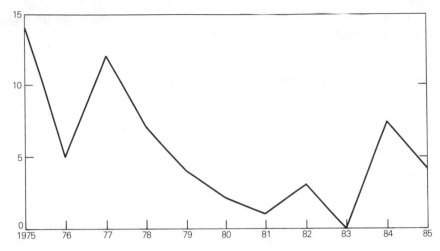

Source: Appendix B.

Figure 6.2   Countervailing duty and antidumping investigations, 1979–85

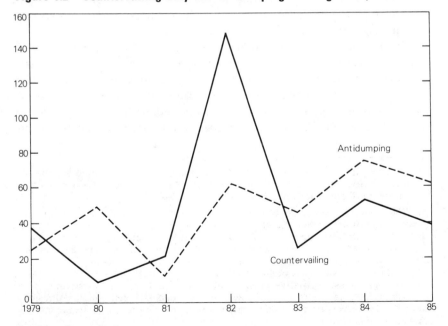

Source: Appendix B.

together an internally consistent set of overall numbers.[32] Yet a look at the numbers that department has supplied—in its semiannual reports to GATT, and in direct response to inquiries—gives the strong initial impression that Congress succeeded in 1979 where it had failed in 1974. Many more cases are being submitted, covering a much greater volume of trade. And many more are being decided in petitioners' favor (although the level of duty imposed is not always sufficient to alter trade flows). For the first time, the process has been a serious one, with the responsible bureaucracy making a strong effort to administer it according to its intended purposes.

There has been an explosion in the volume of cases.[33] In response to industry petitions, Commerce initiated 10 separate CVD investigations in 1980, 27 in 1981, 146 in 1982, 30 in 1983, 55 in 1984, and 43 in 1985. (This compared to one investigation initiated in 1973 and five in 1974.) Parallel antidumping investigation numbers were 26 in 1979, 46 in 1980, 15 in 1981, 65 in 1982, 48 in 1983, 76 in 1984, and 66 in 1985. And these cases involved a much greater magnitude of trade than in previous periods. (Commerce data here arc incomplete, but of those CVD cases where trade figures are provided, the value rose from $494.9 million [31 cases] in 1979 to $2.14 billion [59 cases] in 1982.)

More relief is being granted. As of the second half of 1983, there were 56 countervailing duties in effect, compared to just 13 in 1968. In September 1983, there were 137 antidumping duties operative.

There has also been a modest increase in the frequency of Section 301 petitions. Ironically, one of the most prominent complaints under this "unfair trade" statute—lodged by the stainless steel industry in 1982 against production subsidies in Europe—led President Reagan to request an USITC escape clause review. This resulted the following year in the imposition of tariffs and quotas under the law designed to protect against injury from *fair* trade!

The new industry success with the unfair trade statutes was not accidental. There was now, for the first time, a serious enforcement operation, a core group of professionals organized to give priority to their implementation,

---

32. See US Congress, House, Committee on Ways and Means, *Options,* parts 1 and 2.

33. The numbers that follow are a compilation based on analysis and cross-checking of data from a range of documents, including Commerce reports submitted semiannually to GATT, USTR Trade Action Monitoring System reports, USITC Annual Reports, congressional hearings, other Commerce, USTR, and USITC reports, and the *Federal Register.* These have been supplemented by direct communication with responsible officials to fill gaps and resolve contradictions. I am grateful to my research assistant, Diane T. Berliner, for her persistent and painstaking work in putting these numbers together.

A full list of 1979–1985 CVD and antidumping cases appears in appendix B.

determined to develop methods for the complex calculations required, and ready to decide cases on their merits as set forth in the law.[34]

A large volume of trade business is now being channeled through these procedures. So if the original political logic remained valid, both the petitioning industries and the supporters of liberal trade would be more or less satisfied. The former would be pleased because their cases are at last being judged on their merits, with trade relief the frequent outcome. The latter might be concerned about the increase in import restrictions, but comforted because they were being imposed by apolitical, quasi-judicial procedures that considered each case in isolation, protecting Congress and minimizing the risk of protectionist contagion.

In the real world, alas, almost no one seems happy with the result. Affected industries continue to protest the laws' inadequacy and seek their further elaboration and complication to cover foreign practices that still escape their reach. But the same lack of executive branch discretion which keeps executive officials from denying or diluting relief also prevents them from tailoring it to an industry's needs, whether the goal be protection or adjustment. Industries are thus driven to propose further statutory changes tailored to their specific needs.

Foreign interests are dismayed because the trade-remedy procedures seem arbitrary and unfair to them. And liberal trade advocates are dismayed by one result of such frustrations—the increased use of the trade-remedy laws not to keep decisions "out of politics" but to *raise* their political prominence and force political solutions.

Foreigners are unhappy because the US legal tradition clashes with their more discretionary ways of handling such issues. Our laws are, for the most part, GATT-consistent, proper under the international trade rules that Americans have done so much to create. Indeed, elaborating these rules was one of the prime accomplishments of the Tokyo Round. But other peoples—Europeans, Japanese, Koreans, Brazilians—see "due process" for American domestic interests as a threat to their interests.

They (Europeans above all) are anxious about the real trade effects of US legal decisions: their overall magnitude and how the pain will be distributed among foreign suppliers. They are unwilling to let their fates be determined by procedures that might seem objective and fair and nonpolitical to Americans, but which to foreign eyes appear either unpredictable or skewed in favor of the import-affected petitioner. And these cases inevitably involve

---

34. See Shuman and Verrill, "Recent Developments," *NBER Conference Report*, 1984. See also the candid testimony of former Deputy Assistant Secretary of Commerce Gary Horlick in House Committee on Ways and Means, *Options*, part 2, pp. 535–87.

"a host of arbitrary determinations:"[35] calculating fair value, the full cost of production, the effect of different government programs on export prices, etc. Indeed, expert GATT panels have been meeting since the Tokyo Round to try to establish common standards for such determinations, with little apparent progress.

So it is not surprising that foreign firms and governments press for alternatives. If our processes are going to end up restricting their trade, they want to have a voice in how the pain is allocated.

Actually, the 1979 law did create one new procedure for negotiating an end to a trade-remedy case. In a major departure from previous trade laws, it authorizes "suspension of investigations" through agreements with foreign governments, or with "exporters representing substantially all of the imports of the merchandise"[36] covered by a case. But Congress sought to insure that the purposes of the laws would not be subverted by conditioning such suspension on one of two forms of remedial action: elimination of subsidies or dumping (directly, or through imposition of an offset like an export tax), or elimination of their injurious effect. In other words, the point is to end the subsidy, or at least its trade impact, not to bargain about market share.[37]

Typically, foreign firms and governments want more leeway than this. They may not agree with our legal determination of subsidy or "less-than-fair-value" (dumped) sales, and even if they do, they may have their own political or legal problems in complying.

Forcing Political Solutions

US firms have recognized and exploited this foreign vulnerability. Beginning with the steel antidumping petitions of 1977, they have begun to submit cases that seem aimed less at achieving the specific relief provided by statute than at creating an intolerable situation for foreign competitors, forcing them to come to the bargaining table and cut deals. Once a satisfactory arrangement is reached, the constraints of the law on suspension of investigations are circumvented by a simple device: the complaining industry

---

35. Robert W. Crandall, "The EEC-US Steel Trade Crisis" (paper prepared for Symposium on Euro-American Relations and Global Economic Interdependence, College of Europe, Bruges, Belgium, 13 September 1984). Quoted with permission.

36. House Committee on Ways and Means, *Trade Agreements Act of 1979*, p. 54.

37. For a description and defense of Commerce Department administration of this provision through mid-1984, see Alan F. Holmer and Judith H. Bello, "U.S. Import Law and Policy Series: Suspension and Settlement Agreements in Unfair Trade Cases," *International Lawyer* 18, no. 3 (Summer 1984), pp. 683–97.

withdraws its petition, and Commerce then terminates the investigation, as the law explicitly allows.

A dramatic illustration came in the steel cases of 1982. There was little doubt that foreigners were subsidizing steel that was being shipped to the US market: Europeans were especially guilty, and among them the French and British in particular.[38] So when on 11 January 1982, seven US steelmakers jointly delivered 494 boxes containing 3 million pages of documentation for 132 countervailing and antidumping petitions against foreign (mainly European Community) suppliers, this flood of litigation had a real-world justification. And the remedy sought was the proper one provided under American law. Further petitions followed, bringing the total for 1982 to about 150.[39]

But there was little doubt also that pursuing these cases to their legal conclusion would be highly disruptive to the steel industries of individual EC countries and to the network of political understandings among them. Moreover, in its calculation of foreign subsidies, our law did not distinguish between continuing aid to national producers and one-time adjustment payments aimed at downsizing an industry. The British Steel Corporation, for example, was a regular recipient of government aid. But when Commerce officials announced in June 1982 that they had found subsidies as high as 40 percent on its products, they lumped adjustment payments in with other government subsidies in making their calculations.[40]

---

38. For one comprehensive effort to catalogue such subsidies, see "Government Aid to the Steel Industry of the European Communities: Market Distortion in Europe and Its Impact on the U.S. Steel Industry" (prepared for Bethlehem Steel Corporation and United States Steel Corporation by Verner, Liipfert, Bernhard, McPherson and Hand, Washington, 1984).

It does not follow, however, that foreign subsidies are the primary cause of US industry woes, or that their removal would bring substantial market relief. Robert W. Crandall argues, in fact, that while in an entirely private (nonsubsidized) European steel industry the worth of plants might be very much lower, "no one has presented any convincing evidence that capacity and output would be much lower under such a regime." And even if European output and exports did fall, "Brazil, Taiwan, Korea, and even Canada and Japan have the ability to expand their output and even their capacity substantially in response to any upward movement in export prices." See Crandall, "The EEC-US Steel Trade Crisis," p. 26.

39. USITC, *1982 Annual Report*, Washington, p. x; USTR, *Twenty-sixth Annual Report of the President of the United States on the Trade Agreements Program, 1981–82*, Washington, November 1982, p. 114; Timothy B. Clark, "When Demand is Down, Competition Up, That Spells Trouble for American Steel," *National Journal*, 7 January 1984, p. 9.

40. This is not to say that most European adjustment programs have resulted in substantial movement of workers out of trade-disadvantaged industries. In fact, the impact has been more to help these industries sustain themselves, at the cost of the rest of the economy. See Philip Hayes, "Trade and Adjustment Policies in the European Community (With Special Reference to Textiles and Clothing)," in *Domestic Adjustment and International Trade*, edited by Gary Clyde Hufbauer and Howard F. Rosen (Washington: Institute for International Economics, forthcoming).

Inevitably, the Europeans sought to bargain. This forced US Secretary of Commerce Malcolm Baldrige into the uncomfortable position of brokering between foreign governments and domestic steelmakers for a trade-restricting arrangement he did not particularly like. The end result was a political solution entirely outside established procedures. The EC "voluntarily" restricted carbon steel exports to the United States to 5.44 percent of the US market. And while this overall limit corresponded roughly to what the outcome of enforcing our law would have been, the Europeans distributed the pain among themselves so that the efficient Germans ended up worse off than they would have been, and the inefficient British and French better off.

It was primarily the Europeans who administered the restraint. However, to be on the safe side, the Commerce Department—with the aid of Senator Heinz and over the procedural protests of House Trade Subcommittee leaders—slipped through Congress an amendment to the Tariff Act of 1930 providing that "steel mill products" under arrangements entered into "prior to January 1, 1983" would be denied entry into the United States if they lacked proper foreign government documentation.[41] With these "arrangements" completed, the industry petitioners withdrew their suits.

In the fall of 1983 came another example of a major industry initiating an unfair trade case in order to exert political pressure. This one involved China and textiles. Earlier that year, in retaliation for American textile quota restrictions, Beijing had curtailed its purchases of American grains. Protests from agricultural export interests brought pressure to bear on the Reagan administration, and resulted in the August conclusion of bilateral quota agreement that the US textile industry found insufficient. The textile industry retaliated a month later with an innovative suit, alleging that China's dual exchange rate system constituted a subsidy under the countervailing duty law.

This put US authorities in another bind. They had just reached a deal with a foreign government, but its substance was being threatened by a procedure over which they had little control in the short run. They feared that, to Beijing, the administration would appear either two-faced or impotent at a time when the President was preparing for a major state visit the following spring. And the Chinese government, choosing to treat the matter as an internal US problem, resisted supplying information to contest the suit.

The administration might have ridden it out internationally and domestically. In May 1984, in fact, the Commerce Department would rule that the

---

41. *Congressional Record,* 29 September 1982, pp. S12474–75; *Congressional Record,* 1 October 1982, pp. H8368–71, H8388–89.

CVD law did not apply to imports from nonmarket economy countries.[42] (Without a competitive market as a reference point, the word subsidy loses its meaning.)

But senators from key textile states—Strom Thurmond (R-SC) and Jesse Helms (R-NC)—were up for reelection in 1984. They pressed the White House to do something for the industry. President Reagan, also up for reelection, saw personal political advantage in responding; moreover, in the 1980 campaign, he had made a general commitment to moderate the growth of textile imports. So in December 1983, against the overwhelming advice of his cabinet, he ordered a deal that gave the US textile industry tighter enforcement of existing quota arrangements, not particularly vis-à-vis mainland China but on East Asian imports generally. The industry then withdrew its suit at the last possible moment. Reagan had appeased the textile people without alienating Beijing, but at the cost of further compromise of both trade process and trade policy.

As 1984 began, the steel industry inaugurated a new round with the same old tactics. With European sales fixed at about 5 percent of US consumption and the Japanese informally limiting themselves to about the same amount, the remaining threat was the newly industrializing countries: Brazil, Mexico, and Korea in particular. Again, there was a blizzard of paper, multiple submissions of countervailing duty and antidumping cases. This time no one tried very hard to conceal the political rationale. As David M. Roderick of United States Steel told a press breakfast in early February, US firms planned to file "a tremendous number" of unfair trade complaints, aiming to make the total impact so "burdensome" that the administration, and "all players of substance in the import game . . . would be very pleased to enter into quotas in a negotiated manner."[43] And in a letter to President Reagan he expressed the view that "Enforcement of the trade laws, such as it has been, is simply not doing the job."[44]

The steel industry had been the prime force behind the legislative changes of 1979 and the prime user of the rules on unfair trade practices since then. Now its explicit goal was "temporary" steel import quotas, however they might be achieved or implemented.

---

42. There is, however, substantial authority on the other side of the argument. Harald B. Malmgren, Deputy STR during the enactment of the 1974 act, wrote in support of the American Textile Manufacturers' Institute petition that "there was no doubt whatever in the minds of the drafters of the 1974 Trade Act on the applicability of the countervailing duty statutes to all countries, including Communist or non-market economies." Malmgren, Inc. (Statement, Washington, 28 October 1983; processed.)

43. *Washington Post,* 9 February 1984.

44. *Journal of Commerce,* 2 March 1984.

Other Complications

Thus, trade-remedy laws were being used to exert pressure on foreign governments; at the same time, they were not proving to be the efficient, clinical means for resolving trade cases that their advocates kept trying to make them. There was the never-ending Zenith television case: despite a finding in 1971 of dumping of television sets by Japanese manufacturers, in collaboration with American importers, specific duties were not set until 1978; and the administrative and legal processes on this and related suits continue (at this writing) 15 years later! Efforts to set and collect the duties have been subject to "an extraordinary number of claims and counterclaims," during which litigation "the complexion of the American consumer electronics industry changed irreversibly," as US firms moved offshore and Japanese firms built American plants.[45]

A comprehensive study by the Office of Technology Assessment concluded that this clearly was a case in which "American manufacturers of TVs have been entitled to trade protection but have not yet received it."[46] Hence the case was fuel for those seeking to tighten the trade-remedy laws to provide surer relief, and it underscored even more the difficulty of providing definitive resolutions in such cases.

It also illustrated how legal procedures could be employed for "multiple harassment" of importers. Even as the dumping case was proceeding, US television manufacturers were also pressing, with mixed results, parallel claims against their Japanese counterparts under the antitrust laws, the countervailing duty law, Section 337 of the Tariff Act of 1930 governing unfair practices in import trade, and the escape clause. Critics called this "legal protectionism," suggesting that the trade-remedy procedures, taken as a whole, constituted a substantial US "nontariff barrier."[47] As one report summarized the argument while not quite endorsing it,

The uncertainty of the standards embodied in these laws, particularly the dumping standard, operates to deter competition. Since importers generally cannot predict what prices or practices will be condemned as unfair, price competition is inhibited. Moreover, because American trade laws are sometimes very sweeping and overlap with each other and because different administrative channels are involved, there is an incentive for domestic

---

45. US Congress, Office of Technology Assessment, *International Competitiveness in Electronics,* November 1983, Rept. OTA-ISC-200, pp. 440–41.

46. Ibid., p. 441.

47. See Carl J. Green, "Legal Protectionism in the United States and Its Impact on United States–Japan Economic Relations," in *Appendix to the Report of the Japan-United States Economic Relations Group* (Washington, April 1981), pp. 262–312.

industries to use first one then another statute, seeking relief from different government agencies and harassing their competition. Even if they are unsuccessful in securing relief, they may well impose heavy legal costs upon the future entry into the American market.[48]

And a study by the Secretariat of the United Nations Conference on Trade and Development (UNCTAD) concluded that investigations of unfair trade practices often cut back trade without a final legal resolution. It found evidence of "a very strong export restraining effect of arrangements concluded by exporters to obtain termination of investigations on withdrawal of petitions."

Imports from countries involved in cases resolved in this manner in 1980 United States AD/CVD investigations declined by as much as 46.6 per cent; the decline associated with 1981 United States investigations was even more dramatic: 76.1 per cent. These correlations are particularly disturbing, since they refer to actions in which a final determination of dumping/subsidy or injury was never made.[49]

Designed (in part) to divert political pressures, the unfair trade laws were instead diverting—or deterring—trade.They now offered seemingly endless possibilities for creative lawyers to generate innovative new approaches. Thus, former STR official John C. Greenwald put together the China CVD petition, and an enterprising Washington attorney named Richard Copaken developed an ingenious argument for a once-obscure Florida machine tool firm, alleging Japanese subsidies of its industry derived (in part) from proceeds of community bicycle races. This was, in the end, rejected by the Reagan White House in the spring of 1983, but in the meantime, Copaken made the "Houdaille Case" a household word among trade cognoscenti and a preoccupation within the executive branch for the better part of a year. There was plenty of business for the legal profession, as importers hired also and countered with their own creative rebuttals.

Of course, there were still arguments for living with this system. Perhaps the best one was that advanced by one of America's foremost trade law authorities, John H. Jackson, University of Michigan professor and former STR general counsel. Jackson found the quantifiable costs of the "legalistic system" of import regulation to be substantial but not overwhelming: "less than $250 million" in 1983, or one-tenth of 1 percent of the value of

---

48. *Report of the Japan–United States Economic Relations Group*, January 1981, p. 92.

49. "Protectionism and Structural Adjustment: Anti-Dumping and Countervailing Duty Practices" (draft note by the UNCTAD Secretariat, Geneva, 4 January 1984; processed), p. 9.

imports.[50] After looking at the trade cases of several decades, he found "few instances" of actual multiple harassment, though he recognized that "even the threat of such activity . . . may itself be somewhat inhibiting to foreign exporters." After considering a range of other costs and benefits, Jackson concluded with a cautious affirmative: the system was better than likely alternatives "if we can believe . . . that the US legalistic system—cumbersome, rigid, and costly as it is—in fact provides for an economy more open to imports than virtually any other major industrial economy in the world."[51]

Jackson recognized, however, the evidence that for "very big cases . . . the system breaks down and in fact returns, by one subterfuge or another, to a 'non-rule system' of extensive executive discretion and 'back-room bargaining.' "[52] And the ultimate example of such a breakdown was developing even as his article went to press.

Steel Wins Comprehensive Protection

Interestingly, the process was initiated not by the United States Steel Corporation, whose head had talked of making "all players of substance . . very pleased to enter into quotas," but by US Steel's principal rival, Bethlehem Steel, and their union, the United Steelworkers. Citing an increase in the market share taken by imports from 15 percent in 1979 to 25 percent in early 1984, at a time of decline in domestic production and a 200,000-person drop in steel employment, they submitted an escape clause petition in January 1984, seeking import restrictions so that domestic firms could generate the cash flow to remain in business and finance modernization. (During this same time period, the industry in general was also pushing a quota bill to limit imports to 15 percent of the US market, as well as the flood of CVD and antidumping cases referred to earlier.)

The following July, the USITC found by a 3 to 2 vote that imports had been a substantial cause of serious injury in five of the eight major steel-import categories (though not for bars and rods, or for pipes and tubes). For relief it recommended a mixture of tariffs, quotas, and tariff-rate quotas for five years on those products it determined to have suffered injury from

---

50. This included $44 million in the budgetary costs of the major trade agencies, $97 million in "identifiable attorney and consultant costs," and a roughly equal amount in "costs internal to the firms involved." John H. Jackson, "Perspectives on the Jurisprudence of International Trade: Costs and Benefits of Legal Procedures in the United States," *Michigan Law Review* 82, no. 6 (April–May 1984), pp. 1577–78.

51. Ibid., pp. 1579–80, 1582.

52. Ibid., pp. 1580–81.

imports. Two of the commissioners recommended that the restrictions be conditioned on plans to be presented by the industry to show how the import relief period would be used to promote adjustment. This recommendation came in late July, and under the law, the President had just 60 days to implement, modify, or reject it.

Ronald Reagan's response, in the midst of the general election campaign, was a political master stroke, and a trade policy disaster. He had his trade representative, William E. Brock, announce that the President was rejecting the USITC recommendation. Brock began with strong open-market rhetoric: "The President has clearly determined that protectionism is not in the national interest. It costs jobs, raises prices and undermines our ability to compete here and abroad."[53]

But having hoisted the banner of free trade in the first paragraph, the announcement then "noted," in the second paragraph, that American steel firms and workers faced an "unprecedented and unacceptable" surge of imported steel due both to "massive unfair trade practices" and "diversion of steel imports into the US markets due to quotas and import restraints in other nations."[54] Brock had therefore been instructed, said the third paragraph, to "consult with those nations responsible . . . with a view toward the elimination of such practices." Meanwhile, the government was "to vigorously enforce US fair trade laws."

So far, so good, perhaps. But after further bows to the need "to liberalize world trade" and not "put at risk the exports of our farmers and other workers in export industries," the statement reached the crux of the matter on its third page:

The president's decision assumes the continuation of the US/European Community's arrangement on steel as well as voluntary agreements announced earlier by Mexico and South Africa. Brock . . . added that in some instances the US Trade Representative could be instructed to negotiate voluntary restraint agreements with [other] countries . . . . Such restraint could cover products on which there was no injury determination . . . .

The statement concluded with an expression of "hope" that "this combination of actions, taken without protectionist intention or effect," would

---

53. Office of the United States Trade Representative, Press Release, 18 September 1984, p. 1.

54. Such quotas and import restraints were indeed rife abroad, but the case linking them to diversion of steel here was weak. Were that the case, prices in the US market would have been below those in, say, Japan. In fact, they were higher. The prime cause of increased imports was, rather, the growing competitive disadvantage of US firms in many product lines, exacerbated by the strong dollar.

cause the market to "return to a more normal level of steel imports, or approximately 18½ percent, excluding semi-finished steel."[55]

Brock insisted initially that this market-share figure was a target, not a binding commitment, but steelmen who had just met with the President clearly felt otherwise, and they expressed their gratification with the decision. So too, initially, did steel importers and steel users, who focused on the formal rejection of the USITC's tariff-quota proposal. But the events of the remainder of 1984 made it clear that the President's "national policy for the steel industry," as it came to be labeled, was, if anything, a lot more protectionist than the USITC program he rejected. Asked as in 1982 to provide backup enforcement authority for foreign export restraints, Congress did this and more. It put into statute a target for fair import share: 17 percent to 20.2 percent of the US market, declaring further that in the absence of "satisfactory results within a reasonable period of time, the Congress will consider taking further legislative action."[56]

In the months that followed, agreements were negotiated or reaffirmed with every major foreign seller, whether or not they subsidized sales, whether or not the USITC had found injury from imports of the specific products. What it amounted to was systematic circumvention of the rules for enforcing fair trade, for creating a level playing field, to which the administration, and Congress, claimed to give highest priority! And to buttress his leverage with foreign countries, the President brandished his most flexible import restraining weapon, Section 301 of the Trade Act of 1974.

In the United States, this tendency to exploit unfair trade laws to gain favorable trade-restricting deals left liberal traders and procedural purists isolated and vulnerable. It also put executive officials in a bind. It is hard for them to resist cutting a deal when producing interests on both sides of the border want one—foreign exporters seeking market stability and home firms pressing for import constraint.

Tighter Trade Remedies? Chasing An Illusion

The Chairman of the House Ways and Means Subcommittee on Trade, Sam Gibbons, was in a similar bind in the early 1980s. The Florida Democrat

---

55. This translated into an import-share figure of 20.2 percent when semifinished products were added.

56. Quotations taken from the Trade and Tariff Act of 1984, sec. 803, and US Congress, House, "Joint Explanatory Statement of the Committee of Conference," *Trade and Tariff Act of 1984*, 98th Cong., 2d Sess., 5 October 1984, H. Rept. 98–1156, pp. 197–98.

opposed quotas and trade restrictions generally, but supported those designed to counter unfair foreign trade practices. Gibbons believed they were substantively proper, since victimized firms had a right to offsets for foreign subsidies and dumping. He also valued their political utility. It was important to show responsiveness to those firms facing what they perceived as unfair overseas competition, to show that the system could be fair in redressing their grievances, and to channel relief claimants into objective, fact-finding procedures and thus divert pressures for direct congressional action. Gibbons did not think it proper, however, that the trade-remedy laws be circumvented through negotiation of quota arrangements.

Gibbons also had problems that were specific to his personal situation in the House. As a labeled free-trader, he was vulnerable to the charge that he no longer reflected the prevailing view of House members in general, and House Democrats in particular. This charge threatened the trade leverage of his subcommittee, and of Ways and Means as a whole, at a time of fierce jurisdictional conflict with Energy and Commerce under the aggressive leadership of John D. Dingell (D-Mich.). As described in chapter 4, Dingell had already gotten the "domestic content" bill for autos—a trade measure thinly disguised as a regulation of domestic production—onto the House floor in December 1982 for a favorable vote, over Gibbons's strong opposition. Dingell did so again in 1983.

So Gibbons needed to show that he too could be tough about trade, but in a way that did not undercut the liberal system to which he was devoted.

The course he took was a traditional one. He looked for flaws in the functioning of the trade-remedy laws and vowed to improve them. At the outset of comprehensive hearings he chaired in March through May 1983, Gibbons declared "our concern that US law does not operate as effectively as it should to insure the fair conduct of international trade and the competitiveness of US industries."[57] In the bill his subcommittee proposed in early 1984, he sought to extend the countervailing duty law to previously uncovered foreign practices that industry petitioners saw as damaging subsidies. But he would balance this by insisting that the laws in fact be followed from begining to end; they should not be superseded by political fixes, such as the one Baldrige had negotiated on steel in 1982.

In its most controversial provisions, Gibbons's proposed "Trade Remedies Reform Act" singled out two particular foreign practices, defining them as subsidies subject to countervailing duties. One of these was export targeting, defined broadly as "any government plan or scheme consisting of coordinated actions . . . that are bestowed on a specific enterprise, industry, or group thereof . . . the effect of which is to assist the beneficiary to become more

---

57. House Committee on Ways and Means, *Options*, p. 3.

competitive in the export of any class or kind of merchandise."[58] The object of concern was Japan. The Houdaille machine-tool case and the charges of the Semiconductor Industry Association had brought to prominence the claim that "industrial targeting," singling out specific industrial sectors for government favor to enhance their future export prospects, had been a prime cause of Japanese economic success.[59] The second of these practices was natural resource subsidies: a government such as Mexico would keep the domestic price of, say, oil, below international market levels, conveying a cost advantage to producers of a product like fertilizer. Such subsidies had not been countervailable under US and international practice because they did not meet the specificity test: they were not provided selectively to particular firms or industries, but were available on an economy-wide basis.[60]

But as it emerged from the subcommittee the bill balanced these potentially trade-restrictive steps with an effort to protect the integrity of the rules. It required that the President, not the Secretary of Commerce, make all decisions to suspend or terminate CVD or antidumping investigations, and it provided that any resulting export restraint agreement could not "have an effect on US consumers more adverse" than the imposition of penalty duties through normal operation of the law.[61] As the full committee later explained the concern, "the antidumping and countervailing duty laws have been used as a device to implement quantitative import restrictions, including voluntary restraints, without sufficient consideration of their economic consequences, and contrary to Congressional intent that the primary remedy be offsetting duties."[62]

As trade law, the Gibbons bill presented serious problems. For one thing, it represented unilateral American efforts to extend the scope of counter-

---

58. US Congress, House, Committee on Ways and Means, *Trade Remedies Reform Act of 1984,* 98th Cong., 2d Sess., 1 May 1984, H. Rept. 98–725, p. 26.

59. Semiconductor Industry Association, *The Effect of Government Targeting on World Semiconductor Competition: A Case History of Japanese Industrial Strategy and Its Costs for America* (report prepared by Verner, Liipfert, Bernhard, and McPherson under the direction of Alan Wm. Wolff, Washington, 1983).

60. For detailed treatment of these issues by two lawyers who addressed them in the Department of Commerce, see Alan F. Holmer and Judith Hippler Bello, "The Trade and Tariff Act of 1984: The Road to Enactment," *International Lawyer* 19, no.1, (Winter 1985), pp. 287–320; and Bello and Holmer, "Subsidies and Natural Resources: Congress Rejects a Lateral Attack on the Specificity Test," *George Washington Journal of International Law and Economics* 18, no. 2 (1984), pp. 297–329.

61. US Congress, House, Committee on Ways and Means, Subcommittee on Trade, "Description of H.R. 4784, the Trade Remedies Reform Act, as Ordered Reported," 29 February 1984; processed, p. 2.

62. House Committee on Ways and Means, *Trade Remedies Reform Act,* pp. 17–18.

vailable trade practices well beyond that which commanded international agreement. It raised serious problems of definition. If targeting involved direct government subsidies, it was already subject to CVDs; if it included practices like encouraging favorable access to private bank capital or government-sponsored joint research projects, the benefits of these to particular firms were hard to quantify, as was necessary if an offsetting duty were to be imposed. Moreover, if such rules became the international norm, US exports could become vulnerable—computers as beneficiaries of Pentagon targeting, farm exports because our government subsidized irrigation.

Nevertheless, the trade-remedies bill was a sincere effort, by a protrade congressman, to deal constructively with complex problems under most unfavorable political conditions. It helped Gibbons and the Trade Subcommittee to live through two difficult years, albeit at the cost of alarming many of their liberal trade allies.

But step by legislative step, the Gibbons package came apart in 1984. In the spring, the full Ways and Means Committee, in a 22 to 12 vote, gutted the section of the bill that sought to get a handle on the political fixes. Partly for this reason, the bill lost the support of respected senior Republicans like Barber B. Conable of New York and Bill Frenzel of Minnesota. By late June, prior to action by the full House, a coalition of labor, industry, and agricultural interests forced Gibbons to jettison the export-targeting section. The Business Roundtable and the US Chamber of Commerce had already opposed it as impractical and likely to bring retaliation. Now the AFL-CIO joined them, "since pending domestic content legislation and industrial policy proposals—which they supported—are targeting practices that [the bill] would have branded as unfair."[63]

The natural resource subsidy provision did pass the House, and went to conference that fall as part of the omnibus trade package. But despite the strong backing of ranking Finance Democrat Russell B. Long of Louisiana, Senate conferees—responding to strong administration opposition—rejected it by a 4 to 3, party-line vote. So it, too, was dropped. Of all the proposals in the original Gibbons bill, only the marginal changes became law in 1984.

Taken as a whole, the Gibbons effort was one more illustration of the impossibility of managing volatile trade issues *primarily* through the elaboration of quasi-judicial procedures. One could not make the laws reach potential, borderline subsidies without extending them into uncertain and controversial new areas supported by neither domestic nor international consensus. Thus in the name of strengthening the procedures, the Gibbons approach risked further compromise of them, their use as devices to exert the very political pressure that the rules were supposed to render irrelevant.

---

63. Holmer and Bello, "Trade and Tariff Act of 1984," p. 303.

It was, on its face, a new pursuit of an old illusion—that major trade cases, the really "hot" ones, could somehow be diverted from the political arena, that we could, in the words of Gibbons' predecessor, "run trade on economic law."

But the approach did not die with the bill of 1984. In fact, trade-remedy reform became a central feature of the omnibus trade legislation which came before the House in 1986.

The Omnibus Bill of 1986: Process Protectionism?

Changing the rules might not take specific trade decisions out of politics, but it continued to perform two other important functions. For Congressmen, it offered continued political protection: it was a way for them to respond to industry pressures while pushing the individual case responsibility elsewhere. For private interests, additional elaboration of the trade rules could further tilt the political and policy balance, increasing their odds for obtaining some form of import relief, either within the rules or outside them.

So Ways and Means trade-remedy proposals were an important component of HR 4800, the omnibus measure approved by a 295 to 115 House vote in May 1986. "Resource input subsidies" were made actionable under the countervailing duty law, and "export targeting" was listed as an "unreasonable or unjustifiable" foreign practice under Section 301. That broad section was also amended to mandate retaliation, in most cases, if the US government did not succeed in securing removal of a foreign practice found to be unfair. A separate title aimed at "fully competitive foreign market opportunities" for US telecommunications firms, requiring presidential countermeasures against imports from countries denying such opportunities. The escape clause was amended to allow emergency relief for producers of perishable products, and to transfer final decision authority from the President to the US Trade Representative. Certain Section 301 authorities were transferred to the USTR as well.[64]

The bill did not limit itself to the trade-remedy laws. Among its broader provisions were extension of presidential authority to negotiate tariff and NTB reductions, a requirement that the US Treasury determine the "com-

---

64. See US Congress, House, Committee on Ways and Means, *Comprehensive Trade Policy Reform Act of 1986*, 99th Cong., 2d Sess., 6 May 1986, H. Rept. 99–581, part 1. For comparison of The House omnibus bill with others, see Raymond J. Ahearn et al., "Trade Legislation: Comparative Analyses of H.R. 4800 and Selected Senate Trade Bills" (Report prepared at the request of Senator Lloyd Bentsen [D-Tex.], Congressional Research Service, Washington, 10 June 1986; processed).

petitive exchange rate" and give priority to its achievement, and a provision to impose broad quotas against the products of countries running "excessive" trade deficits with the United States. Its main thrust, however, was to add to the already formidable list of legal rights that US producers could invoke against foreign products or foreign governments, and to reduce executive flexibility in responding to assertions of these rights. Individually, each change could be justified. And as the above list makes clear, many were aimed—in the first instance—at increasing exports, not reducing imports. Nonetheless, if the past were any guide, the practical effect would be to increase trade restrictions—through the laws' direct implementation, and through negotiations forced by suits whose likely legal outcome was unacceptable to important players at home or overseas. The end result, critics argued, might not be another Smoot-Hawley, but it would be import barriers all the same, won through what they came to label "process protectionism."

The Demise of Trade Adjustment Assistance

The incentive to exploit the rules to restrain imports was made all the greater by the discrediting of that pressure-diverting program that had once seemed most promising and constructive: Trade Adjustment Assistance for workers.

When the program was originally proposed, the most sophisticated postwar study of trade policy making lauded it as an approach that "could destroy the political basis of protectionism by giving the injured an alternative way out."[65] It yielded little trade relief in the decade after its enactment in 1962. In the late 1970s, however, following the 1974 act's expansion of benefits and easing of eligibility criteria, this program began at last to be seriously tested. The explosion of claims (mainly from laid-off auto workers), combined with the very generous financial benefits provided, drove the cost to $1.6 billion in fiscal year 1980, six times the previous peak.[66]

---

65. Raymond A. Bauer, Ithiel de Sola Pool, and Lewis Anthony Dexter, *American Business and Public Policy: The Politics of Foreign Trade,* 2d ed. (Chicago, Ill.: Aldine-Atherton, Inc., 1972), p. 43.

66. C. Michael Aho and Thomas O. Bayard, "Costs and Benefits of Trade Adjustment Assistance" in *The Structure and Evolution of Recent US Trade Policy,* edited by Robert E. Baldwin and Anne O. Krueger (Chicago, Ill.: University of Chicago Press, 1984), p. 184.

For a comprehensive assessment of the past and the future of trade adjustment programs, see Gary Clyde Hufbauer and Howard F. Rosen, *Trade Policy for Troubled Industries,* POLICY ANALYSES IN INTERNATIONAL ECONOMICS 15 (Washington: Institute for International Economics, 1986).

Jimmy Carter pointed to this expansion as a humane response to the workers' plight, a constructive alternative to protection. But Ronald Reagan came to power looking for programs to cut and predisposed against the economic interventionism that TAA exemplified. Since analytic studies indicated that TAA was not in practice fulfilling its goals of *adjustment*—helping workers move to other, more competitive industries—it was a vulnerable target for Reagan's new OMB director, David A. Stockman. It took considerable congressional effort to keep the program alive in statute. But the level and duration of benefits were cut and total program funds were slashed. Its life was extended for two years in September 1983, and for six more years in early 1986. But the Reagan administration has not yet been converted to the policy and political case for TAA, notwithstanding the new priority it gave to trade policy in the fall of 1985, and actual benefit levels have remained low.

The Limits of Administrative Remedies

The absence of a credible program to cushion trade injury and to encourage movement of resources away from industries that were losing in world markets simply put more heat on Congress for restrictive action, and on "the rules" for quasi-judicial trade relief.

Yet "the rules" had reached their limits, politically and substantively. To ignore subsidies was doctrinally wrong and politically counterproductive. To be obsessed with them, however, exaggerated their marginal contribution to overall American trade woes, fueling the growing, rather self-indulgent conviction among businessmen and politicians that the international trade game was systematically rigged against the United States. The lack of transparency of nontariff trade barriers, and the welter of conflicting and confusing evidence, allowed great leeway for the eyes of beholders inclined to see how other governments interfered with trade while ignoring how ours did. This weakened the policy tolerance that was central to the international trade system's effective functioning.[67]

To this had to be added the evidence that for trade also, in Justice Holmes's words, "great cases make bad law."[68] When a trade problem involves steel or textiles or automobiles, the political pressures and stakes,

---

67. Richardson, "Currents and Cross-Currents," *NBER Conference Report* (1984), pp. 2–3.

68. Oliver Wendell Holmes, Jr., *Northern Securities Company vs. United States,* 193 US 197, 400 (1904).

abroad as well as at home, become too great to allow "the rules" to operate unimpeded.[69]

What then are our realistic options? One is to go the route of the House bill of 1986—toward more "process protectionism." Another would be to continue our emphasis on "the rules," on standard legal processes for trade relief, but to reduce the relative attractiveness of the "unfair trade practices" statutes that asymmetrically spotlight foreign unfairness by driving US petitioners to prove its existence. This would require making Section 201, the escape clause, into more than a device to put pressure on presidents in the year they seek reelection. There would have to be some tightening of presidential discretion: at minimum, a reduction of the gulf between the narrow criteria applied by the USITC and the broad concerns of "national economic interest" the President is allowed to weigh.

Yet another approach would be to give the executive branch greater discretion in applying all trade remedies. It could be allowed to look broadly at a particular industry case, to determine—in consultation with labor and management—what trade relief, if any, among the various statutory remedies was appropriate and then to provide it. The political disadvantage would be considerable. One reason why "the rules" have been an attractive means of handling trade pressures is that they deny executive branch as well as congressional politicians the power to say "yes" to industry petitions unless regulators first approve.

As this is being written, the United States seems to be moving de facto toward an ad hoc version of the latter: an industry-by-industry response usually resulting, ultimately, in some form of protection, but through a process that ties the hands of executive branch leaders in the meantime. And it puts issues on the political ground where the advocates of restrictions are strongest, since the focus is the plight of an import-affected industry. The question is whether and how much trade should be restricted, without consideration of costs to the overall economy and without a serious adjustment effort by those receiving import protection.

Whatever choice we take, one thing seems clear. We are unlikely to get a more concentrated effort to make "the rules" work than we have seen in the late 1970s and early 1980s. That they have not worked is not the fault of some technical deficiency in drafting or of nefarious foreign cleverness in finding new statutory loopholes. It is evidence, instead, that quasi-judicial procedures will never play more than a marginal role in resolving the "great cases" of US trade policy.

---

69. J. Michael Finger and his colleagues also develop a big case/small case distinction in "The Political Economy of Administered Protection."

7

The National Arena: More Open, More Partisan

Through most of the postwar period, the American trade policy-making system operated within a national political environment that was unusually conducive to liberal policies. There were four basic reasons.

First and foremost, foreign trade was not a major partisan issue. There was competition between Democrats and Republicans for the favor of specific interest groups, but neither party used trade policy as a major means of defining its differences with the other. This both reflected and reinforced a second condition: There was an overwhelming elite consensus in favor of market openness and trade expansion. Given limited interest among the relatively protectionist mass public, this bolstered governmental leaders in their liberal inclinations.

Third, the issue posed by interests seeking import relief was typically a straightforward one—whether to insulate a particular industry's firms and workers from international competition or to make them take their market medicine. This made it easy to label these interests "protectionist," placing them very much on the defensive in the postwar policy environment. Fourth and finally, interest-group initiative was limited and usually followed a simple pattern. A relatively small number of industries sought protection, each on its own track—textiles, shoes, steel, and smaller ones like watchmakers. Other manufacturing and labor interests were typically inactive on trade issues, but many were on call to be mobilized for major liberalizing initiatives.

All four of these conditions made trade policy relatively manageable, facilitating the liberal policies that government leaders wished to pursue. And all four conditions were changing markedly in the 1970s and 1980s.

Trade politics grew more partisan, as a number of prominent Democrats began to see electoral opportunities in assuming a trade-restrictive posture, and as some Republicans reacted by toughening *their* trade stances. Elite leaders, particularly those in business, grew weaker and more qualified in their commitment to liberal trade. New trade-related issues entered the policy debate—industrial policy, misaligned exchange rates. These issues weakened the notion that, on international economic matters, government was best when it intervened least. And they offered broad national-interest rationales for certain trade-restrictive proposals. Finally, interest-group politics became more complex. The AFL-CIO became an across-the-board backer of trade restrictions and a much larger range of interests was seeking government trade action, including segments of frontier, high-tech industries like semiconductors. But the protectionist forces were being countered— albeit hesitantly—by a new antiprotectionist activism among certain exporters and importers and, on occasion, by industrial consumers.

These changes are still in process, and their ultimate import remains unclear. But most of them have tended, on balance, to make the maintenance of open trade policies more difficult. Together with the developments addressed in previous chapters, these changes have undercut time-tested old methods of managing trade issues without substituting reliable new ones.

□ □ □

In 1962, in the key House vote on President John F. Kennedy's Trade Expansion Act, Democrats voted 210 to 44 in support; Republicans lined up 127 to 43 behind a motion to "recommit" (kill) the bill. This was consistent with the basic political alignment of the three prior decades, beginning with Smoot-Hawley in 1930 and the initial Reciprocal Trade Agreements Act of 1934. Democrats backed liberal trade and lower tariffs; Republicans sought to maintain or increase protection for domestic industry.

But little more than a decade after Kennedy's landmark legislative victory, a new alignment seemed to be developing. When authorizing legislation for a new major trade round came before the House in 1973, it was the Democrats who voted 121 to 112 against, while Republicans were almost unanimous, 160 to 19, in favor. For northern Democrats, the turnabout was even greater: 141 to 7 "yea" in 1962; 101 to 52 "nay" in 1973.

An "Amazing Political Reversal"?

At the time, this shift attracted little attention. Trade had not been a prominent source of partisan contention since the 1930s. There was, of course, tactical competition for the support of specific constituencies. Kennedy, for example, promised comprehensive protection for cotton textiles in 1960, strengthening his position in New England and the southern coastal states. Richard M. Nixon, not to be twice outdone, made an even stronger textile promise eight years later. But although these pledges (Nixon's in particular) did have important policy consequences, neither was rooted in a broader trade stance that distinguished one party from its rival. And neither was directed at the national electorate. Similarly, Republicans who voted "protectionist" in 1962 (and Democrats who did so in 1973) were not inclined to advertise that fact. Advocacy of trade restrictions might win plaudits from trade-affected interests, but the mass public was indifferent and opinion leaders were hostile.

Some of the difference between 1962 and 1973, moreover, could be explained by the fact that members were voting on the program of a Democratic President (Kennedy) in the first instance and a Republican (Nixon) in the second. On almost any issue, partisan loyalties pull members toward support of an administration initiative when the White House is occupied by one of their own.

But deeper forces were at work, forces that had been developing for many years. Most important was the shift in the geographic bases of the two political parties. In the first half of the twentieth century, the Republican heartland was the industrial northeast and midwest: Herbert C. Hoover carried Pennsylvania in 1932, but not a single state farther west (and no state south of Delaware). Indeed, from the first Lincoln election until the reign of Franklin D. Roosevelt, not a single Democratic presidential candidate carried either Pennsylvania or Michigan. This general pattern persisted as late as 1948: Harry S Truman scored his upset reelection victory even though his favored Republican rival, Thomas E. Dewey, carried those two states, and New York and New Jersey as well. But the Kennedy-Nixon election of 1960 reversed the pattern. JFK won 303 electoral votes, exactly the same number as Truman. But unlike Truman, he lost badly in the west but *won* Michigan, Pennsylvania, New York, and New Jersey. Since that time, the northeast has become the *Democratic* heartland, while the GOP has flourished in the sunbelt—the West and, increasingly, the South.

This shift reduced Republican dependence on historically protectionist northeastern and midwestern industrialists. By contrast, the Democrats' new heartland was where organized labor was the strongest. It was therefore natural to expect some adjustment of the parties' dominant positions on trade, and in fact Raymond A. Bauer and his colleagues detected signs of an "amazing political reversal" as early as 1953. Closely analyzing a Roper poll taken that year, and looking particularly at respondents with the most polar views, they found that "ultrafree-traders" were "strongly Republican," whereas "ultraprotectionists" tended to be Democrats. And important among the group most committed to trade restrictions were "industrial workers who see a threat to their jobs."[1]

---

1. Raymond A. Bauer, Ithiel de Sola Pool, and Lewis Anthony Dexter, *American Business and Public Policy: The Politics of Foreign Trade* (Chicago: Aldine-Atherton, Inc., 1972), pp. 91–92.

Through the 1950s and 1960s, the major national labor organizations still held to a freetrade position, although the textile unions were an important exception. The AFL-CIO endorsed the Trade Expansion Act of 1962, in part because of its new provisions for trade adjustment assistance to workers. A decade later, however, labor leaders were deriding that program as "burial insurance," and AFL-CIO President George Meany was singing a decidedly different trade tune. Urban Democrats followed him from support to opposition of liberal trade, particularly in the House of Representatives. But with a few iconoclastic exceptions (like Senator Vance Hartke [D-Ind.] of Burke-Hartke fame) they did so quietly. In the Senate, in fact, liberal activists like Walter F. Mondale (D-Minn.) fought the House-passed quota bill of 1970 and backed the Nixon-Ford trade act when it came before them four years later.

It was a Republican, John B. Connally, who was the first postwar presidential aspirant to make trade a prominent issue in his quest for his party's nomination. He won cheers on the campaign circuit in 1979 with his threat to leave Japanese Toyotas rusting on the docks. But his bottom line—exactly one convention delegate in 1980—did not inspire emulation.

By 1982, however, things were suddenly looking very different. The Democrats were again outsiders in the White House and newly a minority in the Senate as well. The economy was suffering its deepest and longest recession in more than forty years. The "frost belt" industrial heartland states like Pennsylvania, Ohio, and Michigan were particularly hard hit, as were their key industries like autos and steel. And US trade was moving deeper into deficit—a victim, in important part, of the strong dollar. Mondale was now seeking the Democratic presidential nomination, and the AFL-CIO had decided, for the first time, to endorse a candidate *before* the primaries. Mondale needed that endorsement; he also needed an issue on which he could take a "tougher" stand than the President. He fastened upon trade. He did not neglect the broader macroeconomic causes of America's distress. But to labor audiences in particular, he went after the Japanese and unfair trade practices, and denounced the Reagan regime for failing to combat them.

The argument went like this: ever since World War II the United States had been operating an open economy, playing by international trade rules. But other countries, Japan in particular, were taking advantage by targeting our industries while insulating their own. The result was record trade deficits and depression in our industrial heartland. We needed to get tough on trade, lest job opportunities for our youth be limited to working at McDonald's hamburger stands and sweeping up around Japanese computers.

For the most part, Mondale avoided concrete commitments to trade protection; he remained at heart an internationalist, and he preferred opening foreign markets to closing American ones. Nevertheless, the United Auto Workers had made its highly restrictive domestic content bill a litmus test for labor Democrats, and Mondale endorsed it. So did the Democratic-controlled House of Representatives in 1982, and again in 1983. In the latter year, only two Democrats from the northeast and industrial midwest voted "no" on final passage. Thus, as the nation marked the fiftieth anniversary of the Reciprocal Trade Agreements Act of 1934, it seemed to be witnessing the reemergence of trade as a highly visible partisan issue, but with the two major parties having switched positions. Senator John H. Chafee (R-RI) remarked, seemingly with some relief, that here was one issue where the Republicans were wearing "the white hats."

The new advocacy of trade restrictions by certain Democrats was not without its logic. Ever since the New Deal, theirs had been the party favoring an active government to redress the imbalances and inequities of the marketplace. Republicans, by contrast, had been critics of government intrusion in business. On trade, however, these positions had been reversed. Would not a new trade realignment make more intellectual sense, then, with the domestic interventionists becoming international interventionists as well?

For all of these reasons, it seemed very possible in early 1983 that trade was on the way to becoming, as in the years before 1930, one of the prime issues dividing and defining our two major political parties.

In the short run, this is not what happened. On the contrary, 1983 and 1984 saw a narrowing of the partisan gap. Mondale found that the "protectionist" label retained its sting, as editorial pages denounced his trade line and internationalist Democrats made known their dismay. Moreover, once Senator Edward M. Kennedy (D-Mass.) withdrew from the contest, he no longer had serious competition for the labor endorsement. So the Democratic challenger backpedaled adroitly. He did not change any specific stand, but from early 1983 onward he deemphasized trade restrictions and highlighted the macroeconomic causes of the trade imbalance. And the Democratic Party platform negotiated by Mondale's aides actually attacked Ronald W. Reagan from the internationalist side, citing as the administration's "most fundamental" mistake its acting "as if the United States were an economic island unto itself." The platform's only specific reference to "trade relief" employed the modifier "temporary," and called for a quid pro quo in the form of industry commitment to "a realistic, hardheaded modernization plan which will restore competitiveness."[2]

---

2. 1984 Democratic Party Platform, reprinted in *Congressional Quarterly,* 21 July 1984, pp. 1748, 1760.

Meanwhile, Reagan was looking more protectionist. The President remained a free-trader in principle, but as noted in chapter 5, he was protecting his political flanks in practice, approving new restraints on heavyweight motorcycles, textiles, and specialty steel, a fourth year of Japanese auto export limits, and—in the middle of the election campaign—a network of voluntary restraint agreements on carbon steel aimed at limiting imports to 20.2 percent of domestic production. His stand was less restrictive than that of Mondale, who called for a 17 percent import share, but the Democrat conditioned his proposal on the industry's commitments to adjust. Not to be outdone, Congress incorporated elements of both candidates' positions— and a modified industry adjustment requirement—into the Trade and Tariff Act of 1984.

So, contrary to widespread expectations, trade did not become a major issue in the 1984 general election. But the threat that it might took its toll in administration policy. Moreover, the issue reemerged in 1985 and 1986, fueled by the unparalleled trade deficit. Democrats, staggering from Reagan's 49-state electoral sweep, needed to counter the administration in its two areas of electoral strength—economic recovery at home and "standing tall" in the world. To those like Representative Tony Coelho of California, Chairman of the House Democratic Campaign Committee, trade seemed the ideal issue, since it met both needs. By targeting the trade deficit, Democrats could highlight the negative side of Reaganomics and attack White House softness toward trade competitors.

In July, three influential mainstream Democrats, Senator Lloyd Bentsen (D-Tex.) and Representatives Dan Rostenkowski (D-Ill.) and Richard A. Gephardt (D-Mo.) introduced a bill imposing a 25 percent tax on imports from countries running large trade surpluses with the United States. In September, after legislators returned to Washington from their home states and districts, House Speaker Thomas P. O'Neill made the declaration (quoted in chapter 4) about trade having become the "number one" issue on Capitol Hill. "President Reagan," he intoned, "seems willing to preside over the de-industrialization of America. We in Congress are not."[3] The following spring, he and other Democratic leaders pushed through the House an "omnibus" trade bill with a decidedly protectionist tilt.

O'Neill was, in fact, exaggerating. Trade was still not the "number one" congressional issue in 1985 and 1986, although its prominence had enormously increased. Nor were Democrats as unified as rhetoric sometimes made it sound. Many who aspired to leadership positions, like Senators Bill Bradley (D-NJ) and Gary Hart (D-Col.), were unwilling to abandon the legacy of Cordell Hull, however much they might criticize the administra-

---

3. Quoted in *Washington Post*, 20 September 1985.

tion's passivity on the trade issue. And as long as Democrats were deeply divided on whether to move in a protectionist direction, the issue could not be a good one for mobilizing and unifying the party against the opposition.

Nor were Republicans prepared to stand still while Democrats decided whether to attack. Just as Reagan had made protectionist concessions in 1984, Senate Finance Republicans were in the forefront of the campaign against Japanese trade practices in the spring of 1985. A year later, 59 House Republicans joined 236 House Democrats in supporting the omnibus legislation.

Still, there had developed in the 1970s and 1980s the *potential* for sharp interparty division on trade in the years to come. And if a future Democratic President were to come to power on a truly protectionist platform, this would remove from the American trade policy-making system the final—and most crucial—pillar of support for open policies, the liberal-leaning leadership of the executive branch.

A Newly Ambivalent Elite

A related development was the weakening of support for liberal trade policies within the American leadership community. As spelled out in chapter 2, open trade policies had never won overwhelming backing from the mass public. Rather, they were sustainable because of mass indifference, combined with strong support from leadership groups. These conditions helped keep trade issues out of the larger public arena, so that specific pressures could be diverted or accommodated by special deals.

Between the 1930s and the 1960s, elite support of liberal trade increased. Postwar prosperity served to confirm the rightness of open trade policy just as the Great Depression had discredited the Smoot-Hawley alternative. Thus, as Judith L. Goldstein has written, liberalism became the dominant ideology because it was associated with the unparalleled prosperity of the years since 1945.[4]

But just as the Munich lesson for security policy was supplanted by Vietnam, the connection between Smoot-Hawley, global depression, and World War II faded also. One reason was time. Another was the afflictions chronicled in chapter 3: increased trade exposure, the American "decline,"

---

4. Judith L. Goldstein, "A Domestic Explanation for Regime Formation and Maintenance: Liberal Trade Policy in the US" (paper prepared for delivery to Annual Meeting of the American Political Science Association, Washington, 30 August–2 September 1984). See also Goldstein, "A Re-examination of American Trade Policy: An Inquiry into the Causes of Protectionism" (Ph.D. diss., University of California, Los Angeles, 1983).

the rise of new competitors, the erosion of the General Agreement on Tariffs and Trade (GATT), stagflation, and the misaligned dollar. Substantial—if not entirely conclusive—evidence from opinion polls tends to confirm what the tone of the recent American trade debate suggests: that leadership backing for liberal trade has weakened significantly since the 1960s, and particularly in the past decade. At the same time, the mass public, which has always been somewhat inclined toward protection, may have grown more concerned about trade and thus more actively supportive of import restrictions.

Available indicators from the murky world of opinion polls offer no single, simple answers. The Roper organization acknowledged as much when it circulated a June 1981 report regarding international economic issues under the heading "Foreign Trade: A Confused View." Similarly, the most thorough analysis of the 1950s underscored "the degree to which apparent expressions of opinion vary according to the way the issue is posed."[5]

Other polling organizations have not always been as careful as Roper in heading the consequent admonition of Bauer, Pool, and Dexter: "to exercise extreme caution in interpreting the poll results."[6] The Harris Survey, for example, used the following headings to report virtually identical public opinion findings: "More Restrictions on Imports Favored Over Traditional US Policy of Free Trade" (15 March 1979); "Americans Favor Restricting Foreign Car Imports" (10 March 1983); and "Americans Want Free, Balanced Trade" (14 March 1983).

Analysis of public opinion is impeded more fundamentally by the lack of any staple questions that were posed consistently by pollsters throughout the postwar period. Gallup asked regularly, during the 1940s and 1950s, whether people favored higher or lower tariffs, and got consistent pluralities for the latter. It also got a consistently positive response to questions about whether people supported continuation of the reciprocal trade agreements program. But these questions are no longer put to the public today.

When questions have been posed in terms of jobs or the desirability of imports per se, mass opinion has shown a consistently protectionist tilt. In 1953, the Roper poll asked, "Would you rather see this country import *more* goods from foreign countries than we do now, or put *more restrictions* on goods imported into this country from abroad?" Of those willing to take a position, 37 percent favored restrictions, and 26 percent favored imports.[7]

---

5. Bauer, Pool, and Dexter, *American Business and Public Policy*, p. 84.

6. Ibid., pp. 85–86.

7. Ibid., p. 85.

Recent surveys suggest a stronger leaning in the restrictive direction. When, between 1977 and 1983, Gallup asked virtually the same question as Roper in 1953—posing a choice between more imports and more restrictions—imports won just 12 percent to 15 percent support, as against 68 percent to 75 percent for restrictions.[8] And most Americans see a direct connection between imports and the loss of jobs. A 10 March 1983 Harris survey found that a 75 percent to 21 percent majority of respondents were convinced that import competition from abroad was harmful to American labor. This was up slightly from 72 percent to 24 percent in 1980. Another Harris survey, released 14 March 1983, found that a 67 percent to 29 percent majority of respondents saw real merit in the claim that "if American workers' jobs are going to be protected, then the US Government must raise the tariffs on competitive products coming in from abroad."

Yet ambivalence remains, and so too does relative lack of interest. Presented in 1983 with the proposition that "we have to produce better products with more efficiency to compete in the world rather than depend on artificial trade barriers, such as tariffs," Americans agreed by 90 percent to 7 percent![9] One expert writing during the congressional trade storm in the spring of 1985 found "not much evidence" of "surging public resentment over our imbalance of trade."[10] A *New York Times/CBS News* poll three months later found "foreign trade" dead last in importance among five listed issues "that people are concerned about,"[11] even though the subject had been in the news more prominently than at any time in postwar memory.

But if mass opinion shows limited change, there is evidence of emerging divisions within leadership groups. William Schneider, a leading public opinion analyst, found a marked shift in the early 1980s. In 1980, only 15 percent of the executives in a Chamber of Commerce poll favored new laws to limit imports. By 1982, that proportion had more than doubled, to 38

---

8. Gallup Report International, October 1983. Roper asked, from 1973 to 1984: "Generally speaking, do you think the government should or should not place restrictions on imports of goods from other countries that are priced lower than American-made goods of the same kind?" Responses fluctuated narrowly, with 61 percent to 68 percent pro-restriction and 21 percent to 31 percent against. The 68 percent pro came in late 1979 and early 1983; the 31 percent against in late 1981. See William Schneider, "Protectionist Push is Coming from the Top," *National Journal*, 27 April 1985, p. 932.

9. "The Harris Survey," 14 March 1983.

10. Schneider, "Protectionist Push," p. 932.

11. "Here are five things that people are concerned about—arms control, foreign trade problems, tax reform, the budget deficit and war in Central America. Which of these is most important right now. . . ." Answers: arms control (19 percent); foreign trade (9 percent); tax reform (19 percent); budget deficit (29 percent); war in Central America (19 percent). (July 1985 Survey, p. 3.)

percent, and opposition to import restrictions among business executives dropped from 78 percent to 44 percent.

In early 1983, Schneider cited Gallup polls of "opinion leaders" indicating "movement in the protectionist direction" between 1978 and 1982, with no comparable shift in the mass public. The polls showed that "top figures in business, labor, government, the media, religion and education were 75 per cent in favor of eliminating tariffs in 1978 but only 67 per cent in favor in 1982. Among labor leaders, the change was quite sharp, from 53 to 42 per cent in favor of tariffs in 1978 to 71 to 21 per cent protariff in 1982." This led Schneider to conclude that "trade protectionism is growing from the top down."[12] Doubtless the recession of the latter year contributed to this shift, but it is unlikely that it explains all of it.

Lending further credence to the Schneider view was a 1983 survey of "opinion leaders" by the Opinion Research Corporation (ORC). It found 75 percent to 20 percent support for "industrial modernization agreements," which might include short-term relief from imports in exchange for management and labor commitments to improve efficiency.[13] And two-thirds of the "Washington thought leaders" interviewed by ORC were in favor of "targeted, temporary measures . . . to persuade other nations to reduce their own trade distortions."[14]

Challenges to Laissez-Faire Trade Doctrine

Both reflecting and contributing to elite ambivalence was the increased questioning of liberal trade ideology, not just in the Washington policy community but at leading intellectual centers. Just as the Great Depression and postwar prosperity had discredited "protectionism," the relative decline of the United States weakened support for "free trade" ideology. An audience was growing for perspectives that held that ideology to be flawed or incomplete. These new perspectives were of two basic sorts. The first, focusing on specific firms and industries, argued that the free trade–protectionist distinction was obsolete in a world characterized by pervasive government intervention in the marketplace. The second, looking at swings in overall trade balances, questioned the compatibility of open market

---

12. "Trade Protectionism is Growing From the Top Down," *National Journal,* 29 January 1983, pp. 240–41.

13. "The Future of America's Basic Industries: A Survey of Opinion Leaders" (conducted for the LTV Corporation by Opinion Research Corporation, 1983).

14. Schneider, "Protectionist Push," p. 933.

policies with exchange rate misalignments that saddled producers with enormous competitive burdens that were not of their making.

At the broadest level, proponents of the first school argued that the actual world economy was not at all that posited by Adam Smith. We did not have autonomous firms jousting for business on their own, with rewards to the most efficient. Rather, other governments rigged the game through a range of actions—subsidies, product standards, procurement regulations—which favored their national producers at the expense of foreign competitors. American firms thus operated not on a level playing field, but on one tilted against them.

For some critics, the challenge was economy-wide. The Labor-Industry Coalition for International Trade (LICIT), comprising eight firms and 11 labor organizations, found that "our nation's industrial base has been weakened across a spectrum ranging from basic industries to the most technologically advanced." It placed much of the blame on "the widening gap between specific industry support efforts in other countries and the absence of such policies and programs in the United States." It argued that the "resulting 'industrial policy gap' has put American industry at a systematic disadvantage." To close the gap, LICIT recommended a range of policy changes aimed at both offsetting the effects of foreign industrial subsidies and providing broader government support to American industrial enterprise.[15] It recognized that not all foreign industrial policy efforts were successful, but even those that were not could hurt American interests. Thus, a comprehensive US response was appropriate.

In essence, the argument was that because other nations subsidize and protect their industries, we must do so, lest we fall behind. But the very comprehensiveness that made the LICIT line attractive for coalition-building purposes made it relatively easy for trade traditionalists to refute. For what made products move in international commerce was *comparative* advantage. No country could gain an across-the-board trade supremacy since one had to import in order to export, and vice versa. A foreign government that subsidized its industries in general would not help any particular one, and

---

15. Labor-Industry Coalition for International Trade, *International Trade, Industrial Policies, and the Future of American Industry* (Washington: Labor-Industry Coalition for International Trade, 1983), pp. iii, iv, 57–66.

For a broad survey of foreign practices in a specific industry, steel, see three reports prepared in 1984 for the Bethlehem Steel Corporation and the United States Steel Corporation by the Washington law firm of Verner, Liipfert, Bernhard, McPherson, and Hand: "Government Aid to the Steel Industry of the European Communities: Market Distortion In Europe And Its Impact On The U.S. Steel Industry," 224 pp.; "Japanese Government Promotion of the Steel Industry: Three Decades of Industrial Policy," 181 pp.; and "The Rise of Steelmaking in the Developing Countries: State Intervention In The Market And Its Effect On International Trade In Steel," 300 pp.

would probably contribute to overall *inefficiency*. Or if it subsidized a particular industry, like steel, costs would be borne by other sectors of its economy and benefits would accrue to consumers of its steel, importers included. For the United States, the choice was then a simple one: accept the subsidy in the form of cheaper steel (which would harm our steelmakers but help steel users), or offset it with a countervailing duty. In this case also, no comprehensive policy response was required.

But what if a nation could prepare the way for market success tomorrow by helping an industry today? Many critics correctly argued that trade theory rested on "static comparative advantage." Trade flowed according to *current* prices, reflecting current production costs. But the process by which producers achieved international competitiveness was a dynamic one, subject to influence by national policies. Governments might, by "targeting" growth sectors, create comparative advantage: they could aid and protect industries that would one day become strong enough to conquer world markets. Japan had done so persistently and successfully, argued scholars such as Ezra Vogel of Harvard and Chalmers Johnson of the University of California, Berkeley, creating what Johnson labeled the "developmental state."[16]

This raised the question of whether, for certain products in certain types of markets, industry-specific trade policy intervention might promote broader national interests, not just those of the specific workers and firms involved. The National Bureau of Economic Research (NBER) inaugurated a major project examining possible economic rationales for interventionist trade policies, export subsidies as well as import barriers, drawing upon oligopoly models of "imperfect" interfirm competition. In a world with a limited number of firms, some drawing support from home governments, the NBER

---

16. Ezra Vogel, *Japan as Number One: Lessons for Americans* (Cambridge, Mass.: Harvard University Press, 1979); Chalmers Johnson, *MITI and the Japanese Miracle: The Growth of Industrial Policy, 1925–1975* (Stanford, Calif.: Stanford University Press, 1982). See also *American Industry in International Competition*, edited by John Zysman and Laura Tyson (Ithaca, NY: Cornell University Press, 1983).

On the critical side, Philip H. Trezise argues that such "models of Japan's postwar economic development are subject to so substantial a discount as to make them largely valueless as guides to understanding. . . . To suppose . . . that politicians and officials in league with businessmen were able to plan and guide Japan's explosive economic growth in detail is neither credible in the abstract nor (as will be seen) supported by the realities." See Trezise, "Politics, Government, and Economic Growth in Japan," in *Asia's New Giant: How the Japanese Economy Works*, edited by Hugh Patrick and Henry Rosovsky (Washington: Brookings Institution, 1976), pp. 753–811. For other critical evaluations of the contribution of industry-specific policies to Japan's economic "miracle," see Edward J. Lincoln, "Japan's Industrial Policy"(prepared for the Japan Economic Institute of America, Washington, April 1984); and Gary R. Saxonhouse, "What Is All This about 'Industrial Targeting' in Japan?" *World Economy*, vol. 6, no. 3 (September 1983), pp. 253–73.

analysts hypothesized, laissez faire might not always be the best policy.[17] And while the initial NBER conclusions were tentative and cautious, centers of political analysis like the Berkeley Roundtable on the International Economy (BRIE) at the University of California, led by John Zysman, were less hesitant in setting forth conceptual rationales for government intervention, which they viewed as essential to meet the Japanese challenge and guide the United States toward a competitive future industrial structure. In 1983 Robert Reich, based at Harvard's John F. Kennedy School of Government, published *The Next American Frontier*, a widely noticed call for thoroughgoing changes in US industrial management which won back-cover blurbs from both Gary Hart and Walter Mondale! Republican George Lodge, from the Harvard Business School across the river, was making a case for activist government industrial policy before business audiences.

Prescriptions varied as to how Americans should respond to government-created comparative advantage. No one in this school called for protection per se; in fact, all warned that a simple defensive response would only make things worse for the United States. Classical liberals like Congressman Sam M. Gibbons (D-Fla.) felt we should take countermeasures aimed at offsetting past industrial targeting by Japan and other nations and deterring such practices henceforth. Interventionists inclined more toward emulation, although their purposes varied. One arresting formulation was that of Reich, who saw a need for the United States to move "beyond free trade." He argued that trade-related US policy should not be *laissez faire* but *proadjustment*. Our goal should be "promoting the rapid transformation of all nations' industrial bases [especially that of the United States] toward higher-value production." Existing US trade policies had, in Reich's view, "just the opposite effect."[18]

The case for activist industrial policy rested on the conviction that the United States faced a deep and pervasive industrial competitiveness problem. As summarized by a trenchant skeptic, Charles L. Schultze, most proponents built their cases on four premises: (1) The United States had been "de-industrializing" and was suffering substantial losses (absolute or relative) in its manufacturing capacity; (2) without assistance, US management and labor might not be capable of making the transition from old heavy to new high-tech industries; (3) the United States was losing its edge in world export markets, with a consequent threat to its global leadership position;

---

17. See, for example, Gene M. Grossman and J. David Richardson, *Strategic U.S. Trade Policy: A Survey of Issues and Early Analysis, NBER Research Progress Report* (Cambridge, Mass.: National Bureau of Economic Research, 1984).

18. Robert Reich, "Beyond Free Trade," *Foreign Affairs,* vol. 61, no. 4 (Spring 1983), p. 790.

and (4) other countries, Japan in particular, had been successful in pursuing industrial policies, "selecting potential winners in the technological race" and nurturing them through a range of policy devices.[19]

If these four premises were correct, the conclusion followed clearly: the United States needed an aggressive industrial policy to manage the transition to a new industrial era, to move resources from declining industries into growth industries, to defend itself in a mercantilist world. Otherwise, this school suggested, our economy might end up a sort of residual comprised of those industries that were left after more purposive nations had chosen theirs. Thus not only did we see proposals like those of financier Felix G. Rohatyn and Representative John S. LaFalce (D-NY) to establish a national industrial bank to channel capital where it was most needed; we also found proposals for at least temporary trade restrictions, which were defended as necessary steps to a better US industrial structure in the future.

As noted in earlier chapters, such ideas were picked up and promulgated by those who would challenge existing centers of trade leadership, by House Energy and Commerce jousting with Ways and Means, and by Senate Democrats seeking to amend the Baldrige-Roth trade reorganization bill in order to put the proposed new trade department into the industrial policy business.

In general, the last two decades have seen the flowering of "issue politics." With decentralization in the Congress and electoral entrepreneurship in individual districts, members get press attention by espousing "new ideas" that differentiate them from their political rivals. Both the internationalization of the US economy and the new forms of (fair and unfair) foreign competition provided ample subject matter for such ideas, particularly among activist Democrats. The ideas of Cordell Hull were no longer at the intellectual cutting edge.

Industrial policy proposals flourished particularly in 1981–82, when the US economy suffered a severe cyclical downturn. But as Schultze noted in his critique, the evolution of international trade in the 1970s did *not*, on balance, support any of the four premises of the "industrial policy" critique. In fact, the US balance of trade in manufactured goods improved markedly during this period.[20]

The case for activist, future-oriented industrial policy carried an added burden. Such policy was far easier to prescribe than to pursue. Was the United States capable of selective mercantilism? Could our political system

---

19. Charles L. Schultze, "Industrial Policy: A Solution in Search of a Problem," *California Management Review* 24, no. 4 (Summer 1983), pp. 5–6.

20. See Robert Z. Lawrence, *Can America Compete?* (Washington: Brookings Institution, 1984).

tilt in favor of industries with future potential and allocate resources to them? Or would political pressure from those *currently* feeling trade pain inevitably channel public resources to the entrenched, embattled industrial "losers"? Alternatively, if economy-wide "industrial policy" was attempted along LICIT-recommended lines, would not this build up, within our government, strong bureaucratic interests in the welfare of specific industrial sectors, interests that would impede economy-wide adjustment and slow down growth for the nation as a whole?[21]

So industrial policy advocates faced double-barreled criticism, on the need for their remedies and on the country's ability to implement them. It is not surprising that the audience for their prescriptions fell off substantially once the US recovery began picking up speed in 1983.

Yet by mid-decade the American industrial trade balance *had* turned enormously negative. And the prime cause was another phenomenon that highlighted the limits of laissez-faire trade doctrine—the incredible, unanticipated surge of the dollar (see chapter 3). By early 1985 the massive international capital inflows that were needed to finance record US budget deficits had driven the dollar to roughly 40 percent above the level that would have brought balance to the US international current (trade and services) account. This meant that in competition with foreign producers, American firms faced the equivalent of a 40 percent tax on their exports and a 40 percent subsidy on competing imports.[22] Under these circumstances, we did begin to see a trade-induced "deindustrialization," concentrated in those industries most exposed to international competition, but spreading by mid-decade to the industrial sector taken as a whole.

US manufacturing employment peaked at 21.1 million workers in the spring of 1979, then fell 3 million in the subsequent recession. As of summer 1986, it stood at just 19.1 million. Only one-third of those lost industrial jobs had returned, and manufacturing payrolls actually had a half million fewer on their payrolls than at the start of 1985.[23]

---

21. For a comprehensive argument linking the rise of "distributional coalitions" seeking maximum income for their members to slowdowns in national economic growth, see Mancur Olson, *The Rise and Decline of Nations* (New Haven, Conn.: Yale University Press, 1982).

22. John Williamson, *The Exchange Rate System,* POLICY ANALYSES IN INTERNATIONAL ECONOMICS 5, 2nd ed. (Washington: Institute for International Economics, June 1985); Stephen Marris, *Deficits and the Dollar: The World Economy at Risk,* POLICY ANALYSES IN INTERNATIONAL ECONOMICS 14 (Washington: Institute for International Economics, December 1985).

23. See *Economic Report of the President,* January 1981, table B-35, and *Economic Indicators,* Washington, September 1986, p. 14.

As the French economist Albert Bressand put it, we seemed afflicted with " 'good things' that do not go together," a free-market currency regime that wreaked havoc on the free market in trade.[24] And, as C. Fred Bergsten noted as early as 1981, the trade imbalance produced by a strong dollar was bound to generate enormous pressure for trade restrictions as it expanded the ranks of the "trade losers" in the American industrial economy.[25] At the urging of such international economic policy analysts, organizations like the Business Roundtable began to make the overvalued dollar (and the undervalued yen) one of their chief "trade" policy priorities.

As in the case of industrial malaise, a focus on the exchange rate did not yield a persuasive, broadly supported, general-interest alternative for US *trade* policy. On the contrary, its message was that the required measures lay outside the trade sphere: like the Group of Five initiative of September 1985 which helped move the dollar down, and like the still-urgent need to reduce the federal budget deficit.

More generally, misaligned exchange rates, like intensified industrial competition, have spawned an intellectual challenge that puts free-market purists on the ideological defensive. Liberal values continue, of course, to be widely held; no competing doctrine for trade policy has yet won comparable acceptance. Still, recent challenges have muted the liberal-protectionist dichotomy that served as an enormous political advantage to trade-expanders throughout the postwar period. Thus, intellectually as well as politically and procedurally, the trade policy game has become more open, and this has added to the unpredictability of policy outcomes.

New Patterns of Interest-Group Politics

There have been important modifications in the pattern of trade politics that predominated in the early postwar period. During that time, a modest number of industries typically sought protection, each more or less on its own. Executive and congressional leaders encouraged each to go it alone, in order to avert log-rolling of the Smoot-Hawley variety. They pointed the smaller industries toward the Tariff Commission (now the US International Trade Commission) and the quasi-judicial trade remedy procedures. Larger ones, mainly textiles, cut separate deals for themselves, part of which involved promises not to obstruct broader trade-liberalizing initiatives like

---

24. Albert Bressand, "Mastering the 'Worldeconomy,' " *Foreign Affairs,* vol. 61, no. 4 (Spring 1983), p. 762.

25. C. Fred Bergsten, "The Costs of Reaganomics," *Foreign Policy,* no. 44 (Fall 1981), pp. 24–36.

the Kennedy and Tokyo rounds. No important groups took across-the-board protectionist stances.

Nor was there much self-initiated interest-group activism on the liberal trade side. National business and labor organizations were generally on call to endorse major new trade-expanding initiatives; yet once particular legislative battles were fought and won, the coalitions supporting them faded away. Nor were those who benefited specifically from open trade—importers, industrial consumers, and retail consumers—inclined to enter the political fray.[26]

The last fifteen years have brought at least three significant changes in this pattern.

First and most important, the number and range of industries seeking trade relief has increased. Substantial protection has been achieved not just by the textile-apparel coalition, but by other mature industries such as steel and automobiles. Adding up just these three and a few minor product categories like motorcycles, we have reached a situation in which the relatively traditional, standardized products now benefiting from quota arrangements account for well over one-fourth of the total value of US imports of manufactured goods.

Nor is pressure on trade policy any longer limited to those who are clearly current trade losers, the low-tech sectors whose manufacturing processes can be widely replicated around the world. The old rule was that losers enter trade politics while winners stick to business. But beginning in the late 1970s, producers of high-technology products like semiconductors, telecommunications, and machine tools were beginning to press for governmental action. The Semiconductor Industry Association went to Capitol Hill with its concerns about Japanese competition. Executives of Corning Glass Company, a leader in fiber-optics, expressed concern that Japanese industrial targeting was making international trade a losing proposition for them. An important electronics firm, Motorola, began in 1982 to place a series of 20 full-page advertisements in the *Wall Street Journal* under the heading, "Meeting Japan's Challenge." And in early 1985, even David Packard, Chairman of the Board of the successful high-tech Hewlett-Packard Company and cochair of the US-Japan Advisory Commission, suggested

---

26. Those whose overall interests tilted toward open trade but who might at some point want protection for certain products were influenced by the long-established practice of "reciprocal noninterference," which induced them, in the words of E. E. Schattschneider, "to accept the incidental burdens" of others' protection without protest. See Schattschneider, *Politics, Pressures and the Tariff* (New York, NY: Prentice-Hall, 1935), p. 284. Those actively involved in the import business felt disadvantaged in the political arena, since they could be charged with helping foreign interests take away American jobs. In both cases, abstention from politics therefore seemed the wisest course.

that the United States consider imposing temporary quotas to "decrease the growth of Japan's exports to the U.S."[27]

What moved Motorola and other firms in technology-intensive industries was a new mix of export market interest and import market anxiety. As a group, they had done very well in the international marketplace; as noted in chapter 3, they were disproportionately responsible for the explosion of US exports in the 1970s. But they had suffered trade losses also, particularly in 1982–86, and they worried about competing, as solitary private actors, against what they feared as a government-industry combine headquartered in Tokyo. They contrasted the inroads Japanese producers were making in American markets with their own problems in selling across the Pacific. Their call was seldom for out-and-out protection (although the machine tool industry did win import limits in 1986 on grounds of national security interests). Rather, they became advocates of what trade specialists call "sectoral reciprocity." If by hard negotiations, the United States government could not persuade other nations—above all Japan—to open up their markets for US products, to limit subsidies, to establish a "level playing field" for trade, then the United States should take protective action in return.

By and large, trade-afflicted firms still pursued their campaigns for protection separately, on behalf of their particular industry groupings, though (as noted in chapter 6), they did join in coalitions seeking revision of the general trade-remedy laws. There was a textile-shoe alliance formed in 1970 to win statutory import quotas, but it dissolved as soon as the textile firms won new protection by traditional (executive-negotiated) means. At the same time, there did emerge in the 1970s and 1980s a major national, cross-industry organization—a coalition, more accurately—which took an across-the-board trade-restrictive stance. That was, of course, organized labor, whose shift from early postwar trade liberalism was the second major development in interest-group politics.

In its direct impact on trade legislation, labor's new protectionism was limited. After a decade and a half, it had virtually nothing in statute to show for its major trade stands: for the Burke-Hartke quota bill of 1971, against the Nixon-Ford trade bill in 1973–74, for domestic content for autos in 1981–84, and against extension of trade preferences to advanced developing countries in 1974 and 1984. An older labor priority, trade adjustment assistance for workers was inaugurated in 1962 and expanded in 1974; however, it was gutted in 1981. Steel unions were able to obtain in the trade bill of 1984 a provision requiring firms to reinvest net cash flow in steel facilities and worker training. But more generally, as discussed in

---

27. Letter from Packard to Stephen R. Levy, Chairman, International Committee, American Electronics Association, 5 March 1985, released by AEA.

chapter 4, labor failed to exploit the vulnerability of that bill by extracting concessions on any of a number of its longstanding concerns.

What labor did achieve was indirect: it neutralized important potential supporters of liberal trade. The hearts and minds of many UAW Democrats who voted for domestic content were elsewhere, but House members unwilling to buck labor on a proposal which had so little other support were not going to be spear-carriers for trade liberalization more generally. Instead, they would either look for issues on which they could take a trade-restrictive stance, or confine their activism to other policy areas. Similarly, organizations like the Consumer Federation of America (CFA), an umbrella group that counted the UAW among its members, found the union "calling in some old debts" to extract an endorsement of domestic content. "On the surface, this might appear to go against consumer interests" in lower prices and in variety and quality of products, admitted the CFA's Executive Director to *The Wall Street Journal*. But "we appreciate all the work for consumer issues that the UAW has done over the years."[28]

More generally, consumers did not fulfill the hopes of liberal traders who saw them as a natural domestic constituency for international openness. Consumers Union did file a suit that contributed to temporary abandonment of US-EC-Japanese steel export restraint in the early 1970s. But the more politically activist consumer advocates like Ralph Nader did not play, lest labor be offended. (A symptom of this difficulty is the fact that Consumers for World Trade, a dedicated antiprotectionist lobbying group in Washington, has a Board of Directors that is impressive in its international economics and business expertise but limited in its connections to the domestic US consumer movement.)

There did emerge, however, an activist group on the trade-expanding side, the Emergency Committee for American Trade (ECAT) created in 1967. Unlike labor, this industry-backed organization kept a relatively low profile but cultivated congressional power centers skillfully, supplying needed analysis and argumentation and alert to the timing of trade action (as labor often was not). Also becoming more active were general-purpose industry organizations like the Business Roundtable, the Chamber of Commerce, and the National Association of Manufacturers. But by the mid-1980s, such general business groups became subject to cross-pressures within their memberships, due to increased US trade exposure and the record trade deficit.

Finally, the third new development in trade politics was that general liberal trade groups were increasingly joined on specific issues by "special

---

28. *Wall Street Journal,* 3 September 1982.

interests" who, benefiting from exports or imports, were driven, by the prospect of economic losses, to do direct battle against seekers of protection.[29]

One example came in mid-1983. The Reagan administration, unable to win Chinese adherence to stringent textile restraints, imposed quotas unilaterally. The government in Beijing, urged on by Washington-based liberal trade advocates, retaliated by withholding purchases of American grain. This brought farm organizations—and Senate Finance Committee Chairman Robert J. Dole—into the fray in a campaign to soften the administration's stance.

In mid-1984, again under industry pressure, the administration moved to tighten enforcement of "country of origin" rules under the textile quota regime. Importers and retailers charged that this would "steal Christmas" by making them unable to fill their orders for the holiday season. They raised such a howl that the administration first deferred implementation of the new rules, and then adjusted them to ease their impact.

In that same summer, after the USITC found that imports had injured the US copper industry, fabricators of wire and other copper products protested that this would simply lead to increased import competition for *them* without giving the producers more than temporary relief. They made it clear to the White House, facing decision in the midst of the election campaign, that they had more workers than did the copper mines, and that their workers were more strategically placed insofar as electoral college votes were concerned. Their argument was a factor in the President's decision not to grant protection to the copper producers. A year later, shoe retailers mobilized against a USITC recommendation for footwear import quotas, getting 19 Republican senators to sign a letter in opposition. Reagan said "no" to shoe protection as well.[30]

How far such an antiprotectionist backlash might develop was unclear. Some groups, like mass-market retailers, remained basically local community people, with their chief executive officers not very aggressive in pushing congressmen on national trade issues. As for industrial users of imports, the norm was for them to operate quietly, as when IBM worked within the Semiconductor Industry Association to counter those Silicon Valley-based firms inclined to favor semiconductor import restrictions.

But if the antiprotectionist activism of the mid-1980s was not exactly a match for the textile or steel industries, it did communicate one important political point. As firms seeking trade relief escalated their demands, they

---

29. I. M. Destler and John S. Odell, *The Politics of Anti-Protection* (Washington: Institute for International Economics, forthcoming).

30. An early analysis of this phenomenon can be found in Boyd France, "An Antiprotectionist Backlash Is Gathering Strength on the Hill," *Business Week*, 17 September 1984, p. 40.

could no longer be assured that adversely affected business interests would stay on the sidelines. Politicians were likely to feel pressure from more than one direction.

Conclusions

Trade politics has become more partisan. The elite has grown less committed to liberal trade. Intellectual challenges to open-market policies have grown. Patterns of trade politics have become more complex. All these changes have weakened the old system for diverting and managing trade policy pressures, and most have increased the political weight of those backing trade restrictions.

The greatest risk, at least potentially, is that posed by the threat of a new party competition on trade policy. If the Democrats were in fact to become an out-and-out protectionist party, this would risk for trade policy the fate that has recently befallen policy toward the Soviet Union and arms control. A new President would represent not continuity but drastic change. And this would remove the strongest anchor of the old trade-management system—the liberal-leaning executive branch. A lesser effect of trade partisanship may already be evident: Democrats may have driven Republicans to a more restrictive stance, as evidenced, for example, in the disturbing steel-trade precedent of the Trade and Tariff Act of 1984 (see chapters 4 and 6).

There is a more subtle risk in the present political alignment. The trade policy management system has worked best under executive leaders who were open traders internationally but politically interventionist at home, as in the Kennedy-Johnson administration and later under the leadership of Carter's special trade representative, Robert S. Strauss. This enabled government officials to take the lead, to shape issues, to encourage counterpressures, rather than to wait—as the Reagan administration did on steel—until the protection-seeking industry defined the problem and amassed broad support. Thus, if trade policy polarization proceeds, Americans may be faced with a choice between a party inclined toward protectionism and a liberal-trade party indisposed to the very sort of activist management necessary to put its convictions into practice. (The increased trade activism of the Reagan administration since September 1985 offers modest hope that this tendency may *not* reach its logical conclusion.)

At minimum, these changes have combined with changes in the congressional, executive, and regulatory domains to make trade politics a much more open, unpredictable game. Possible consequences are considered in chapter 8; what we might do about it is addressed thereafter.

8

Summing Up: Stronger Pressure, Weaker System

Taken together, the four previous chapters depict an American trade policy-making system that shows serious erosion. Not only is Congress feeling more pressure from import-impacted industries, but it has become less protected from such pressure, and thus less able to resist proposals for trade-restrictive action.

These changes increase the political burden of the executive branch. Now, more than ever, there is need for a strong, "presidential" trade broker with solid ties to Capitol Hill. Yet, as the experience of the office of the Trade Representative shows, successive presidents have been reluctant to give such an official their consistent backing.

The "rules," or trade-remedy procedures, have become more consequential economically. But, as a direct result, they have been transformed politically, from means of diverting protectionist pressure to handy vehicles for asserting it, particularly for large industries.

The national politics of trade is becoming more open, but what new alignments may emerge remains unclear. In the early 1980s, there seemed to be movement toward a new partisan split—a reversal of the 1920s—with labor Democrats tilting protectionist and the Republicans uncertain about whether to try to beat them or to join them. In 1984, presidential candidate Walter F. Mondale apparently had second thoughts, for he stressed the macroeconomic sources of American trade woes and urged changes in fiscal, monetary, and exchange rate policies. But in 1985 and 1986, many Democrats were tempted anew by the notion that a "tough" trade stance could score points against the Republican administration and win back blue-collar and ethnic constituencies that have been drifting away from the Democratic camp.

This institutional and political erosion has not yet been punctuated by any single dramatic event like the Smoot-Hawley Act of 1930. Congress has become increasingly active on trade issues, but it has not reclaimed its constitutional primacy over "commerce with foreign nations." In fact, legislative leaders have repeatedly worked at patching up the old system. Congress has continued to seek alternatives to product-specific legislation by rewriting and then re-rewriting the trade-remedy laws and by protecting the "executive broker," the trade representative's office, against the threats of White House reorganizers. With strong executive branch help, legislators removed most of the restrictive proposals from the Trade and Tariff Act of 1984. And the congressional trade explosion of the years that followed can be explained, in part, as a reaction to the *inattention* that the subject was receiving at the other end of Pennsylvania Avenue.

Most important of all, both branches responded to the big institutional and political problem of the 1970s—the incapacity of the system to negotiate and implement nontariff trade agreements—with a notable political innovation, the "fast-track" procedures assuring expeditious congressional action on legislation to implement such agreements. These made it possible for the United States to act constructively in *the* major trade negotiation of that decade, the Tokyo Round.

But the new procedures could not help when the problem was myriad specific trade pressures, with no comprehensive international negotiation within which they might be packaged. And unfortunately, the system increasingly yielded to this sort of pressure.

The Growth of Trade Protection

The 1980s have brought acceleration of a well-established postwar pattern: pressure for trade restrictions led not to statutory protection but to a growing number of "special deals" for "special cases," arranged by the executive branch. Automobiles, the largest and long the proudest of US manufacturing industries, sought and won protection in 1981, as Japan enforced "voluntary" export restraints at the Reagan administration's behest. Sugar import quotas were reimposed in 1982. Carbon steel restraints were negotiated with the European Community (EC) in 1982 and with other major exporters two years later. Meanwhile, producers of motorcycles, specialty steel, and wood shingles gained temporary protection through escape clause proceedings, machine tool makers got a presidential import-relief decision on national security grounds, and the textile industry won several tightenings of the rules for enforcing quota restrictions.

These cases meant, in total, a substantial expansion of the proportion of the US market governed by "managed trade." Precise measures of this trend are elusive. In 1984, Bela and Carol Balassa published one careful effort to analyze the extent and growth of nontariff import protection in the United States, the European Community, and Japan, focusing particularly on changes in 1981–83. They found that just 6.2 percent of US manufactured imports in 1980 were subject to visible quantitative restrictions, compared to 7.2 percent for Japan and 10.8 percent for the EC. But in the next three years, an additional 6.52 percent of our imports came under such restraints. We surpassed Japan (which added no such overt barriers in 1981–83) and reduced the gap between ourselves and the EC. Or if the measure is the proportion of manufactured products consumed in the United States whose import is subject to nontariff restrictions, the figure for 1980 was 20.3 percent, and an additional 14.7 percent in the next three years.[1]

These 1981–83 numbers were dominated by the new Japanese restraint on automobiles. President Ronald W. Reagan's decision not to ask for continuation of this restraint after March 1985 helped to ease its protective effect: Japan's Ministry of International Trade and Industry did not abandon controls on auto exports but did raise the volume limit by 24 percent.

On the other hand, the Balassa numbers were computed before the most important trade-restrictive precedent of the 1980s, the move of the administration—with congressional cheers and reinforcement—to negotiate a network of voluntary export restraints on steel, which aimed at limiting total steel product imports to 20.2 percent of the US market. The Trade and Tariff Act of 1984 backed these restraints with new enforcement powers and a threat of direct statutory action if negotiations fell short of this target (see chapters 4 and 6).

From recent trade statistics one can derive a simple but telling measure. In 1985, US imports of "iron and steel mill products" totaled $9.7 billion. If one adds to this the amounts for the other major, already-restricted products—textiles ($4.9 billion), apparel ($14.9 billion), and new passenger cars ($36.5 billion)—one reaches a total of $66.0 billion. In the three major statistical categories of manufactured goods, 1985 imports totaled $232.3

---

1. Bela and Carol Balassa, "Industrial Protection in the Developed Countries," *World Economy* (June 1984), p. 187. For the product breakdown, see their "Levels of Protection on Manufactured Goods: The U.S., EC, Canada, Japan," 1984; processed.

Applying somewhat different criteria, William R. Cline concludes that 45.1 percent of US manufactured imports were "affected" by major nontariff barriers in 1981. By his measure, 34.1 percent of US consumption of manufactured goods consists of products whose import is restrained. Since Cline includes all steel imports in his calculations, owing to the "trigger price mechanism" inaugurated in late 1977, his numbers would not be much affected by post-1981 developments. (*Exports of Manufactures from Developing Countries* [Washington: Brookings Institution, 1984], p. 60.) See Balassa and Balassa, p. 188, and Cline, p. 60n, for dialogue on their respective measures.

Note that, in comparisons between countries, a higher ratio of quota-controlled imports may reflect looser protection. For example, Japanese car sales are limited to about 20 percent of the auto market in the United States, compared to 3 percent in France. The result is that the value of these restricted auto purchases is much greater in the United States, as is their share of total US imports.

billion.[2] Thus, without even counting lesser items such as motorcycles, one reaches a total of more than one-fourth of US manufactured imports in products now subject to major quantitative restraint. Import controls on all of these products were initiated, or tightened, since 1980. When the "special cases" in trade policy reach this magnitude, they begin to look less like the exception and more like an emerging rule. It becomes hard to resist concluding, as did a 1985 *New York Times* editorial, that "Industry by industry, the battle to maintain open markets is being lost."[3]

The Skewing of the Trade Balance

It is conceivable, of course, that the *Times* was misreading the situation. It might be that the greater disorder and noisiness of US trade politics, and the increased imposition of legal impediments to imports, represent simply a rear-guard reaction to the ongoing internationalization of our economy. Increased protection would be, in this view, a defensive phenomenon, and thus a testimony to the success of liberal policies rather than a harbinger of their failure.[4] Such would be an apt interpretation for the decade ending in 1980. For in that period, though the system of trade politics was subject to growing strains and though the number of US trade restrictions increased, so did the volume of US international commerce.

Measured in current dollars, US merchandise exports rose, as a proportion of our total production of goods, from 9.2 percent in 1970 to 19.7 percent in 1980. The proportion of imports rose from 8.7 to 21.9 percent over this same period.[5] Due to greater inflation in tradable goods prices, these numbers

---

2. Numbers are general imports taken from US Department of Commerce, Bureau of the Census, "Highlights of US Export and Import Trade," Rept. FT 990, December 1985, table 2, p. C-6. The three categories of imports from which the $232.3 billion total was derived are "manufactured goods classified chiefly by material" (which include iron and steel products and textiles), $46.5 billion; "machinery and transport equipment," $137.3 billion; and "miscellaneous manufactured articles" (which include apparel), $48.5 billion. Statistics are customs value basis.

3. "Even Out the Free Trade Pain," *New York Times*, 14 January 1985.

4. A related interpretation is that of Charles Lipson, who asked in 1982 why "world trade has continued to grow while trade restraints have been tightened." He concluded that the new barriers were in mature, basic industries, while trade expansion had come mainly in growth sectors where industries have differentiated products and high R&D expenditure. See "The Transformation of Trade: The Sources and Effects of Regime Change," *International Organization*, vol. 36, no. 2 (Spring 1982), pp. 417–55.

5. Exports are f.a.s., imports at customs value. Percentages were obtained by dividing merchandise exports (or imports) by total US production of goods for the same year, as reported in *Economic Report of the President*, Washington, February 1985, tables B-98 and B-6.

exaggerate changes in the actual volume of trade, particularly on the import side.[6] But if one employs a better measure of the changing real impact of trade, statistics using constant (1972) dollars, the export share of US goods production rose from 9.3 percent in 1970 to 13.9 percent in 1980. On the same price-deflated basis, imports went up from 9.3 percent in 1970 to 11.2 percent in 1980.[7] This growth was part of an enormous expansion in the volume of trade worldwide.

If this trade story had persisted after 1980—if trade as a share of our economic activity had continued to increase—one could rest comfortably. Given the actual expansion of commerce, the increasing political noise about trade, and the intermittent actual steps to restrict it, could be considered a modest price to pay. One could take particular comfort from the rising importance of foreign sales for American producers; this would surely drive export interests to become a stronger constituency for open trade policies, and thus reduce if not eliminate the endemic political advantage of import-competing interests. (And in fact, as noted in chapter 7, there has been evidence of some increase in protrade political activity by economic interests with strong export or import stakes.)

But the early and mid-1980s brought a very different pattern. Globally, total trade stagnated. The dollar figure actually declined for three consecutive years, from 1981 to 1983, before it rebounded in 1984 and 1985 to roughly the level of the decade's beginning.[8] For the United States, *exports* followed a similar pattern—$224.3 billion in 1980, $214.4 billion five years later. But imports shot up from $249.8 to $338.9 billion.[9] The 1985 trade deficit

---

6. The most important reason, of couse, is the thirteenfold incrcase in the price of petroleum imports during the decade. Thus, while in current dollars imports of oil and oil products rose from $2.9 billion in 1970 to $79.3 billion in 1980, the increase in constant (1972) dollars was from $3.3 to $6.8 billion, a "mere" doubling. Import numbers ibid., table B-99; price deflators from Data Resources, Inc.

7. Computed from data in *Economic Report of the President,* February 1985 and February 1986; and *Survey of Current Business,* various issues.

8. *Economic Report of the President,* February 1985, table B-105; and February 1986, table B-6.
This stagnation was the product, in major part, of the recession which afflicted the world economy in the wake of the second "oil shock." And it was what one would have expected. For example, C. Fred Bergsten and William R. Cline found, for 1961–81, a direct correlation between increases in real gross domestic product (GDP) and the growth of nonoil imports for the OECD countries taken as a whole. "Below 1 ½ percent GDP growth, nonoil imports decline instead of growing. . . . For each percentage point rise in GDP growth, nonoil imports rise by more than three percentage points." See "Trade Policy in the 1980s: An Overview," in *Trade Policy in the 1980s,* edited by William R. Cline (Washington: Institute for International Economics, 1983), p. 75.

9. Joint Economic Committee, *Economic Indicators,* June 1986, p. 36. Exports are f.a.s.; imports are customs basis.

exceeded $124 billion. The overall US current account deficit, trade plus services transactions, topped $117 billion. Such a magnitude was, in the words of Arthur Burns, "awesomely different from anything experienced in the past," by any country.[10]

Of course, the dollar value of US trade had grown almost sixfold between 1970 and 1980, so it was not surprising that the trade deficits of the 1980s were larger. Indeed, due importantly to inflation, virtually all US economic aggregates—gross national product, government spending, etc.—had ballooned beyond previous comprehension. What was alarming was that our imbalance was extreme even when adjusted for increased trade volume. In 1972, our merchandise imports had been 113 percent of exports. In 1978, the next peak year, they rose to 124 percent. But in 1985, the value of US imports was 158 percent that of exports!

Not only was this imbalance unprecedented for modern America; it was also worse than any other advanced industrial nation had experienced since the 1940s. To finance the trade deficit—and the related federal budget deficit—the United States was "going into debt faster than any major developed country since World War II, and faster than the average of the seven major developing-country debtors on the eve of the debt crisis."[11]

And for this period, unlike the 1970s, the current-dollar trade figures *understated* the real changes in product flows, since the super-strong dollar depressed the prices of imports as denominated in our currency. Hence, measured on a price-deflated basis, total merchandise imports rose from 11.4 percent to 15.7 percent of US goods production between 1980 and 1985. Over this same period, exports declined as a share of goods production from 13.9 percent to 10.3 percent, a drop even greater than that precipitated fifty years earlier by the Great Depression and the Smoot-Hawley Act.[12] Thus those American producer interests who normally had the strongest stakes in trade expansion were finding themselves at a serious disadvantage in overseas markets, even as foreign products were surging into our own.

---

10. Burns notes that prior to 1983 "the biggest current account deficit that any country had ever experienced in a single year was about $15 billion." "The American Trade Deficit," *Foreign Affairs,* vol. 62, no. 5 (Summer 1984), p. 1068.

11. Stephen Marris, *Deficits and the Dollar: The World Economy at Risk,* POLICY ANALYSES IN INTERNATIONAL ECONOMICS 14 (Washington: Institute for International Economics, December 1985), p. 94.

12. See footnote 7, with 1985 merchandise trade data from June 1986 *Economic Indicators.* Between 1929 and 1933, price-deflated merchandise exports dropped from roughly 8 percent to 6.4 percent, or by 20 percent, as a share of US goods production. Between 1980 and 1985 they dropped by 26 percent. (Calculations for 1929–33 draw upon data in US Department of Commerce, Bureau of the Census, *Historical Statistics of the United States,* p. 889, and *National Income and Product Accounts of the United States,* 1929–76, Statistical Tables, pp. 360–63.)

So, even as many more industries hurt by imports were seeking trade protection, the political counterweight was weakened as exporters lost market share and grew demoralized.

The American trade policy-making system was thus feeling, in the mid-1980s, a unique "double-whammy": the erosion of its institutions and a wrenching trade imbalance that skewed our politics very much in the trade-restrictive direction. In the short term, product-specific protection was not preventing overall imports from growing very rapidly. Even in textiles and apparel, the most elaborately regulated sector, imports rose by 40 percent worldwide in 1984,[13] sucked in by the strong recovery and by the strong dollar, the largest single cause of the overall import explosion. And political pressure increased apace.

This was clearly an enormously disruptive variation in the cyclical politics of trade. The ebb and flow of protectionist pressures was nothing new: as the Continental Grain Company recurrently reminds us in its advertisements on the back cover of *Foreign Affairs*, attitudes toward free trade bear some resemblance to a roller coaster, going "up and down, up and down" with changes in the economic climate. Certainly, the late 1970s and early 1980s were an economic "downer" for Americans. First, inflation hit double-digit levels and the prime interest rate topped 20 percent. Then, in a recession deepened by the Federal Reserve Board's tough new anti-inflation stance, the unemployment rate hit double digits in September 1982 for the first time since the World War II, and it remained at 10 percent or above until the following July.

By late 1984, however, unemployment had dropped by 3 percentage points, and real GNP growth for that year was at its highest level since 1951. Yet, in the words of US International Trade Commission Chairwoman Paula Stern, these better overall economic years nonetheless brought "the most serious campaign for protection ever to have been waged in a recovery period."[14] And the reason was all too clear: the skewed trade balance. This was driven above all by the strong dollar,[15] but it would be 18 months to

---

13. Imports of textiles rose from $3.2 billion in 1983 to $4.5 billion in 1984 (and $4.9 billion in 1985). Imports of apparel jumped from $9.6 billion to $13.5 billion (and, for 1985, $14.9 billion). US Department of Commerce, Commerce, FT 990: "Highlights," Rept. FT 990, December 1984 and December 1985, pp. C-6 and C-7.

14. Paula Stern, "Trade and Recovery: Where Do We Stand in 1984?" (remarks at the General Accounting Office, Washington, 8 February 1984).

15. C. Fred Bergsten argued in 1982 that, from the early 1970s onward, exchange rate misalignment was a better "leading indicator" of protectionist pressure in the United States and overall U.S.-Japan trade tensions than the unemployment rate or any other macroeconomic variable. See "What to Do About the U.S.-Japan Economic Conflict," *Foreign Affairs*, vol. 60, no. 5 (Summer 1982), pp. 1059–75. See also C. Fred Bergsten and William R. Cline, "Overview," in Cline, *Trade Policy in the 1980s*, pp. 86–87. The dollar reached its peak value on 25 February 1985.

two years after the exchange rate began its decline before the overall trade balance was likely to improve.

The enormous economic pain caused by wrenching trade balance changes was bound to precipitate strong pressures for trade restrictions. One can even wonder why the American policy-making system has withstood them as much as it has, for as long as it has. But its condition has become serious, if not critical, and the prognosis must remain, at best, "guarded."

Procedural norms and pressure-diverting devices cannot be expected to survive overwhelming political assault. They are useful at the margins, for calling in counter-forces, for muting certain influences and encouraging others. They are helpful for riding out tough economic and political periods. But if export as well as import-competing interests stop believing that open international trade is serving their interests, then there may be no way that the old trade policy processes can be restored. At minimum, we may be in for a rather bleak trade future.

Some Bleak Prospects

With our weakened policy-making system forced to respond to the current excruciating trade imbalance, we are likely to see, at the very least, two extensions of recent trends: a further spread of negotiated barriers to imports, or "managed trade," and an ever more fractious trade diplomacy, as our embattled officials demand more of foreign governments—and offer them less in return.

"Special deals for special cases" were standard practice in the postwar American policy-making system. And the major new trade protection of the 1980s has come in the same old way. The executive branch, responding to industry pressure reinforced by Congress, has responded by "working something out," usually by pressuring foreign suppliers to institute "voluntary" export restraints.

But the situation of 1981–85 differed from that of earlier decades in that these trade restrictions were not being balanced by major market-opening initiatives. Nor were they coming within a broader context of rapidly expanding world trade. Without these offsetting forces, "special deals for special cases" are transformed from a means of shielding a generally liberal trade-policy regime to a threat to that regime's core purpose. So even as US trade officials labored to develop new global initiatives, to once again lead the world toward more open trade, they found themselves acquiescing in a slide toward managed trade. The just-inaugurated "Uruguay Round" offers an opportunity to reverse this trend, but the still-record trade deficit provides both pressure and rationale for tightening old import restraints and imposing new ones.

Moreover, while such measures were less than totally effective in the world of the super-strong dollar, this only drove their supporters to get them tightened. Now, ironically, as the dollar comes down and the petitioners' economic need for these restrictions diminishes, they will come to have more bite.

Seeking to limit such US trade restrictions, to retain some room for maneuver, liberal-minded executive and congressional leaders must focus more than ever on attacking other governments' import barriers and export subsidies. In this way also they are walking in the footsteps of their predecessors. Beginning with the bargaining tariff of the 1930s, government leaders have found the pursuit of expanded markets abroad a principal means of fighting protection at home. In the 1980s, we have seen a toughening of US tactics, as illustrated by the Reagan administration's subsidies for grain exports, congressional threats to restrict the American market unless granted reciprocal foreign-market access for specific products like telecommunications, and the administration's recent initiation of several Section 301 cases alleging unreasonable or unjustifiable foreign trade practices.

Such tactics can sometimes be very useful in international trade bargaining. And under current circumstances, they are critical to the administration's domestic credibility. The problem is one of policy balance. One needs carrots to offer other nations, not just sticks. If our domestic political situation forces our leaders to demand the moon without offering much earthly value in return, we should not be astonished if the response of foreign governments is limited and grudging. The Uruguay Round offers an opportunity to reverse this trend also, to return to the tradition of balanced, reciprocal trade bargaining. But until the trade deficit shrinks, executive branch leaders will not be politically able to seize this opportunity.

Nor are marginally increased protection at home, and more fractious trade diplomacy abroad, our worst current trade prospects. At least three bleaker possibilities now confront us.

One is the tried-and-true bogeyman of the liberal trade community, a *return to legislative protectionism à la Smoot-Hawley.* The combination of much stronger trade pressures and weaker congressional resistance could bring an end to the half century of "voluntary legislative restraint" on trade matters. There has been ample evidence of Capitol Hill's increased vulnerability to trade-restrictive initiatives involving major industries. The United Auto Workers pushed the "domestic content" bill through the House twice, although a range of interests opposed it, and although many who voted "aye" thought it bad legislation. Enforcement of steel protection was a popular add-on to the Trade and Tariff Act of 1984. And the past two years have brought an explosion of congressional trade initiatives, with the

Jenkins bill to roll back textile imports winning strong House and Senate majorities. President Reagan vetoed the bill, and a House vote to override him fell eight votes shy of the required two-thirds. But the bill represented the most substantial breach to date of the postwar congressional tradition of avoiding product-specific trade legislation.

Could the future bring a return to legislative log-rolling on trade matters, with protection-seeking interests forming alliances—"We'll back your quota if you'll back ours"—and Congress ratifying the result? The system has not disintegrated to this point, *yet*. But the longer the current imbalance continues, the more likely that industries will be driven to form protectionist coalitions. A modest example was the Senate's addition of shoe quotas and a copper protection initiative to the Jenkins bill.

A second danger is a *new surge of what has been labeled "process protectionism,"* an expansion of opportunities for import relief under the trade-remedy laws, particularly the "unfair trade" statutes, and a further reduction of executive branch discretion in resolving such cases. This approach is attractive to legislators because it allows them to be responsive to petitioners while keeping the final responsibility off their backs—the specific protection is worked out elsewhere. And it is, in fact, the approach taken by the omnibus trade legislation passed by the House of Representatives in May 1986, many of whose provisions find parallels in prominent Senate bills. It is almost certain, therefore, to be an important feature of future legislative initiatives.

In form, this simply involves further refinement of the rules that insulated the system from political pressures earlier in the postwar period. But in practice, the elaboration of these quasi-judicial rules in the 1970s and 1980s has not taken such product-specific decisions "out of politics," for reasons spelled out in chapter 6. On the contrary, it has increased the opportunities for industries to use the trade-remedy laws to force political solutions, as did the steel industry in 1982 and 1984. The further that legislation goes in creating "rights" to trade protection of statutorily specified magnitudes, the more it will drive governments to negotiate more flexible—but nonetheless protectionist—trade arrangements.

A third disturbing possibility, treated in chapter 7, is *a new ideological debate on trade,* featuring a philosophical division between our two political parties not seen on this issue since the 1940s. Republicans would hold to free market policies in principle, as an extension of their stance against industry-specific government intervention. Democrats—under the pressure of organized labor and seeking to renew their party tradition of active government engagement in the economy—would be disposed to employ trade protection as one of several tools to nurture and strengthen US competitiveness. So far, Democratic "protectionism" has in fact proved muted. But if a future President were to come to office on a protectionist platform, we could then begin to see the sort of oscillation in US trade policy that has occurred since 1970 on defense and arms control matters, and on international monetary policy.[16] The system of trade politics would lose its last and most critical pillar, the liberal-leaning executive.

Can the American trade policy-making system be saved from outcomes such as these? Can we reverse the trend toward managed trade and get back on the trade expansion track?

It will be very, very hard to do so without a shift in the macroeconomic situation, the confluence of forces that has generated those record trade imbalances. This requires attention to actions outside of the "trade policy" sphere, and it is the subject of chapter 9.

If a balanced and stable economic environment can be restored, the prospects for constructive trade policy will be very much better. Still, executive and congressional leaders will need to cope, as constructively as possible, with the pressures that will assuredly remain. Chapter 10 proposes organizational and policy changes that might better the odds of coping successfully.

Both chapters assume that, even in a world where many foreigners are "unfair" and some are gaining on us, a basically liberal trade approach remains the best policy option for today's United States.

---

16. On the contrast between US policy oscillation on monetary-macroeconomic issues and continuity on trade issues, see C. Fred Bergsten, "America's Unilateralism," pp. 3–14 in *Conditions for Partnership in International Economic Management*, A Task Force Report to The Trilateral Commission by Bergsten, Etienne Davignon, and Isamu Miyazaki, Triangle Papers: 32 (New York, NY: Trilateral Commission, 1986).

III Prescription

9

Nontrade Responses to Trade Problems

In August 1984, on taking her oath as Chairwoman of the United States International Trade Commission (USITC), Paula Stern lamented the fact that economic problems with broader causes were regularly being dumped on the trade system's doorstep. "The Commission," she noted, "does not make macroeconomic policy. But we do deal, one by one, with its industrial victims."[1]

Stern was alluding, of course, to the record US budget deficits that had helped make the dollar so strong and the trade balance so weak. The practice of scapegoating trade policy had a longer history. In any economy undergoing wrenching economic change, "foreign imports" offer a tempting target, and trade restrictions an appealing remedy. At the industry-specific level, executives and labor leaders in the business like textiles will fight bitterly over whether plants should be unionized, yet lobby together for measures to block foreign competitors. For that is one thing on which they can agree. Or looking at the American economy as a whole, a severe trade imbalance is, by definition, the summation of a host of specific markets that are being lost to US products at home and overseas.

It is hardly surprising that the "industrial victims" seek redress, or that they focus particularly on trade measures as a cure. What is surprising, perhaps, is just how ineffective trade measures generally are in addressing those trade problems that afflict an entire economy. Nowhere is this truer than in the case of the gross excess of imports over exports that has confronted the United States in 1984–1986.

Common sense argues the opposite. It is hard, at first glance, not to blame an overall trade imbalance on unfair foreign competition or on weak-kneed American trade bargaining. If we are selling less than we are buying, it must be because our market is open, drawing others' goods in while they

---

1. Remarks on Reaffirmation of Oath of Office, 9 August 1984, p. 2.

are blocking ours out. If the situation is to be corrected, it seems to follow that the United States will have to "get tough," really tough, with its trading partners.

But on this issue, common sense turns out to be wrong. There are good reasons for tough trade bargaining, but correcting large trade imbalances is not one of them. The spring 1985 congressional response to the Japan problem offers an apt illustration.

Trade With Japan: Right Problem, Wrong Solution

By mid-decade, the US trade condition had become severe. No longer was the nation running modest trade imbalances offset by investment earnings from abroad, as was generally the case in 1971–82. By calendar year 1984, the US trade deficit had topped $100 billion by the most conservative measure, and the value of imports had ballooned to 50 percent above that of exports. In volume (price-deflated) terms, imports jumped from 11.2 percent to 15.2 percent of total US goods production between 1980 and 1984. Exports dropped from 13.9 percent to 10.8 percent during the same period.[2]

Little wonder that producers of internationally traded goods flocked to Washington—not just those feeling pressure from imports, but those like Caterpillar, Inc., who were losing out in formerly lucrative export markets. And they did not flock solely, or mainly, to the USITC. In early 1985, they came particularly to the United States Congress. They saw the trade imbalance growing even worse, with projections approaching $150 billion for 1985 and 1986. They saw the dollar continuing to rise. They saw a flood of imports here and continued import resistance in foreign markets. Perhaps worst of all, they saw an administration with no credible program for dealing with the trade crisis, headed by a President who, to judge by his words, looked upon the American economic landscape and saw nothing but good. Finding the White House deaf to their appeals, just as it had been in the years before as the imbalance was starting to grow, they redoubled their efforts at the other end of Pennsylvania Avenue.

The response there was sharp, and in the Senate it centered (at least initially) on Japan. This was hardly surprising either. US exports to that country had risen moderately in 1984, from $21.9 billion to $23.6 billion, but imports had shot up from $41.2 billion to $57.1 billion, again conservatively measured. This meant a deficit in bilateral trade of $33.6 billion, a

---

2. Computed from data in *Economic Report of the President,* Washington, February 1985 and February 1986; and *Survey of Current Business,* various issues.

deficit that was far greater than any the United States had ever run with a single trading partner.[3]

Imports of Japanese products were expected to grow further in 1985, as in fact they did; for one thing, Ronald W. Reagan was in the process of deciding not to ask the Tokyo government to extend the "voluntary" restraints that had held down their auto exports since 1981. Yet despite the public commitments of Prime Minister Yasuhiro Nakasone, ongoing negotiations to open certain hard-to-crack Japanese markets—telecommunications, paper and wood products, etc.—were proceeding slowly, with uncertain results. Thus both import-competing and export interests were frustrated with the Japanese. So, too, were trade officials in the Office of the United States Trade Representative (USTR) and the Department of Commerce, who believed that Japanese market barriers were blocking at least $10 billion in American export sales. Commerce even had a list, its "guesstimates" of "potential additional US exports" to the Japanese market of forest products, telecommunications and electronics equipment, cigarettes, and other manufactured goods.[4]

So senators unloaded on Japan, with double-barrelled rhetoric and the threat of retaliatory action. By a 92 to 0 vote on 28 March 1985, they passed a resolution centering on the "bilateral trade imbalance" that was "costing the United States hundreds of thousands of jobs every year." Japan had "extensive access to the United States market," the resolution declared. US exporters "lack access to the Japanese market for manufactured goods, forest products, key agricultural commodities, and certain services in which the United States has a comparative advantage." Years of market-access negotiations with Japan had been "largely unsuccessful." Therefore, the resolution called upon the President to retaliate against unfair Japanese trading

---

3. Senators preferred the higher trade deficit figure of $36.8 billion, rounded upward to $37 billion, which was derived from the c.i.f. (cost-insurance-freight) import total of $60.4 billion. For 1985, the Japan deficit number would rise to $46.2 billion (customs value) and $49.8 billion c.i.f. (As noted in chapter 3, Senator Russell B. Long [D-La.] had insisted for years that the c.i.f. figures were a truer measure of imports, and, at his initiative, the Trade Agreements Act of 1979 required Commerce to report its monthly and cumulative c.i.f. import figures 48 hours before the "customs value" statistics it had previously emphasized. This meant that, for global trade, senators inveighed against a deficit of *$123* billion, not the $107 billion [later adjusted to $114 billion] yielded by the traditional measure.)

These and subsequent trade figures for 1983–85 are taken from publications of the Department of Commerce, International Trade Administration, esp. "United States Foreign Trade: Flash Tables," December 1984, and Bureau of the Census, "Highlights of U.S. Export and Import Trade," Rept. FT 990, December 1984 and December 1985.

4. For the "list" and an analysis, see C. Fred Bergsten and William R. Cline, *The United States–Japan Economic Problem*, POLICY ANALYSES IN INTERNATIONAL ECONOMICS 13 (Washington: Institute for International Economics, October 1985), pp. 109–116.

practices, asking him to act to counter the effects of the "elimination or relaxation of the voluntary restraints on Japanese automobile exports," either with additional US sales to Japan or with action "against competitive Japanese exports including, but not limited to, automobiles, telecommunication products, and electronics products."[5]

"Debate" on the measure consisted, in the main, of a stream of denunciations of Japanese trade practices and of the supineness of American responses. Among the more moderate were those of Trade Subcommittee Chairman John C. Danforth (R-Mo.) who declared that "the administration's trade policy" was "a failure" because it lacked credibility: no one believed there was "ever any possibility . . . that the United States [would] ever . . . do anything to retaliate." Regarding Japan, he declared that "the time has come to act—not talk, not complain, not insult, but act."

Danforth's Democratic counterpart, Lloyd Bentsen (D-Tex.) declared himself "a reluctant supporter of this resolution . . . because I do not think it goes far enough." "We are in a trade war, and we are losing it," Bentsen declared. Full Finance Committee Chairman Bob Packwood (R-Ore.) announced he had reached "the limits of my patience with the Japanese. . . . As far as I am concerned . . . I am going to do everything I can to retaliate in kind to any of their products that come to this country." And while the resolution adopted that afternoon was nonbinding, the Finance Committee followed in early April by reporting out a mandatory bill that would require the President to take retaliatory action.

Like concern over the US global trade imbalance, congressional frustration with Japan had ample factual basis. Tokyo was running a growing global trade surplus, totaling $44 billion in 1984. And its market did not thwart only Americans. To quote one oft-cited statistic, in 1984 Japan took just 8 percent of the manufactured exports of the developing countries, compared to 58 percent taken by the United States. While Japan had dismantled most of its formal trade barriers rapidly in the 1970s, strong import resistance clearly remained, and it was entirely proper for us to press a country that had so benefited from liberal trade to practice at home what it took such adept advantage of abroad.

But there was one small difficulty. Japanese trade policies had very little relation to the American trade imbalance that was generating such enormous pressures on Capitol Hill. Japan had not created it, and improvements in its trade behavior would not solve it, however desirable they might be on other grounds.

---

5. The text of Senate Concurrent Resolution 15 appears in *Congressional Record,* Daily Edition, 28 March 1985, p. S3573. The quotes below come from the debate that preceded its adoption, pp. S3556–73.

☐ The trade deficit with Japan was America's largest, but it had not worsened any faster during the years between 1981 and 1984 than our trade balances with Europe or the developing countries. Even between 1983 and 1984, when the Japanese deficit did jump alarmingly, US trade with the European Community (EC) deteriorated in nearly the same measure.[6] This suggested that the trade imbalance was, in essence, "made in America." And it was. But it was not a product of US *trade* policies. For these had in fact grown more restrictive since 1981, when the overall US "current account" was in balance.

☐ Instead, experts generally agreed, the $80 billion increase in the US trade deficit between 1981 and 1984 was the product of three macroeconomic developments. Listed in order of ascending importance, these were: the developing-country debt crisis, which caused Latin American purchases of US exports to plummet; the "growth gap" of 1983 and 1984, with the United States leading the advanced industrial world in emerging from recession (and therefore in growth of its import demand); and the remarkable rise in the value of the dollar.[7]

☐ Of these three forces, the first two had largely played themselves out by early 1985, although they were unlikely to operate powerfully in reverse very soon. This meant that if the US trade deficit were to be reduced, the dollar would have to come down substantially in value.

☐ Why had the dollar risen, despite growing US trade deficits? The operative force had been international capital flows—the readiness of both domestic and foreign investors to shift their funds out of foreign currencies and into our own. We needed them to do so in order to finance our suddenly enormous budget deficits without "crowding out" private business in-

---

6. US exports to the European Community went up 6 percent in 1984, compared to 7.8 percent for our sales to Japan. Imports from the EC rose by 30.7 percent, compared to 38.7 from Japan. Exports to Hong Kong, Korea, and Taiwan rose 6.8 percent; imports went up 30.9 percent.

Comparing US bilateral trade balances with 24 major trading nations, Bergsten and Cline found that for 17 of them, the proportionate change from 1980–81 to 1984 was greater than that with Japan. *United States–Japan Economic Problem*, p. 23.

7. For the most comprehensive analysis, see Stephen Marris, *Deficits and the Dollar: The World Economy at Risk*, POLICY ANALYSES IN INTERNATIONAL ECONOMICS 14 (Washington: Institute for International Economics, December 1985), ch. 1. Bergsten and Cline, (*United States–Japan Economic Problem*, p. 50) find that "the main driving force behind the growing imbalance in the bilateral US-Japanese trade relationship has been the overvaluation of the dollar," followed by the slowdown in Japan's growth relative to the United States.

See chapters 3 and 8 for more on the apparent causes of exchange rate misalignment and its impact on trade flows.

vestment. High real US interest rates were a powerful inducement. These were being encouraged by the relatively tight monetary policy of a Federal Reserve Board determined to quench inflation. Also attracting funds was a surge of foreign confidence in the American economy as the Reagan boom gathered steam, together with the relative stagnation and "Euro-pessimism" that discouraged investment in the EC nations.

☐ Finally, during the same period when the United States had been developing a capital shortage, Japan and the European Community had been developing capital surpluses. They had been *cutting* their government budget deficits. In Japan, this had created a substantial excess of savings. Its outflow, much of it directly to this country, helped us finance our deficit and the Reagan boom, but it weakened the yen and thereby fueled the very Japanese trade surplus that was bringing denuniciation down upon Tokyo.

Given this situation, suppose that Japan had, in 1985, made the sort of broad, immediate trade concessions that Americans sought. Suppose that the Commerce Department list was right, that opening Japanese markets could bring $10 billion in additional US sales. Suppose that Japan had taken the requisite steps, and suppose further that the predicted increment in American sales had resulted. Suppose also that these openings benefited other exporting nations, to the tune of an additional $10 billion. But suppose that the Japanese savings-capital surplus remained substantially unchanged. The increased import demand, combined with the continuing capital outflow, could be expected to weaken the yen further, reducing other imports and increasing exports until most or all of the trade balance improvement was offset.[8] The volume of Japanese trade would almost certainly be larger, the world economy would be more efficient, and US exporters would benefit. But the *balance* of trade would be little changed.

One could, by this logic, still criticize the Japanese government for policies that resulted in large and growing worldwide trade surpluses, just as one could criticize the Reagan administration for doing the opposite. But the policies needing alteration would be macroeconomic. As Secretary of State George P. Shultz put it in that trade-contentious spring, "Japan must deal with its saving-investment imbalance if its chronic imbalance in trade is to be corrected."[9]

---

8. By definition, a nation's net capital outflow has to be equaled by its current account surplus. Or in the case of the United States, the present current account deficit has to be equal to, and financed by, an inflow of capital.

9. George P. Shultz, "National Policies and Global Prosperity" (address prepared for delivery 11 April 1985 at the Woodrow Wilson School of Public and International Affairs, Princeton University, Princeton, NJ).

Similarly, if the United States were to impose trade barriers without reducing the savings-investment imbalance that was causing us to import capital, we might succeed in reallocating the trade pain among import-impacted industries, and between them and the export sector. But we would not, in a floating exchange rate regime, reduce our trade deficit to any significant degree.[10]

Interestingly, the spring 1985 trade debate in the United States gave growing recognition to these realities. Senators had downplayed them in March, but when on 1 April, the House Ways and Means Committee reported out its trade resolution, it gave the exchange rate much greater emphasis. It too focused substantially on Japan, and called for strong trade measures vis-à-vis Tokyo. But it gave top billing not to the bilateral imbalance but to the "global United States merchandise trade deficit," which it declared "partially the result of the strong dollar," which it related in turn to "the large fiscal deficit" and the "foreign capital needed to finance this deficit." It thus called for "concerted action by both the President and the Congress to reduce the fiscal deficit and thereby bring the dollar down to a level which will help restore United States trade competitiveness." Otherwise, the House resolution declared, "the ability of the United States to resist broad-scale import protection . . . will be substantially reduced."[11] This resolution passed the House by a vote of 394 to 19.

---

10. A variant, proposed recurrently by Lester Thurow, would be an attempt to limit the overall bilateral US-Japan trade imbalance to, say, $2.5 billion a quarter. When it reached this level, we would block further imports. There is some question about whether such comprehensive value limit could be enforced. Even if it could, it would be incredibly disruptive to consumers and marketers and industrial users of Japanese goods. And assuming no change in the two nations' savings-investment balances, all or most of the bilateral deficit reduction would be offset by changes in the two nations' trade accounts with other nations, leaving the global US deficit (and the global Japanese surplus) little changed.

For a fuller critique, see I. M. Destler, "The Wrong Approach to Japanese Trade," *Washington Post,* 16 March 1983. For evidence of the idea's resurfacing, see Hobart Rowen, *Washington Post,* 16 December 1985.

11. See House Concurrent Resolution 107, "To express the sense of the Congress that the President take action to reduce the growing United States merchandise trade deficit and that he take action to respond to unfair international trade practices of Japan." See also US Congress, House, Committee on Ways and Means, 99th Cong., 1st Sess., 1 April 1985, H. Rept. 99–35, reporting the bill favorably for floor action.

Senator Danforth stressed the dollar and its links to the US budget deficit in his April 1985 speech to the National Press Club, as did the Bentsen-chaired "Senate Democratic Working Group on Trade Policy" in its preliminary report issued the same month.

Getting Serious About Trade Imbalances

No trade imbalance endures forever. And hard though it was for the trade players of mid-decade to believe, this American deficit too would pass. It is useful, then, to extract lessons from that experience that will remain relevant when the American trade crisis of mid-decade is history.

Concerning huge trade imbalances, the key needs fall into two broad categories. The first is *education*, specifically the need to spread understanding of their causes and why trade actions cannot cure them. The second, at the boundaries of this book's reach, concerns *macroeconomic policy*, or specifically what might be done to set such imbalances aright.

Education

Experience may be a hard school, but the 1980s brought many learners. By early 1983, for the first time in memory, a major US industry group, the Business Roundtable, was pointing to the dollar-yen rate as a primary source of trade ills. At first, the analysis was primitive: the Japanese were alleged to be "manipulating" their currency to keep it weak and to keep their exports competitive. As evidence for this thesis proved elusive, the emphasis shifted to the way the broad macroeconomic policies of Japan and the United States had combined to create a misaligned yen-dollar relationship. A 1984 Harris–*Business Week* survey found 64 percent of business executives naming the strong dollar as the reason for the trade deficit.[12]

By 1985, precious few trading interests were still insensitive to the impact of exchange rates on their international competiveness. And as noted below, this new awareness bought time for US trade policymakers when, in the fall of 1985, the yen began a sharp rise. But this connection, however crucial, is not all that needs learning and remembering. The larger lesson is that in a world of floating exchange rates and large-scale capital flows, *trade imbalances are largely immune to treatment by trade policy measures.* They can be reached only by other means, mainly macroeconomic measures that influence total demand and affect the savings-investment balance within trading nations. Also, when circumstances are favorable, trade imbalances can be influenced by official intervention in foreign exchange markets.

Trade measures can affect the volume of trade. They can influence the composition of that trade. But unless coupled with other measures, they will have little impact on the overall surplus or deficit run by a nation.

---

12. William Schneider, "Protectionist Push is Coming from the Top," *National Journal,* 27 April 1985, p. 933.

This negative lesson has its limits. It is, as earlier noted, counter-intuitive. If Japan restricts market access *and* runs trade surpluses, it is an uphill argument to assert that the two phenomena are essentially independent. If the United States is running record trade deficits and its firms are facing trade barriers abroad and subsidized foreign competition at home, it is hard to resist arguments that the former are *caused* by the latter. Even businessmen and politicians who find the contrary logic persuasive when it is presented to them, will often revert to the simpler old trade-deficit–trade-barrier connection once the presenter has departed.

More important, it is not enough, in responding to industries under stress and to politicians feeling their heat, to argue that a particular remedy will *not* minister to their ills. For in policy, as in sports, it is hard to beat something with nothing. Politicians facing daily pressure need at some point to respond, to "do something." If constructive action is not available, they may be driven to destructive actions. To repeat the words of the House resolution of April 1985: when the strong dollar is undermining American trade competitiveness, "the ability of the United States to resist broad-scale import protection [is] substantially reduced."

So one must ask further: if trade measures will not reduce trade imbalances, what will? The short answer is what Chairwoman Stern referred to in the quotation that opened this chapter: changes in macroeconomic policy.

Macroeconomic Policy

Just as the huge US trade deficits of mid-decade were at bottom a product of the need to import capital to finance record budget deficits, measures to reduce the trade imbalance could be effective only insofar as they diminished that international borrowing. It was capital inflow that had bid up the dollar's value: if we reduced our need for it, real US interest rates could drop off, making our currency less attractive on foreign-exchange markets. Or if, perhaps encouraged by governments and central banks, currency markets bid the dollar's value down, this would tend to drive US interest rates up (absent offsetting monetary or fiscal policy changes), reducing our total demand for savings and cutting the international capital inflow that way.

The best way to reduce US international borrowing was to cut the federal budget deficit. The larger the cuts could be, the more they would reduce our need for capital inflow. The sooner these cuts came, the less would be the ultimate magnitude of the debt that the United States would accumulate and be required to finance. This would mean, over the longer term, that the dollar would not have to fall as far to bring balance to our international accounts.

After a fashion, Congress responded to this need in the fall of 1985, by enacting the Gramm-Rudman-Hollings legislation designed to force regular, annual deficit cuts, through mandatory spending reductions if required. The credibility of this effort has been diluted by problems of constitutionality (the Supreme Court invalidated one important provision in the summer of 1986), and by the President's persistent failure to grasp (or acknowledge) Gramm-Rudman's numerical logic: that reaching its deficit-reduction targets would require either a severe slash in defense spending or a substantial rise in taxes. And in the fall of 1986, both branches conspired to postpone that logic one more year, satisfying the law's demands for fiscal 1987 through a combination of one-year budget gimmicks, selective spending reductions, and minor tax increases. The legislation nonetheless offered strong testimony to the political potency of the deficit issue, and the political need that both Congress and the White House now felt at least to appear to be taking significant action. And the fiscal 1987 deficit *was* expected to be substantially below the previous year's.

Before Gramm-Rudman was enacted, however, the major industrial countries began employing another means of moving the dollar downward. On 22 September 1985, Secretary of the Treasury James A. Baker III, acting on a belated Reagan administration recognition of the dollar-trade-protectionist problem, met with his Group of Five Finance Minister colleagues in New York. Jointly they declared their desire for an "orderly" dollar decline.[13] Central banks, particularly that in Tokyo, helped nudge the market downward with exchange market intervention. The yen moved up smartly, from roughly 240 to the dollar to 200 by year's end and below 160 by summer 1986. The major European currencies rose significantly as well. The German mark, which traded at 2.84 on 20 September 1985 (and near 3.5 the previous February), moved below 2.0 in October 1986.

Yet even with this substantial exchange rate adjustment, the US trade deficit grew worse in 1986. Projections suggested that it would shrink somewhat in 1987 and 1988, perhaps by $35 billion to $40 billion per year, but this would only bring it down to slightly less than $100 billion. A further dollar decline would be necessary for the United States to achieve balance in its current account by the end of this decade.[14] (However, the

---

13. The dollar had receded gradually over the spring and summer from its February peak. So the ministers in September could endorse continuation of that trend, calling for a "further orderly appreciation of the major nondollar currencies against the dollar." (The other Group of Five countries were France, Germany, Japan, and the United Kingdom.)

14. C. Fred Bergsten, "The Outlook for the Trade Deficit and for America as a Debtor Country" (statement before the Subcommittee on Trade, House Ways and Means Committee, 24 September 1986; processed).

substantial foreign debt that the United States was accumulating during the high-deficit years might well force the nation, by the 1990s if not sooner, to start running trade *surpluses* in order to meet the interest payments.)

Having suffered the wrenching effects of the strong dollar, American producers of internationally traded goods now stood to gain from its decline. So, too, did US trade policy. Embattled administration and congressional trade leaders could now anticipate an easing of protectionist pressures, coming roughly in three stages. Most immediately, the weakening of the dollar brought *expectations* of a better competitive future, particularly vis-à-vis Japan as the yen shot upward. For the first time in years, there was reason to see better trade times ahead, and this anticipation of improvement served to lower Washington's trade temperature in the fall of 1985, particularly where Tokyo was concerned. Second, as the currency realignment proceeded, American firms could expect to find improvement in their *real competitive positions*. Exporters could lower their foreign-currency prices, or increase their profit margins, or both; import-competers saw their foreign competitors forced to do the opposite: raise dollar prices, or cut into profits, or both. Such improvements were likely to reduce industry pressure on trade officials, just as their opposites had increased it. And in fact, in the nine months of 1986, American companies began to report increases in export and domestic orders. Across the Pacific, their Japanese counterparts were now feeling a squeeze: a surge in the volume of imports and even a decline, albeit slight, in *real* exports.

But during this same period, the dollar trade balance remained skewed due to "*J*-curve" effect,[15] in which the immediate result of a devaluation is to worsen a nation's trade accounts. The continuation of 12-digit trade deficits gave proponents of restrictions a numerical basis to claim that the

---

The International Monetary Fund MERM (trade-weighted) index for the dollar rose from 100 during its base year (1980) to a 143.7 average for 1984 and 150.2 for 1985. By 25 September 1986, the index had dropped back to 118.2. As of that date, the dollar had declined 29.2 percent from its 25 February peak. Still, projections by the Institute for International Economics indicated that if the dollar fell no further, the US trade deficit would not drop below about $80 billion. Absent significantly faster growth in Japan and Europe, the dollar would have to decline at least 10 percent more, by these projections, to achieve current account balance by the end of the decade. (Updated calculations based on the model developed by Marris in *Deficits and the Dollar*.)

15. For the United States, a weaker dollar would first increase the total spent for imports by raising the dollar prices of imported goods. This would add to the trade deficit. Dollar decline would, over time, cut significantly into the volume of imports, and this deficit-reducing effect—added to that of the increase in dollar exports— would, over 12 to 24 months, come to exceed the import price effect, making the trade deficit lower than it would have been had the dollar not fallen. But in the meantime the current-dollar trade figures would look as bad as ever, or worse.

trade situation was as bad as ever. This posed a continuing threat in the congressional election year. It would likely be 1987 before US trade politics would experience the third major political benefit from devaluation, an actual drop in that trade deficit.[16] And for this benefit to be strong the drop would have to be substantial—to below the symbolic $100 billion annual rate (with imports measured c.i.f.), with further improvement expected in the months ahead. Such a number might well not be reached before late 1987, or 1988.

In practice, of course, neither the economics nor the politics of dollar decline would proceed in a tidily sequential fashion. Bringing down the dollar was not, alas, akin to the landing of an airplane. The available policy controls were crude, and foreign-exchange markets were volatile, driven by expectations of future values as well as by current interest returns. Moreover, the extent and persistence of the 1982–85 misalignment increased the chances that the dollar would, sooner or later, swing too far in the downward direction.

The imbalance had gotten so great, and had persisted for so long, that there were no easy answers. This increased the appeal of more extreme measures. Prominent among these, in early 1985, was the idea of an across-the-board surcharge on all US imports, either as a substitute or as a supplement for conventional budget measures. Its attraction was that it appeared to attack both our deficits simultaneously. It would reduce the volume of imports by raising their price. And if the surcharge rate were 20 percent, a frequently proposed figure, it would generate revenues of around $60 billion a year.

If one looked simply at its trade effects, such a measure would clearly seem counterproductive: by reducing demand for imports, it would tend to strengthen the dollar. But as a deficit-cutting tax it would reduce the need for capital imports, lessening the US savings-investment imbalance. Thus, it might, by some analyses, prove a net contributor to dollar decline. It would, of course, be inflationary, since it would raise import prices. Still, as a macroeconomic policy measure, a surcharge was not entirely without appeal, *if* one assumed there were no other way of raising taxes or otherwise getting the federal budget under control. And for politicians, could there be a less painful measure than one that, at least in the first instance, taxed foreigners and not Americans?

As international trade and economic policy, however, such a surcharge would be an enormous risk. It was, at best, very hard to square with our obligations under the General Agreement on Tariffs and Trade (GATT). It

16. The lag would result not just from the *J*-curve effect, but from the fact that the dollar had needed to fall so far just to stop the trade deficit from getting worse.

might well bring across-the-board retaliation, and thus precipitate a real trade war. And it would prove hard to sustain worldwide. Would we really be willing to inflict such a sudden blow on Canada, two-thirds of whose exports (and 16 percent of whose entire GNP) were sold in US markets? Could we reasonably ask debt-ridden developing countries to hold to their stringent repayment obligations, if we seemed to be breaching our trade obligations, and with a measure that undercut their ability to earn in export markets the money they required to pay their debts? Yet if we excluded Canada (20 percent of US imports) and the developing countries (29 percent of US imports, excluding those from members of the Organization of Petroleum Exporting Countries [OPEC]), a surcharge would lose half of its economic bite, and constitute trade discrimination on a massive scale.

Finally, econometric analyses have tended to conclude that while a global tax on imports would probably reduce the US trade deficit, at least in the short run, "Any gains in output and employment made by import-competing industries" would be "outweighed by losses in the wider economy," even without foreign retaliation.[17] It offered, therefore, no magic solution. Nor did conceivable alternatives aimed directly at international transactions, such as a tax on capital inflows. So the far better course was the conventional if painful one of attacking the budget deficit.

Over the longer term, once we exit from the current imbalance, the need is to avoid creating another one at some future date. This requires, by definition, not just attention to US fiscal and monetary policy, but to its interaction with the policies of America's trading partners. The strong dollar was the product not only of American governmental actions that drew capital in, but also of actions in Europe and Japan that tended to drive capital out—increased fiscal stringency combined with money management that resulted in interest rates below our own.

The Japanese, in particular, may come to see the need for greater policy balance. For the alternative is for Tokyo to expose itself, time after time, to the international political assaults that its growing trade surpluses inevitably produce.[18]

---

17. Craig K. Elwell, "The Macroeconomic Consequences of a Temporary Tariff on Imports," Congressional Research Service Report No. 85–103E, 29 April 1985, p. 3. Elwell uses the Data Resources, Inc., econometric model. Other studies included Lawrence R. Klein, Peter Pauly, and Christian E. Petersen, "Import Surcharges, US Deficits, and the World Economy," Project LINK, Department of Economics, University of Pennsylvania, April 1985.

For a broad policy analysis, see Julius L. Katz, A Tax on Imports: Can It Cure The Deficits? (Washington: Council on U.S. International Trade Policy, September 1985).

18. Moreover, as the rising yen slows growth in Japan by halting the rise in the volume of exports, as it has in fact for January–June 1986, business pressure for domestic stimulus can be expected to increase.

A more ambitious goal is to move toward *more structured cooperation on exchange rates*, a set of international rules for coordinated intervention policies to constrain speculative movements. Without a much more dependable medium-term relationship among currency values, we risk a recurrence of egregious trade imbalances like that which, as this is written, so threatens support for open trade policies in the United States. This is not the book to offer detailed prescriptions in this sphere. But one should not underestimate either the economic and political difficulty of such international monetary reform, or the urgency of trying.[19]

Is there any way, within the US governmental process, to *institutionalize* consideration of such policy linkages? Can we, through some sort of structural reform, increase the chances that our leaders will address the connection between trade and macroeconomic policies in a timely manner? There is certainly a clear need for the President's senior advisers to focus on the *global* impact of such far-reaching measures as the Reagan tax-and-budget package of 1981. To this end, various cabinet-level committees have been proposed. The 1983 trade reorganization bill included, for example, a provision authored by Senator Charles McC. Mathias (R-Md.) to establish a Council on International Trade, Economic and Financial Policy whose aim would be "harmonizing these policy areas."[20]

The problem is that one cannot legislate presidential advisory processes. In 1981 the Reagan administration did establish a senior committee that *ought to have* addressed these policy connections, the Cabinet Council on

---

19. See John Williamson, *The Exchange Rate System*, POLICY ANALYSES IN INTERNATIONAL ECONOMICS 5 (Washington: Institute for International Economics, September 1983, rev. June 1985). Williamson makes the case for a system where countries cooperate to keep the values of their respective currencies within agreed-upon target zones. Interest in the target-zone idea burgeoned following the Group of Five's September 1985 New York meeting.

For a proposal that goes a long step further and calls for making exchange rate stability the primary target of overall national monetary policies, see Ronald I. McKinnon, *An International Standard for Monetary Stabilization*, POLICY ANALYSES IN INTERNATIONAL ECONOMICS 8 (Washington: Institute for International Economics, March 1984).

President Ronald W. Reagan declared in his 1986 State of the Union Address, "We must never again permit wild currency swings to cripple our farmers and other exporters," and announced that he had asked Baker "to determine if the nations of the world should convene to discuss the role and relationship of our currencies." (Reprinted in *New York Times*, 5 February 1986.) At the Tokyo economic summit the following May, the seven participating leaders agreed to enhance their efforts at surveillance of exchange rates and related economic policies.

20. US Congress, Senate, Committee on Governmental Affairs, *Trade Reorganization Act of 1983*, 98th Cong., 2d Sess., 3 April 1983, S. Rept. 98–374, pp. 13–17. For a history of foreign economic policy coordinating institutions and proposals, see I. M. Destler, *Making Foreign Economic Policy* (Washington: Brookings Institution, 1980), esp. chs. 1 and 13.

Economic Affairs. The fact that it did not reflected not lack of jurisdiction but lack of understanding and will: administration minds and priorities were elsewhere. However, any administration ought to place within its policy coordination staff a senior aide with presidential access and a broad international economic policy mandate.[21]

Finally, could changes in congressional procedures encourage legislators to target the real causes of unbalanced trade? One reason they have stressed trade policy responses may be that they have clear power to impose them, whereas the exchange rate, for example, is beyond legislative reach. Senators and representatives might be encouraged to address the real problem if there were a procedure by which Congress set "targets for the US current account and the dollar," based on recommendations from the Secretary of the Treasury and the Chairman of the Federal Reserve Board, and then monitored progress toward their achievement.[22] This would be somewhat similar to the process that has evolved on domestic monetary policy, with the Fed testifying regularly before Congress on its monetary growth targets and strategies for meeting them.

Such an approach could not be too inflexible, since exchange rates and trade balances are, after all, determined multilaterally, not unilaterally. But such a procedure could put constructive pressure on an administration, and could channel congressional energy away from the wrong answers and toward the right ones. Of course, it would be committees other than Finance and Ways and Means that would have the primary action.

Using corrective macroeconomic policy measures, as well as reforms in structure and process like those suggested here, government can attack those large imbalances that so burden trade policymakers. For these economy-wide "trade" problems have, by their nature, no trade policy solutions. If macroeconomic policy changes help bring an end to dollar misalignment, and if national policies and international cooperation can reduce future

---

21. For considerations governing where this aide can best be placed, see *Making Foreign Economic Policy*, pp. 217–28.

The Economic Policy Council (EPC) of the second Reagan administration began to operate more effectively in the summer of 1985, after a restructuring which eliminated most of the other cabinet councils established by Presidential Assistant Edwin Meese III in 1981. But while the EPC contributed to development of a series of *trade*-policy initiatives, the dollar intervention strategy was reportedly developed in a more restricted circle.

22. C. Fred Bergsten, "Correcting the Dollar and Reforming the International Monetary System" (statement before the Subcommittee on International Finance, Trade and Monetary Policy, House Committee on Banking, Finance and Urban Affairs, 19 November 1985; processed), p. 12.

Title IV of HR 4800, the omnibus trade bill passed by the House in May 1986, would require the Treasury to determine the "competitive exchange rate" consistent with current account balance, and to make its achievement a top policy priority.

exchange rate fluctuations, American firms and workers can function in a far more stable, predictable economic environment. If adjustment within the US economy were then smooth, so that workers and capital could flow efficiently into enterprises with international comparative advantage, then trade policymakers could rest truly easy.

Unfortunately, major adjustment is seldom smooth. And the plight of those hurt by economic change—whether its cause be "fair or "unfair" trade or broader economic forces—necessarily commands our attention. This is particularly so when hardship reaches near-depression levels, as it did in the American midwest in 1981–82. The plight of key "rust belt" industries, autos and steel above all, does much to explain why, for a time, "industrial policy" became a prime focus of debate for many deeply concerned about the American place in the international economy. Thus industrial policy is the second important sphere of nontrade policy that requires attention here.

Microeconomic Policy: Promoting Adjustment by Labor and Industry

In 1984, even as the US economy was rebounding, steel, a venerable basic industry, continued to lag. Employment remained more than 200,000 below that of the late 1970s, a cut of roughly half. Imports poured in, with large volumes coming from nations whose steel plants had gotten hefty public subsidies. And the old, integrated manufacturing facilties faced rising competition at home as well—from "mini-mills" that employed new production technology to make important steel products much more cheaply than could Bethlehem or US Steel.

This basic industry was just one of a number whose specific plight had won public attention. Autos had been even more visible in 1980 and 1981; consumer electronics had had its crisis in the years before. At the high-technology end of the spectrum, alarms were regularly voiced about semiconductors or telecommunications. Could the US economy have much of a future if such frontier industries were being bested in their home market by foreign competitors, particularly Japanese? This was intertwined with the broader question of deindustrialization, the thesis that international trade was relentlessly transforming the nation into a postindustrial, service economy. This was demonstrably not true in the late 1970s, when the issue was first raised. But in the decade following, the trade deficit came to cut seriously into manufacturing employment. As of summer 1986, in the fourth year of economic recovery, US factory jobs totaled 2 million less than at their peak level seven years before.

As discussed in chapter 7, these developments raised the question of *industrial* policy: whether the United States should invest public resources to influence the sectoral composition of our economy, to buttress certain industries viewed as important for the national future. Other nations had clearly done so, albeit with mixed effectiveness. So, willy-nilly, had we. Agriculture had long benefited from research and educational support and from programs to aid producers of specific commodities. Aircraft, computer, and semiconductor firms had gained enormously from Pentagon research funding. Our textile and apparel industries were larger because of quota protection. But all this was ad hoc. Unlike countries such as Japan and France, we had never targeted particular industries or sectors for purposes of economic development. In the early 1980s, there were many who saw such action by foreign governments as a threat to the United States. They felt that we should counter other nations' industrial policies or respond in kind to their governmental efforts to create future comparative advantage, or both.[23]

Much of the campaign focused on trade action: making industrial targeting an unfair trade practice under our countervailing duty law, as proposed by Representative Sam M. Gibbons (D-Fla.), or threatening import restrictions for products like telecommunications from nations whose markets denied our firms reciprocal access. Or, for basic industries, the policy advocated was frequently one of protection, because imports were subsidized and this was unfair or because the industry needed time to restructure itself so it could face foreign competition more effectively in the future, or both.

From the vantage point of a particular industry, such an approach has substantial attractions. An industry loses when foreign competitors are subsidized, as in certain cases they have been; it gains, at least in the short run, from any form of benefit bestowed by its government, whether it be a direct subsidy, import protection, or favorable treatment in the tax code. There will also be, from time to time, strong welfare arguments for providing import relief and related assistance to individuals and communities absorbing acute trade pain.[24] If, for certain large industries, the burden of trade impact is regionally concentrated in the northeast-midwest rust belt; if plant closings have a multiplier effect by drying up businesses that depend on their spending and that of their employees; and if the geographic mobility of many residents of these communities is limited, this may argue for redevelopment programs with a geographic focus.[25]

---

23. See, for example, *International Trade, Industrial Policies, and the Future of American Industry* (Washington: Labor–Industry Coalition for International Trade, April 1983).

24. The role and limits of trade-specific adjustment assistance are treated in chapter 10.

25. It has sometimes been argued that this rust belt adjustment is part of a broader, more disturbing development: a reversal of gains in American income distribution

But such programs need to be limited to cases of very severe need. For their net impact will almost always be to weaken, not strengthen, the American economy taken as a whole.

From an economy-wide perspective, any help to a particular industry represents resources diverted from other uses, however the subsidy may be provided. If the aim is to arrest or slow an industry's decline, it is, by definition, a grant to the competitively inefficient, to a current economic loser. Even at the high-tech, high-growth end of the industrial spectrum, public support makes economic policy sense only if it promises to spur future productivity or market gains commensurate with public investment. And if it does, one must then ask why government is better able than private capitalists to anticipate these gains and finance them.

There will be instances, of course, in which a particular industry produces spillover benefits, "external economies" in economists' lingo, meaning that its success produces gains for the broader economy and society beyond those captured by the firms' owners. Such public gains can justify public investments. But these gains must be weighted against negative spillovers. If government policies result in our steel (or semiconductor) prices' being substantially above international norms, for example, these will create international competitive *disadvantages* for firms that use these products as inputs, such as makers of autos and computers. Moreover, while public help can increase the capacity of an industry to compete internationally, it can reduce the incentive to make the hard, cost-cutting decisions that will ultimately prove necessary.

To the limits of industry-specific interventions in terms of overall economic efficiency must be added problems of political efficacy. Will our system of government allow officials to allocate resources to those select cases in which the spillover gains for the overall economy are strongest? It may when these gains are coincident with other policy purposes: certain defense research, for example. But the normal political process tends to produce the opposite result. It is the losers (Chrysler Corporation, the steel industry) that come to Washington for help, and government frequently responds to them—

---

achieved earlier in this century. Technological change, it is suggested, is replacing middle-class union jobs in industries like steel and autos with a mix of high-paying positions for the technology-literate and low-paying jobs for others, with adverse implications not just for displaced industrial workers but also for educationally disadvantaged racial and ethnic minorities.

This would certainly be an unhappy development. But although such a redistribution is no doubt occurring in particular communities, broader indicators do not show a clear nationwide trend. Robert Z. Lawrence, for example, finds that the percentage of middle-income jobs in high-technology manufacturing is marginally greater than that for manufacturing as a whole. He also finds, however, a decline (between 1969 and 1979) in the proportion of overall manufacturing jobs paying middle-income wages. *Can America Compete?* (Washington: Brookings Institution, 1984), p. 80.

See ch. 3, footnote 10, this volume, for Lawrence's statistics.

because of their evident hardship, as well as their political power. Even in Japan, it is agriculture that wins the most blatant government favor, to the detriment of the economy as a whole. In the United States, where we lack a policy tradition of even *trying* to generate visions of our future industrial structure and bring these visions into being, the losers are likely to do even better.

For all these reasons, even strong proponents of an industrial policy focus tend to see sector-specific policy actions as the final recourse, not the initial one. As Laura Tyson and John Zysman put it, "When we confront either a sector problem or a shift in international trade that is of broad national concern, there should be a clear order of policy preferences: aggregate policies first; policies to improve the workings of markets second; and finally—and only as a last resort—industry-specific policies."[26] And in undertaking such interventions, to repeat the words of another industrial policy advocate, the motivation should be pro-adjustment, supportive of the "transformation of all nations' industrial bases toward higher-value production."[27]

But this is not to say that all concern about American industrial competitiveness is misplaced. In the world of international trade, a nation cannot, by definition, be competitive in all industries. The whole purpose of trade is to benefit from the international division of labor, to buy from abroad what is less expensive there, to produce what we produce most efficiently here. But the position of the US economy overall, and the living standard of American citizens, are ultimately functions of the productivity of our economic enterprises. Unless their output per worker continues to increase, there is no way, in the long run, for the real incomes of Americans to grow. And there is no way to avoid falling behind, in relative terms, if productivity in other nations, broadly defined, is increasing faster.

Here there is reason for long-term worry. In the mid-1980s, the overriding immediate problem has been the strong dollar and the trade imbalance. But looking to a future when that is behind us, slow productivity growth seems likely to pose the most serious threat to US economic and trade performance. Careful analysis suggests that, with reasonable exchange rates, the United States can hold its own in industrial trade.[28] But our overall record in productivity growth has not been particularly encouraging (though the

26. "Conclusions: What to Do Now?" in *American Industry in International Competition: Government Policies and Corporate Strategies,* edited by John Zysman and Laura Tyson (Ithaca, NY: Cornell University Press, 1983), p. 423.

27. Robert Reich, "Beyond Free Trade," *Foreign Affairs,* vol. 61, no. 4 (Spring 1983), p. 790.

28. Lawrence, *Can America Compete?* The author offers a telling rebuttal to those who argue that, over the 1970s, the United States was deindustrializing relative to its primary trading partners. However, to maintain the US share in manufactured goods

innovativeness of our high-tech industries is a positive harbinger for the future).[29]

We therefore need policies to speed adjustment by industry and labor, to encourage movement of resources from less productive to more productive enterprises and regions. This should be joined with efforts to increase productivity growth for the economy as a whole. There is a strong need for policies, in Charles Schultze's words, "designed to make the economy in general more flexible, more dynamic, more productive, and more capable of adjustment to technological change."[30] Such policies need to focus on labor markets, increasing training opportunities for workers and improving market information about job openings. They can include more support of general and specialized education and encouragement of research where the benefits to society exceed those recoverable by a firm. They can include tax code changes that favor productivity-enhancing forms of investment, and that favor the domestic savings that must ultimately finance such investment.

Among liberal trade advocates, it is common to view industrial policy as a stalking horse for protection. Often it is. A label like "industrial policy" can lend respectability to trade-restrictive proposals for politicians who view "protectionism" as something bad. And industrial policy involves, by definition, government microeconomic intervention that may well prove unwise from an economy-wide perspective. Even if no trade protection is initially involved or intended, it can create a governmental stake in a particular industry's prosperity that may lead to such protection in the future.

But the focus on our industrial productivity can be enormously constructive. It can turn American attention away from nefarious-seeming foreigners, toward self-help at home. It can focus our energies on creating an appropriate, stimulative policy environment for our productive enterprises. It can encourage a creeping recognition that many of the problems of American producers are, in important part, "made in USA."

---

exports, "a lower exchange rate was required." Thus, "in this sense, the U.S. lost competitiveness" (p. 95).

In future years, unless our relative productivity performance improves, this pattern is likely to be repeated. The United States could return to, and maintain, a reasonable export-import balance, but this would require a gradual, continuing devaluation of the dollar, which would mean lower (relative) living standards for the American people.

29. For various indicators of competitiveness, see *Global Competition: The New Reality*, Report of the President's Commission on Industrial Competitiveness, vol. 2, Washington, January 1985, pp. 6–16.

30. Charles L. Schultze, "Industrial Policy: A Solution in Search of a Problem," *California Management Review*, vol. 24, no. 4 (Summer 1983), p. 6.

10

Coping with Trade Pressures

Changes in macroeconomic policy can help redress huge trade imbalances and ease the enormous pressure they generate for import restrictions. Steps to improve overall industrial competitiveness can help make adjustment to economic dislocations more humane and efficient, and reduce the temptation to blame foreign devils for domestic ills.

By contrast, *trade* policy is not an effective instrument for addressing these broad, economy-wide problems. Changes in the level of import barriers can have little impact on the size of a nation's trade deficit, or trade surplus, at least in a world of floating exchange rates. Import barriers can, of course, affect the *composition* of trade, and thus, indirectly, the sectoral composition of the domestic economy. Any industry with relatively high protection will have greater output, profits, and wages as a result, at least in the short run. But these gains will be at the expense of other industries, and the economy as a whole will suffer from such favoring of enterprises that are less competitive internationally.

Present losses might be offset if protection helped foster tomorrow's economic winners. But in practice it is extraordinarily difficult to use trade policy as a tool to favor "industries of the future." Not only does this require an ability to know, better than the market, what these industries are and will be; it demands a political capacity to favor likely future "winners" over those industries that suffer the greatest current pain and are therefore most active politically. Postwar experience offers no reason to believe that our system can do this.

What Trade Policy Can Do

We are left, then, with one primary *positive* trade policy goal and one *negative* one. The positive aim is to increase the *volume* of trade, through opening markets abroad and at home, and thus to increase the gains from trade to the American economy as a whole.[1] The negative aim is damage limitation—minimizing the harm to our overall economy, and the international trading system, from successful attempts by special interests to win import protection.[2] Both are important. Both, particularly the second, will require higher priority to trade issues than US presidents have typically given. But trade policy is *not* the key to righting huge economic imbalances like that of 1983–1986, nor is it the key to future U.S. industrial leadership.[3]

Realism about what trade policy can and cannot do leads directly to conclusions about how our government should be structured to handle it. Proponents of a department of trade have had ambitious goals: to redress the trade imbalance, to bolster industrial competitiveness generally.[4] Their reach exceeds trade policy's grasp. But much of the congressional trade frustration and activism at mid-decade reflected the fact that the Reagan administration was not doing what has for a half century been the executive branch's primary political job in the trade arena. It was not coping credibly with industry pressures. So all of the heat came down on Capitol Hill.

Such pressures have been atypically intense in 1985 and 1986, of course: the trade imbalance guaranteed that. But even after the current storm passes,

---

1. Of course, an expansion of exports through subsidization is just as trade-distorting as a restriction of imports. Thus, countervailing duties to offset foreign subsidies have an economic, as well as a political, rationale.

2. There are foreign-policy interests at stake also. In today's world, these generally reinforce the argument for US openness on *imports* (oil perhaps excepted), since this smooths relations with the European Community, Japan, and the newly industrializing countries of the Third World. On the export side, pressing for foreign-market openness can create political frictions with allies in the short run, as it forces on their governments the choice between resisting US demands and confronting politically potent, protected home constituencies. Over the long run, however, successful campaigns to open foreign markets are likely to strengthen economic interdependence and the sense of common stakes in a liberal world trade order.

For more on the short-run tension between market-opening trade policies and bilateral political harmony with one major ally, see *Coping With U.S.-Japanese Economic Conflicts*, edited by I. M. Destler and Hideo Sato (Lexington, Mass.: Lexington Books, 1982), ch. 7.

3. For one lucid explanation why, see Rachel McCulloch and J. David Richardson, "U.S. Trade and the Dollar: Evaluating Current Policy Options," in *Current U.S. Trade Policy: Analysis, Agenda, and Administration*, edited by Robert E. Baldwin and J. David Richardson, *NBER Conference Report* (Cambridge, Mass.: National Bureau of Economic Research, 1986), pp. 49–75.

4. See, for example, the opening statements of Senator William V. Roth, Jr. (R-Del.) and his colleagues in US Congress, Senate, Committee on Governmental Affairs, *Trade Reorganization Act of 1983*, 98th Cong., 2d Sess., 17 March 1983, S. Hrg. 98–474, pp. 1–10.

even after the value of American exports comes once again to resemble the value of our imports, substantial demands for trade restrictions will remain. Our economy is more exposed internationally than it was 15 or 20 years ago, and hence more US industries are hurt by import competition. So, too, are communities depending on these industries—and trade policy *can* matter to them, since it can give them some relief from the pain of adjustment. Such relief has a political legitimacy that government protection from domestic rivals does not have. For products like steel, the case for protection is strengthened by the widespread actions of foreign governments to subsidize and protect their own domestic producers.

In form, this is basically the Schattschneider problem that opened this book: the problem of political imbalance. The US Congress, recognizing its vulnerability to one-sided pressure for import restrictions, cooperated with successive administrations in developing means of coping: a range of devices that facilitate voluntary legislative restraint on product-specific trade policy. America's leaders developed a system to divert and channel pressures, and to deal separately with the most trade-afflicted among our major industries. Throughout the postwar period, this system has generally avoided major public confrontations on trade that pit industry against industry or political party against political party. It has tilted policy outcomes toward open trade by tilting process toward closed politics.

Can The System Be Salvaged?

Can such an approach still work for the United States in the 1980s and 1990s? At least four trends, spelled out in the body of this book, make the going harder. Trade has become more important economically; Congress is now more open procedurally; the trade-remedy procedures have proved more exploitable politically; and politicians have brought the issue back into the national electoral arena.

Taken together, these four trends have made trade policy a much more public matter. Rhetoric has escalated. Legislative activity has increased, whether it is measured in numbers of bills introduced or in numbers given committee or floor consideration. There are more efforts to draw trade policy lines for partisan advantage.

Such developments might lead to a judgement that the old system has run its course, that it is futile to keep trying to patch it up, that we should instead look to create an entirely different set of trade policy institutions.

Yet even the less protected Congress of today, faced with a trade imbalance beyond previous imagination, has been reluctant to seize product-specific trade responsibility. In fact, most congressional trade leaders have sought not weaker but stronger executive branch leadership. Senator John C. Danforth (R-Mo.) suggested openly in his spring 1985 Japan offensive that his prime target was the White House: he wanted *the administration* to take the trade problem seriously. When it finally did act on trade and the dollar the following September, Danforth's counterpart on Senate Finance, Lloyd Bentsen (D-Tex.), was quick to claim some of the credit. He said that Congress had finally "gotten their attention," and he, too, meant not the government in Tokyo but the one in Washington. Congress did pass a textile quota bill that fall, but with the comfort of knowing that the President was committed to veto it. In the summer of 1986, 276 House members did vote to override that veto but somehow their number fell short of the two-thirds required.

This suggests a strong current market on Capitol Hill for political insulation, a will to continue a trade policy-making relationship in which legislators can make noise, pressure the administration, claim credit for specific actions it takes, but avoid final responsibility themselves. It suggests that the idea of "protection for Congress" on trade may have life in it still. It suggests that the system may yet be salvagable.

If a system that insulates Congress continues to reflect political reality on Capitol Hill, it also represents political necessity for those who favor open trade policies. As illustrated by House votes for domestic content in 1982 and 1983 and the substantial margins in both chambers for Jenkins textile bill in 1985, legislators remain vulnerable to unbalanced pressure for import restrictions. In neither autos nor textiles was the number of representatives who wanted the legislation to become law anywhere near equal to the number who voted "aye" at roll call time.

Many of them, in fact, would much rather not have voted at all. But the erosion of internal congressional constraints makes it harder today for leaders to protect members by stopping such proposals before they reach the floor. Nor can the heavy trade pressures be absorbed through quasi-judicial trade remedy procedures, however much legislators may seek to refine them. "The rules" have been transformed, in the large industry cases, from means for politicians to divert the heat to means for petitioners to stoke it up.

All of this places even more burdens on the "executive broker," in the double meaning of that phrase, as the central *function* that needs buttressing and as the downtown *institution* that must perform it. Both damage-limitation at home and trade-expansion abroad require the balancing of economic interests and policy concerns. When an industry seeks protection from imports, government needs to seek out other interests that would be affected by such protection—industrial users of a product, retailers, exporters, household consumers—and encourage them to enter the political arena.[5] And ever since the "bargaining tariff" of the 1930s, one of the best ways to resist closing markets at home has been to press for opening markets overseas.

Not by coincidence, successive congressional trade leaders have created, strengthened, and protected an executive branch brokering institution—the Office of the US Trade Representative (USTR). They placed it where they hoped its chief would have the ear of the President and the leeway to balance domestic and foreign concerns, micro and macro issues, legislative and executive branches. But while presidents have been consistent backers of liberal trade policies, they have more often than not failed to provide the sort of consistent support the USTR needs to do *confident* battle against protectionist pressures. This has contributed to the Representative's periodic turf struggles with other cabinet officials, and led Senators like Roth to conclude that a cabinet-level department could exercise stronger trade policy leadership. Indeed, the Reagan administration endorsed this view in 1983–84, though largely because of a prior commitment by senior aide Edwin Meese III to Secretary of Commerce Malcolm Baldrige.

The argument here is that the trade department advocates are right, at least in part, about the problem but wrong about the solution. The growing importance of trade, and the increase in pressures on our trade policy-making system, do call for an organizational response. There is a need for stronger, more centralized management and coordination. Cabinet and working-level tension between USTR and Commerce is unnecessary and counterproductive. And USTR has had recurrent problems in maintaining its role of executive branch trade leader. If a new cabinet Department of Trade were likely to prove stronger, there would be a good case for creating one.

In fact, however, a Secretary of Trade would more likely become what most heads of executive departments currently are: an official with a prestigious title but modest power, all too close to the interests his department affects, and distant from the President. On trade, this would mean a department overly responsive to the protection-seeking complainers and unable or disinclined to balance their concerns against those of others. Moreover, a new department of trade would raise serious jurisdictional problems on Capitol Hill, buttressing the commerce committees vis-à-vis the tax committees in the struggle for the primary trade role.

---

5. The role of such interests will be treated in greater detail in I. M. Destler and John S. Odell, *The Politics of Anti-Protection* (Washington: Institute for International Economics, forthcoming, 1987).

The better answer is to build on what has been, for all its limitations, an organizational success story—the office of the White House trade representative—and to do so in a way that might improve the incumbent's presidential connection.

A USTR-Based Trade Reorganization

One recurrent argument for trade reorganization is the dispersion of trade responsibilities within the US government. This is, for the most part, a bogus argument. The problem with current executive branch trade organization is *not* that "no less than 25" departments and agencies have some slice of trade responsibility, to employ Roth's oft-repeated phrase. This simply reflects the range of governmental concerns that trade policy affects. In any conceivable organizational arrangement, we would have the State Department and the National Security Council stressing trade's importance to alliance relations, the Defense Department worrying about technological leakage to the Soviet Union, Treasury and the Council of Economic Advisers responsible for linking trade policy to the overall domestic economy and Third World debt, and the Department of Agriculture stressing the connection of grain exports to commodity programs and overall farm welfare.

Nor are other governments fundamentally different. Americans negotiating trade issues with Japan during the past decade have dealt not only, and not always mainly, with the Ministry of International Trade and Industry. They have found themselves confronting the Agriculture Ministry on beef and citrus, the Ministry of Posts and Telecommunications on the deregulation of Nippon Telephone and Telegraph, and the Finance Ministry on a range of matters, not to mention the Foreign Ministry and, intermittently, a special Minister for International Economic Relations.

All government activities with a "trade" label do not require a common home. As a day-to-day matter, export promotion through technical aid to firms need not be housed in the same agency that handles import regulation or trade negotiations. And, since decisions on East-West trade are bound to have a heavy security-foreign policy component, it is unrealistic to expect that the dominant role in such matters will fall to the same official who leads in "mainstream" trade negotiations with Japan and the European Community (EC).

But if substantial dispersion of US governmental trade responsibility is inevitable, the current bifurcation of trade leadership is not. In fact, the current organization has at least four serious flaws:

□ The current USTR-Commerce division of labor asks for trouble. Putting "policy," "coordination," and "negotiations" one place and "nonagricultural operational trade responsibilities" in a separate and formally coequal agency invites competition and conflict.

☐ This is exacerbated by the fact that international trade is the only subject in the Commerce Secretary's portfolio that offers an opportunity for important policy leadership. Thus, any ambitious incumbent with decent White House connections becomes a rival of the US Trade Representative.

☐ The numerical expansion of USTR in 1980 created an organizational hybrid, too large for a flexible coordinating-negotiating staff but too small to be the central executive branch repository of line expertise and responsibility. And USTR's size makes it a target of White House reorganizers seeking to trim overall staff.

☐ Presidential support for USTR, particularly important at times of trade policy crisis, has often been tenuous.

The last of these problems is, at bottom, personal and political more than it is organizational. But one can address the first three in a way that should make the trade representative fit better within the Executive Office of the President (EOP). Three simple steps are needed:

☐ Convert USTR into a small, elite EOP unit, with a professional staff totaling about 25, with responsibility for leading international negotiations, brokering on Capitol Hill, and coordinating interagency trade.

☐ Create outside the EOP, as a noncabinet executive branch agency, a United States Trade Administration (USTA) headed by a Deputy USTR for Operations, and merge within this new unit the remaining staff of the current USTR and that of Commerce's International Trade Administration.[6]

☐ Abolish the Department of Commerce.[7]

---

6. This proposal draws upon two ideas that arose during the Carter administration's trade reorganization deliberations. The first, a tentative proposal put forward under Strauss's name, called for a Trade Policy Council in the Executive Office of the President and a Board of Trade outside it, both to be headed by the President's Trade Representative. The second, a fallback proposal put to President Carter by Secretary of State Cyrus R. Vance and Secretary of the Treasury W. Michael Blumenthal, called for a US Trade Policy Administration *and* a US Export Corporation, both headed by deputy STRs.

7. This final step would not be required for *trade* reorganization, since removal of the department's trade functions would presumably end the Secretary's threat to USTR primacy. But it would be a logical step, for what remained would be a set of autonomous technical agencies: the National Oceanic and Atmospheric Administration

Replacing the current "two-headed monster"[8] with a two-tiered USTR-USTA structure would have several obvious advantages. It would build on an organization with a generally successful track record, one that retains substantial support on Capitol Hill and in the broader trade community. It would establish the US Trade Representative as the *only* cabinet-level official for whom international trade was the primary policy responsibility. It would reduce conflict below his level by consolidating, under one of his deputies, the staffs responsible for providing detailed backup to negotiations and enforcing the trade laws. Within the executive branch, trade policy would continue to be an interagency process at both the USTR and the USTA level, but management of this process would be easier with a clear locus of leadership.

Such a reorganization should also help strengthen the trade representative's White House connection. Not only would it eliminate his prime rival for the presidential trade mandate, but it would also make his immediate USTR office a smaller, more flexible unit, increasing its "fit" within the Executive Office of the President in terms of both size and operational style. This would help particularly during presidential transitions, when the trade office has been especially vulnerable. Under the current arrangement, any future Edwin Meese looking to rationalize EOP operations and cut staff in his boss's name would find USTR a juicy target, with nearly twice as many official employees as the National Security Council.[9] Making it a lean, senior-level trade brokering staff would render the office less vulnerable numerically and more compatible functionally.

Could such a small USTR handle the enormous range of specific negotiations with which today's trade policymakers must cope? It obviously could not do most of the detailed work by itself. It would have to draw heavily on the proposed USTA for expertise and negotiating support. Some negotiations would need to be managed, on a day-to-day basis, either by senior USTA officials or by representatives of such departments as Agriculture and State, which would continue to have strong involvement in executive branch

---

(13,908 employees as of 1 January 1985), the Bureau of the Census (8,324), the National Bureau of Standards (3,282), and the Patent and Trademark Office (3,256) are the largest. They could exist as a free-standing federal agency or agencies, but cabinet status would be inappropriate. (Staff numbers are taken from US Senate Committee on Governmental Affairs, "Organization of Federal Executive Departments and Agencies," GPO: 1985 0–44–340, 1 January 1985.)

8. The phrase is Senator Roth's. See, for example, *Trade Reorganization Act of 1983*, p. 2.

9. As of 1 January 1985, USTR had 140 employees on EOP rolls, compared to 77 at the National Security Council, 40 at the Office of Policy Development, and 29 for the Council of Economic Advisers.(Senate Governmental Affairs Committee, *Organization of Federal Executive Departments.*)

trade policy making. But these agencies and officials need to see themselves, and be seen, not primarily as rivals to USTR for trade policy influence, but as allies—allies with somewhat differing perspectives, to be sure, but sharing the basic objective of working to open markets abroad and at home.

An example of how this can work was supplied by the Reagan administration in September 1986, when USTR Clayton K. Yeutter led, at the successful Punta del Este talks of the General Agreement on Tariffs and Trade (GATT), a cabinet-level delegation that included the Secretaries of Commerce and Agriculture. By buttressing the USTR's status and authority, the changes proposed here could help make such cross-governmental leadership the rule, not the exception.

This reorganization would not deal directly with the problem stressed in chapter 9: the need for a strong trade input into the macroeconomic policies that so influence the import-export balance. But by enhancing his status within the White House, it should make it easier for the US Trade Representative to press the trade policy interest in administration economic policy debates, by participating in such forums as the President and his chief economic aides have established. He would still need, of course, to cultivate ties with such aides, for no USTR is likely to be, himself, a prime presidential adviser on monetary or fiscal policy. If Congress, however, were to legislate a process for setting dollar or exchange rate targets, as urged in chapter 9, it should require that the Secretary of the Treasury consult with the trade representative before determining his recommended target levels.

Making the USTR more at home in the White House is clearly preferable to an oft-proposed alternative: seeking to strengthen his authority by transferring to *him* major trade authorities now assigned the President, such as decisions on escape clause cases.[10] That is clearly unworkable: no chief executive could allow such formal autonomy in a White House official to become real independence. He would have to rein the USTR in, cut him down to size. Congress could not protect his authority, since it is the President who hires the USTR and can fire him. So in seeking such autonomy, all Congress would achieve would be to weaken the trade representative's presidential connection, when what Congress really wants is the opposite— for the President to support the USTR and build him up.

---

10. For example, the omnibus trade legislation passed by the House of Representatives in May 1986 shifts to the USTR final authority over Section 201 decisions, and certain intermediate authorities under Section 301. See US Congress, House, Committee on Ways and Means, *Comprehensive Trade Policy Reform Act of 1986*, 99th Cong., 2d Sess., 6 May 1986, H. Rept. 99–581, part 1. For comparison of the 1986 House bill with others, see Raymond J. Ahearn et al., "Trade Legislation: Comparative Analyses of H.R. 4800 and Selected Senate Trade Bills" (Report prepared at the request of Senator Lloyd Bentsen [D-Tex.], Congressional Research Service, Washington, 10 June 1986; processed).

But like many legislative proposals that would be unwise to adopt, this one contains a clear message that presidents ignore at their peril. Such current congressional frustration reflects a view that chief executives have given short shrift to trade policy: not just that they have been reluctant to "get tough" with foreign competitors, although that is part of it, but that they have given low priority to the effective, responsive management of domestic trade pressures on which the overall system ultimately depends.

Congress cannot, of course, legislate executive branch decision making, and no President will or can always decide issues as his Trade Representative recommends. But when an administration is egregiously unresponsive to trade concerns, as Ronald W. Reagan's was for most of 1981–85, it invites congressional efforts to tie its hands, as a number of current bills would do. Conversely, the executive branch gets leeway from Capitol Hill when there is confidence about the trade priorities of an administration and about its capacity to pursue them effectively. STR's legislative successes in 1974 and 1979 are cases in point.

Trade policy making could also benefit from modest reforms at the other end of Pennsylvania Avenue. USTR has been, in important respects, a creature and ally of the Senate Finance and House Ways and Means committees. A strong role for these committees remains critical, particularly for Ways and Means, which has faced increasing jurisdictional challenge. But it cannot regain the dominance of Wilbur D. Mills's day. With increased congressional interest in trade, and with major trade-affecting action now involving spheres like exchange rate or industrial policy, other committees will inevitably play important roles; for instance, other committees participated in review of the MTN agreements of 1979. To coordinate action on the omnibus trade legislation in 1986, Congressman Don Bonker (D-Wash.) proposed that the Speaker of the House create an Ad Hoc Committee on Trade to "facilitate the consideration of complex trade legislation without limiting the House's ability to draw on the expertise of the standing committees." Bonker cited the model of the Ad Hoc Select Committee on Energy, created in 1977 to oversee and integrate the work of several committees on high priority Carter administration legislation.[11]

The danger of such a proposal is that it would further weaken Ways and Means. Once the omnibus legislation and the Ad Hoc committee passed into history, it would be hard for that committee to reestablish its primacy

---

11. Letter of 5 November 1985, from Bonker to Speaker Thomas P. O'Neill, Jr., reprinted in *Congressional Record*, 7 November 1985. For analysis of the experience on energy legislation, see Bruce I. Oppenheimer, "Congress and the New Obstructionism: Developing an Energy Program," in *Congress Reconsidered*, 2nd ed., edited by Lawrence C. Dodd and Bruce I. Oppenheimer (Washington: Congressional Quarterly Press, 1981), pp. 286–88.

in trade policy. The need is to protect that central role while accommodating pressures for broader participation. The way House Democrats actually handled the omnibus bill was better. Majority Leader James C. Wright, Jr., (D-Tex.) played the role of bringing together the bill, whose provisions had been reported out by several House committees, but Ways and Means made the most substantial contribution, and its Chairman, Dan Rostenkowski (D-Ill.), served as floor leader for the bill as a whole. For future general trade legislation, it might be useful for the Speaker to formalize this first-among-equals role by designating Rostenkowski or his successor as head of a House Trade Steering Group that included representatives from: Banking, Finance and Urban Affairs (to cover international monetary issues); Energy and Commerce; Foreign Affairs; and others as appropriate. Such a group could farm out sections of a bill to the appropriate panels, with the Ways and Means chair retaining overall policy responsibility for coordinating their work and managing the bill that emerged.

Another possible congressional reform would be a trade reconciliation procedure parallel to that employed on budget matters since 1974. Bills and amendments diverging from existing trade policy (as interpreted by Senate Finance, House Ways and Means, the Steering Group, or another committee with established authority over its subject matter) would be subject to a point of order on the Senate or House floor. Through such a procedure, congressional leaders could block floor votes on product-specific, trade-restrictive proposals that had not been recommended by the committee with jurisdiction.

What the Trade Broker Must Do

If experience has shown the costs of the USTR-Commerce division, it has shown equally the benefits of choosing trade representatives like Robert S. Strauss and William E. Brock, adroit senior *politicians* with strong ties on Capitol Hill. Their successes illustrate how important it is for the incumbent to immerse himself in the *politics* of trade, above all in its congressional aspects.

Experience suggests also the range of policy and political initiatives an executive branch trade leader must undertake if he is to cope with competing demands and return US trade policy to its forward-tilting course. First of all, he needs to look for ways to cultivate, respond to, and reinforce his congressional allies—the senior members of Senate Finance and House Ways and Means above all.

In cases of major industry campaigns for import relief, like steel in 1984 or textiles in 1985–86, he needs to tilt against them, to encourage all major interests affected by proposed trade restrictions to make their voices heard. When the political game is broadened to include players on the other side—industrial users of imports, retailers, exporters, foreign governments—an administration gains leeway to resist extreme demands and to opt for moderate trade restrictions when some action is required.

By contrast, in cases in which industries seek legal trade remedies, the USTR needs to show sympathy and empathy, with overt presidential backing—to press Section 301 cases where egregious foreign practices are involved; to lean toward granting temporary relief under the escape clause (Section 201) where it would seem to make a nontemporary difference for a trade-injured industry; to show responsiveness to industries that use established trade procedures, and to take their situations—and the laws—seriously. (Beginning in the fall of 1985, the Reagan administration has shown much greater sensitivity to this need than it did during the President's first term.)

More generally, an administration's trade leader needs to establish credibility as defender of US interests; only then will broad business support for a liberal trade regime and market-expanding policies be restored and maintained. There is a need to woo the export-oriented portion of the "fair trade" constituency away from protectionism, by showing business people that the government in Washington will really fight for *their* rights.

This requires the aggressive and visible practice of "export politics," pressing particular foreign-market issues in which there are good prospects for success and issues in which the United States can maintain a tough stance—a stance that includes trade sanctions if we are not successful in winning meaningful foreign concessions.

Finally, trade policy needs to be managed, insofar as is possible, in a bipartisan manner—as STRs and USTRs generally have done. A bipartisan approach is necessary because the immediate electoral payoffs will often seem to be on the trade-restrictive side, and the alternative is a bidding war in which Democrats and Republicans compete for special-interest support at the expense of overall national welfare. A bipartisan approach remains possible because protectionism is still a risky party platform, costly in respect and in reputation—as John Connally learned in the late 1970s in his quest for the Republican presidential nomination, and as Democrats have discovered more than once in the 1980s.

Policy Tools: The "Uruguay Round"

The old trade policy-making system leaned heavily on international negotiations to achieve global reductions in trade barriers. Such negotiations remain the most obvious political means of expanding the volume of trade.

They also perform three valuable functions in US trade politics. They offer a basis for bringing export interests actively into the political process, offsetting the ever-present pressure from producers who would restrict imports. They provide a rationale for resisting that protectionist pressure. And they reinforce the position of the central trade broker who has the lead in conducting them.

Thus, USTR William Brock was advancing both national and institutional interests when, during Reagan's first term, he sought to initiate a new global trade negotiation. His successor, Clayton Yeutter, brought this goal to fruition. In September 1986, the delegation which he led to the GATT ministerial conference at Punta del Este won agreement to launch the "Uruguay Round" of multilateral trade talks, with services and agricultural trade—major US priorities—among the central agenda items.[12]

There remains the problem of domestic political timing: when to seek congressional backing. The administration will need new authority to conduct the round. The fast-track procedures, assuring expeditious legislative action to implement new nontariff barrier (NTB) agreements, expire in January 1988. But it is hardly promising politics to seek new trade authority while the trade deficit remains at stratospheric heights. Over the past fifteen years, the major legislative successes on trade policy (1973–74, 1979) have come under the opposite circumstances: at times when, largely as a consequence of prior decline in the dollar, the US trade balance was improving. So, too, did the actual negotiation of the final multilateral trade negotiation (MTN) agreements. The congressional trade explosion of 1985, on the other hand, took place in the context of record, and rapidly growing trade deficits.

In calendar year 1986, therefore, the administration understandably resisted congressional efforts to legislate on trade. Instead, it gave priority to macroeconomic and exchange rate steps like those discussed in chapter 9: bringing the dollar down further; and encouraging stronger economic growth stimulus by our major trading partners. It also continued its new aggressiveness on product-specific issues, especially attacking foreign-market barriers. The aim was to establish at long last the administration's credibility as defender of US trade interests, while buying time for exchange rate adjustment to affect the trade balance. This policy package had one grievous flaw—presidential and congressional failure, in practice, to mount

12. For comprehensive treatment of the substance of such a round and suggested priorities, see Gary Clyde Hufbauer and Jeffrey J. Schott, *Trading for Growth: The Next Round of Trade Negotiations*, POLICY ANALYSES IN INTERNATIONAL ECONOMICS 11 (Washington: Institute for International Economics, September 1985). See also C. Michael Aho and Jonathan David Aronson, *Trade Talks: America Better Listen!* (New York, NY: Council on Foreign Relations, 1985).

a serious attack on the federal budget deficit. Nonetheless, it did succeed in two important senses: there was further downward dollar adjustment, and there was no protectionist legislation.

There was also, however, no reduction in the trade deficit. By summer 1986 it had stopped growing, but was holding steady at a record annual rate—$145 billion on the traditional basis, over $170 billion with imports valued c.i.f. In economic terms, this was not surprising. Due to the J-curve effect, it normally takes at least 12 to 18 months for exchange rate changes to bring significant trade-balance improvement.[13] And there were reasons to believe that the lag this time might be greater: because the dollar had been misaligned so much, for so long; because even though it had peaked on February 1985, markets had no special reason to believe that the succeeding drop would prove sizeable and lasting until late fall, after the Group of Five initiative.[14]

But if the persistence of the deficit was explicable economically, it was an enormous burden politically. Against the logic of mainstream economics, and notwithstanding a heightened understanding of macroeconomic factors like the exchange rate, the merchandise trade imbalance is still widely seen on Capitol Hill as reflecting *trade* policy failure. Its persistence undercuts those who argue that nontrade responses are the proper policy cure. And even legislators who reject the trade deficit–trade policy link intellectually must cope with it politically, for record imports and sluggish exports mean more firms and workers hurt by trade, and fewer who are being helped. Until the deficit declines appreciably, until business people begin telling their senators and representatives that their own bottom lines are improving, the reception for any liberalizing trade bill is bound to be hostile. It will almost certainly be encumbered with major, trade-restrictive amendments: "process protectionism" like that in the 1986 House bill, and quite likely a new restrictive textile provision as well.

But a substantial shift in the trade balance could transform this political atmosphere. It could give new political life to long-received economic wisdom. Moreover, such an improvement can be expected over the next two years. Trade policy leaders should tailor their domestic strategy to this expectation. They should prepare to ride the wave of improved US trade

13. A weaker dollar has an immediate impact on the *volume* of trade, depressing imports and strengthening exports. Thus, it eases the plight of US producers of traded goods from the start. But because devaluation also raises the dollar price of imports, the net favorable impact on the dollar trade balance does not come until the drop in imports, together with the rise in exports, is sufficient to more than offset this price increase. This generally takes at least a year.

14. C. Fred Bergsten, "The Outlook for the Trade Deficit and for America as a Debtor Country." Statement before the Subcommittee on Trade, House Committee on Ways and Means, 24 September 1986; processed.

performance, but not force congressional action before this wave reaches the shore.

The administration should, therefore, *not seek authorization for the new Uruguay Round until there is a substantial, noticeable decline in the merchandise trade deficit.* The trend must be clear. The reduction must be significant. And it must reverse, in important part, the 1980–85 market-share losses of US producers of traded goods. For these three criteria to be met, *the deficit's annual rate will need to drop below $100 billion, for at least one quarter* (with imports measured c.i.f., since that is the number legislators now watch). *And the deficit will need to continue to fall, generating expectations of steadily improving US trade prospects.*

Renewal of Fast-Track Authority: The Case for Waiting

Why the threshold of $100 billion? The short answer is that no improvement that falls short of that level is likely to have the necessary political impact.

Research into the politics of economics suggests that what matters above all are *trends:* how players with influence see the direction in which critical variables are moving. Voters, for example, are affected not so much by the absolute level of their income as by changes over the past 12 months. Politicians recognize this fact, and respond to it.[15] This suggests, by analogy, that the same 12-digit number that spelled trade disaster when we crossed it going up could come to symbolize hope when we pass it going down.

The prospect that this will be viewed as a positive development is enhanced by the fact that getting there from here (from the trade position of the United States in late 1986) will require a notable improvement. Not once since the beginning of 1985 has the notoriously volatile monthly trade deficit statistic dropped below $8.3 billion, the number necessary to meet our target. For the first nine months of 1986, it averaged over $14 billion. Thus, getting back down below $100 billion would represent a nontrivial change.

For business and labor, the real change would be even greater. For the improvement in the dollar trade balance would come on top of the volume trade gains they are already experiencing from the better exchange rate. Precision in such matters is impossible, but projections indicate that reaching

---

15. Edward R. Tufte finds "yearly change in real disposable income per capita" to be the economic indicator best linked to voting in congressional elections, arguing that such a trend measures citizens' perceptions of the recent past and hence their expectations for the future under current political leadership. For his findings, and a discussion of other work in this area, see his *Political Control of the Economy* (Princeton, NJ: Princeton University Press, 1978), ch. 5, and "Determinants of the Outcomes of Midterm Congressional Elections," *American Political Science Review*, Vol. 69, no. 3 (September 1975), pp. 812-26.

$100 billion would have a marked impact on one useful, simple measure of import pressure, the ratio of imports (price-deflated) to US goods production. This ratio, which shot up from 11.2 percent to 15.7 percent between 1980 and 1985, would drop to about 13.6 percent with the trade deficit at about the $100 billion rate. The ratio for exports, which plummeted from 13.9 percent to 10.3 percent over 1980–85, would recover to around 12.1 percent.[16] Both exporters and import-competers, then, would regain roughly half of what they lost, in real trade-competitive position, during the devastating first half of the decade. Once they have rebounded this much, and expect to gain more, they should send to Capitol Hill messages very different from those they delivered in 1985! And they will begin to see gain, not just pain, in a new trade round.

The problem is that such improvements will take time. The trade deficit should begin shrinking very soon, but its annual rate is unlikely to drop below the $100 billion threshold before the closing months of 1987, at the very earliest. More probably, it will not reach this point until sometime in 1988. If the administration, as urged here, waits until then to seek renewal of fast-track authority, there will likely be a gap, a time period when USTR is negotiating abroad with no statutory assurance of quick legislative action on agreements reached.

Could our negotiators live with such a gap? With foreign governments, there could be difficulty: representatives of our trading partners would certainly hold back major concessions until they felt confident that their US counterparts could deliver on their end of a deal. But the first two years of the new round are unlikely to produce major results.[17] During the early,

---

16. These percentages draw upon a projection by Stephen Marris, based on his model in *Deficits and the Dollar,* but employed for purposes here as a rough indicator of US import and export volumes associated with meeting the interim $100 billion deficit target posited here, assuming exchange rates like those of August–September 1986. Marris projects, under specified assumptions, a calendar 1988 US trade deficit of $83.1 billion (balance of payments basis), which corresponds roughly to $100 billion with imports measured c.i.f. Using the model's estimates of real changes in national product, exports, and imports, and assuming that goods production retains its current share of GNP, merchandise exports (in 1972 dollars) would rise from $80.3 billion in 1985 to $107.5 billion in 1988, and imports would drop, over the same period, from $123.0 billion to $120.7 billion. Projected price-deflated goods production rises from $783.3 billion in 1985 to $886 billion in 1988.

For discussion of such ratios in earlier years, and statistical sources, see chapter 8.

17. It is possible that a free trade agreement with Canada will be concluded and ready for legislative action in 1988. There could be serious political difficulty if US implementation action were not completed before the next Canadian election, which must take place no later than September 1989, and the expiration date for the general fast-track authority applies also to such bilateral deals. It might therefore be necessary, if general action were delayed, to seek a special extension of the fast-track deadline limited to bilateral free trade agreements, or specifically to the Canada case.

necessarily exploratory phase of the talks, foreign officials ought to be willing to proceed on the basis of an understanding that US authorities will seek authority when trade balance improvement vindicates their basic approach and reduces the protectionist price they will have to pay.

More difficult will be making such a strategy work at home. Congress could refuse to accept the administration's timetable and move a trade bill anyway, as the House did in 1986. To pursue the approach suggested above, the President and the US Trade Representative will need congressional cooperation: not just of House Democrats, but of similarly minded senators of both political persuasions, legislators whose trade experience in the 1980s has made them enormously skeptical of both administration trade serious-ness and likely trade results. Administration rhetoric like that of 1986, attacking not just the legislative product but legislators' motives, would surely prove counterproductive in 1987 and 1988. Moreover, USTR Yeutter can build the political foundations for future favorable action only if he has a clear presidential mandate to work with key trade senators and represen-tatives, during the preliminaries as well as the main legislative event.

This suggests that the two branches might well begin 1987 with strikingly different, but not necessarily incompatible postures. That of Congress would be skeptical, one of "show me." Legislators have lived through years of egregious trade imbalances and what they see as weak administration trade leadership. They will have to be shown that the United States can hold its own it today's world while keeping to the postwar liberal trade tradition. As the One-hundredth Congress of 1987–88 comes to Washington next January, the trade balance will still be very bad; its members will believe in its improvement when they see it, not before. In the meantime, major hearings could explore not just liberal trade strategies like that spelled out here, but radical alternatives. The administration would participate actively in such hearings, using them as a forum to make the case for its broad trade strategy and the value of the Uruguay Round. USTR would also seek congressional advice on how best to engage the private sector in the Round.

The administration posture would be that the trade balance was going to improve. Authorizing legislation for the new round was not immediately necessary, and it would be preferable if Congress waited: until trade balance improvement vindicated the exchange rate emphasis, and until there was time to make the full case, with private interests as well as legislators, for the new trade round. But USTR would, of course, need extension of fast-track authority at some point. If Congress passed an otherwise acceptable bill including such a provision, the President would happily sign it. But he would defer submitting an administration bill.

Such a posture would give USTR and the administration a chance to begin rebuilding trade relations with Capitol Hill, to develop the sort of ties that Strauss and Brock had when *they* needed them, in 1979 and 1984. It might lead to fast-track extension sometime in 1988, or this might be left as a priority task for the new administration that took over in 1989. The legislators' posture would give them full opportunity to put forward their own proposals, represent their constitutents, and express their reservations. In the end, they would extract some price for the new negotiating authority. But the greater the improvement in the trade situation faced by American firms, the less protectionist that price would be. And the reduced intensity of trade-political pressures would be welcomed at both ends of Pennsylvania Avenue.

For this strategy to succeed, the trade balance will, of course, need to improve—significantly, steadily. Projections as of September 1986, based on exchange rates of that date, suggest that it is likely to do so—but barely enough to reach the $100 billion mark. Thereafter, the deficit could even rise again. To prevent this—surely a disaster for trade and trade politics—will require a further push on "nontrade" policy measures discussed in chapter 9.

But assuming such a push, US trade policymakers can look forward to a somewhat brighter political future. Better trade times will be on the way. Legislative initiatives should be timed to make the most of that coming good news.

As it takes steps to right the macroeconomic imbalance and to prepare for global trade negotiations, the US government will also be pursuing bilateral trade negotiations, particularly with Japan. Here, too, the need is to tilt talks in the trade-expanding direction wherever possible.

High-Technology Issues: Sectoral Reciprocity?

A particular challenge is posed by the growing trade in high-technology products such as telecommunications equipment and semiconductors. Increasingly there are calls for "sectoral reciprocity," linking Japanese access to the American market to the openness of Japanese markets to comparable US products. Senator Danforth has sought to apply this principle to telecommunications trade, linking what other nations' firms can sell here with what ours can sell there. Legislation to this end has won committee approval in the Senate, and was incorporated in the ominbus House trade bill of 1986. And the Reagan administration completed, in July, a very difficult, year-long bilateral semiconductor negotiation with an agreement to end below-cost sales by Japanese firms in the US market, and to increase market access for US products in Japan.

Carried to its logical extreme, "sectoral reciprocity" makes little trade sense. If negotiators must limit themselves to a series of narrow bargains within sectors—balancing US import restrictions on wine against those of the European Community, for example—the chance for broad, mutually beneficial, cross-industry trade-offs disappears, and with it the prospect for major trade liberalization.

There is, however, a strong circumstantial case for selective application of the "sectoral reciprocity" principle in negotiations with Japan. If one believes, for example, that industries like semiconductors and telecommunications are important to future US industrial strength, and that the ability to sell in the second biggest national market is an important contributor to their strength, then it follows that these products should have priority in our bilateral trade talks. In the quest for leverage over the Tokyo government on these issues, the question arises of how to affect the interests of Fujitsu or Nippon Electric or Hitachi, integrated electronics firms that will have an important influence on Japanese policy. Generally speaking, they will have no interest in opening their home markets to competitive imports unless failure to do so is likely to cost them sales in the lucrative *American* market. Thus, a capacity to threaten market closure here can be important in achieving market openness across the Pacific. This certainly proved true in the just-concluded semiconductor talks, although the long-term effectiveness of that agreement remains to be proven.

The risk of sectoral reciprocity, as William R. Cline has pointed out, is that if we actually come to deliver on such threats, the likely outcome is greater protection and lower welfare in both countries.[18] Or it may lead to a market-sharing, cartel-type arrangement, as critics charged the United States and Japan with concluding on semiconductors in 1986. There is no way to eliminate such risks, but adroit political leadership can minimize them by the timely selection of subjects. The 1985 Market-Oriented Sector-Specific (MOSS) talks with Japan employed at least a tacit threat of trade sanctions on telecommunications, given congressional concerns. And five years earlier, the United States won its initial concessions from Japan on telecommunications by threatening to deny Japanese firms the right to bid on US government contracts under the just-completed MTN government procurement code.[19]

---

18. *Reciprocity: A New Approach to World Trade Policy*, POLICY ANALYSES IN INTERNATIONAL ECONOMICS 2 (Washington: Institute for International Economics, September 1982).

19. Timothy J. Curran, "Politics and High Technology: The NTT Case," in *Coping with U.S.-Japanese Economic Conflicts*, edited by I. M. Destler and Hideo Sato (Lexington, Mass.: Lexington Books, 1982), pp. 231–39.

One outgrowth of the "reciprocity" movement is the requirement, in the Trade and Tariff Act of 1984, for the USTR to report every year on the significant foreign barriers to American products. The first *Annual Report on National Trade Estimates* was released on 30 October 1985 (Washington: USTR).

Revitalizing the Private Advisory Committees

An important instrument of USTR leadership for both global and bilateral talks would be a rejuvenated private sector advisory committee system. This network of agricultural, business, and labor representatives was important to Robert Strauss in building consensus support for the MTN.

But it became harder to make the committees work effectively thereafter, without the target of a grand central negotiation. In part, it reflected increased use of committee positions for second-order political patronage, to reward faithful partisans. But it also reflected a tendency in the first-term Reagan administration to wait for trade issues to come to it, to pursue not just laissez-faire economics but laissez-faire politics as well. On a few negotiations, like high-technology trade talks with Japan, committees of business representatives were regularly and usefully engaged. But in cases like the steel industry's drive for import relief, protection seekers within the industry were allowed to define the issue; by the time the administration became really active, these interests had defined the policy question not as whether to increase protection but as how and how much.

Effective use of advisory committees to balance such pressures requires executive officials to take the initiative, anticipating the emergence of major trade-restrictive proposals and developing ties to a range of business interests so that policy is not captured by any single one. It involves bringing in not just producers of goods but users and marketers as well, those who benefit from imports as well as those who suffer from them.

There is also a need to structure the advisory process around actual decisions. Not only will this encourage trade officials and group members to take the process seriously, but it will also encourage officials and business leaders to place the appropriate, representative people on the committees in the first place. Fortunately, the inauguration of the Uruguay Round offers an opportunity to revitalize the committees and their role in the trade policy process.

Policy Tools: New Approaches to Trade Adjustment

Just as trade policymakers need opportunities to expand our markets abroad, they need alternatives at home for firms and workers fighting losing battles against import competition.

In principle, of course, the plight of a worker displaced by foreign competition is no different from that of one whose job disappears because his firm moves to Texas or South Carolina. In practice, however, "foreign" competition creates pressure for government intervention, while domestic competition does not. When there are no alternatives, that intervention is likely to be restrictions on imports. Thus, the argument for treating trade-generated displacement differently is that our political system treats trade differently.

In the 1960s and 1970s, the United States recognized this difference by establishing and expanding the program known as Trade Adjustment Assistance (TAA). This broadened support for major trade legislation, and provided Presidents Gerald R. Ford and Jimmy Carter something to give industries like shoes and automobiles while denying or deferring import relief. TAA did not, however, prove very effective in retraining workers and helping them move out of the trade-injured industry. Many auto workers, for example, seem to have used the program to maintain an income near that to which they had become accustomed, while waiting for their old companies to hire them back! No wonder many of TAA's former congressional champions turned skeptical, or that it proved an easy target for the budget-cutting initiative of the incoming Reagan administration. Since 1981, the authorizing legislation has twice been extended, but funding and eligibility have been curtailed.

TAA's demise was unfortunate for two important reasons. First of all, government *should* be seeking ways to facilitate workers' adjustment to economic change. These workers are losers in a broader international competitive process which brings large overall benefits to their nation. In return, that nation ought to give some attention to helping these workers train for and find other jobs. Public officials have not found this easy to do, but the federal government should continue to experiment in this area, together with private firms and state agencies. A moderately financed TAA program can carry out such experimentation, and approaches that prove successful can then be extended also to workers displaced by home-grown economic change.

The second reason to regret TAA's decline is political: it dilutes pressure for trade restrictions, and thus it strengthens our national capacity to pursue open trade policies, which produce gains for the nation far greater than TAA's costs.

But how could one hope to fund trade adjustment at more than a token level, at a time when the Gramm-Rudman-Hollings amendment is threatening the budgets of far more established programs? It might be possible to find enough money to help trade-displaced employees of relatively small industries, but to deal with the larger cases—textiles, steel, automobiles—a new departure is clearly required.

One promising approach, developed in detail by Gary Clyde Hufbauer and Howard F. Rosen,[20] applies particularly to those industries to which trade protection is also being provided. They would channel revenues from tariffs to the financing of adjustment programs. If the protection were in the form of quotas, these would be auctioned off and the proceeds devoted to the same purpose.[21] The aim would be not to invest public funds in new production facilities but to facilitate downsizing, a movement of resources out of the industry. This approach is easiest to apply in cases of new protection. By opting to participate in such a program, firms and workers would get temporary import relief, but it would be degressive, diminishing over time. And they would have to choose between this sort of comprehensive but temporary protection and other remedies such as the unfair trade statutes.

Proposals containing elements of such an approach have been put forward on Capitol Hill. As part of a comprehensive Senate initiative, John Heinz (R-Pa.) has introduced legislation amending Section 201 of the Trade Act of 1974 (the escape clause) to provide an adjustment option. An industry could accompany its petition for trade relief with a revitalization plan developed by a tripartite labor-business-government panel; if the USITC found that trade injury existed and that the plan offered was "likely to result in . . . sufficient adjustment," the president would have to approve it—and institute the commission's trade-relief plan—unless he persuaded Congress to enact an alternative.[22] The omnibus House bill of 1986 included a similar provision. Senators William V. Roth (R-Del.) and Daniel Patrick Moynihan (D-NY) have addressed the funding side by proposing that trade adjustment assistance be financed by a surtax of 1 percent applied to all US imports.[23]

The political risk of such a program, addressed to (and shaped by) a particular industry or sector, is that of capture by antiadjustment industry and labor interests, who might convert it into an instrument of indefinite protection and support. It would then no longer facilitate an orderly outflow

---

20. *Trade Policy for Troubled Industries*, POLICY ANALYSES IN INTERNATIONAL ECONOMICS 15 (Washington: Institute for International Economics, March 1986), ch. 5. See also Robert Z. Lawrence and Robert E. Litan, *Saving Free Trade: A Pragmatic Approach* (Washington: Brookings Institution, 1986).

21. A full analysis of this subject will appear in C. Fred Bergsten and Jeffrey J. Schott, *Auction Quotas and US Trade Policy* (Washington: Institute for International Economics, forthcoming).

22. Comments by Heinz on submission of S. 1863, in *Congressional Record*, 20 November 1985, p. S15990. An earlier version of the Heinz proposal appears in *Congressional Record*, 18 March 1983.

23. The Roth-Moynihan bill is S. 1544, the proposed Trade Adjustment Assistance Reform and Extension Act of 1985.

of resources from the industry; it would instead become a means to remain uncompetitively large with perpetual government help. European adjustment programs have frequently experienced such capture. One means of resisting this tendency would be to insure that antiprotection interests, including users of an industry's products, were represented in the development and oversight of any adjustment program. Also important is active monitoring by executive branch trade leaders determined to limit trade restrictions—leaders committed to the proposition that, in the words of one trade authority, "Our laws should be lubricants, rather than sand, in the gears of change."[24] This is another argument for housing executive branch leadership in the White House-based USTR, rather than in a department that would be vulnerable to special-interest pressure and disadvantaged in mobilizing counterweights.

By providing a comprehensive alternative, such adjustment approaches might reverse the trend lamented in chapter 6: the use of "the rules" by potent industries not to obtain the requisite statutory relief but to create a political crisis and force a negotiated, market-sharing solution. "The rules" have failed to address the adjustment needs of major industries like textiles, steel, and autos, and they have not "depoliticized" the process of trade relief. If petitioners were in fact required to choose among remedies, and if by entering the comprehensive adjustment track they renounced the right to initiate countervailing duty or antidumping suits, this problem could be diminished though assuredly not eliminated.[25] In particularly egregious subsidy or dumping cases, it would still be possible for suits to be "self-initiated" by the administration, as authorized in the Trade Agreements Act of 1979 and undertaken recently, in selected cases, by the Reagan administration.

In balancing pressures for import relief in specific industry cases, one final device would be most helpful: an analytic agency, free of short-run dependence on either the White House or the Congress, whose job would be to measure, as objectively as possible, the real impact of present and prospective cases of trade protection on all major affected US interests and on the economy as a whole.

As an operating agency, USTR could not give priority to such analysis, nor would the proposed USTA sitting under it. The US International Trade Commission must, under present law, limit its injury investigations to the petitioning industry, although it can and does consider broader effects when

---

24. Peter D. Ehrenhaft, "New Directions for the Trade Laws," *George Washington Journal of International Law and Economics*, vol. 18, no. 3 (1985), p. 706.

25. A precedent is the Carter administration's trigger price mechanism for steel protection, which was conditioned on the industry's withdrawing its antidumping suits, and whose enforcement was suspended when they resubmitted them.

it decides what form of trade relief to recommend. One approach would be to widen the USITC's mandate so it would be required to publish a more comprehensive assessment of the impact of import restrictions, as well as the industry-specific findings on which its injury determination is based. This would include, but go beyond, the proposal of Senator John H. Chafee (R-RI) that the USITC evaluate the impact of trade relief on consumers.

If it were judged difficult for the USITC to pursue such contrasting analytic tacks simultaneously, an alternative would be to create a new Trade Barrier Assessment Agency. Its task would be to issue annual, public reports on the extent and impact of existing US trade restrictions, and ad hoc reports when specific new cases arose. A model would be the Industries Assistance Commission of Australia, which has performed this function with high credibility in that country.[26] (It has not, however, kept that nation from pursuing relatively protectionist trade policies.)

In Defense of Trade Brokering

In the end, much will depend on the quality and assertiveness of the trade leadership of the executive branch. Greater decentralization and activism on Capitol Hill have increased the USTR's burden and his need to keep the initiative. To cope with trade policy pressures effectively requires building confidence in the system, so that it is responsive to trade-created problems even when resisting the relief sought. It requires knowing the petitioners and their political patrons.

As in other policy areas, brokering in the trade sphere is not an end in itself, but a means to maintaining relatively open US policies. It is an appropriate means for trade because achieving this goal is importantly a matter of avoiding or limiting government interventions in the US economy. Such a trade-expanding purpose is what gives officials a basis for taking the initiative and a capacity to deal with specific interests without being engulfed by them. If they act as if government policy is simply a function of the balance of outside pressures, they will invite still more pressure, together with contempt for their weakness. But if they demonstrate commitment to this purpose, and skill in its pursuit, they will command respect—as have, in fact, many US trade officials in the half century since Cordell Hull.

Their posture should be one of knowing where they want the trade policy train to go, and one of political capacity to steer it in that direction, together

---

26. Lawrence B. Krause, "Australia's Comparative Advantage in International Trade," in *The Australian Economy: A View from the North,* edited by Richard E. Caves and Lawrence B. Krause (Washington: Brookings Institution, 1984), p. 290.

with readiness to plan and execute the journey in ways that maximize the gain and minimize the pain for special interests. Only then will private actors find it to their advantage to climb on board. Only with a balance of strength and responsiveness can trade leaders cope effectively with the inevitable pressures of an internationalized American economy.

In the end, there is no attractive alternative to the classic, liberal-leaning trade policy that was pursued by those who shaped the old American trade policy-making system. Now, as in earlier decades, we need institutions designed to limit and balance restrictive pressures while leading the United States and the world toward a more open and mutually rewarding international economy. Yet these institutions must be adapted to changes in our economics and our politics. If we are to maintain the benefits of trade and the stimulus of a relatively open international system, we must continue to find ways of coping with trade pressures, ways of converting import-reducing issues to export-expanding issues when we can, and putting together limited protection packages when we must.

Finally, if Americans are to support continuation of such policies, they must believe that they can compete and prosper in today's difficult trade world.

Most critical to restoring such a belief are the macroeconomic measures stressed in chapter 9, for only when our imports no longer dwarf our exports will it be possible to sell the notion that we are "holding our own." Also important, however, is a sustained effort by government and business leaders to put forward a broad, protrade rationale that can play in the domestic arena.

The rationale would go something like this. The world is a tough place, with a great deal of unfairness (here as well as overseas), but:

☐ *America is competing and can compete with any nation in the world*, as long as our macroeconomic policies keep currency relationships in reasonable balance.

☐ *The way we will keep competing is by maintaining a dynamic, flexible economy that rewards our industrial winners, not our losers*

☐ *In the long run, the more we import the more we can export, and this means a better life for Americans*; therefore, we should keep our economic borders as open as possible and press other nations to do likewise.

☐ *To those hurt by the economic change that trade will bring, we should offer aid to facilitate adjustment, but not lock ourselves into outmoded production facilities or overpriced products.*

With persistence and our share of luck, we Americans can hold our own in a relatively open trade world. We ought to be able to handle our internal politics so as to make that happy outcome possible. And day by day, as they grapple with the specifics of trade politics, executive branch and congressional trade leaders could do worse than bear in mind the admonition with which E. E. Schattschneider closed his book about Smoot-Hawley 51 years ago: "To manage pressures is to govern; to let pressures run wild is to abdicate."[27]

27. *Politics, Pressure and The Tariff* (New York, NY: Prentice-Hall, Inc., 1935), p. 293.

Appendices

Appendix A 1984 and 1985:
The Leadership Difference

In October 1984, just a month before the fall election, Congress managed to act comprehensively on trade. The Senate and the House pulled together a range of pending proposals in what became the Trade and Tariff Act of 1984. Even expert observers were surprised, first by the emergence of the broad trade bill, and then by the capacity of congressional trade leaders, working with the Reagan administration, to eliminate most (though not all) of the restrictive provisions that had passed one house or the other.

In the spring of 1985, Washington was again surprised, but this time by the sudden explosion of congressional concern about trade and the drive to enact protectionist legislation.

Chapter 4 treats this contrast, and offers as one important explanation the exceptional effectiveness of executive branch trade leadership in the first case, and its virtual absence in the second. This explanation is important to the broader argument developed in this book: about the erosion of trade policy-making institutions, and the consequent need for more centralized and politically sensitive executive branch trade institutions. By telling the story of 1984 and 1985 at greater length, this appendix offers added documentation for this conclusion, and provides in the process some new information about the trade-political events of those two frenetic years.[1]

The Trade and Tariff Act of 1984

The broad context was forbidding. The US trade deficit continued to grow, with all projections for 1984 now exceeding $100 billion. The causes were macroeconomic, most notably the soaring dollar, whose continued strength

---

1. The following pages draw substantially on confidential interviews with persons involved in the enactment of the Trade and Tariff Act of 1984, and to a lesser degree on similar discussions with trade players of 1985.

virtually assured that this deficit would stay very large at least through 1986. But the result put advocates of open trade very much on the defensive.

As the overall trade picture grew bleaker, as the Ninety-eighth Congress moved toward adjournment, both House and Senate wrestled with a range of relatively modest legislative issues. For the liberal trade community, there was one "must" item, action on trade preferences for developing countries, or "GSP." In the Trade Act of 1974, the United States had, pursuant to an international agreement, granted these countries duty-free access to our market for a range of their products for a 10-year period. This period ended on 3 January 1985.

Few executive branch or congressional trade specialists were enthusiastic about preferences, which constituted a departure from the nondiscriminatory, most-favored-nation (MFN) principle of treating all countries alike. Moreover, GSP had precious little support among American economic interests, even though, due to exclusion of sensitive articles (for example, textiles, shoes) and ceilings on benefits available to any one country in a specific product, only 3 percent of total US imports were affected. But Third World nations attached great symbolic importance to GSP's continuation. It would therefore be very difficult for the United States to negotiate with the newly industrializing countries on matters increasingly important to interests here—copyright protection, access to *their* markets—if preferences were simply allowed to die.

The prospects for passing GSP extension on its own were dim: organized labor opposed it, particularly for the "big three" newly industrializing countries (NICs)—Korea, Taiwan, and Hong Kong—most of whose products were clearly competitive in the United States without special treatment. In fact, so unpopular was the cause that the administration was unable, in 1983, to find a single House member to sponsor its GSP renewal proposal. So, the House Ways and Means Committee deferred action. There was on the table, however, a trade vehicle more popular not only in the Congress (it had *163* House sponsors) but in the Reagan White House as well: a bill authorizing negotiation of a bilateral free trade agreement with Israel.

On 31 July, with the support and encouragement of US Trade Representative William E. Brock, the Senate Finance Committee voted to join the two with a number of other trade proposals, and to attach the whole package on the floor as an amendment to a minor tariff-adjustment bill (HR 3398) already passed by the other chamber. Such legerdemain was necessary because trade bills, being "revenue bills" under the Constitution, were supposed to originate in the House of Representatives. But internal divisions and labor opposition had kept the Ways and Means Committee from moving. Thus, if there was to be broad trade legislation in 1984, particularly legislation including GSP, the Senate would have to go first.

Trade Subcommittee Chairman John C. Danforth (R-Mo.) began pressing the Senate Majority Leader, Howard H. Baker, Jr. (R-Tenn.), to give him floor time to bring up the bill. Baker was skeptical. Danforth had not been able to negotiate a "unanimous consent" agreement limiting time for debate or amendments that might be proposed. The leader feared, therefore, that Danforth would not be able to maintain control on the floor, and that his bill would be tied up procedurally or loaded with protectionist baubles for a wide range of industries. But due to a House-Senate-administration impasse on budget legislation, there was floor time available in mid-September, so Baker gave Danforth his chance. The tacit understanding, however, was that if he lost control—if opponents were able to threaten indefinite delay, or attach major protectionist provisions that could not be shed in conference—then the bill would be pulled off the floor, never to return.

The Senate took up the bill on 17 September, and Danforth had precious little room for maneuver. He had been given one floor day and had reason to anticipate a second. But he had to keep things moving, avoid any impasse. The only way to do this was to bargain with almost every protection-seeking interest: from copper and bromine producers to winemakers to textile manufacturers and even, at the behest of Minority Leader Robert C. Byrd (D-W.Va.), manufacturers of ferroalloy products. In one particularly egregious case, an effort by certain West Coast fishing interests to overturn an unfavorable USITC decision, the Senate did reject, by 73 to 22, a proposal to raise the tariff on water-packed tuna from 6 percent to 35 percent. But the typical pattern was to bargain, in a manner at least faintly reminiscent of Smoot-Hawley. Wine interests, in fact, won acceptance of a proposal by Senator Pete Wilson (R-Cal.) allowing producers of grapes to seek quasi-judicial remedies in *wine* import cases. Not only was this contrary to GATT rules, which stipulated that only producers of a like product could claim injury from imports. It was also clearly harmful to the export interests of US agriculture, since the European Community, the target of the provision, was likely to retaliate. But farm lobbies were in disarray, with some deferring to California interests in this issue, others apparently taken by surprise.

The bargaining dragged on. Six amendments were added to the committee bill on Monday, 14 on Tuesday. With the grant of additional floor time, there were 12 more on Wednesday and 11 on Thursday. The typical pattern was to negotiate for flexibility in language, with the expectation that unwanted provisions could be further diluted (or deleted) when the bill went to conference with the House. But the apparent ease with which proposals were attached to the bill did not please trade specialists like Senator John Heinz (R-Pa.), who had spent months and years developing the trade law reform proposals which were added to the bill in modified, prenegotiated form. Conversely, it favored those like wine-amendment sponsor Wilson who played individualistic hardball.

Danforth carried the main bargaining burden, working with ranking Democratic subcommittee member Lloyd Bentsen (D-Tex.). On the two latter days, they were aided by the presence of US Trade Representative William Brock, who had just returned from South America and who, as a former senator, had the right of access to floor deliberations. He exploited this to join aggressively in the legislative bargaining process. (For example, he sought, where possible, to substitute letters of commitment from the administration for statutory changes: a key success came when this strategy assuaged the concerns of the US textile industry about the Israel free trade agreement.)

Two other factors improved the legislation's prospects. One was the administration announcement on Tuesday, the second day of the Senate trade debate, that it would seek to negotiate restraint agreements with steel-exporting nations with the aim of reducing imports to about 18.5 percent of the US market (20.2 percent including semifinished products). Brock said this figure was simply a target, but steel leaders coming from a meeting with President Reagan referred to it as a commitment. When the trade bill was promptly amended to give the administration legal authority to enforce such restraints, it gained one important additional source of support.

The second factor, harder to explain, was the ineffectiveness of organized labor. Labor could have caused great difficulty for Danforth and Brock, perhaps even destroyed the bill's prospects, by exploiting its procedural vulnerability, proposing attractive amendments and undertaking to debate them at length if they were not accepted. In fact, labor did just about nothing. The UAW, preoccupied with a major wage negotiation, did not push domestic content for autos. The AFL-CIO was essentially inactive, according to numerous inside reports, until the final day of the Senate debate, when union representatives suddenly contracted their Hill allies and expressed alarm at what they suddenly perceived was happening.

One reason labor was slow to move was its prior success in keeping trade legislation off the floor. The Senate operates, on most procedural matters, by unanimous consent, which means that a single member can delay consideration of a bill to which he objects. And one of labor's Senate allies, Howard M. Metzenbaum (D-Ohio) had placed a hold on HR 3398 and maintained it for much of the year. Labor had also gotten holds placed on Danforth's reciprocity bill in 1982 and 1983. But it is hard for a senator to keep such a hold on indefinitely, particularly if another of his key constituencies is interested in having the bill considered. For Metzenbaum, the American Jewish community—which wanted the Israeli free trade title enacted—met that description. So Metzenbaum lifted his objection to the Senate's taking up the bill.

Labor was plainly unprepared for this: despite the wide-open procedural situation on the floor, not a single labor amendment was proposed during the four-day debate. Nor did labor representatives perform one of the basic lobbying tasks, preparing information and argumentation for sympathizers so they were armed to do battle for labor interests.

Labor did not, of course, need to push all the items on its wish list. It might make sense for the UAW to hold off on a "domestic content" amendment, since the vote would likely be less favorable in the Senate than it had been in the House, and might in any case embarrass the labor-endorsed Democratic presidential standard-bearer, Walter F. Mondale, who (notwithstanding his endorsement of that legislation) was seeking to limit his national identification with protectionist causes. But other proposals cherished by labor had broader potential support: eliminating trade references for the "big three" East Asian NICs, for example, or deleting provisions aimed at facilitating direct foreign investment by US firms. Even if majorities were unavailable on these, senators sympathetic to labor might have threatened to drag out the debate indefinitely—the one thing the bill's managers could not abide—unless their concerns were satisfied. But labor simply did not have its act together.[2] In fact, the GSP renewal as passed by the Senate (and as later enacted into law) was less restrictive than the authority originally granted in 1974.

So aided by astute management and labor neglect, the bill survived, passing the Senate late Thursday, the fourth day of debate, by a vote of 96 to 0. The margin reflected also the number of interests that had been bought off, at least temporarily, in the bill itself or through agreements negotiated on the side. These included provisions or understandings aimed at protecting producers of steel, footwear, copper, ferroalloys, wine, textiles, bromine, and dairy products. An alarmed *Washington Post* lambasted the result in an editorial entitled "The Anti-Trade Bill":

The losers in every major trade case of the past year—the copper producers, the shoemakers, the wine producers—have managed to insert language to try to win in Congress what they lost in litigation. . . . the wine industry . . . wants protection but can't meet the current law's first requirement— to show that imports are actually hurting it. The bill would change the law to say that the wine makers don't have to show that they are being hurt; they would only have to show that their suppliers—the perenially distressed grape growers—need to sell more grapes. . . .

---

2. One close observer, paraphrasing John L. Lewis who had said labor's primary goal was to "organize the unorganized," suggested that labor's problem on trade was inability to "organize the organized": to bring together, behind a viable trade legislative strategy, labor's considerable political assets. One cause of this failure was thin trade staffing at AFL-CIO headquarters. Another factor was labor's tendency to take a strong position and stick to it rather than seek compromise. Hence, for example, domestic content was not used as a lever to extract an administration (or a Japanese) commitment to continue restraints on auto imports after their scheduled expiration in March 1985.

There was originally some good legislation in this bill. . . . but it has long since been grievously outweighed by its burden of bad amendments. If the bill gets to President Reagan, he will have a clear and urgent responsibility to let it go no farther.[3]

But the Congress was now moving. As the Senate moved forward with a bill containing two reasonably popular items—authority to negotiate with Israel and authority to enforce steel restraints—the logjam at Ways and Means was broken. The Thursday following, 27 September, that committee reported out four separate trade bills: GSP renewal, US-Israel free trade, "steel import stabilization," and "wine equity." Six days later, the House passed each of these separately, defeating in the process, by a surprisingly wide 233 to 174 margin, a Gephardt amendment that would have eliminated preferences for the big three NICs. It then attached the four bills as amendments to the Senate-passed HR 3398. The House also attached several previously enacted bills, the most important being the Trade Remedies Reform Act developed by Trade Subcommittee Chairman Sam M. Gibbons, so that they would go to conference as well. Interestingly, the domestic content bill was not among them, one reason being that Ways and Means— which had the dominant conference role—had opposed it both substantively and procedurally.

At this point, time was very, very short: the target for sine die adjournment of the Ninety-eighth Congress was the coming weekend. While the House bill was making its way to the floor, there had been—as one would expect— preliminary Senate-House-administration meetings discussing whether a compromise satisfactory to all three parties was feasible. Danforth and Robert J. Dole (R-Kan.), Chairman of the full Finance Committee, were basically administration allies: they were willing (even in some instances eager) to give up most product-specific protectionist provisions. The problem was that, on most of the other substantive issues—trade remedies, the formula for extending preferences, key details on Israeli free trade—they needed the House to yield. What could House representatives get in return? What, among the matters to be resolved in the conference, could they claim credit for, justifying concessions on other matters?

The answer was to be found, it soon became clear, in the provisions on steel. Ways and Means Chairman Rostenkowski had pushed through his committee and the House a bill which, in the name of implementing Reagan's just-announced "national policy for the steel industry," incorporated two proposals advocated by Mondale and other Democratic critics of the President's action. One was a lower market share for imports, 17 percent

---

3. *Washington Post*, 28 September 1984.

as opposed to the administration's 18.5 percent. The second, strongly pushed by steel labor, was an adjustment requirement for steel firms: they had to reinvest all net cash flow in steel operations, and allocate 1 percent of earnings to worker retraining. Could something close to these be accepted by the administration? In early meetings in Dole's Capitol "cubbyhole" office with Brock and Danforth, and thereafter with the two senators plus Rostenkowski and Gibbons, the Ways and Means Chairman made it clear that without steel language along these lines, there would be no bill. Trade Representative Brock then signaled the administration's reluctant assent: with modifications, they could live with the steel adjustment provisions. Gibbons indicated, in turn, that he would be willing to drop the most controversial trade-remedy law changes in the House bill, provisions the administration considered unacceptable.

Still, time was very short. After a night of staff preparation, the formal House-Senate conference began Thursday, 4 October, at 3 P.M.[4] The target adjournment day was 5 October, and no votes could be taken after 6 P.M. on account of the Jewish holiday of Yom Kippur. Two very different bills had to be reconciled and a compromise statute agreed to. Dole, a protagonist in the budget struggle that was tying up the Senate, was not present when the session opened and it was the Senate's turn to chair the conference, so Rostenkowski nominated Danforth—who had no experience at running such a meeting. He commenced to play that role in front of four hundred or so lobbyists, and after winning agreement that any issue, once closed, would not be reopened, he proposed that, as previously arranged with Gibbons, they drop one controversial trade-remedy change and take the teeth from another. But one Senator not party to the bargaining objected, at least until he could see the language. Fearing that such visible disagreement would invite the heavy lobbying they were working to avoid, the conferees quickly moved their ostensibly open session to a room in the Capitol so small that, as one participant remembers it, the "public" audience was limited to two pool reporters and one to three others, including, as it turned out, the American Iron and Steel Institute representative.

Most issues were quickly settled on the basis of prior consultations among members and staff. But some remaining, essentially second-order matters proved tricky. One was the structure of the GSP title. The two bills were philosophically similar, with both seeking to increase administration discretion and, in some instances, maximum benefits in order to give the

---

4. The conference was originally scheduled to begin at noon, but the Senate had met very late for the two previous nights due to bitter conflicts on the omnibus continuing resolution that was funding most government activities for the year: until 2:38 A.M. Wednesday, and then until 9:32 A.M. Thursday. So the senators sought postponement in order to get some sleep.

United States bargaining leverage with recipient countries. This created a modest constituency for GSP among those interests who sought changes in NIC policies (for example, concerning copyright protection). But the approaches of the two chambers differed markedly in detail, and one Congressman, Donald J. Pease (D-Ohio), had worked assiduously on the House formula and was tenacious in pressing its specific merits. He had to be persuaded that the Senate version, favored by the administration, served the ends that *he* sought and was therefore a reasonable basis for compromise. This was accomplished through language reportedly put forward by the administration and carefully negotiated by the Finance Committee staff.

Another issue, a House provision authorizing countervailing duties against "natural resource subsidies" which had the backing also of ranking Finance Democrat Russell B. Long (D-La.), was resolved by procedural collaboration: Danforth polled the Senate conferees, who opposed it in a 4 to 3 party-line vote, but Rostenkowski did not poll the House conferees, a majority of whom would probably have supported it. Thus it was possible for the House to recede. (Long signaled his unhappiness by refusing to sign the conference report but did not impede final Senate action on the bill.)

As typically occurs in the rush to adjournment, personal factors—fatigue, resentment—intruded. When the exhausted senators decided to break up and go to bed Thursday evening, House members hit the ceiling: they were being asked to yield on several sensitive issues but the senators were not even willing to stay around and talk to them! And Gibbons, cooperative in giving way on trade remedies, grew stubborn on a detail of the Israeli title. As was standard practice with tariff agreements, the House bill provided that any negotiated duty changes could be put into effect by presidential proclamation, without further congressional action. Gibbons, backed by ranking Trade Subcommittee Republican Bill Frenzel (R-Minn.), stood by this provision as a matter of trade principle. The Senate bill, however, required that the tariff reductions be approved legislatively, under the fast-track procedures, and Danforth and Brock had used this provision to reassure a number of interests—textile and bromine manufacturers among them—that they would have a shot at whatever agreement was reached. In the final bargaining, Senate conferees decided that this was the one last House concession they absolutely needed. The House conferees never met on this; rather, Representative Thomas J. Downey (D-NY), the principal House sponsor of the Israeli free trade bill, conducted a telephone poll of House conferees, apparently at Rostenkowski's suggestion. A majority agreed to recede, and by about 5 P.M. Friday afternoon this final difference was resolved.

Fortunately for the bill's prospects, congressional leaders had by this time been forced to abandon their weekend adjournment target, and both houses would in fact stay in session until the following Friday, 12 October. This not only made it possible for the staffs to prepare the conference report and have the compromise bill enacted by both houses the following Tuesday, but it also allowed time for a follow-on bill—House Concurrent Resolution 372—"to correct the enrollment of H.R. 3398." For inevitably the rush had brought mistakes, like the complete omission of the language of a section devoted to protecting intellectual property rights, or confusion as to the definition of the "steel" that was being restrained. It had also brought eleventh-hour misunderstandings which were fought out frenetically, like the "green tube" controversy pitting Oklahoma against Texas.[5]

The result was widely applauded, with even the *Post* expressing its pleasure and surprise that "the omnibus trade bill was transformed in the House-Senate conference into pretty respectable legislation. . . . most of the bad stuff got thrown out and all of the good stuff stayed." Singled out for special praise was "William E. Brock, who worked mightily and, as it turned out, highly effectively to change the thrust of this bill."[6]

Somewhat surprisingly, therefore, the system worked. Notwithstanding the dispersion of power, the vulnerability to special interests, the inability of Ways and Means to act first in the traditional manner, it did prove possible for the Congress to produce a general trade bill that extended an unpopular program (GSP), while omitting or gutting most of the protectionist language that had made it through one chamber or the other. Provisions designed to benefit copper, ferroalloys, shoes, and dairy products were deleted or watered down. On preferences, in fact, the bill represented a move in the liberal, negotiating, internationalist direction, when compared with the 1974 law it replaced. It encouraged the administration to negotiate with the NICs for market access and intellectual property rights, and offered the NICs inducements as well as penalties.

The bill was not comparable to those of 1974 and 1979. It included no general new authority for multilateral trade negotiations, save on services and investment, nor did it include major provisions implementing prior trade agreements. It did include a watered-down but still objectionable precedent on wine, allowing producers of grapes to challenge wine imports. Most serious was the protectionist provision that originated in the administration, the new steel policy. Once the White House suggested that it would seek to limit total steel imports to a certain level, in a way that the industry read as a promise, the way was cleared for the bill to incorporate

---

5. The issue here, put very briefly, was whether an Oklahoma plant would be allowed, as an exception to the steel restraints, to continue to import green tube, a form of semifinished steel, for final processing.

6. "On Trade, a Happy Ending," *Washington Post*, 12 October 1984.

a global import target, something even the textile people had been unable to achieve. It was written as a bipartisan compromise—between 17 percent (Mondale) and 20.2 percent (Reagan), reflecting only the "sense of Congress." But it threatened to have bite, for the bill spoke of considering "such legislative actions concerning steel and iron ore products as may be necessary," if the Reagan program did not "produce satisfactory results within a reasonable period of time."[7] The entire steel title was enacted hastily, without hearings or serious review of the language in either body; in fact, it was embraced by Senate conferees because it was something to give the House, to make the whole bill go.

The fact that even this bill was passed, that preferences got extended and other useful things were enacted, was due no little to chance. On several occasions, a determined opponent might have blocked it: in the Finance Committee, on the Senate floor, during conference, and when the conference report (subject to a House point of order because it did not simply compromise differences but rewrote key sections) came up for final action. Labor might have scuttled it by clever, time-wasting Senate floor amendments, Long by signaling his unhappiness about natural resource subsidies with more than the withholding of his signature.

The success of the bill depended on a confluence of particular personalities: Brock, Danforth, and Rostenkowski most of all. Each, in a different way, wanted the legislation and each was skilled in moving it forward. And each was a key to its success. But the single indispensable person was clearly the US Trade Representative. He had immersed himself in the legislative struggle, drawing lines, making deals, fighting for statutory flexibility, working personally with senators and representatives. With the bill essentially cobbled together—first on the Senate floor, then in conference—an astute political manager was needed. Brock met that need.

The Trade Explosion of 1985

The Trade and Tariff Act of 1984 cleared the decks of major trade issues requiring statutory attention. Aside from the adjustment assistance program expiring in September 1985 (whose extension in the House bill was not agreed to by the conference), there was nothing that Congress *had* to do on trade until the NTB negotiating authority expired in January 1988. So having labored intensively on trade in 1984, Congress was expected in the year ahead to take a rest. Such an expectation was reinforced by President Ronald W. Reagan's landslide reelection victory, over an adversary who had sought to make the trade deficit an important campaign issue.

---

7. Trade and Tariff Act of 1984, Section 803.

Instead, 1985 would bring an outpouring of rhetoric and proposed legislation on trade more substantial, and more threatening, than anything America had seen in the postwar period. And the primary target was a nation hardly mentioned in the 1984 act, Japan.

It began with a New Year's summit conference between the President and a leader with whom he had a particularly congenial personal relationship, Yasuhiro Nakasone. The Prime Minister, with a new leadership mandate from his Liberal-Democratic Party, wanted to buttress his Reagan connection. So he proposed to fly to the United States and see the President. A meeting was arranged for 2 January in Los Angeles.

US trade officials, concerned about the growing US trade deficit with Japan, developed proposals to press Tokyo harder to open its markets. One idea that gained support was to negotiate specific targets for increases in imports of manufactured goods. But not only did Reagan reject this proposal; he also decided, reportedly, not even to give priority to trade in his meeting. It was Nakasone who raised the subject and stressed the need to do something, after which American and Japanese officials quickly shaped a program of Market-Oriented Sector-Specific (MOSS) talks focused on four product areas where the United States felt it had strong export potential: telecommunications, forestry products, electronics, and pharmaceuticals. The aim was to negotiate important Japanese market-opening measures before the end of the year.

At the close of that same January, the US Department of Commerce released trade figures for 1984. They featured the long expected 12-digit global merchandise trade deficit—$107 billion customs value, $123 billion c.i.f. They also included a rise in the bilateral deficit with Japan considerably greater than anticipated—from $19.3 billion to $33.6 billion customs value. The c.i.f. trade deficit was even greater, $36.8 billion. US exports to Japan had been $23.6 billion, up from $21.9 billion in 1983. But imports (c.i.f.) had skyrocketed from $41.2 billion to $60.4 billion.

In 1980–83, the deficit with Japan had grown, but at a lesser rate than those with most other U.S. trading partners. In 1984, however, it grew more rapidly. And all projections were that it would continue to increase in 1985.[8]

The congressional trade community saw, therefore, an imbalance with Japan that was growing alarmingly fast, and a White House that was not giving priority to reversing the trend. Reagan had not pushed Nakasone on trade issues. Moreover, the budget deficit his policies had created was, most

---

8. Statistics are those reported by the US Commerce Department. For a thorough analysis of the bilateral deficit and its sources, see C. Fred Bergsten and William R. Cline, *The United States–Japan Economic Problem*, POLICY ANALYSES IN INTERNATIONAL ECONOMICS 13 (Washington: Institute for International Economics, October 1985).

believed, a major contributor to the continuing rise of the dollar (which would hit its peak that February).

The stage was set, therefore, for strong congressional action. What forced the action was an already established target date for major trade-related decisions, 1 April. This was when the fourth year of voluntary restraints on auto exports would come to an end. It was also when, through legislation enacted by the Diet in December, Japan's government telecommunications monopoly, Nippon Telephone and Telegraph (NTT), would be transformed into a private firm.

In early March, Reagan announced that, unlike in previous years, he would not ask Japan to restrain auto exports. This alarmed legislators in general and Danforth in particular, who had important car manufacturing plants in his state and who saw the lifting of VERs as bound to drive the deficit still higher. And through that same month, the MOSS talks focused on telecommunications, driven by the 1 April deadline. US producers saw hope they might make greater sales to a privatized NTT. But they also feared that its transformation would negate painfully won prior concessions from the Japanese government concerning official procurement from foreign sources. And Japanese negotiators were typically slow in clarifying matters and making significant concessions.

So the Senate heated up. At an 8 March Finance Committee hearing, senator after senator denounced Japan for what they saw as intransigence on imports. Two weeks later, Senator John H. Chafee (R-RI), a longstanding free-trader, introduced a bill that would block all Japanese telecommunications sales to the United States until US trade officials certified that American makers of telecommunications products had "equal access to the markets of Japan." And all joined in support of a Danforth resolution calling for retaliation against Japan—telecommunications as well as autos were among the product areas suggested—unless import markets expanded to offset the anticipated increase in car sales from the lifting of quotas.

There was an element of executive branch encouragement in this congressional movement—USTR and Commerce trade negotiators, frustrated by the limited support they were getting from the White House, saw the threat of statutory protectionism as strengthening their leverage with Tokyo, and were willing to nurture that threat, up to a point. But it was a risky game, and a strong executive hand was needed to keep the lid on. This point seemed lost on the President and his new Chief of Staff, former Treasury Secretary Donald T. Regan. For just at the time they should have been dispatching USTR Brock to Capitol Hill on a damage-limiting mission, they were instead pressuring him to move to another job, Secretary of Labor! He agreed with extreme reluctance. The announcement was made 20 March. So, just as the Senate was getting ready to explode, the administration was removing the only man it had with the stature and experience to cope.[9] It was also giving one more telling signal that trade policy was very, very low on the list of presidential priorities.

Finally, on the very day that the Danforth resolution was up for a vote in the Senate, Japan's Ministry of International Trade and Industry announced that it would continue voluntary auto export restraints, but at a level 25 percent above that of 1984. This decision, aimed at limiting the political damage from increased imports to the United States, was apparently timed to buttress MITI's limited leverage over Japan's auto manufacturers. It got everybody in Washington angry. The White House, seeing the continuation of quotas as a rebuff to the President's policy (and perhaps as commentary on his political judgement in abandoning them), denounced the action. Members of Congress, focusing on the large quota increase, saw it as a flagrant example of Japanese export aggressiveness. The Danforth resolution sailed through the Senate 92 to 0, with the debate punctuated by virulent, bipartisan denunciation of the Japanese. The House of Representatives followed on 2 April, passing by 394 to 19 a resolution similar in content, though giving greater emphasis to the global trade imbalance.

The Missouri Senator might have been content to stop here, at least for a time. He would say publicly, on more than one occasion, that his real target was not Japan but the White House. He wanted to jolt the administration into taking trade seriously. Having sent a strong message, it made sense to pause for a time and assess the reaction. But Danforth's Finance colleagues were up in arms, and Senator Bob Packwood (R-Ore.), Chairman of the full committee, pressed forward with a mandatory version of the Danforth resolution. This won committee endorsement on 4 April by a vote of 12 to 4.

The Senate then did pause on the trade and Japan front, in part because its leadership got seriously engaged in efforts to reduce the budget deficit. But as the White House continued seemingly indifferent, month after month, other proposals threatening trade restrictions moved forward:

□ A textile industry bill that would roll back import quotas, originally introduced to toughen the administration's stance in the upcoming Multi-Fiber Arrangement (MFA) negotiations, surprised its proposers by accumulating close to three hundred cosponsors in the House. With protectionist provisions added for shoes and copper, it would later pass both houses by strong majorities, forcing a presidential veto in December.

---

9. Two days before, the White House had undercut its *other* senior trade spokesman, Secretary of Commerce Malcolm Baldrige, by announcing that it was abandoning his proposal for a Department of Trade "at this time."

- Three prominent Democrats with leadership positions on trade, Senator Bentsen and Congressmen Rostenkowski and Richard A. Gephardt (D-Mo.), introduced in July a radical bill that would impose an import surcharge on products of countries running large trade surpluses with the United States. As submitted, it would have affected not just Japan but Korea, Taiwan, and Brazil as well.

- In September, after members had returned from the August recess, House Speaker Thomas P. (Tip) O'Neill declared, "Based on what I hear from members in the cloak room, trade is the number one issue."[10]

- Senate Finance also cleared for floor action a revised version of Danforth's telecommunications bill, linking access to the US market to liberalization of import barriers overseas.

- Meanwhile, while House Ways and Means was preoccupied with tax reform, the Energy and Commerce Committee moved ahead with bills on telecommunications and trade remedies, to make it easier for firms to qualify for trade relief.

- In December, Senate Majority Leader Robert Dole sought floor action on trade bills targeted at Japan, only to be blocked by textile industry champion Ernest F. Hollings (D-SC), who was retaliating for the Finance Committee's lack of procedural cooperation on the textile quota bill.

Legislators were driven toward restrictive action on trade because of the unprecedented unfavorable trade balance. With such a wrenching shift in trade flows, as documented in chapter 8, pressure for statutory relief was bound to increase. They were moved also by partisan interests—a sense of opportunity on the part of Democrats, who saw trade as "a key jobs and pro-America issue" with which to attack the Reagan administration; a fear of vulnerability on the part of Republicans, which was one reason why Danforth and his colleagues seized the initiative in early 1985.

But they were driven also by the broad, bipartisan conviction that the White House was a prime contributor to the trade problem and was doing nothing to solve it. Through the summer, the President's position remained that the strong dollar was a good thing, and he was undercutting Senate efforts at compromise to reduce the budget deficit legislators saw as a prime cause of the strong dollar. The White House was neglecting trade-specific policy: it was more than three months before a successor to Brock was proposed to the Senate and confirmed, and the new choice—while a senior

---

10. *Washington Post,* 19 September 1985.

man with substantial prior trade experience—lacked the congressional standing Brock or Strauss had possessed when they had entered the position.

Because of its lack of credibility on trade, the administration was not performing its primary political function under the old trade policy-making system. It was not protecting Congress by absorbing and managing pressures for trade restrictions. Indeed, it was doing the opposite, diverting those pressures to Capitol Hill. So representatives of trade-impacted industries, rebuffed when they took their plight to the White House, lobbied with double force at the other end of Pennsylvania Avenue.

Some of the contrast between 1984 and 1985, therefore, can be attributed to the leadership difference, the strong administration presence on Capitol Hill in 1984 in the person of USTR William Brock; the absence of such a presence in 1985, particularly before September.

There was change for the better in 1985's waning months. President Reagan announced an aggressive response to what he labelled "unfair" foreign trade actions, initiating several trade complaints and creating a "strike force" to develop more. His new USTR, Clayton K. Yeutter, got more deeply into trade policy and trade politics. Most important, Secretary of the Treasury James A. Baker III not only led in an effort to respond to trade policy pressures, but also won endorsement of a policy to bring down the value of the dollar. This new policy was announced on 22 September 1985 by Baker and the finance ministers of the four other leading industrial economies: France, the Federal Republic of Germany, Japan, and the United Kingdom. The policy was crowned with success, as the dollar did, at long last, decline substantially.

As 1986 began, there was still much trade policy work to be done. A large number of legislators in both houses had become aroused on trade, and coalitions were moving to pass a comprehensive bill before the year was out. The administration did not have its own bill to serve as a reference point and basis for bargaining. The legislative action would take place in the shadow of the new-record trade deficit of 1985—roughly $150 billion worldwide (c.i.f.), and $50 billion (c.i.f.) with Japan. There was also ahead what was viewed as a particularly critical mid-term election, with Republicans facing a challenge to retain control of the Senate and Democrats seeing trade as a promising issue to use against them.

The Reagan administration had retained the trade initiative in 1984 through Brock's adroit engagement in the legislative process. It had lost that initiative in the spring and summer of 1985, and entered 1986 struggling to regain it.

Appendix B Administrative Trade Cases

B-1 ESCAPE CLAUSE INVESTIGATIONS, 1975–85

Product	Date initiated	Initiator	Action taken
Birch plywood door skins (TA–201–01)	18 Apr 1975	Columbia Plywood Corp.	USITC negative determination, case terminated (20 Oct 1975)
Metal fasteners (bolts, nuts, and screws of iron or steel) (TA–201–02)	22 May 1975	Russell, Burdsall & Ward, Inc.; Industrial Fasteners Institute; Cap, Screw, and Special Threaded Products Bureau	USITC negative determination, case terminated (24 Nov 1975)
Wrapper tobacco (TA–201–03)	25 May 1975	Cigar Leaf Tobacco Foundation, Inc.	USITC negative determination, case terminated (5 Nov 1975)
Asparagus (TA–201–04)	10 Jul 1975	California Asparagus Growers Assn., Incorporated; Washington Asparagus Growers Assn.; unaffiliated asparagus growers	USITC equally divided (12 Jan 1976); President decided to accept USITC decision as negative (10 Mar 1976)
Stainless steel and alloy tool steel (TA–201–05)	16 Jul 1975	Tool and Stainless Steel Industry Committee for Import Relief; United Steelworkers of America; AFL-CIO	USITC affirmative determination; President granted Orderly Marketing Agreements, quotas, and adjustment assistance (16 Mar 1976)
Slide fasteners and parts (TA–201–06)	18 Aug 1975	Slide Fastener Assn.	USITC equally divided (18 Mar 1976); President decided to accept USITC decision as negative, but granted expedited adjustment assistance (14 Apr 1976)
Footwear (TA–201–07)	20 Aug 1975	American Footwear Industries Assn.; Boot and Shoe Workers' Union; United Shoe Workers of America	USITC affirmative determination (20 Feb 1976); President granted expedited adjustment assistance (16 Apr 1976)

Product (case no.)	Date	Petitioner(s)	Outcome
Stainless steel table flatware (TA–201–08)	28 Aug 1975	Stainless Steel Flatware Manufacturers Assn.	USITC affirmative determination; President granted expedited adjustment assistance (30 Apr 1976)
Certain gloves (TA–201–09)	8 Sep 1975	Work Glove Manufacturers' Assn.	USITC negative determination, case terminated (8 Mar 1976)
Mushrooms (TA–201–10)	17 Sep 1975	Mushroom Canners Committee of the Pennsylvania Food Processors Assn.; Mushroom Processors Tariff Committee	USITC affirmative determination: President granted expedited adjustment assistance (17 May 1976)
Ferrocyanide and ferrocyanide blue pigments (TA–201–11)	2 Oct 1975	American Cyanamid Company	USITC affirmative determination (2 Apr 1976); President determined import restraints not in the national economic interest (1 Jun 1976)
Shrimp (TA–201–12)	17 Nov 1975	National Shrimp Congress	USITC affirmative determination, recommended import relief; President granted expedited adjustment assistance (7 Jul 1976)
Round stainless steel wire (TA–201–13)	12 Dec 1975	Stainless Steel Wire Industry Committee	USITC negative determination, case terminated (12 Jun 1976)
Honey (TA–201–14)	29 Dec 1975	Mid-US Honey Producers Marketing Assn., Inc.; Great Lakes Honey Marketing Assn.; Michigan Beekeepers Assn.; others	USITC affirmative determination (29 Jun 1976); President determined import restraints not in the national economic interest (28 Aug 1976)
Plant hangers (TA–201–15)	22 Jun 1976	Knots to You, Inc.	USITC negative determination, case terminated (22 Dec 1976)
Sugar (TA–201–16)	17 Sep 1976	Senate Committee on Finance	USITC affirmative determination, recommended reduced quotas (17 Mar 1977); President rejected USITC recommendation (4 May 1977)[1]

Appendix B was researched and written by Diane T. Berliner.

[1] On 4 May 1977, President Jimmy Carter announced that he would not accept the USITC recommendations for reduced quotas of US sugar imports. He announced that, in accordance with the provisions of the Agricultural Adjustment Act of 1949, he would attempt to provide a payment to farmers of up to 2 cents per pound for sugar whenever the market price fell below 13.5 cents per pound. (USITC, *1977 Annual Report*, p. 7).

B-1 ESCAPE CLAUSE INVESTIGATIONS, 1975–85 (continued)

Product	Date initiated	Initiator	Action taken
Mushrooms (TA–201–17)	20 Sep 1976	Special Representative for Trade Negotiations (STR)	USITC affirmative determination, recommended tariff-rate quotas (10 Jan 1977); President determined import restraints not in the national economic interest, STR was directed to monitor imports (11 Mar 1977)
Footwear (TA–201–18)	28 Sep 1976	Senate Committee on Finance	USITC affirmative determination; President granted adjustment assistance and Orderly Marketing Agreements (1 Apr 1977)
Television receivers, color and monochrome, assembled or not assembled, finished or not finished, and subassemblies thereof (TA–201–19)	21 Oct 1976	Industrial Union Department; AFL-CIO; American Flint Glass Workers Union of North America; Allied Industrial Workers of America; and others	USITC affirmative determination; President granted Orderly Marketing Agreements (20 May 1977)
Low carbon ferrochromium (TA–201–20)	21 Jan 1977	Committee of Producers of Low Carbon Ferrochromium	USITC negative determination, case terminated (8 Jul 1977)
Cast-iron cooking ware (TA–201–21)	12 Feb 1977	Atlanta Stove Works, Inc.; General Housewares Corp.; Lodge Manufacturing Company	USITC negative determination, case terminated (8 Jul 77)
Fresh cut flowers (TA–201–22)	12 Feb 1977	Growers Division of the Society of American Florists and Ornamental Horticulturalists	USITC negative determination, case terminated (14 Jul 1977)

Date	Product	Petitioner	Determination
22 Feb 1977	Certain headwear (TA–201–23)	Empire State Cloth, Hat & Cap Manufacturing Assn.; United Hatters, Cap and Millinery Workers International Union	USITC negative determination, case terminated (18 Aug 1977)
23 Mar 1977	Stoves and stove parts, and fireplace grates (TA–201–24)	Atlanta Stove Works, Inc.; Washington Stove Works; US Stove Company; Portland Stove Foundry, Inc.; Martin Industries, Inc.	USITC equally divided (25 Jul 1977); President chose to accept USITC decision as negative, no import relief granted (23 Sep 1977)
26 Mar 1977	Live cattle and certain edible meat products of cattle (TA–201–25)	National Assn. of American Meat Promoters; the Meat Promoters of South Dakota, North Dakota, Montana and Wyoming	USITC negative determination, case terminated (30 Aug 1977)
13 Apr 1977	Malleable cast-iron pipe and tube fittings (TA–201–26)	American Pipe Fittings Assn.	USITC negative determination, case terminated (22 Sep 1977)
22 Jun 1977	Bolts, nuts, and large screws of iron or steel (TA–201–27)	US Fastener Manufacturing Group; United Steelworkers of America; International Assn. of Machinists and Aerospace Workers	USITC affirmative determination, recommended increased tariffs (12 Dec 1977); President rejected USITC recommendation, no import relief granted (10 Feb 1978)
8 Jul 1977	High-carbon ferrochromium (TA–201–28)	Committee of Producers of High Carbon Ferrochrome	USITC affirmative determination, recommended increased tariffs (1 Dec 1977); President determined import restraints not in the national economic interest (28 Jan 1978)
11 Aug 1977	Citizens band (CB) radio transceivers (TA–201–29)	E.F. Johnson Company	USITC affirmative determination; President granted tariff increase for three years (27 Mar 1978)
16 Dec 1977	Stainless steel flatware (TA–201–30)	Stainless Steel Flatware Manufacturers Assn.	USITC affirmative determination, recommended increased tariffs (12 May 1978); President rejected USITC recommendation, no import relief granted (30 Jun 1978)

B-1   ESCAPE CLAUSE INVESTIGATIONS, 1975–85 (continued)

Product	Date initiated	Initiator	Action taken
Unalloyed, unwrought zinc (TA–201–31)	29 Dec 1977	Lead Zinc Producers Committee	USITC negative determination, case terminated (1 Jun 1978)
Unalloyed, unwrought copper (TA–201–32)	23 Feb 1978	Anaconda Company; Asarco, Inc.; Cities SVC Minerals Group; and nine other producers	USITC affirmative determination, recommended quotas for five-year period (23 Aug 1978); President determined import restraints not in the national economic interest (24 Oct 1978)
Bicycle tires and tubes (TA–201–33)	2 Mar 1978	Carlisle Tire and Rubber Company	USITC affirmative determination, recommended increased tariffs for five years (1 Sep 1978); President determined import restraints not in the national economic interest (2 Nov 1978)
Fishing tackle (TA–201–34)	29 Mar 1978	American Fishing Tackle Manufacturers Assn.; Tackle Representatives Assn.	USITC affirmative determination, recommended suspension of GSP designation (28 Sep 1978); President determined import restraints not in the national economic interest (27 Nov 1978)
High-carbon ferrochromium (TA–201–35)	21 Jun 1978	House Committee on Ways and Means	USITC affirmative determination; President granted tariff increase for three years (15 Nov 1978)
Clothespins (TA–201–36)	27 Jul 1978	USITC	USITC affirmative determination; President granted global quotas for three years (8 Feb 1979)
Bolts, nuts, and large screws of iron or steel (TA–201–37)	15 Aug 1978	House Committee on Ways and Means	USITC affirmative determination; President granted tariff increase for three years (26 Dec 1978)

Product (TA number)	Date	Petitioner	Outcome
Certain machine needles (TA–201–38)	25 Aug 1978	The Torrington Company	USITC negative determination, case terminated (16 Jan 1979)
Nonelectric cooking ware (TA–201–39)	5 May 1979	General Housewares Corp.	USITC affirmative determination; President granted tariff increase for four years (3 Jan 1980)
Leather wearing apparel (TA–201–40)	3 Aug 1979	National Outerwear Sportswear Assn.; Amalgamated Clothing and Textile Workers Union; International Ladies' Garment Workers Union; United Food and Commercial Workers Union; Tanners' Council of America, Inc.	USITC affirmative determination, recommended increased tariffs for three years; President rejected USITC recommendation, but granted expedited adjustment assistance (26 Mar 1980)
Certain ground fish (TA–201–41)	11 Sep 1979	Fishermen's Marketing Assn. of Washington, Incorporated; Coast Draggers Assn.	USITC negative determination, case terminated (28 Jan 1980)
Fresh cut roses (TA–201–42)	29 Nov 1979	Roses, Inc.	USITC negative determination, case terminated (23 Apr 1980)
Mushrooms (TA–201–43)	24 Mar 1980	American Mushroom Institute	USITC affirmative determination; President granted tariff increase for three years (3 Nov 1980)
Certain motor vehicles and certain chassis and bodies therefor (TA–201–44)	30 Jun 1980	International Union, United Automobile Aerospace and Agricultural Implement Workers of America	USITC negative determination, case terminated (28 Dec 1980)
Fishing rods and parts thereof (TA–201–45)	27 Jul 1981	21 US fishing rods and parts manufacturers	USITC negative determination, case terminated (25 Nov 1981)
Tubeless tire valves (TA–201–46)	29 Apr 1982	Nylo-Flex Manufacturing Company; Schrader Automotive Products Division of Scoville Manufacturing Company; Eaton Corp.	USITC negative determination, case terminated (29 Sep 1982)
Heavyweight motorcycles, engines, and power train subassemblies (TA–201–47)	16 Sep 1982	Harley-Davidson Motor Company and Harley-Davidson of York, Inc.	USITC affirmative determination; President granted tariff increase for five years (2 Apr 1983)

B-1 ESCAPE CLAUSE INVESTIGATIONS, 1975–85 (continued)

Product	Date initiated	Initiator	Action taken
Stainless steel and alloy tool steel (TA–201–48)	10 Dec 1982	US Trade Representative	USITC affirmative determination; President granted tariff increase (5 Jul 1983)
Stainless steel table flatware (TA–201–49)	5 Jan 1984	Domestic manufacturers of stainless steel table flatware	USITC negative determination, case terminated (13 Jun 1984)
Nonrubber footwear (TA–201–50)	23 Jan 1984	Footwear Industries of America, Inc.	USITC negative determination, case terminated (18 Jul 1984)
Carbon and certain alloy steel products (TA–201–51)	24 Jan 1984	United Steelworkers of America; Bethlehem Steel Corp.	USITC affirmative determination for certain products, recommended five-year program of tariffs and quotas (1 Aug 1984); President granted Voluntary Restraint Agreements (VRAs) (20 Sep 1984)
Unwrought copper (TA–201–52)	26 Jan 1984	Anaconda Minerals Company	USITC affirmative determination, recommended a 5 cents per pound duty for five years (25 Jul 1984); President determined import restraints not in the national economic interest (5 Sep 1984)
Tuna, prepared or preserved in any manner, in air-tight containers (TA–201–53)	15 Feb 1984	United States Tuna Foundation; C.H.B. Foods, Inc.; American Tuna Boat Assn.; United Industrial Workers; Fishermen's Union of America	USITC negative determination, case terminated (29 Aug 1984)
Potassium Permanganate (TA–201–54)	30 Nov 1984	Carus Chemical Company	USITC negative determination, case terminated (8 May 1985)

Product	Date	Petitioner	Outcome
Nonrubber footwear (TA–201–55)	31 Dec 1984	Footwear Industries of America	USITC affirmative determination, recommended five-year quota program (1 Jul 1985); President denied import relief, instructed Department of Labor to develop work plans (30 Aug 1985)
Wood shingles and shakes (TA–201–56)	25 Sep 1985	Domestic Wood Shingles and Shakes Producers	USITC affirmative determination, recommended increased tariffs (25 Mar 1986); President granted tariffs of 35 percent (20 May 1986)
Electric shavers, parts thereof, and certain blades and cutting heads (TA–201–57)	27 Sep 1985	Remington Products, Inc.	USITC negative determination, case terminated (27 Mar 1986)
Certain metal castings (TA–201–58)	2 Dec 1985	Cast Metals Federation	USITC negative determination, case terminated (2 Jun 1986)
Apple juice (TA–201–59)	27 Dec 1985	US Trade Representative	USITC negative determination, case terminated (27 Jun 1986)

B-2 COUNTERVAILING DUTY INVESTIGATIONS, 1979–85

Product	Date initiated	Country involved	Initiator	Action taken
Dextrines and soluble or chemically treated starches derived from potato starch (701–TA–22)	30 Jan 1979	Belgium	Corn Refiners Assn.	Affirmative final subsidy determination (19 Dec 1979); negative final injury determination, case terminated (14 Aug 1980)
Dextrines and soluble or chemically treated starches derived from potato starch (701–TA–23)	30 Jan 1979	Denmark	Corn Refiners Assn.	Affirmative final subsidy determination (19 Dec 1979); negative final injury determination, case terminated (14 Aug 1980)
Dextrines and soluble or chemically treated starches derived from potato starch (701–TA–24)	30 Jan 1979	Germany (FR)	Corn Refiners Assn.	Affirmative final subsidy determination (19 Dec 1979); negative final injury determination, case terminated (14 Aug 1980)
Dextrines and soluble or chemically treated starches derived from potato starch (701–TA–25)	30 Jan 1979	France	Corn Refiners Assn.	Affirmative final subsidy determination (19 Dec 1979); negative final injury determination, case terminated (14 Aug 1980)
Dextrines and soluble or chemically treated starches derived from potato starch (701–TA–26)	30 Jan 1979	Ireland	Corn Refiners Assn.	Affirmative final subsidy determination (19 Dec 1979); negative final injury determination, case terminated (14 Aug 1980)
Dextrines and soluble or chemically treated starches derived from potato starch (701–TA–27)	30 Jan 1979	Italy	Corn Refiners Assn.	Affirmative final subsidy determination (19 Dec 1979); negative final injury determination, case terminated (14 Aug 1980)
Dextrines and soluble or chemically treated starches derived from potato starch (701–TA–28)	30 Jan 1979	Luxembourg	Corn Refiners Assn.	Affirmative final subsidy determination (19 Dec 1979); negative final injury determination, case terminated (14 Aug 1980)

Product	Date	Country	Petitioner	Determination
Dextrines and soluble or chemically treated starches derived from potato starch (701–TA–29)	30 Jan 1979	Netherlands	Corn Refiners Assn.	Affirmative final subsidy determination (19 Dec 1979); negative final injury determination, case terminated (14 Aug 1980)
Dextrines and soluble or chemically treated starches derived from potato starch (701–TA–30)	30 Jan 1979	United Kingdom	Corn Refiners Assn.	Affirmative final subsidy determination (19 Dec 1979); negative final injury determination, case terminated (14 Aug 1980)
Canned tomatoes and tomato concentrates	30 Jan 1979	Belgium	Canners League of California	Affirmative final subsidy determination (22 Aug 1979); negative final injury determination, case terminated (18 Jun 1980)
Canned tomatoes and tomato concentrates	30 Jan 1979	Denmark	Canners League of California	Affirmative final subsidy determination (22 Aug 1979); negative final injury determination, case terminated (18 Jun 1980)
Canned tomatoes and tomato concentrates	30 Jan 1979	Germany (FR)	Canners League of California	Affirmative final subsidy determination (22 Aug 1979); negative final injury determination, case terminated (18 Jun 1980)
Canned tomatoes and tomato concentrates	30 Jan 1979	France	Canners League of California	Affirmative final subsidy determination (22 Aug 1979); negative final injury determination, case terminated (18 Jun 1980)
Canned tomatoes and tomato concentrates	30 Jan 1979	Ireland	Canners League of California	Affirmative final subsidy determination (22 Aug 1979); negative final injury determination, case terminated (18 Jun 1980)
Canned tomatoes and tomato concentrates	30 Jan 1979	Italy	Canners League of California	Affirmative final subsidy determination (22 Aug 1979); negative final injury determination, case terminated (18 Jun 1980)

B-2 COUNTERVAILING DUTY INVESTIGATIONS, 1979–85 (continued)

Product	Date initiated	Country involved	Initiator	Action taken
Canned tomatoes and tomato concentrates	30 Jan 1979	Luxembourg	Canners League of California	Affirmative final subsidy determination (22 Aug 1979); negative final injury determination, case terminated (18 Jun 1980)
Canned tomatoes and tomato concentrates	30 Jan 1979	Netherlands	Canners League of California	Affirmative final subsidy determination (22 Aug 1979); negative final injury determination, case terminated (18 Jun 1980)
Canned tomatoes and tomato concentrates	30 Jan 1979	United Kingdom	Canners League of California	Affirmative final subsidy determination (22 Aug 1979); negative final injury determination, case terminated (18 Jun 1980)
Pig iron (701–TA–2)	13 Feb 1979	Brazil	Ad Hoc Committee of Merchant Pig Iron Producers of America	Affirmative final subsidy and injury determinations, cash deposit on case-by-case basis (4 Apr 1980); cash deposit 7 percent f.o.b. value (15 Feb 1983)
Ferrochrome, ferromanganese, ferrosilicone manganese, and ferrosilicone	6 Mar 1979	Spain	Ferroalloys Federation (10 members)	Affirmative final subsidy determination, cash deposit 2.4 percent ad valorem (2 Jan 1980); case terminated (31 Oct 1984)
Certain industrial fasteners	23 Mar 1979	Japan	Industrial Fasteners Institute	Affirmative final subsidy determination, cash deposit 4 percent (4 Jun 1979); waiver of deposit (29 Oct 1981)
Certain scale and weighing machinery	29 Mar 1979	Japan	Reliance Electric Company	Negative final injury determination, case terminated (7 May 1980)

Product	Date	Country	Petitioner	Status
Taps, cocks, valves, and similar devices and parts thereof (701–TA–4)	29 Mar 1979	Japan	Valve Manufacturers Assn.	Petition withdrawn, case terminated (21 Feb 1980)
Rifles, shotguns and combination rifles and shotguns and parts (701–TA–8)	5 Apr 1979	Brazil	Harrington, Richardson and Company	Petition withdrawn, case terminated (19 Mar 1980)
Certain ferroalloys (701–TA–10)	11 May 1979	Brazil	Ferroalloy Assn.	Petition withdrawn, case terminated (19 May 1980)
Chain of iron or steel or parts thereof	22 May 1979	Japan	National Assn. of Chain Manufacturers	Affirmative final subsidy determination, cash deposit of 2 percent f.o.b. value (9 Apr 1980); petition withdrawn, case terminated (6 Mar 1985)
Frozen potato products (701–TA–3)	25 May 1979	Canada	Frozen Potato Products Institute	Negative preliminary injury determination, case terminated (21 Feb 1980)
Viscose rayon staple fiber (701–TA–6)	18 Jun 1979	Austria	Avtex Fibers	Petition withdrawn, case terminated (26 Feb 1980)
Taps, cocks, valves and similar devices and parts thereof (701–TA–4)	3 Jul 1979	Italy	Valve Manufacturers Assn.	Petition withdrawn, case terminated (21 Feb 1980)
Certain textile and textile products	20 July 1979	Pakistan	US Treasury	Negative final injury determination, case terminated (24 Jul 1980)
Malleable pipe fittings of iron or steel (701–TA–9)	28 Aug 1979	Japan	American Pipe Fittings Associates	Petition withdrawn, case terminated (2 Apr 1980)
Dextrines and solubles or chemically treated starches derived from corn starch	18 Sep 1979	Denmark	Henkel Corp.	Negative final injury determination, case terminated (7 May 1980)
Dextrines and solubles or chemically treated starches derived from corn starch	18 Sep 1979	Germany (FR)	Henkel Corp.	Negative final injury determination, case terminated (7 May 1980)

B-2 COUNTERVAILING DUTY INVESTIGATIONS, 1979–85 (*continued*)

Product	Date initiated	Country involved	Initiator	Action taken
Dextrines and solubles or chemically treated starches derived from corn starch	18 Sep 1979	France	Henkel Corp.	Negative final injury determination, case terminated (7 May 1980)
Dextrines and solubles or chemically treated starches derived from corn starch	18 Sep 1979	Ireland	Henkel Corp.	Negative final injury determination, case terminated (7 May 1980)
Dextrines and solubles or chemically treated starches derived from corn starch	18 Sep 1979	Italy	Henkel Corp.	Negative final injury determination, case terminated (7 May 1980)
Dextrines and solubles or chemically treated starches derived from corn starch	18 Sep 1979	Luxembourg	Henkel Corp.	Negative final injury determination, case terminated (7 May 1980)
Dextrines and solubles or chemically treated starches derived from corn starch	18 Sep 1979	Netherlands	Henkel Corp.	Negative final injury determination, case terminated (7 May 1980)
Dextrines and solubles or chemically treated starches derived from corn starch	18 Sep 1979	United Kingdom	Henkel Corp.	Negative final injury determination, case terminated (7 May 1980)
Wool top	21 Sep 1979	Australia	American Textile Manufacturers Institute	Negative final subsidy determination, case terminated (20 Mar 1980)
Fresh cut roses (701–TA–21)	1 Feb 1980	Netherlands	Roses, Inc.	Negative preliminary injury determination, case terminated (4 Sep 1980)

Product	Date	Country	Petitioner	Determination
Fresh cut roses (701–TA–22)	1 Feb 1980	Israel	Roses, Inc.	Affirmative final subsidy determination, duty of 2 percent f.o.b value (4 Sep 1980); cash deposit of 12 percent ad valorem (9 Feb 1983); cash deposit of 23 percent ad valorem (6 Jan 1984)
Industrial fasteners	25 Feb 1980	India	Industrial Fasteners Institute	Affirmative preliminary and final subsidy determinations, duty 18 percent ad valorem (21 Jul 1980); order revoked (6 Oct 1982); cash deposit 20 percent f.o.b. value (17 Oct 1983)
Certain iron-metal castings (701–TA–37)	14 Mar 1980	India	Pinkerton Foundary, Inc.	Affirmative final subsidy and injury determinations, cash deposit on case-by-case basis (16 Oct 1980); duty of 2.6 percent ad valorem (18 Oct 1984)
Spirits (104–TAA–3)	28 Mar 1980	Ireland	Not available	Affirmative final subsidy determination; final administrative review results: cash deposit required (25 Jun 1981); negative final injury determination, CVD order revoked (3 Sep 1981)
Plastic animal identification tags (303–TA–1)	25 Aug 1980	New Zealand	Y—Tex Corp.	Affirmative final subsidy determination (15 Jan 1981); negative final injury determination, case terminated (5 Mar 1981)
Leather wearing apparel (701–TA–68)	12 Nov 1980	Uruguay	Ralph Edwards Sportswear, Inc.	Affirmative preliminary subsidy determination, cash deposit 26 percent f.o.b. value; affirmative final subsidy and injury determinations, cash deposit of 2.4 percent f.o.b. value (16 Jul 1982)

B-2 COUNTERVAILING DUTY INVESTIGATIONS, 1979–85 (continued)

Product	Date initiated	Country involved	Initiator	Action taken
Leather wearing apparel	12 Nov 1980	Mexico	Ralph Edwards Sportswear, Inc.	Affirmative final subsidy determination, cash deposit 5 percent f.o.b. value (10 Apr 1981); cash deposit 13 percent f.o.b. value (21 Jan 1983); subsidy of 2.7 percent ad valorem (4 Oct 1984)
Leather wearing apparel	12 Nov 1980	Colombia	Ralph Edwards Sportswear, Inc.	Affirmative final subsidy determination, Suspension Agreement negotiated (2 Apr 1981)
Leather wearing apparel	14 Nov 1980	Argentina	RES, Inc.	Affirmative final subsidy determination, Suspension Agreement negotiated (23 Apr 1981); duty of 4 percent ad valorem (18 Mar 1983)
Optic liquid sensing systems (104–TAA–2)	12 Mar 1981	Canada	Skully Electronic Systems, Inc.	Negative final injury determination, duty of 12 percent ad valorem from previously initiated case revoked (25 Aug 1981)
Lamb meat	18 May 1981	Australia	National Wool Growers Assn.; National Lamb Feeders Assn.	Petition withdrawn, case terminated (1 Oct 1981)
Lamb meat (701–TA–80)	18 May 1981	New Zealand	National Wool Growers Assn.; National Lamb Feeders Assn.	Petition withdrawn, case terminated (12 Jun 1982)

Sodium gluconate (701–TA–69)	19 Jun 1981	Belgium	Pfizer, Inc.	Affirmative preliminary subsidy and injury determinations (16 Sep 1981); suspension of investigation based on Suspension Agreement, case terminated (30 Nov 1981)
Sodium gluconate (701–TA–70)	19 Jun 1981	Denmark	Pfizer, Inc.	Affirmative preliminary subsidy and injury determinations (16 Sep 1981); suspension of investigation based on Suspension Agreement, case terminated (30 Nov 1981)
Sodium gluconate (701–TA–71)	19 Jun 1981	Germany (FR)	Pfizer, Inc.	Affirmative preliminary subsidy and injury determinations (16 Sep 1981); suspension of investigation based on Suspension Agreement, case terminated (30 Nov 1981)
Sodium gluconate (701–TA–72)	19 Jun 1981	France	Pfizer, Inc.	Affirmative preliminary subsidy and injury determinations (16 Sep 1981); suspension of investigation based on Suspension Agreement, case terminated (30 Nov 1981)
Sodium gluconate (701–TA–73)	19 Jun 1981	Ireland	Pfizer, Inc.	Affirmative preliminary subsidy and injury determinations (16 Sep 1981); suspension of investigation based on Suspension Agreement, case terminated (30 Nov 1981)
Sodium gluconate (701–TA–74)	19 Jun 1981	Italy	Pfizer, Inc.	Affirmative preliminary subsidy and injury determinations (16 Sep 1981); suspension of investigation based on Suspension Agreement, case terminated (30 Nov 1981)

B-2 COUNTERVAILING DUTY INVESTIGATIONS, 1979–85 (continued)

Product	Date initiated	Country involved	Initiator	Action taken
Sodium gluconate (701–TA–75)	19 Jun 1981	Luxembourg	Pfizer, Inc.	Affirmative preliminary subsidy and injury determinations (16 Sep 1981); suspension of investigation based on Suspension Agreement, case terminated (30 Nov 1981)
Sodium gluconate (701–TA–76)	19 Jun 1981	Netherlands	Pfizer, Inc.	Affirmative preliminary subsidy and injury determinations (16 Sep 1981); suspension of investigation based on Suspension Agreement, case terminated (30 Nov 1981)
Sodium gluconate (701–TA–77)	19 Jun 1981	United Kingdom	Pfizer, Inc.	Affirmative preliminary subsidy and injury determinations (16 Sep 1981); suspension of investigation based on Suspension Agreement, case terminated (30 Nov 1981)
Sodium gluconate (701–TA–78)	19 Jun 1981	Greece	Pfizer, Inc.	Affirmative preliminary subsidy and injury determinations (16 Sep 1981); suspension of investigation based on Suspension Agreement, case terminated (30 Nov 1981)
Bicycle tires and tubes	3 Aug 1981	Taiwan	Carlisle Tire and Rubber Company	Affirmative final subsidy determination, subsidy de minimus (28 Oct 1981); cash deposit 1 percent ad valorem (17 Feb 1982)
Ski lifts and parts thereof (104–TAA–5)	19 Aug 1981	Italy	Delegation of the Commission of the European Community	Petition withdrawn, case terminated (9 Dec 1981)

Product (case number)	Date	Country	Petitioner	Determination
Hard-smoked herring fillets (701–TA–81)	2 Oct 1981	Canada	McCurdy Fish Company	Petition withdrawn, case terminated (29 Oct 1981)
Refrigerators, freezers, and other refrigerating equipment and parts	26 Oct 1981	Italy	White Consolidated Industries, Inc.	Negative preliminary injury determination, case terminated (13 Jan 1982)
Ceramic tiles	30 Oct 1981	Mexico	Tile Council of America, Inc.	Affirmative preliminary and final subsidy determinations, cash deposit 17 percent ad valorem (23 Feb 1982); cash deposit 19 percent f.o.b. invoice price (26 Sep 1983); subsidy of 2.1 percent ad valorem (31 Oct 1984)
Hard-smoked herring fillets (701–TA–82) (701–TA–81 revised and reinitiated)	17 Nov 1981	Canada	McCurdy Fish Company	Negative preliminary injury determination, case terminated (23 Dec 1981)
Carbon steel plate	18 Nov 1981	South Africa	US Treasury (trigger price mechanism)	Petition withdrawn, case terminated (8 Feb 1982)
Carbon steel plate (701–TA–83)	18 Nov 1981	Belgium	US Treasury (trigger price mechanism)	Petition withdrawn, case terminated (8 Feb 1982)
Carbon steel plate (701–TA–84)	18 Nov 1981	Brazil	US Treasury (trigger price mechanism)	Petition withdrawn, case terminated (8 Feb 1982)
Hot-rolled carbon steel sheet (701–TA–85)	18 Nov 1981	France	US Treasury (trigger price mechanism)	Petition withdrawn, case terminated (8 Feb 1982)
Structural steel shapes	19 Nov 1981	Spain	US Treasury (trigger price mechanism)	Petition withdrawn, case terminated (8 Feb 1982)
Prestressed concrete steel wire strand (701–TA–164)	2 Dec 1981	Spain	Five domestic manufacturers of prestressed concrete strand	Negative final injury determination, case terminated (1 Sep 1982)

B-2 COUNTERVAILING DUTY INVESTIGATIONS, 1979–85 (*continued*)

Product	Date initiated	Country involved	Initiator	Action taken
Prestressed concrete steel wire strand	4 Dec 1981	South Africa	Four domestic manufacturers of prestressed concrete strand	Suspension of investigation based on Suspension Agreement, cash deposit 27 percent f.o.b. value (28 Apr 1982); affirmative final subsidy determination (2 Aug 1983); case terminated (29 Oct 1985)
Potassium permanganate (701–TA–183)	4 Dec 1981	Spain	Carus Chemical Company	Affirmative final subsidy and injury determinations (21 Jul 1982); petition withdrawn, case terminated (11 Aug 1982)
Hot-rolled carbon steel plate (701–TA–86)	11 Jan 1982	Belgium	US Steel, Bethlehem Steel, and other steel corporations	Affirmative preliminary injury determination (3 Mar 1982); petition withdrawn, case terminated (29 Oct 1982)
Hot-rolled carbon steel plate (701–TA–87)	11 Jan 1982	Brazil	US Steel, Bethlehem Steel, and other steel corporations	Affirmative preliminary subsidy determination, subsidy 12 percent ad valorem (20 Jan 1983); affirmative final subsidy determination (16 Mar 1983)
Hot-rolled carbon steel plate (701–TA–88)	11 Jan 1982	France	US Steel, Bethlehem Steel, and other steel corporations	Affirmative preliminary injury determination (3 Mar 1982); petition withdrawn, case terminated (29 Oct 1982)
Hot-rolled carbon steel plate (701–TA–89)	11 Jan 1982	Italy	US Steel, Bethlehem Steel, and other steel corporations	Affirmatiave preliminary injury determination (3 Mar 1982); petition withdrawn, case terminated (29 Oct 1982)

Hot-rolled carbon steel plate (701–TA–90)	11 Jan 1982	Luxembourg	US Steel, Bethlehem Steel, and other steel corporations	Affirmative preliminary injury determination (3 Mar 1982); petition withdrawn, case terminated (29 Oct 1982)
Hot-rolled carbon steel plate (701–TA–91)	11 Jan 1982	Netherlands	US Steel, Bethlehem Steel, and other steel corporations	Affirmative preliminary injury determination (3 Mar 1982); petition withdrawn, case terminated (29 Oct 1982)
Hot-rolled carbon steel plate (701–TA–92)	11 Jan 1982	United Kingdom	US Steel, Bethlehem Steel, and other steel corporations	Affirmative preliminary injury determination (3 Mar 1982); petition withdrawn, case terminated (29 Oct 1982)
Hot-rolled carbon steel plate (701–TA–93)	11 Jan 1982	Germany (FR)	US Steel, Bethlehem Steel, and other steel corporations	Affirmative preliminary injury determination (3 Mar 1982); petition withdrawn, case terminated (29 Oct 1982)
Hot-rolled carbon steel sheet and strip (701–TA–94)	11 Jan 1982	Belgium	US Steel, Bethlehem Steel, and other steel corporations	Affirmative preliminary injury determination (3 Mar 1982); petition withdrawn, case terminated (29 Oct 1982)
Hot-rolled carbon steel sheet and strip (701–TA–95)	11 Jan 1982	Brazil	US Steel, Bethlehem Steel, and other steel corporations	Affirmative preliminary injury determination (3 Mar 1982); petition withdrawn, case terminated (29 Oct 1982)
Hot-rolled carbon steel sheet and strip (701–TA–96)	11 Jan 1982	Italy	US Steel, Bethlehem Steel, and other steel corporations	Affirmative preliminary injury determination (3 Mar 1982); petition withdrawn, case terminated (29 Oct 1982)
Hot-rolled carbon steel sheet and strip (701–TA–97)	11 Jan 1982	Luxembourg	US Steel, Bethlehem Steel, and other steel corporations	Affirmative preliminary injury determination (3 Mar 1982); petition withdrawn, case terminated (29 Oct 1982)

B-2 COUNTERVAILING DUTY INVESTIGATIONS, 1979–85 (continued)

Product	Date initiated	Country involved	Initiator	Action taken
Hot-rolled carbon steel sheet and strip (701–TA–98)	11 Jan 1982	France	US Steel, Bethlehem Steel, and other steel corporations	Affirmative preliminary injury determination (3 Mar 1982); petition withdrawn, case terminated (29 Oct 1982)
Hot-rolled carbon steel sheet and strip (701–TA–99)	11 Jan 1982	United Kingdom	US Steel, Bethlehem Steel, and other steel corporations	Affirmative preliminary injury determination (3 Mar 1982); petition withdrawn, case terminated (29 Oct 1982)
Hot-rolled carbon steel sheet and strip (701–TA–101)	11 Jan 1982	Germany (FR)	US Steel, Bethlehem Steel, and other steel corporations	Affirmative preliminary injury determination (3 Mar 1982); petition withdrawn, case terminated (29 Oct 1982)
Cold-rolled carbon steel sheet and strip (701–TA–102)	11 Jan 1982	Belgium	US Steel, Bethlehem Steel, and other steel corporations	Affirmative preliminary injury determination (3 Mar 1982); petition withdrawn, case terminated (29 Oct 1982)
Cold-rolled carbon steel sheet and strip (701–TA–103)	11 Jan 1982	Brazil	US Steel, Bethlehem Steel, and other steel corporations	Affirmative preliminary injury determination (3 Mar 1982); petition withdrawn, case terminated (29 Oct 1982)
Cold-rolled carbon steel sheet and strip (701–TA–104)	11 Jan 1982	France	US Steel, Bethlehem Steel, and other steel corporations	Affirmative preliminary injury determination (3 Mar 1982); petition withdrawn, case terminated (29 Oct 1982)

Product	Date filed	Country	Petitioner	Status
Cold-rolled carbon steel sheet and strip (701–TA–105)	11 Jan 1982	Italy	US Steel, Bethlehem Steel, and other steel corporations	Affirmative preliminary injury determination (3 Mar 1982); petition withdrawn, case terminated (29 Oct 1982)
Cold-rolled carbon steel sheet and strip (701–TA–106)	11 Jan 1982	Luxembourg	US Steel, Bethlehem Steel, and other steel corporations	Affirmative preliminary injury determination (3 Mar 1982); petition withdrawn, case terminated (29 Oct 1982)
Cold-rolled carbon steel sheet and strip (701–TA–107)	11 Jan 1982	Netherlands	US Steel, Bethlehem Steel, and other steel corporations	Affirmative preliminary injury determination (3 Mar 1982); petition withdrawn, case terminated (29 Oct 1982)
Cold-rolled carbon steel sheet and strip (701–TA–108)	11 Jan 1982	United Kingdom	US Steel. Bethlehem Steel, and other steel corporations	Affirmative preliminary injury determination (3 Mar 1982); petition withdrawn, case terminated (29 Oct 1982)
Cold-rolled carbon steel sheet and strip (701–TA–109)	11 Jan 1982	Germany (FR)	US Steel, Bethlehem Steel, and other steel corporations	Affirmative preliminary injury determination (3 Mar 1982); petition withdrawn, case terminated (29 Oct 1982)
Galvanized carbon steel sheet (701–TA–110)	11 Jan 1982	Belgium	US Steel, Bethlehem Steel, and other steel corporations	Affirmative preliminary injury determination (3 Mar 1982); petition withdrawn, case terminated (29 Oct 1982)
Galvanized carbon steel sheet (701–TA–111)	11 Jan 1982	France	US Steel, Bethlehem Steel, and other steel corporations	Affirmative preliminary injury determination (3 Mar 1982); petition withdrawn, case terminated (29 Oct 1982)
Galvanized carbon steel sheet (701–TA–112)	11 Jan 1982	Italy	US Steel, Bethlehem Steel, and other steel corporations	Affirmative preliminary injury determination (3 Mar 1982); petition withdrawn, case terminated (29 Oct 1982)

B-2 COUNTERVAILING DUTY INVESTIGATIONS, 1979–85 *(continued)*

Product	Date initiated	Country involved	Initiator	Action taken
Galvanized carbon steel sheet (701–TA–113)	11 Jan 1982	Luxembourg	US Steel, Bethlehem Steel, and other steel corporations	Affirmative preliminary injury determination (3 Mar 1982); petition withdrawn, case terminated (29 Oct 1982)
Galvanized carbon steel sheet (701–TA–114)	11 Jan 1982	Netherlands	US Steel, Bethlehem Steel, and other steel corporations	Affirmative preliminary injury determination (3 Mar 1982); petition withdrawn, case terminated (29 Oct 1982)
Galvanized carbon steel sheet (701–TA–115)	11 Jan 1982	United Kingdom	US Steel, Bethlehem Steel, and other steel corporations	Affirmative preliminary injury determination (3 Mar 1982); petition withdrawn, case terminated (29 Oct 1982)
Galvanized carbon steel sheet (701–TA–116)	11 Jan 1982	Germany (FR)	US Steel, Bethlehem Steel, and other steel corporations	Affirmative preliminary injury determination (3 Mar 1982); petition withdrawn, case terminated (29 Oct 1982)
Carbon steel structural shapes (701–TA–117)	11 Jan 1982	Belgium	US Steel, Bethlehem Steel, and other steel corporations	Petition withdrawn, case terminated (10 Feb 1982)
Carbon steel structural shapes (701–TA–118)	11 Jan 1982	Brazil	US Steel, Bethlehem Steel, and other steel corporations	Petition withdrawn, case terminated (10 Feb 1982)
Carbon steel structural shapes (701–TA–119)	11 Jan 1982	France	US Steel, Bethlehem Steel, and other steel corporations	Petition withdrawn, case terminated (10 Feb 1982)

Product (case number)	Date	Country	Respondent	Status
Carbon steel structural shapes (701–TA–120)	11 Jan 1982	Italy	US Steel, Bethlehem Steel, and other steel corporations	Petition withdrawn, case terminated (10 Feb 1982)
Carbon steel structural shapes (701–TA–121)	11 Jan 1982	Luxembourg	US Steel, Bethlehem Steel, and other steel corporations	Petition withdrawn, case terminated (10 Feb 1982)
Carbon steel structural shapes (701–TA–122)	11 Jan 1982	Netherlands	US Steel, Bethlehem Steel, and other steel corporations	Petition withdrawn, case terminated (10 Feb 1982)
Carbon steel structural shapes (701–TA–123)	11 Jan 1982	United Kingdom	US Steel, Bethlehem Steel, and other steel corporations	Petition withdrawn, case terminated (10 Feb 1982)
Carbon steel structural shapes (701–TA–124)	11 Jan 1982	Germany (FR)	US Steel, Bethlehem Steel, and other steel corporations	Petition withdrawn, case terminated (10 Feb 1982)
Hot-rolled carbon steel bar (701–TA–125)	11 Jan 1982	Belgium	US Steel, Bethlehem Steel, and other steel corporations	Affirmative preliminary injury determination (3 Mar 1982); petition withdrawn, case terminated (29 Oct 1982)
Hot-rolled carbon steel bar (701–TA–126)	11 Jan 1982	Brazil	US Steel, Bethlehem Steel, and other steel corporations	Affirmative preliminary injury determination (3 Mar 1982); petition withdrawn, case terminated (29 Oct 1982)
Hot-rolled carbon steel bar (701–TA–127)	11 Jan 1982	France	US Steel, Bethlehem Steel, and other steel corporations	Affirmative preliminary injury determination (3 Mar 1982); petition withdrawn, case terminated (29 Oct 1982)
Hot-rolled carbon steel bar (701–TA–128)	11 Jan 1982	United Kingdom	US Steel, Bethlehem Steel, and other steel corporations	Affirmative preliminary injury determination (3 Mar 1982); petition withdrawn, case terminated (29 Oct 1982)

B-2 COUNTERVAILING DUTY INVESTIGATIONS, 1979–85 (continued)

Product	Date initiated	Country involved	Initiator	Action taken
Hot-rolled carbon steel bar (701–TA–129)	11 Jan 1982	Germany (FR)	US Steel, Bethlehem Steel, and other steel corporations	Affirmative preliminary injury determination (3 Mar 1982); petition withdrawn, case terminated (29 Oct 1982)
Hot-rolled alloy steel bar (701–TA–130)	11 Jan 1982	France	US Steel, Bethlehem Steel, and other steel corporations	Affirmative preliminary injury determination (3 Mar 1982); petition withdrawn, case terminated (29 Oct 1982)
Hot-rolled alloy steel bar (701–TA–131)	11 Jan 1982	Italy	US Steel, Bethlehem Steel, and other steel corporations	Affirmative preliminary injury determination (3 Mar 1982); petition withdrawn, case terminated (29 Oct 1982)
Hot-rolled alloy steel bar (701–TA–132)	11 Jan 1982	United Kingdom	US Steel, Bethlehem Steel, and other steel corporations	Affirmative preliminary injury determination (3 Mar 1982); petition withdrawn, case terminated (29 Oct 1982)
Hot-rolled alloy steel bar (701–TA–133)	11 Jan 1982	Germany (FR)	US Steel, Bethlehem Steel, and other steel corporations	Affirmative preliminary injury determination (3 Mar 1982); petition withdrawn, case terminated (29 Oct 1982)
Cold-formed carbon steel bar (701–TA–134)	11 Jan 1982	Belgium	US Steel, Bethlehem Steel, and other steel corporations	Affirmative preliminary injury determination (3 Mar 1982); petition withdrawn, case terminated (29 Oct 1982)
Cold-formed carbon steel bar (701–TA–135)	11 Jan 1982	Brazil	US Steel, Bethlehem Steel, and other steel corporations	Affirmative preliminary injury determination (3 Mar 1982); petition withdrawn, case terminated (29 Oct 1982)

Product	Date	Country	Petitioner	Disposition
Cold-formed carbon steel bar (701–TA–136)	11 Jan 1982	France	US Steel, Bethlehem Steel, and other steel corporations	Affirmative preliminary injury determination (3 Mar 1982); petition withdrawn, case terminated (29 Oct 1982)
Cold-formed carbon steel bar (701–TA–137)	11 Jan 1982	Italy	US Steel, Bethlehem Steel, and other steel corporations	Affirmative preliminary injury determination (3 Mar 1982); petition withdrawn, case terminated (29 Oct 1982)
Cold-formed carbon steel bar (701–TA–138)	11 Jan 1982	United Kingdom	US Steel, Bethlehem Steel, and other steel corporations	Negative preliminary subsidy determination, petition withdrawn, case terminated (7 Sep 1982)
Cold-formed carbon steel bar (701–TA–139)	11 Jan 1982	Germany (FR)	US Steel, Bethlehem Steel, and other steel corporations	Affirmative preliminary injury determination (3 Mar 1982); petition withdrawn, case terminated (29 Oct 1982)
Cold-formed alloy steel bar (701–TA–140)	11 Jan 1982	France	US Steel, Bethlehem Steel, and other steel corporations	Affirmative preliminary injury determination (3 Mar 1982); petition withdrawn, case terminated (29 Oct 1982)
Cold-formed alloy steel bar (701–TA–141)	11 Jan 1982	Italy	US Steel, Bethlehem Steel, and other steel corporations	Affirmative preliminary injury determination (3 Mar 1982); petition withdrawn, case terminated (29 Oct 1982)
Cold-formed alloy steel bar (701–TA–142)	11 Jan 1982	United Kingdom	US Steel, Bethlehem Steel, and other steel corporations	Affirmative preliminary injury determination (3 Mar 1982); petition withdrawn, case terminated (29 Oct 1982)
Cold-formed alloy steel bar (701–TA–143)	11 Jan 1982	(FR) Germany	US Steel, Bethlehem Steel, and other steel corporations	Affirmative preliminary injury determination (3 Mar 1982); petition withdrawn, case terminated (29 Oct 1982)

B-2 COUNTERVAILING DUTY INVESTIGATIONS, 1979–85 (continued)

Product	Date initiated	Country involved	Initiator	Action taken
Cold-formed alloy steel bar (701–TA–144)	11 Jan 1982	Belgium	US Steel, Bethlehem Steel, and other steel corporations	Affirmative preliminary injury determination (3 Mar 1982); petition withdrawn, case terminated (29 Oct 1982)
Barley (104–TAA–6)	15 Jan 1982	France	USITC	Affirmative final subsidy determination (no date recorded)
Certain steel wire nails (701–TA–145)	19 Jan 1982	Republic of Korea	Atlantic Steel Company; Florida Wire and Nail Company; others	Affirmative preliminary injury determination, cash deposit on case-by-case basis (19 Mar 1982); negative final subsidy determination, case terminated (9 Sep 1982)
Hot-rolled carbon steel plate	1 Feb 1982	Brazil	US Steel, Bethlehem Steel, and other steel corporations	Affirmative preliminary and final subsidy determinations, suspension of liquidation, net subsidy 12 percent ad valorem (20 Jan 1983); order revoked (18 Sep 1985)
Certain carbon steel products	1 Feb 1982	Germany (FR)	US Steel, Bethlehem Steel, and other steel corporations	Affirmative preliminary injury determination (3 Mar 1982); petition withdrawn, case terminated (29 Oct 1982)
Certain carbon steel products	1 Feb 1982	Italy	US Steel, Bethlehem Steel, and other steel corporations	Affirmative preliminary injury determination (3 Mar 1982); petition withdrawn, case terminated (29 Oct 1982)

Product	Date	Country	Parties	Action
Certain carbon steel products	1 Feb 1982	Luxembourg	US Steel, Bethlehem Steel, and other steel corporations	Affirmative preliminary injury determination (3 Mar 1982); petition withdrawn, case terminated (29 Oct 1982)
Certain carbon steel products	1 Feb 1982	Brazil	US Steel, Bethlehem Steel, and other steel corporations	Affirmative preliminary injury determination (3 Mar 1982); petition withdrawn, case terminated (29 Oct 1982)
Certain carbon steel products	1 Feb 1982	France	US Steel, Bethlehem Steel, and other steel corporations	Affirmative preliminary injury determination (3 Mar 1982); petition withdrawn, case terminated (29 Oct 1982)
Certain carbon steel products	1 Feb 1982	Netherlands	US Steel, Bethlehem Steel, and other steel corporations	Affirmative preliminary injury determination (3 Mar 1982); petition withdrawn, case terminated (29 Oct 1982)
Certain carbon steel products	1 Feb 1982	United Kingdom	US Steel, Bethlehem Steel, and other steel corporations	Affirmative preliminary injury determination (3 Mar 1982); petition withdrawn, case terminated (29 Oct 1982)
Certain carbon steel products (701–TA–154)	1 Feb 1982	South Africa	US Steel, Bethlehem Steel, and other steel corporations	Affirmative preliminary and final subsidy determinations (1 Sep 1982); order revoked (6 Aug 1985)
Certain carbon steel products (701–TA–155)	1 Feb 1982	Spain	Eight US producers of stainless steel bar and wire	Affirmative final subsidy and injury determinations, cash deposit on case-by-case basis (3 Jan 1983); order revoked (21 Aug 1985)
Certain carbon steel products (701–TA–156)	1 Feb 1982	Spain	Eight US producers of stainless steel bar and wire	Affirmative final subsidy and injury determinations, cash deposit on case-by-case basis (3 Jan 1983); order revoked (21 Aug 1985)

B-2 COUNTERVAILING DUTY INVESTIGATIONS, 1979–85 *(continued)*

Product	Date initiated	Country involved	Initiator	Action taken
Certain carbon steel products (701–TA–157)	1 Feb 1982	Spain	Eight US producers of stainless steel bar and wire	Affirmative final subsidy and injury determinations, cash deposit on case-by-case basis (3 Jan 1983); order revoked (21 Aug 1985)
Certain carbon steel products (701–TA–158)	1 Feb 1982	Spain	Eight US producers of stainless steel bar and wire	Affirmative final subsidy and injury determinations, cash deposit on case-by-case basis (3 Jan 1983); order revoked (21 Aug 1985)
Certain carbon steel products (701–TA–159)	1 Feb 1982	Spain	Eight US producers of stainless steel bar and wire	Affirmative final subsidy and injury determinations, cash deposit on case-by-case basis (3 Jan 1983); order revoked (21 Aug 1985)
Certain carbon steel products (701–TA–160)	1 Feb 1982	Spain	Eight US producers of stainless steel bar and wire	Affirmative final subsidy and injury determinations, cash deposit on case-by-case basis (3 Jan 1983); order revoked (21 Aug 1985)
Certain carbon steel products (701–TA–161)	1 Feb 1982	Spain	Eight US producers of stainless steel bar and wire	Affirmative final subsidy and injury determinations, cash deposit on case-by-case basis (3 Jan 1983); order revoked (21 Aug 1985)
Certain carbon steel products (701–TA–162)	1 Feb 1982	Spain	Eight US producers of stainless steel bar and wire	Affirmative final subsidy and injury determinations, cash deposit on case-by-case basis (3 Jan 1983); order revoked (21 Aug 1985)

Product	Date	Country	Petitioner	Determination
Certain carbon steel products (701–TA–163)	1 Feb 1982	Spain	Eight US producers of stainless steel bar and wire	Affirmative final subsidy and injury determinations, cash deposit on case-by-case basis (3 Jan 1983); order revoked (21 Aug 1985)
Prestressed concrete steel wire strand (701–TA–164)	1 Feb 1982	Spain	Five domestic manufacturers of prestressed concrete strand	Affirmative final subsidy and injury determinations, cash deposit on case-by-case basis (3 Jan 1983)
Hot-rolled carbon steel bar (701–TA–146)	3 Feb 1982	Italy	US Steel, Bethlehem Steel, and other steel corporations	Affirmative preliminary injury determination (3 Mar 1982); petition withdrawn, case terminated (29 Oct 1982)
Hot-rolled carbon steel bar (701–TA–147)	3 Feb 1982	Luxembourg	US Steel, Bethlehem Steel, and other steel corporations	Affirmative preliminary injury determination (3 Mar 1982); petition withdrawn, case terminated (29 Oct 1982)
Carbon steel wire rod (701–TA–148)	10 Feb 1982	Brazil	Seven US producers of carbon steel	Petition withdrawn, case terminated (9 Nov 1982)
Carbon steel wire rod (701–TA–149)	10 Feb 1982	Belgium	Seven US producers of carbon steel	Petition withdrawn, case terminated (9 Nov 1982)
Carbon steel wire rod (701–TA–150)	10 Feb 1982	France	Seven US producers of carbon steel	Petition withdrawn, case terminated (9 Nov 1982)
Certain nuts, bolts and screws (701–TA–151)	22 Feb 1982	Japan	US Fasteners Manufacturing Group	Petition withdrawn, case terminated (24 Mar 1982)
Prestressed concrete steel wire strand (701–TA–152)	4 Mar 1982	Brazil	Six domestic manufacturers of prestressed concrete strand	Affirmative preliminary subsidy and injury determinations, suspension of investigation based on Suspension Agreement (22 Oct 1982)
Prestressed concrete steel wire strand (701–TA–153)	4 Mar 1982	France	Six domestic manufacturers of prestressed concrete strand	Affirmative final subsidy determination (22 Oct 1982); negative final injury determination, case terminated (15 Dec 1982)

B-2 COUNTERVAILING DUTY INVESTIGATIONS, 1979–85 *(continued)*

Product	Date initiated	Country involved	Initiator	Action taken
Carbon steel wire rod	4 Mar 1982	South Africa	US industry producing carbon steel wire rod	Affirmative final subsidy determination, subsidy 8 percent ad valorem (27 Sep 1982); order revoked (7 Oct 1985)
Carbon steel wire rod	4 Mar 1982	Argentina	US industry producing carbon steel wire rod	Suspension of investigation (27 Sep 1982)
Hot-rolled stainless steel bar (701–TA–176)	10 Mar 1982	Spain	US industry producing stainless steel bar and wire rod	Affirmative final subsidy determination, cash deposit on case-by-case basis (15 Nov 1982); negative final injury determination, case terminated (5 Jan 1983)
Cold-formed stainless steel bar (701–TA–177)	10 Mar 1982	Spain	US industry producing stainless steel bar and wire rod	Affirmative final subsidy determination, cash deposit on case-by-case basis (15 Nov 1982); negative final injury determination, case terminated (5 Jan 1983)
Stainless steel wire rod (701–TA–178)	10 Mar 1982	Spain	US industry producing stainless steel bar and wire rod	Affirmative final subsidy determination, cash deposit on case-by-case basis (15 Nov 1982); negative final injury determination, case terminated (5 Jan 1983)
Michelin X-Radial steel belted tires (104–TAA–9)	11 Mar 1982	Canada	Rubber Manufacturers Assn., USITC	Petition withdrawn, case terminated (16 Jun 1982)
Certain tomato products (104–TAA–23)	16 Mar 1982	Greece	USITC	Negative final injury determination, case terminated (7 Nov 1982)

Product (case number)	Date	Country	Petitioner	Determination
Large diameter and small diameter welded carbon steel pipes and tubes (701–TA–168)	13 May 1982	Republic of Korea	US Steel Corp.	Affirmative final injury determination, cash deposit on case-by-case basis (18 Feb 1983); order revoked (29 Oct 1985)
Hot-rolled carbon steel plate (701–TA–170)	19 May 1982	Republic of Korea	US Steel Corp.	Affirmative final subsidy and injury determinations, cash deposit on case-by-case basis (18 Feb 1983); order revoked (10 Oct 1985)
Hot-rolled carbon steel sheet (701–TA–171)	19 May 1982	Republic of Korea	US Steel Corp.	Affirmative final subsidy and injury determinations, cash deposit on case-by-case basis (18 Feb 1983); order revoked (10 Oct 1985)
Galvanized carbon steel sheet (701–TA–173)	19 May 1982	Republic of Korea	US Steel Corp.	Affirmative final subsidy and injury determinations, cash deposit on case-by-case basis (18 Feb 1983); order revoked (10 Oct 1985)
Toy balloons (including pinchballs and playballs)	26 May 1982	Mexico	National Latex Products Company	Affirmative final subsidy determination, cash deposit 6 percent of f.o.b. invoice prices (29 Dec 1982); cash deposit 4 percent and 10 percent ad valorem (19 Mar 1984); subsidy of 4 percent and 9 percent ad valorem (14 Nov 1984); subsidy of 5 percent and 3 percent ad valorem (11 Mar 1986)
Welded carbon steel pipes and tubes (701–TA–165)	3 Jun 1982	Brazil	US Steel Corp.	Negative preliminary subsidy determination (affirmative for small diameter) (12 Oct 1982); petition withdrawn, case terminated (29 Oct 1982)
Large diameter and small diameter welded carbon steel pipes and tubes (701–TA–166)	3 Jun 1982	France	US Steel Corp.	Affirmative preliminary subsidy determination (negative for large diameter) (12 Oct 1982); petition withdrawn, case terminated (29 Oct 1982)

B-2 COUNTERVAILING DUTY INVESTIGATIONS, 1979–85 (continued)

Product	Date initiated	Country involved	Initiator	Action taken
Large diameter and small diameter welded carbon steel pipes and tubes (701–TA–167)	3 Jun 1982	Italy	US Steel Corp.	Affirmative preliminary subsidy determination (negative for large diameter) (12 Oct 1982); petition withdrawn, case terminated (29 Oct 1982)
Large diameter and small diameter welded carbon steel pipes and tubes (701–TA–169)	3 Jun 1982	Germany (FR)	US Steel Corp.	Petition withdrawn, case terminated (29 Oct 1982)
Certain commuter airplanes (701–TA–174)	4 Jun 1982	France	Commuter Aircraft Corp.	Negative preliminary injury determination, case terminated (21 Jul 1982)
Certain commuter airplanes (701–TA–175)	4 Jun 1982	France	Commuter Aircraft Corp.	Negative preliminary injury determination, case terminated (21 Jul 1982)
Deformed steel bars of concrete reinforcement	10 Jun 1982	South Africa	Industrial Siderurgica, Inc.	Affirmative final subsidy determination (28 Oct 1982); cash deposit based on f.o.b. invoice price (13 Apr 1984); tentative order to revoke (3 Jul 1985)
Hot-rolled stainless steel bar (701–TA–179)	23 Jun 1982	Brazil	Seven domestic manufacturers of stainless steel	Affirmative final subsidy and injury determinations, subsidy 15 percent ad valorem (13 May 1983)
Cold-formed stainless steel bar (701–TA–180)	23 Jun 1982	Brazil	Seven domestic manufacturers of stainless steel	Affirmative final subsidy and injury determinations, subsidy 15 percent ad valorem (13 May 1983)

Product	Date	Country	Petitioner	Determination
Stainless steel wire rod (701–TA–181)	23 Jul 1982	Brazil	Seven domestic manufacturers of stainless steel	Affirmative final subsidy and injury determinations, subsidy 15 percent ad valorem (13 May 1983)
Steel wire rope	2 Jul 1982	South Africa	Committee of Domestic Steel Wire Rope and Specialty Cable Manufacturers	Affirmative preliminary subsidy determination (13 Sep 1982); Suspension Agreement negotiated (26 Jan 1984)
Certain imported unfinished subway cars and parts thereof or railcars (701–TA–182)	6 Jul 1982	Canada	The Budd Company	Affirmative preliminary subsidy determination (29 Nov 1982); petition withdrawn, case terminated (15 Feb 1983)
Cotton sheeting and sateen	6 Jul 1982	Peru	American Textile Manufacturers Institute	Affirmative preliminary subsidy determination, cash deposit 34 percent of f.o.b. value (19 Nov 1982); cash deposit 30 percent f.o.b. value (1 Feb 1983); affirmative final subsidy determination, subsidy 35 percent ad valorem (3 Mar 1983); subsidy 21 percent ad valorem (31 Aug 1984)
Cotton yarn	6 Jul 1982	Peru	American Yarn Spinners Assn.	Affirmative preliminary and final subsidy determinations, subsidy 30 percent f.o.b. value (1 Feb 1983); subsidy 20 percent ad valorem (31 Aug 1984)
Litharge, red lead and lead stabilizers	12 Jul 1982	Mexico	US industry producing litharge, red lead, and lead stabilizers	Affirmative preliminary and final subsidy determinations, subsidy 4 percent ad valorem (6 Dec 1982); subsidy 5 percent ad valorem (10 Sep 1985)
Pectin	14 Jul 1982	Mexico	Hercules, Inc.	Affirmative preliminary and final subsidy determinations, subsidy 11 percent ad valorem (4 Apr 1983)

B-2   COUNTERVAILING DUTY INVESTIGATIONS, 1979–85 (continued)

Product	Date initiated	Country involved	Initiator	Action taken
Polypropylene film	14 Jul 1982	Mexico	Hercules, Inc.	Affirmative preliminary and final subsidy determinations, subsidy 6 percent ad valorem (4 Apr 1983)
Frozen concentrated orange juice (701–TA–184)	21 Jul 1982	Brazil	Florida Citrus Mutual	Affirmative final subsidy and injury determinations, subsidy 3 percent ad valorem (27 Jul 1983)
Fireplace mesh panels (701–TA–185)	26 Jul 1982	Taiwan	Justesen Industries, Inc.	Affirmative preliminary injury determination (15 Sep 1982); negative final subsidy determination, case terminated (17 Mar 1983)
Steel rails (701–TA–186)	28 Jul 1982	European Community	CP&I Steel Corp.	Petition withdrawn, case terminated (28 Sep 1982)
Certain tool steels (701–TA–187)	30 Jul 1982	Brazil	Nine US producers of tool steel bar and rod; United Steelworkers of America	Affirmative final injury determination, cash deposit 18 percent f.o.b. invoice price (13 Jan 1983); suspension of investigation based on Suspension Agreement (30 Mar 1983); subsidy 18 percent to 77 percent ad valorem (6 Jun 1983)
Certain commuter airplanes or turbo prop aircraft (701–TA–188)	13 Aug 1982	Brazil	Fairchild Swearingen	Negative preliminary injury determination, case terminated (6 Oct 1982)
Certain dairy products (104–TAA–10)	27 Aug 1982	European Community, Brazil	USITC	Negative preliminary injury determination, case terminated (22 Dec 1982)

Product	Date	Country	Petitioner	Disposition
Roses and other cut flowers	1 Sep 1982	Colombia	US industry producing roses and other cut flowers	Suspension of investigation based on Suspension Agreement, subsidy 5 percent f.o.b. value after 1 October 1983 (18 Jan 1983)
Steel rails (701–TA–189)	9 Sep 1982	European Community	CP&I Steel Corp.	Petition withdrawn, case terminated (28 Sep 1982)
Yarns of polypropylene	21 Sep 1982	Mexico	Quaker Textile Corp.	Affirmative preliminary and final subsidy determinations, cash deposit 4 percent ad valorem (4 Apr 1983)
Industrial nitrocellulose (701–TA–190)	22 Sep 1982	France	Hercules, Inc.	Affirmative final subsidy and injury determinations, cash deposit of 4 percent ad valorem (23 Jun 1983)
Steel rails (701–TA–191)	29 Sep 1982	Germany(FR)	CP&I Steel Corp.	Petition withdrawn, case terminated (29 Oct 1982)
Steel rails (701–TA–192)	29 Sep 1982	France	CP&I Steel Corp.	Petition withdrawn, case terminated (29 Oct 1982)
Steel rails (701–TA–193)	29 Sep 1982	United Kingdom	CP&I Steel Corp.	Petition withdrawn, case terminated (29 Oct 1982)
Steel rails (701–TA–194)	29 Sep 1982	Luxembourg	CP&I Steel Corp.	Petition withdrawn, case terminated (29 Oct 1982)
Certain iron-metal construction castings	30 Sep 1982	Mexico	Eleven domestic manufacturers of iron-metal construction castings	Affirmative preliminary and final subsidy determinations, subsidy 3 percent ad valorem (2 Mar 1983); subsidy .08 percent ad valorem (20 Mar 1986)
Stainless steel sheet and strip (701–TA–195)	7 Oct 1982	United Kingdom	The tool and stainless steel industry	Affirmative final subsidy determination, negative final injury determination, cash deposit 19 percent ad valorem (23 Jun 1983)

B-2 COUNTERVAILING DUTY INVESTIGATIONS, 1979–85 (continued)

Product	Date initiated	Country involved	Initiator	Action taken
Stainless steel plate (701–TA–196)	7 Oct 1982	United Kingdom	The tool and stainless steel industry	Affirmative final subsidy determination (20 Apr 1983); negative final injury determination (15 Jun 1983); cash deposit 19 percent ad valorem (23 Jun 1983)
Softwood fence lumber (701–TA–197)	7 Oct 1982	Canada	US Coalition for Fair Canadian Lumber Imports	Negative final subsidy determination, case terminated (31 May 1983)
Softwood fence shingles (701–TA–198)	7 Oct 1982	Canada	US Coalition for Fair Canadian Lumber Imports	Negative final subsidy determination, case terminated (31 May 1983)
Softwood fence shakes (701–TA–199)	7 Oct 1982	Canada	US Coalition for Fair Canadian Lumber Imports	Negative final subsidy determination, case terminated (31 May 1983)
Float glass (104–TAA–11)	8 Oct 1982	Belgium	US Treasury	Public hearings (16 Dec 1982)
Float glass (104–TAA–12)	8 Oct 1982	Italy	US Treasury	Public hearings (16 Dec 1982)
Wool	18 Oct 1982	Argentina	National Wool Growers Assn., Inc.	Affirmative preliminary and final subsidy determinations, cash deposit 5 percent ad valorem (4 Apr 1983); cash deposit 7 percent ad valorem (21 Feb 1984); subsidy 7 percent ad valorem (17 Sep 1985)

Product	Date	Country	Petitioner	Determination
Certain carbon steel pipe and tube products	29 Oct 1982	South Africa	The Committee on Pipe and Tube Imports	Affirmative final subsidy determination, cash deposit on case-by-case basis (12 Sep 1983); suspension of investigation based on Suspension Agreement, case terminated (1 Jun 1983); cash deposit on case-by-case basis (14 Aug 1984); order revoked (4 Sep 1985)
Certain automated fare collection equipment and parts thereof (701–TA–200)	1 Nov 1982	France	Cubic Western Data, Inc.	Negative preliminary injury determination, case terminated (8 Dec 1982)
Rayon staple fiber (104–TAA–13)	16 Nov 1982	Sweden	USITC	Affirmative preliminary injury determination (23 Mar 1983)
Anhydrous and aqua ammonia	26 Nov 1982	Mexico	US industry producing anhydrous and aqua ammonia	Negative final subsidy determination, case terminated (22 Jun 1983)
Fresh asparagus	30 Nov 1982	Mexico	Four associations of asparagus growers	Negative final subsidy determination, case terminated (13 May 1983)
Carbon black	3 Dec 1982	Mexico	US industry producing carbon black	Affirmative preliminary and final subsidy determinations, subsidy 2 percent ad valorem (27 Jun 1983)
Galvanized steel wire strand	7 Dec 1982	South Africa	Three domestic manufacturers of wire strand	Affirmative preliminary subsidy determination, cash deposit 23 percent f.o.b. value (15 Feb 1983); suspension of investigation based on Suspension Agreement (29 Apr 1983)
Bicycle tires and tubes (104–TAA–14)	10 Jan 1983	Republic of Korea	US Treasury	Negative preliminary injury determination, CVD order revoked, case terminated (6 Jun 1983)

B-2 COUNTERVAILING DUTY INVESTIGATIONS, 1979–85 (continued)

Product	Date initiated	Country involved	Initiator	Action taken
Bicycle tires and tubes (104–TAA–15)	10 Jan 1983	Taiwan	US Treasury	Negative preliminary injury determination, CVD order revoked, case terminated (9 Jun 1983)
Certain nonrubber footwear (104–TAA–16)	25 Jan 1983	Brazil	USITC	Negative preliminary injury determination, CVD order revoked, case terminated (21 Jun 1983)
Certain nonrubber footwear (104–TAA–17)	25 Jan 1983	India	USITC	Negative preliminary injury determination, CVD order revoked, case terminated (21 Jun 1983)
Certain nonrubber footwear (104–TAA–18)	25 Jan 1983	Spain	USITC	Negative preliminary injury determination, CVD order revoked, case terminated (21 Jun 1983)
Portland cement and cement clinker	1 Apr 1983	Mexico	US industry producing portland cement	Affirmative preliminary and final subsidy determinations, subsidy 6 percent ad valorem (12 Sep 1983); subsidy 3.5 percent ad valorem (19 Dec 1985)
Canned tuna	5 Apr 1983	Philippines	The Tuna Research Foundation	Affirmative final subsidy determination, subsidy 1 percent ad valorem (31 Oct 1983)
Pork rind pellets	8 Apr 1983	Mexico	Evans Food Products Company	Negative final subsidy and injury determinations, case terminated (29 Aug 1983)

Product	Date	Country	Petitioner	Determination
Forged undercarriage components (semi-finished links and rollers, semi-finished segments, finished articles) (701–TA–201)	29 Apr 1983	Italy	Seven American producers	Affirmative final subsidy and injury determinations, subsidy 1.4 percent ad valorem (29 Dec 1983)
Carbon steel wire rod	15 Jun 1983	Trinidad and Tobago	US producers of carbon steel wire rod	Affirmative preliminary and final subsidy determinations, subsidy 7 percent ad valorem (4 Jan 1984); tentative order to revoke (9 May 1985)
Certain refrigeration compressors	23 Jun 1983	Singapore	Tecumseh Products Company	Affirmative preliminary subsidy determination, subsidy 5 percent ad valorem (29 Aug 1983); suspension of investigation based on Suspension Agreement (7 Nov 1983)
Certain scissors and shears (104–TAA–19)	11 Jul 1983	Brazil	USITC	Negative preliminary injury determination, CVD order revoked, case terminated (1 Mar 1984)
Cotton shop towels (701–TA–202)	27 Jul 1983	Pakistan	Milliken and Company	Affirmative final subsidy and injury determinations, subsidy 18 percent ad valorem (30 Sep 1985)
Certain castor oil products (104–TAA–20)	21 Sep 1983	Brazil	USITC	Affirmative preliminary injury determination (8 Feb 1984)
Textiles, apparel and related products	3 Oct 1983	People's Republic of China	American Textile Manufacturers Institute	Petition withdrawn, case terminated (9 Dec 1983)
Unprocessed float glass	6 Oct 1983	Mexico	PPG Industries, Inc.	Affirmative preliminary and final subsidy determinations, subsidy 2.5 percent ad valorem (4 Jun 1984)
Certain fresh cut flowers	20 Oct 1983	Mexico	US industry producing fresh cut flowers	Negative final subsidy determination, case terminated (16 Apr 1984)

B-2 COUNTERVAILING DUTY INVESTIGATIONS, 1979–85 *(continued)*

Product	Date initiated	Country involved	Initiator	Action taken
Pads for woodwind instrument keys (701–TA–203)	7 Nov 1983	Italy	Prestini Musical In-struments Corp.	Negative final subsidy determina-tion, case terminated (25 Apr 1984)
Carbon steel plate (701–TA–204)	10 Nov 1983	Brazil	US Steel Corp.	Affirmative final subsidy and injury determinations, cash deposit on case-by-case basis (26 Apr 1984)
Carbon steel coils (701–TA–205)	10 Nov 1983	Brazil	US Steel Corp.	Affirmative final subsidy and injury determinations, cash deposit on case-by-case basis (22 Jun 1984); order revoked (6 Sep 1985)
Hot-rolled carbon steel sheet (701–TA–206)	10 Nov 1983	Brazil	US Steel Corp.	Affirmative final subsidy and injury determinations, cash deposit on case-by-case basis (22 Jun 1984); order revoked (6 Sep 1985)
Cold-rolled carbon steel sheet (701–TA–207)	10 Nov 1983	Brazil	US Steel Corp.	Affirmative final subsidy and injury determinations, cash deposit on case-by-case basis (22 Jun 1984); order revoked (6 Sep 1985)
Bricks	14 Nov 1983	Mexico	Brick Institute of Texas	Affirmative preliminary and final subsidy determinations, net subsidy 3.5 percent ad valorem (8 May 1984)
Continuous cast iron bars (701–TA–208)	15 Nov 1983	Brazil	Wells Manufacturing Company	Negative preliminary injury deter-mination, case terminated (11 Jan 1984)

Product	Date	Country	Petitioner	Disposition
Carbon steel wire rod (701–TA–209)	23 Nov 1983	Spain	Six domestic steel producers	Affirmative final subsidy and injury determinations, suspension of liquidation, cash deposit on case-by-case basis (8 May 1984); suspension of liquidation no longer effective (10 Jul 1984)
Certain carbon steel products	8 Dec 1983	Mexico	US Steel Corp.	Affirmative preliminary subsidy determination, subsidy 5 percent ad valorem (10 Feb 1984); petition withdrawn, case terminated (25 Apr 1984)
Cold-rolled carbon steel sheet	8 Dec 1983	Argentina	US domestic industry producing steel	Affirmative final subsidy determination, cash deposit on case-by-case basis (26 Apr 1984)
Carbon steel wire rod	13 Dec 1983	Spain	Carbon steel wire rod industry	Affirmative final subsidy and injury determinations, net subsidy 13 percent ad valorem, cash deposit on case-by-case basis (8 May 1984); tentative order to revoke duty (4 Jun 1985)
Carbon steel wire rod	13 Dec 1983	Poland	Carbon steel wire rod industry	Negative final subsidy determination, case terminated (7 May 1984)
Carbon steel wire rod	13 Dec 1983	Czechoslovakia	Carbon steel wire rod industry	Negative final subsidy determination, case terminated (7 May 1984)
Cotton yarn (104–TAA–21)	18 Jan 1984	Brazil	USITC	Affirmative preliminary injury determination (23 May 1984)
Bottled green olives (104–TAA–22)	19 Jan 1984	Spain	USITC	Negative preliminary injury determination, CVD order revoked (7 Jun 1984)
Certain table wine (701–TA–210)	27 Jan 1984	France	American Grape Growers Alliance for Fair Trade	Negative preliminary injury determination, case terminated (21 Mar 1984); decision reversed to affirmative (12 Dec 1985)

B-2 COUNTERVAILING DUTY INVESTIGATIONS, 1979–85 (continued)

Product	Date initiated	Country involved	Initiator	Action taken
Certain table wine (701–TA–211)	27 Jan 1984	Italy	American Grape Growers Alliance for Fair Trade	Negative preliminary injury determination, case terminated (21 Mar 1984); decision reversed to affirmative (12 Dec 1985)
Galvanized carbon steel sheet (701–TA–212)	10 Feb 1984	Australia	US Steel Corp.	Negative final subsidy determination, case terminated (25 Jul 1984)
Lime	21 Mar 1984	Mexico	US lime manufacturers	Affirmative preliminary and final subsidy determinations, cash deposit on case-by-case basis (11 Sep 1984)
Cotton shop towels	28 Mar 1984	Peru	Milliken and Co.	Affirmative preliminary subsidy determination, subsidy 44 percent ad valorem (27 Jun 1984); investigation suspended (12 Sep 1984)
Potassium chloride (701–TA–213)	30 Mar 1984	Spain	Amax Chemical, Inc.; Ken McGee Chemical Corp.	Affirmative final subsidy determination, subsidy 8 percent ad valorem (17 Sep 1984); negative final injury determination (7 Nov 1984)
Potassium chloride	30 Mar 1984	Germany (DR)	Amax Chemical, Inc.; Ken McGee Chemical Corp.	Rescission of initiation, petition dismissed (6 Jun 1984)
Potassium chloride	30 Mar 1984	USSR	Amax Chemical, Inc.; Ken McGee Chemical Corp.	Rescission of initiation, petition dismissed (6 Jun 1984)

Product	Date	Country	Petitioner	Determination
Potassium chloride (303–TA–15)	30 Mar 1984	Israel	Amax Chemical, Inc.; Ken McGee Chemical Corp.	Affirmative final subsidy determination, subsidy 4 percent ad valorem (14 Sep 1984); negative final injury determination (7 Nov 1984)
Hot-rolled carbon steel bars and hot-rolled carbon steel barsize shapes	6 Apr 1984	Mexico	Labor Management Committee for Fair Foreign Competition, Inc.	Affirmative preliminary and final subsidy determinations, subsidy 1.7 percent to 105 percent ad valorem (17 Aug 1984)
Lamb meat (701–TA–214)	18 Apr 1984	New Zealand	American Lamb Company	Negative preliminary injury determination, case terminated (13 Jun 1984)
Portland hydraulic cement	1 Jun 1984	Costa Rica	Puerto Rican Cement Company; San Juan Cement Company	Affirmative preliminary subsidy determination, subsidy 15 percent ad valorem (21 Sep 1984); suspension of investigation (3 Dec 1984)
Oil country tubular goods (701–TA–215)	13 Jun 1984	Brazil	Lone Star Steel Co.	Affirmative final subsidy and injury determinations, subsidy of 11 percent to 25 percent ad valorem (27 Nov 1984); order revoked (21 Aug 1985)
Oil country tubular goods	13 Jun 1984	Mexico	Lone Star Steel Co.	Affirmative final subsidy determination, net subsidy 6 percent ad valorem (30 Nov 1984); order revoked (31 Jul 1985)
Oil country tubular goods (701–TA–216)	13 Jun 1984	Republic of Korea	Lone Star Steel Co.	Affirmative final subsidy determination, net subsidy 1 percent ad valorem (28 Nov 1984); negative final injury determination (16 Jan 1985)
Oil country tubular goods (701–TA–217)	13 Jun 1984	Spain	Lone Star Steel Co.	Affirmative final subsidy and injury determinations, cash deposit on case-by-case basis (30 Nov 1984); order revoked (31 Jul 1985)

B-2 COUNTERVAILING DUTY INVESTIGATIONS, 1979–85 (continued)

Product	Date initiated	Country involved	Initiator	Action taken
Oil country tubular goods	13 Jun 1984	Argentina	Lone Star Steel Co.	Affirmative final subsidy determination, net subsidy 1 percent ad valorem (27 Nov 1984)
Cold-rolled carbon steel sheet (701–TA–218)	18 Jun 1984	Republic of Korea	US Steel Corp.	Affirmative final subsidy and injury determinations, net subsidy 3.6 percent ad valorem (3 Dec 1984); order revoked (10 Oct 1985)
Cold-rolled carbon steel structural shapes (701–TA–219)	18 Jun 1984	Republic of Korea	US Steel Corp.	Negative final subsidy determination, case terminated (3 Dec 1984)
Certain carbon steel pipes and tubes (701–TA–220)	17 Jul 1984	Spain	Committee on Pipe and Tube Imports	Affirmative preliminary subsidy and injury determinations, suspension of liquidation, net subsidy 1 percent ad valorem (17 Oct 1984); petition withdrawn, case termination (11 Feb 1985)
Certain textiles and textile products	19 Jul 1984	Peru	American Textile Manufacturers Assn.	Affirmative final subsidy determination, net subsidy 22.3 percent ad valorem for textiles; 19.9 percent for apparel (12 Mar 1985)
Certain textiles and textile products	19 Jul 1984	Singapore	American Textile Manufacturers Assn.	Negative final subsidy determination, case terminated (12 Mar 1985)
Certain textiles and textile products	20 Jul 1984	Malaysia	American Textile Manufacturers Assn.	Affirmative final subsidy determination, net subsidy 0.6 percent ad valorem (21 Dec 1985)

Product	Date	Country	Petitioner	Disposition
Certain textiles and textile products	20 Jul 1984	Thailand	American Textile Manufacturers Assn.	Affirmative final subsidy determination, net subsidy 1.2 percent ad valorem, suspension of investigation (12 Mar 1985)
Certain textiles and textile products	20 Jul 1984	Sri Lanka	American Textile Manufacturers Assn.	Affirmative final subsidy determination, net subsidy 3 percent ad valorem for textiles and 5 percent ad valorem for apparel (12 Mar 1985)
Certain textiles and textile products	20 Jul 1984	Portugal	American Textile Manufacturers Assn.	Petition withdrawn, case terminated (21 Dec 1984)
Certain textiles and textile products	20 Jul 1984	Indonesia	American Textile Manufacturers Assn.	Affirmative preliminary subsidy determination, net subsidy 1 percent ad valorem (21 Dec 1984); petition withdrawn, case terminated (17 Apr 1985)
Certain textiles and textile products	20 Jul 1984	Argentina	American Textile Manufacturers Assn.	Affirmative final subsidy determination, net subsidy 4.5 percent ad valorem for textiles and 16 percent ad valorem for apparel (12 Mar 1985)
Certain textiles and textile products	20 Jul 1984	Turkey	American Textile Manufacturers Assn.	Affirmative preliminary subsidy determination, net subsidy 17 percent ad valorem (21 Dec 1984); petition withdrawn, case terminated (17 Apr 1985)
Certain textiles and textile products	20 Jul 1984	Panama	American Textile Manufacturers Assn.	Petition withdrawn, case terminated (4 Dec 1984)
Certain textiles and textile products	23 Jul 1984	Colombia	American Textile Manufacturers Assn.	Affirmative preliminary subsidy determination, net subsidy 7 percent to 14 percent ad valorem (31 Dec 1984); suspension of investigation (12 Mar 1985)

B-2 COUNTERVAILING DUTY INVESTIGATIONS, 1979–85 (*continued*)

Product	Date initiated	Country involved	Initiator	Action taken
Certain textiles and textile products	24 Jul 1984	Mexico	American Textile Manufacturers Assn.	Affirmative final subsidy determination, net subsidy 4 percent ad valorem (18 Mar 1985)
Fabricated automotive glass	31 Jul 1984	Mexico	PPG Industries, Inc.	Affirmative final subsidy determination, net subsidy 4.7 percent ad valorem (14 Jan 1985)
Certain textiles and textile products	2 Aug 1984	Philippines	American Textile Manufacturers Assn.	Affirmative preliminary subsidy determination, average subsidy 1.4 percent ad valorem (11 Jan 1985); petition withdrawn, case terminated (17 Apr 1985)
Certain cast-iron pipe fittings (701–TA–221)	18 Sep 1984	Brazil	Cast Iron Pipe Fittings Committee	Affirmative final subsidy determination, net subsidy 14 percent ad valorem (5 Mar 1985); negative final injury determination (24 Apr 1985)
Certain cast-iron pipe fittings (701–TA–222)	18 Sep 1984	India	Cast Iron Pipe Fittings Committee	Petition withdrawn, case terminated (17 Oct 1984)
Agricultural tillage tools (701–TA–223)	28 Sep 1984	Brazil	Ingersoll Products Corp.	Affirmative preliminary and final subsidy and injury determinations, net subsidy 8 percent ad valorem (22 Oct 1985)
Welded carbon steel pipe and tube products	25 Oct 1984	Mexico	Committee on Pipe and Tube Imports	Affirmative preliminary subsidy determination, net subsidy 1 percent to 24 percent ad valorem (31 Jan 1985); petition withdrawn, case terminated (2 Apr 1985)

Product	Date	Country	Petitioner	Determination
Live swine and fresh, chilled and frozen pork (701–TA–224)	2 Nov 1984	Canada	National Pork Producers Council	Affirmative final injury and subsidy determinations, cash deposit of C$0.04/pound (15 Aug 1985)
Converted paper related school and office supplies	16 Nov 1984	Mexico	Stationery International Trade Committee	Affirmative preliminary subsidy determination, net subsidy 1 percent to 24 percent ad valorem (31 Jan 1985)
Oleoresins	12 Dec 1984	India	Kalamazoo Spice Extraction Co.	Affirmative final subsidy determination, petition withdrawn, case terminated (13 Mar 1985)
Oleoresins of paprika	12 Dec 1984	Spain	Kalamazoo Spice Extraction Co.	Affirmative final subsidy determination, petition withdrawn, case terminated (13 Mar 1985)
Carbon steel plates (701–TA–225)	19 Dec 1984	Sweden	US Steel Corp.	Affirmative final subsidy determination, net subsidy 8.8 percent ad valorem (19 Aug 1985); negative final injury determination (3 Oct 1985)
Carbon steel plates (701–TA–226)	19 Dec 1984	Venezuela	US Steel Corp.	Affirmative preliminary subsidy determination, net subsidy 76 percent ad valorem (20 Mar 1985)
Hot-rolled carbon steel sheet (701–TA–227)	19 Dec 1984	Austria	US Steel Corp.	Affirmative final subsidy determination, net subsidy 2 percent ad valorem (19 Aug 1985); negative final injury determination (3 Oct 1985)
Hot-rolled carbon steel sheet (701–TA–228)	19 Dec 1984	Sweden	US Steel Corp.	Affirmative final subsidy determination, net subsidy 8.8 percent ad valorem (19 Aug 1985); negative final injury determination (3 Oct 1985)
Hot-rolled carbon steel sheet (701–TA–229)	19 Dec 1984	Venezuela	US Steel Corp.	Affirmative preliminary subsidy and injury determinations, net subsidy 76 percent ad valorem (20 Mar 1985); petition withdrawn, case terminated (19 Jul 1985)

B-2 COUNTERVAILING DUTY INVESTIGATIONS, 1979–85 (continued)

Product	Date initiated	Country involved	Initiator	Action taken
Cold-rolled carbon steel sheets and plates (701–TA–230)	19 Dec 1984	Austria	US Steel Corp.	Affirmative preliminary and final subsidy and injury determinations, subsidy 2 percent ad valorem (3 Oct 1985); tentative order to revoke subsidy (14 Mar 1986)
Cold-rolled carbon steel sheets and plates (701–TA–231)	19 Dec 1984	Sweden	US Steel Corp.	Affirmative preliminary subsidy and injury determinations, net subsidy 3.4 percent ad valorem (20 Mar 1985); affirmative final injury and subsidy determinations, subsidy of 8.8 percent ad valorem (11 Oct 1985)
Cold-rolled carbon steel sheets and plates (701–TA–232)	19 Dec 1984	Venezuela	US Steel Corp.	Affirmative preliminary subsidy and injury determinations, net subsidy 76 percent ad valorem (20 Mar 1985); petition withdrawn, case terminated (19 Jul 1985)
Galvanized carbon steel sheets (701–TA–233)	19 Dec 1984	Austria	US Steel Corp.	Negative preliminary injury determination, case terminated (13 Feb 1985)
Galvanized carbon steel sheets (701–TA–234)	19 Dec 1984	Venezuela	US Steel Corp.	Negative preliminary injury determination, case terminated (13 Feb 1985)

Product (case number)	Date	Country	Petitioner	Action
Iron-ore pellets (701-TA-235)	20 Dec 1984	Brazil	Cleveland-Cliffs Iron Company; United Steelworkers of America	Affirmative preliminary injury and subsidy determinations, subsidy 5 percent ad valorem (22 Mar 1985); investigation suspended (19 Jun 1985)
Tapered tubular steel transmission structures (701-TA-236)	11 Feb 1985	Republic of Korea	Not available	Petition withdrawn, case terminated (7 Mar 1985)
Low-fuming brazing copper wire and rod (701-TA-237)	19 Feb 1985	France	American Brass Co.	Negative preliminary injury determination (10 Apr 1985)
Low-fuming brazing cooper wire and rod (701-TA-238)	19 Feb 1985	South Africa	American Brass Co.	Negative preliminary and final subsidy determinations (5 Aug 1985)
Low-fuming brazing copper wire and rod	19 Feb 1985	New Zealand	American Brass Co.	Affirmative preliminary and final subsidy determinations, suspension of liquidation, cash deposit of 9.17 percent ad valorem (5 Aug 1985)
Certain ethyl alcohol (701-TA-239)	25 Feb 1985	Brazil	Ad Hoc Committee of Domestic Fuel Ethanol Producers	Affirmative final subsidy determination, net subsidy 2.6 percent ad valorem (27 Jan 1986); negative final injury determination (19 Mar 1986)
Oil country tubular goods (701-TA-240)	28 Feb 1985	Austria	US Steel Corp.	Affirmative preliminary injury and subsidy determinations, net subsidy 1.82 percent ad valorem (3 Jun 1985); petition withdrawn, case terminated (8 Jan 1986)

B-2   COUNTERVAILING DUTY INVESTIGATIONS, 1979–85 (continued)

Product	Date initiated	Country involved	Initiator	Action taken
Oil country tubular goods (701–TA–241)	28 Feb 1985	Venezuela	US Steel Corp.	Affirmative preliminary injury determination (24 Apr 1985); petition withdrawn, case terminated (13 Nov 1985)
Certain welded carbon steel pipes and tubes (701–TA–242)	28 Feb 1985	Venezeula	Committee on Pipe and Tube Imports	Affirmative preliminary injury determination (24 Apr 1985); petition withdrawn, case terminated (13 Nov 1985)
Certain circular welded carbon steel pipes and tubes	28 Feb 1985	Thailand	Committee on Pipe and Tube Imports	Affirmative preliminary and final subsidy determinations, suspension of liquidation, cash deposit of 1.79 percent ad valorem (14 Aug 1985)
Lamb meat	25 Mar 1985	New Zealand	American Lamb Co.	Affirmative final subsidy determination, suspension of liquidation, net subsidy NZ$0.36 (17 Sep 1985)
Portable aluminum ladders and certain components of ladders	26 Mar 1985	Mexico	R.D. Werner Co.	Petition withdrawn, case terminated (24 May 1985)
Carbon steel wire rod (701–TA–243)	8 Apr 1985	Portugal	Several domestic steel companies	Affirmative preliminary injury determination (30 May 1985); negative preliminary subsidy determination (11 Jul 1985); petition withdrawn, case terminated (10 Dec 1985)

Product	Date	Country	Petitioner	Determination
Carbon steel wire rod (701–TA–244)	8 Apr 1985	Venezuela	Several domestic steel companies	Affirmative preliminary injury and subsidy determinations, net subsidy 70.98 percent ad valorem (11 Jul 1985); petition withdrawn, case terminated (12 Aug 1985)
Offshore platform jackets and piles (701–TA–248)	18 Apr 1985	Republic of Korea	Kaiser Steel Corp.	Affirmative preliminary injury and subsidy determinations, net subsidy 9.58 percent and 4.14 percent ad valorem (19 Jul 1985)
Iron construction castings (701–TA–249)	13 May 1985	Brazil	Municipal Castings Fair Trade Council	Affirmative preliminary injury and subsidy determinations for heavy castings, negative preliminary injury determination and affirmative preliminary subsidy determination for light castings, suspension of liquidation, net subsidy 4.56 percent ad valorem (12 Aug 1985); affirmative final subsidy determination, subsidy 3.4 percent ad valorem (19 Mar 1986)
Converted paper related school and office supplies	14 May 1985	Mexico	Stationery International Trade Committee	Petition withdrawn, case terminated (7 Jun 1985)
Lime oil (303–TA–16)	29 May 1985	Peru	Parmann-Kendall, Inc.	Negative preliminary injury determination (24 Jul 1985)
Carbon steel wire rod	12 Jun 1985	Saudi Arabia	Atlantic Steel Co. and others	Affirmative preliminary and final subsidy determinations, net subsidy 5.5 percent ad valorem (30 Feb 1986)

B-2 COUNTERVAILING DUTY INVESTIGATIONS, 1979–85 (continued)

Product	Date initiated	Country involved	Initiator	Action taken
Deformed steel concrete reinforcing bars	13 Jun 1985	Peru	Florida Steel Corp.; Chaparral Steel Co.	Affirmative preliminary and final subsidy determinations, net subsidy 1.82 percent ad valorem (27 Nov 1985)
Certain welded carbon steel pipes and tubes (701–TA–251)	16 Jul 1985	India	Committee on Pipe and Tube Imports	Affirmative preliminary injury and subsidy determinations, net subsidy 5 percent ad valorem (16 Oct 1985); negative final injury and subsidy determinations, case terminated (15 Jan 1986)
Certain welded carbon steel pipes and tubes (701–TA–252)	16 Jul 1985	Taiwan	Committee on Pipe and Tube Imports	Affirmative preliminary injury and subsidy determinations, net subsidy 1.15 percent ad valorem (16 Oct 1985); negative final subsidy determination (31 Dec 1985); case terminated (15 Jan 1986)
Certain welded carbon steel pipes and tubes	16 Jul 1985	Yugoslavia	Committee on Pipe and Tube Imports	Affirmative preliminary and final subsidy determinations, net subsidy 74.5 percent ad valorem (31 Dec 1985)
Certain welded carbon steel pipes and tubes (701–TA–253)	16 Jul 1985	Turkey	Committee on Pipe and Tube Imports	Affirmative preliminary injury and subsidy determinations, cash deposit 23.64 percent ad valorem (28 Oct 1985); affirmative final subsidy and injury determinations, net subsidy 18.81 percent ad valorem (3 Mar 1986)

Product	Date	Country	Petitioner	Determination
Certain red raspberries (701–TA–254)	18 Jul 1985	Canada	Washington Raspberry Commission	Affirmative preliminary injury and subsidy determinations, net subsidy 0.99 percent ad valorem (21 Oct 1985); investigation suspended (9 Jan 1986)
Oil country tubular goods (701–TA–255)	22 Jul 1985	Canada	Lone Star Steel Co.	Affirmative preliminary injury and subsidy determinations, net subsidy 0.72 percent ad valorem (30 Dec 1985)
Oil country tubular goods (701–TA–256)	22 Jul 1985	Taiwan	Lone Star Steel Co.	Affirmative preliminary injury determination (11 Sep 1985); negative preliminary subsidy determination (6 Dec 1985)
Certain fresh Atlantic groundfish (701–TA–257)	5 Aug 1985	Canada	North Atlantic Fisheries Task Force	Affirmative preliminary injury and subsidy determinations, net subsidy 6.85 percent ad valorem (9 Jan 1986); affirmative final subsidy determination, net subsidy 5.8 percent ad valorem (24 Mar 1986)
Carbon steel wire rod	9 Aug 1985	Singapore	Atlantic Steel Company	Negative preliminary and final subsidy determinations (27 Jan 1986)
Certain table wine (701–TA–258)	10 Sep 1985	Italy	American Grape Growers Alliance for Fair Trade	Negative preliminary injury determination (30 Oct 1985)
Certain table wine (701–TA–259)	10 Sep 1985	France	American Grape Growers Alliance for Fair Trade	Negative preliminary injury determination (30 Oct 1985)
Certain table wine (701–TA–260)	10 Sep 1985	Germany (FR)	American Grape Growers Alliance for Fair Trade	Negative preliminary injury determination (30 Oct 1985)

B-2 COUNTERVAILING DUTY INVESTIGATIONS, 1979–85 (continued)

Product	Date initiated	Country involved	Initiator	Action taken
Carbon steel wire rod	23 Sep 1985	New Zealand	Atlantic Steel Co.	Affirmative final subsidy determination, net subsidy 25.7 percent ad valorem (7 Mar 1986)
Rice	24 Sep 1985	Thailand	Rice Millers Assn.	Affirmative preliminary subsidy determination, cash deposit of 1.6 percent ad valorem (27 Jan 1986)
In-shell pistachio nuts	26 Sep 1985	Iran	California Pistachio Commission	Affirmative final subsidy determination, net subsidy 99.5 percent ad valorem (11 Mar 1986)
Welded steel wire fabric for concrete reinforcement (701–TA–261)	24 Oct 1985	Italy	Wire Reinforcement Institute	Petition withdrawn, case terminated (14 Nov 1985)
Welded steel wire fabric for concrete reinforcement (701–TA–262)	24 Oct 1985	Republic of Korea	Wire Reinforcement Institute	Petition withdrawn, case terminated (14 Nov 1985)
Welded steel wire fabric for concrete reinforcement (701–TA–263)	24 Oct 1985	Mexico	Wire Reinforcement Institute	Petition withdrawn, case terminated (14 Nov 1985)
Welded steel wire fabric for concrete reinforcement (701–TA–264)	24 Oct 1985	Venezuela	Wire Reinforcement Institute	Petition withdrawn, case terminated (14 Nov 1985)
Welded steel wire fabric for concrete reinforcement (701–TA–261A)	20 Nov 1985	Italy	Wire Reinforcement Institute	Negative preliminary injury determination (15 Jan 1986)

Welded steel wire fabric for concrete reinforcement (701–TA–263A)	20 Nov 1985	Mexico	Wire Reinforcement Institute	Negative preliminary injury determination (15 Jan 1986)
Welded steel wire fabric for concrete reinforcement (701–TA–264A)	20 Nov 1985	Venezuela	Wire Reinforcement Institute	Negative preliminary injury determination (15 Jan 1986)
Porcelain on steel cooking ware (701–TA–265)	4 Dec 1985	Taiwan	General Housewares Corp.	Affirmative preliminary injury determination, negative preliminary subsidy determination (7 Mar 1986)
Porcelain on steel cooking ware (701–TA–266)	4 Dec 1985	Mexico	General Housewares Corp.	Affirmative preliminary injury and subsidy determinations, net subsidy 2.3 percent ad valorem (7 Mar 1986)

B-3 ANTIDUMPING INVESTIGATIONS, 1979–85

Product	Date initiated	Country involved	Initiator	Action taken
Spun acrylic yarn (731–TA–1)	2 Jan 1979	Japan	American Yarn Spinners Assn.	Affirmative final SLFV determination, cash deposit on case-by-case basis; final review results: 18.3 percent cash deposit (26 Mar 1982)[1]
Carbon steel plate	9 Jan 1979	Belgium	Lukens Steel Co. (trigger price mechanism)	Petition withdrawn, case terminated (25 Jun 1979)
Carbon steel plate	9 Jan 1979	France	Lukens Steel Co. (trigger price mechanism)	Petition withdrawn, case terminated (25 Jun 1979)
Carbon steel plate	9 Jan 1979	Germany (FR)	Lukens Steel Co. (trigger price mechanism)	Petition withdrawn, case terminated (25 Jun 1979)
Carbon steel plate	9 Jan 1979	Italy	Lukens Steel Co. (trigger price mechanism)	Petition withdrawn, case terminated (25 Jun 1979)
Carbon steel plate	9 Jan 1979	United Kingdom	Lukens Steel Co. (trigger price mechanism)	Petition withdrawn, case terminated (28 Feb 1979)
45 R.P.M. adaptors (flat and round spindle)	2 Feb 1979	United Kingdom	Aldisher Manufacturing Company	Negative preliminary injury determination, case terminated (20 Mar 1979)
Carbon steel light weight T-beams	9 Feb 1979	Belgium	Connors Steel Company	Negative final SLFV determination, case terminated (20 Sep 1979)
Sodium acetate	29 Mar 1979	Canada	Niacet Corp.	Negative final injury determination, case terminated (3 Jan 1980)

Product	Date	Country	Petitioner	Determination
Sodium hydroxide, in solution (light caustic soda) (731–TA–8)	20 Apr 1979	Germany (FR)	Linden Chemicals and Plastics	Negative preliminary injury determination, case terminated (21 Feb 1980)
Sodium hydroxide, in solution (light caustic soda) (731–TA–9)	20 Apr 1979	France	Linden Chemicals and Plastics	Negative preliminary injury determination, case terminated (21 Feb 1980)
Sodium hydroxide, in solution (light caustic soda) (731–TA–10)	20 Apr 1979	Italy	Linden Chemicals and Plastics	Negative preliminary injury determination, case terminated (21 Feb 1980)
Sodium hydroxide, in solution (light caustic soda) (731–TA–11)	20 Apr 1979	United Kingdom	Linden Chemicals and Plastics	Negative preliminary injury determination, case terminated (21 Feb 1980)
Steel wire coat and garment hangars	20 Apr 1979	Canada	Laidlow Corp.	Negative preliminary injury determination, case terminated (19 Jun 1979)
Certain steel wire nails (731–TA–26)	26 Apr 1979	Republic of Korea	U.S. Treasury (trigger price mechanism)	Negative final injury determination, case terminated (13 Aug 1980)
Sugar and syrups (731–TA–3)	30 Apr 1979	Canada	Amstar Corp.	Affirmative final SLFV determination (16 Oct 1981); final administrative review results: 17.33 percent cash deposit (11 Jun 1982); cash deposit on case-by-case basis (25 Oct 1983)
Melamine in crystal form (731–TA–13)	1 May 1979	Austria	Melamine Chemicals, Inc.	Negative final injury determination, case terminated (14 May 1980)
Melamine in crystal form (731–TA–14)	1 May 1979	Italy	Melamine Chemicals, Inc.	Negative final injury determination, case terminated (14 May 1980)

---

[1] SLFV refers to "sales at less than fair value."

B-3 ANTIDUMPING INVESTIGATIONS, 1979–85 (continued)

Product	Date initiated	Country involved	Initiator	Action taken
Melamine in crystal form (731–TA–16)	1 May 1979	Netherlands	Melamine Chemicals, Inc.	Negative final SLFV determination, case terminated (25 Apr 1980)
Portable electric typewriters (731–TA–12)	18 May 1979	Japan	SCM Corp.	Cash deposit on case-by-case basis; administrative review results: cash deposit 0.60 percent; waiver of deposit (24 Feb 1983); cash deposit on case-by-case basis (9 Sep 1983)
Ply worsted spun acrylic machine knitting yarn (731–TA–2)	2 Jul 1979	Italy	American Yarn Spinners Assn.	Affirmative final SLFV determination, duty of 48 percent ad valorem (8 Apr 1980); admin. review results: cash deposit on case-by-case basis (4 Feb 1982); review results: same as above (4 Sep 1985)
Countertop microwave ovens (731–TA–4)	29 Aug 1979	Japan	Assn. of Home Appliance Manufacturers	Affirmative final SLFV determination, suspension of liquidation (15 Jul 1980); case terminated (11 Dec 1980)
Certain industrial electric motors (between 150 and 500 HP) (731–TA–7)	3 Oct 1979	Japan	National Electrical Manufacturers Assn.	Affirmative final SLFV determination, cash deposit on case-by-case basis (18 Jun 1982); review results: cash deposit on case-by-case basis (5 Apr 1983); review results: same as above (15 Aug 1984)
Tomatoes, peppers, cucumbers, squash (731–TA–15)	19 Oct 1979	Mexico	S.W. Florida Winter Vegetable Growers Assn.	Negative final SLFV determination, case terminated (28 Mar 1980)

Product	Date	Country	Petitioner	Determination
Railway passenger cars and parts thereof, intended for use as original equipment in the United States (731–TA–5)	27 Nov 1979	Italy	Budd Company (Railway Division)	Negative preliminary injury determination, case terminated (22 Feb 1980)
Railway passenger cars and parts thereof, intended for use as original equipment in the United States (731–TA–6)	27 Nov 1979	Japan	Budd Company (Railway Division)	Negative preliminary injury determination, case terminated (22 Feb 1980)
Pipes and tubes of iron or steel (731–TA–15)	28 Feb 1980	Japan	Babcock and Wilcox Company	Petition withdrawn, case terminated (16 Jul 1980)
Clams in airtight containers (731–TA–17)	6 Mar 1980	Canada	A.M. Look Canning Company	Negative preliminary injury determination, case terminated (30 Apr 1980)
Carbon steel cold-rolled sheet (731–TA–18)	17 Apr 1980	Belgium	US Steel Corp.	Affirmative preliminary injury determination (1 May 1980); petition withdrawn, case terminated (1 Oct 1980)
Carbon steel cold-rolled sheet (731–TA–19)	17 Apr 1980	Germany (FR)	US Steel Corp.	Affirmative preliminary injury determination (1 May 1980); petition withdrawn, case terminated (1 Oct 1980)
Carbon steel cold-rolled sheet (731–TA–20)	17 Apr 1980	France	US Steel Corp.	Affirmative preliminary injury determination (1 May 1980); petition withdrawn, case terminated (1 Oct 1980)
Carbon steel cold-rolled sheet (731–TA–21)	17 Apr 1980	Italy	US Steel Corp.	Affirmative preliminary injury determination (1 May 1980); petition withdrawn, case terminated (1 Oct 1980)
Carbon steel cold-rolled sheet (731–TA–23)	17 Apr 1980	Netherlands	US Steel Corp.	Affirmative preliminary injury determination (1 May 1980); petition withdrawn, case terminated (1 Oct 1980)

B-3 ANTIDUMPING INVESTIGATIONS, 1979–85 (continued)

Product	Date initiated	Country involved	Initiator	Action taken
Carbon steel cold-rolled sheet (731–TA–24)	17 Apr 1980	United Kingdom	US Steel Corp.	Affirmative preliminary injury determination (1 May 1980); petition withdrawn, case terminated (1 Oct 1980)
Carbon steel galvanized sheet (731–TA–18)	17 Apr 1980	Belgium	US Steel Corp.	Affirmative preliminary injury determination (1 May 1980); petition withdrawn, case terminated (1 Oct 1980)
Carbon steel galvanized sheet (731–TA–19)	17 Apr 1980	Germany (FR)	US Steel Corp.	Affirmative preliminary injury determination (1 May 1980); petition withdrawn, case terminated (1 Oct 1980)
Carbon steel galvanized sheet (731–TA–20)	17 Apr 1980	France	US Steel Corp.	Affirmative preliminary injury determination (1 May 1980); petition withdrawn, case terminated (1 Oct 1980)
Carbon steel galvanized sheet (731–TA–21)	17 Apr 1980	Italy	US Steel Corp.	Affirmative preliminary injury determination (1 May 1980); petition withdrawn, case terminated (1 Oct 1980)
Carbon steel galvanized sheet (731–TA–23)	17 Apr 1980	Netherlands	US Steel Corp.	Affirmative preliminary injury determination (1 May 1980); petition withdrawn, case terminated (1 Oct 1980)
Carbon steel galvanized sheet (731–TA–24)	17 Apr 1980	United Kingdom	US Steel Corp.	Affirmative preliminary injury determination (1 May 1980); petition withdrawn, case terminated (1 Oct 1980)

Product	Date	Country	Petitioner	Determination
Carbon steel hot-rolled sheet (731–TA–18)	17 Apr 1980	Belgium	US Steel Corp.	Affirmative preliminary injury determination (1 May 1980); petition withdrawn, case terminated (1 Oct 1980)
Carbon steel hot-rolled sheet (731–TA–19)	17 Apr 1980	Germany (FR)	US Steel Corp.	Affirmative preliminary injury determination (1 May 1980); petition withdrawn, case terminated (1 Oct 1980)
Carbon steel hot-rolled sheet (731–TA–20)	17 Apr 1980	France	US Steel Corp.	Affirmative preliminary injury determination (1 May 1980); petition withdrawn, case terminated (1 Oct 1980)
Carbon steel hot-rolled sheet (731–TA–21)	17 Apr 1980	Italy	US Steel Corp.	Affirmative preliminary injury determination (1 May 1980); petition withdrawn, case terminated (1 Oct 1980)
Carbon steel hot-rolled sheet (731–TA–23)	17 Apr 1980	Netherlands	US Steel Corp.	Affirmative preliminary injury determination (1 May 1980); petition withdrawn, case terminated (1 Oct 1980)
Carbon steel hot-rolled sheet (731–TA–24)	17 Apr 1980	United Kingdom	US Steel Corp.	Affirmative preliminary injury determination (1 May 1980); petition withdrawn, case terminated (1 Oct 1980)
Carbon steel plate (731–TA–18)	17 Apr 1980	Belgium	US Steel Corp.	Affirmative preliminary injury determination (1 May 1980); petition withdrawn, case terminated (1 Oct 1980)
Carbon steel plate (731–TA–19)	17 Apr 1980	Germany (FR)	US Steel Corp.	Affirmative preliminary injury determination (1 May 1980); petition withdrawn, case terminated (1 Oct 1980)

B-3 ANTIDUMPING INVESTIGATIONS, 1979–85 (continued)

Product	Date initiated	Country involved	Initiator	Action taken
Carbon steel plate (731–TA–20)	17 Apr 1980	France	US Steel Corp.	Affirmative preliminary injury determination (1 May 1980); petition withdrawn, case terminated (1 Oct 1980)
Carbon steel plate (731–TA–21)	17 Apr 1980	Italy	US Steel Corp.	Affirmative preliminary injury determination (1 May 1980); petition withdrawn, case terminated (1 Oct 1980)
Carbon steel plate (731–TA–23)	17 Apr 1980	Netherlands	US Steel Corp.	Affirmative preliminary injury determination (1 May 1980); petition withdrawn, case terminated (1 Oct 1980)
Carbon steel plate (731–TA–24)	17 Apr 1980	United Kingdom	US Steel Corp.	Affirmative preliminary injury determination (1 May 1980); petition withdrawn, case terminated (1 Oct 1980)
Carbon steel structural shapes (731–TA–18)	17 Apr 1980	Belgium	US Steel Corp.	Affirmative preliminary injury determination (1 May 1980); petition withdrawn, case terminated (1 Oct 1980)
Carbon steel structural shapes (731–TA–19)	17 Apr 1980	Germany (FR)	US Steel Corp.	Affirmative preliminary injury determination (1 May 1980); petition withdrawn, case terminated (1 Oct 1980)
Carbon steel structural shapes (731–TA–20)	17 Apr 1980	France	US Steel Corp.	Affirmative preliminary injury determination (1 May 1980); petition withdrawn, case terminated (1 Oct 1980)

Product	Date	Country	Petitioner	Determination
Carbon steel structural shapes (731–TA–21)	17 Apr 1980	Italy	US Steel Corp.	Affirmative preliminary injury determination (1 May 1980); petition withdrawn, case terminated (1 Oct 1980)
Carbon steel structural shapes (731–TA–23)	17 Apr 1980	Netherlands	US Steel Corp.	Affirmative preliminary injury determination (1 May 1980); petition withdrawn, case terminated (1 Oct 1980)
Carbon steel structural shapes (731–TA–24)	17 Apr 1980	United Kingdom	US Steel Corp.	Affirmative preliminary injury determination (1 May 1980); petition withdrawn, case terminated (1 Oct 1980)
Anhydrous sodium metasilicate (731–TA–25)	10 Jun 1980	France	PQ Corp.	Affirmative final SLFV determination, duty 60 percent ad valorem (7 Jan 1981); review results: cash deposit of 60 percent (8 Oct 1982); waiver of deposit (31 Oct 1984)
Natural or synthetic menthol (731–TA–27)	2 Jul 1980	Japan	Haarman and Reimar Corp.	Negative final injury determination, case terminated (17 Jun 1981)
Natural or synthetic menthol (731–TA–28)	2 Jul 1980	People's Republic of China	Haarman and Reimar Corp.	Affirmative preliminary injury and SLFV determinations, cash deposit 14 percent f.o.b. value (14 Jan 1981); negative final injury determination, case terminated (17 Jun 1981)
Potassium chloride (751–TA–3)	1 Aug 1980	Canada	Texasgulf, Inc.	Negative final SLFV and injury determinations, case terminated (15 Apr 1981)
Asphalt roofing shingles (731–TA–29)	17 Sep 1980	Canada	Asphalt Roofing Manufacturers Assn.	Negative preliminary injury determination, case terminated (16 Oct 1980)

B-3 ANTIDUMPING INVESTIGATIONS, 1979–85 (continued)

Product	Date initiated	Country involved	Initiator	Action taken
Unrefined montan wax (731–TA–30)	30 Sep 1980	Germany (DR)	American Lignite Products Company	Affirmative final SLFV and injury determinations (28 Jul 1981); cash deposit of 13 percent ex factory value (10 Sep 1981); waiver of deposit (15 Aug 1983); tentative determination to revoke order (22 Jun 1984)
Precipitated barium carbonate (731–TA–31)	30 Sep 1980	Germany (FR)	FMC Corp., Chemicals Products Corp.; Sherwin-Williams Company	Affirmative final SLFV and injury determinations, duty of 10 percent f.o.b. value (24 Jun 1981); cash deposit of 39 percent ad valorem (24 Feb 1984); no dumping duties assessed since November 1984 (22 Apr 1985)
Strontium carbonate (731–TA–32)	30 Sep 1980	Germany (FR)	FMC Corp., Chemicals Products Corp., Sherwin-Williams Company	Negative final SLFV determination, case terminated (24 Jun 1981)
Strontium nitrate (731–TA–33)	6 Oct 1980	Italy	FMC Corp.	Affirmative final SLFV determination (7 May 1981); security deposit (24 Sep 1981); deposit waived (23 Jun 1983); tentative determination to revoke order (14 May 1984)
Portable electric nibblers (731–TA–34)	6 Oct 1980	Switzerland	Widder Corp.	Petition withdrawn, case terminated (3 Dec 1980)
Latchet hook kits (731–TA–35)	13 Nov 1980	United Kingdom	A&H Shillman Company, Inc.; Ann Company, Inc.	Petition dismissed (10 Dec 1980)

Product (investigation number)	Date	Country	Petitioner	Determination
Snow grooming vehicles, and parts and assemblies thereof (731–TA–36)	5 Dec 1980	Germany (FR)	Delorean Manufacturing Company	Negative preliminary injury determination, case terminated (5 Jan 1981)
Certain iron-metal castings (731–TA–37)	12 Dec 1980	India	Pinkerton Foundary, Inc.	Affirmative final SLFV determination, negative final injury determination, case terminated (5 Aug 1981)
Synthetic L-Menthio Nine (751–TA–4)	15 Dec 1980	Japan	USITC	Negative final SLFV determination, case terminated (29 Jul 1981)
Truck trailer axles and assemblies and parts thereof (731–TA–38)	19 Feb 1981	Hungary	Rockwell International Corp.	Affirmative preliminary injury and SLFV determinations, cash deposit 68 percent of f.o.b. value (17 Sep 1981); investigation suspended (4 Jan 1982)
Secondary aluminum alloy in unwrought form (731–TA–40)	8 Apr 1981	United Kingdom	Aluminum Recycling Assn., Inc.	Negative preliminary SLFV and injury determinations, case terminated (20 May 1981)
Tubeless tire valves (731–TA–41)	27 Apr 1981	Germany (FR)	Nylo-Flex Manufacturing Company	Negative final SLFV determination, case terminated (30 Nov 1981)
Motorcycle batteries (731–TA–42)	1 May 1981	Taiwan	Yuasa General Battery	Affirmative preliminary injury and SLFV determinations, cash deposit on case-by-case basis (14 Oct 1981); negative final SLFV determination, case terminated (31 Mar 1982)
Fresh cut roses (731–TA–43)	8 Jun 1981	Colombia	Roses, Inc.	Petition withdrawn, case terminated (30 Jun 1981)
Sorbitol (731–TA–44)	19 Jun 1981	France	Pfizer, Inc.	Affirmative final SLFV and injury determinations, cash deposit of 7 percent to 9 percent f.o.b. value (7 Apr 82); review results: cash deposit of 4 percent and 17 percent (15 Sep 1983)

B-3 ANTIDUMPING INVESTIGATIONS, 1979–85 *(continued)*

Product	Date initiated	Country involved	Initiator	Action taken
Certain steel wire nails (731–TA–45)	1 Jul 1981	Japan	US Treasury (trigger price mechanism)	Negative preliminary injury determination, case terminated (19 Aug 1981)
Certain steel wire nails (731–TA–46)	1 Jul 1981	Republic of Korea	US Treasury (trigger price mechanism)	Affirmative preliminary SLFV determination, cash deposit of 4 percent (3 Feb 1982); affirmative final SLFV determination (11 Aug 1982); order revoked (1 Oct 1985)
Certain steel wire nails (731–TA–47)	2 Jul 1981	Yugoslavia	US Treasury (trigger price mechanism)	Negative preliminary injury determination, case terminated (26 Aug 1981)
Certain amplifier assemblies and parts thereof or high-power microwave amplifiers and components thereof (731–TA–48)	5 Aug 1981	Japan	Aydin Corp.; MCL Inc.	Affirmative final SLFV and injury determinations, cash deposit on case-by-case basis (20 July 1982); average duty 0.3 percent (19 Jun 1984)
Fireplace mesh panels (731–TA–49)	19 Aug 1981	Taiwan	International Management Services Assn.	Affirmative final SLFV and injury determinations, cash deposit of 6 percent to 10 percent f.o.b. value (9 Apr 1982); duties of 5 percent to 6 percent assessed (7 Jun 1982); cash deposit of 6.4 percent (21 May 1984)
Stainless steel clad plate (731–TA–50)	6 Oct 1981	Japan	Luken's Steel Company	Affirmative final SLFV and injury determinations (29 July 1982); cash deposit of 2 percent ad valorem (8 Mar 1984); order revoked (20 Sep 1985)

Product (case number)	Date	Country	Petitioner	Outcome
Carbon steel plate (731–TA–51)	18 Nov 1981	Romania	US Treasury (trigger price mechanism)	Petition withdrawn, case terminated (8 Feb 1982)
Steel sheet piling (731–TA–52)	19 Nov 1981	Canada	US Treasury (trigger price mechanism)	Suspension Agreement (15 Sep 1982)
Stainless steel plate (731–TA–53)	30 Dec 1981	Sweden	Not available	Affirmative final SLFV determination, cash deposit of 5.2 percent (6 May 1982); cash deposit on case-by-case basis (16 Jan 1984)
Hot-rolled carbon steel plate (731–TA–54)	11 Jan 1982	Luxembourg	US Steel, Bethlehem Steel, and other steel corporations	Affirmative preliminary injury determination (3 Mar 1982); petition withdrawn, case terminated (29 Oct 1982)
Hot-rolled carbon steel plate (731–TA–55)	11 Jan 1982	Italy	US Steel, Bethlehem Steel, and other steel corporations	Affirmative preliminary injury determination (3 Mar 1982); petition withdrawn, case terminated (29 Oct 1982)
Hot-rolled carbon steel plate (731–TA–56)	11 Jan 1982	France	US Steel, Bethlehem Steel, and other steel corporations	Affirmative preliminary injury determination (3 Mar 1982); petition withdrawn, case terminated (29 Oct 1982)
Hot-rolled carbon steel plate (731–TA–57)	11 Jan 1982	Brazil	US Steel, Bethlehem Steel, and other steel corporations	Affirmative preliminary injury determination (3 Mar 1982); petition withdrawn, case terminated (29 Oct 1982)
Hot-rolled carbon steel plate (731–TA–58)	11 Jan 1982	Romania	US Steel, Bethlehem Steel, and other steel corporations	Affirmative preliminary injury determination (3 Mar 1982); petition withdrawn, case terminated (29 Oct 1982)
Hot-rolled carbon steel plate (731–TA–59)	11 Jan 1982	Netherlands	US Steel, Bethlehem Steel, and other steel corporations	Suspension of investigation based on Suspension Agreement (29 Dec 1982)

B-3 ANTIDUMPING INVESTIGATIONS, 1979–85 (*continued*)

Product	Date initiated	Country involved	Initiator	Action taken
Hot-rolled carbon steel plate (731–TA–60)	11 Jan 1982	Germany (FR)	US Steel, Bethlehem Steel, and other steel corporations	Affirmative preliminary injury determination (3 Mar 1982); petition withdrawn, case terminated (29 Oct 1982)
Hot-rolled carbon steel sheet and strip (731–TA–61)	11 Jan 1982	Germany (FR)	US Steel, Bethlehem Steel, and other steel corporations	Affirmative preliminary injury determination (3 Mar 1982); petition withdrawn, case terminated (29 Oct 1982)
Hot-rolled carbon steel sheet and strip (731–TA–62)	11 Jan 1982	United Kingdom	US Steel, Bethlehem Steel, and other steel corporations	Affirmative preliminary injury determination (3 Mar 1982); petition withdrawn, case terminated (29 Oct 1982)
Hot-rolled carbon steel sheet and strip (731–TA–63)	11 Jan 1982	Netherlands	US Steel, Bethlehem Steel, and other steel corporations	Affirmative preliminary injury determination (3 Mar 1982); petition withdrawn, case terminated (29 Oct 1982)
Hot-rolled carbon steel sheet and strip (731–TA–64)	11 Jan 1982	Luxembourg	US Steel, Bethlehem Steel, and other steel corporations	Affirmative preliminary injury determination (3 Mar 1982); petition withdrawn, case terminated (29 Oct 1982)
Hot-rolled carbon steel sheet and strip (731–TA–65)	11 Jan 1982	Italy	US Steel, Bethlehem Steel, and other steel corporations	Affirmative preliminary injury determination (3 Mar 1982); petition withdrawn, case terminated (29 Oct 1982)

Hot-rolled carbon steel sheet and strip (731–TA–66)	11 Jan 1982	France	US Steel, Bethlehem Steel, and other steel corporations	Affirmative preliminary injury determination (3 Mar 1982); petition withdrawn, case terminated (29 Oct 1982)
Hot-rolled carbon steel sheet and strip (731–TA–67)	11 Jan 1982	Belgium	US Steel, Bethlehem Steel, and other steel corporations	Affirmative preliminary injury determination (3 Mar 1982); petition withdrawn, case terminated (29 Oct 1982)
Cold-rolled carbon steel sheet and strip (731–TA–68)	11 Jan 1982	United Kingdom	US Steel, Bethlehem Steel, and other steel corporations	Affirmative preliminary injury determination (3 Mar 1982); petition withdrawn, case terminated (29 Oct 1982)
Cold-rolled carbon steel sheet and strip (731–TA–69)	11 Jan 1982	Germany (FR)	US Steel, Bethlehem Steel, and other steel corporations	Affirmative preliminary injury determination (3 Mar 1982); petition withdrawn, case terminated (29 Oct 1982)
Cold-rolled carbon steel sheet and strip (731–TA–70)	11 Jan 1982	Netherlands	US Steel, Bethlehem Steel, and other steel corporations	Affirmative preliminary injury determination (3 Mar 1982); petition withdrawn, case terminated (29 Oct 1982)
Cold-rolled carbon steel sheet and strip (731–TA–71)	11 Jan 1982	Luxembourg	US Steel, Bethlehem Steel, and other steel corporations	Affirmative preliminary injury determination (3 Mar 1982); petition withdrawn, case terminated (29 Oct 1982)
Cold-rolled carbon steel sheet and strip (731–TA–72)	11 Jan 1982	Italy	US Steel, Bethlehem Steel, and other steel corporations	Affirmative preliminary injury determination (3 Mar 1982); petition withdrawn, case terminated (29 Oct 1982)
Cold-rolled carbon steel sheet and strip (731–TA–73)	11 Jan 1982	Belgium	US Steel, Bethlehem Steel, and other steel corporations	Affirmative preliminary injury determination (3 Mar 1982); petition withdrawn, case terminated (29 Oct 1982)

B-3   ANTIDUMPING INVESTIGATIONS, 1979–85 (*continued*)

Product	Date initiated	Country involved	Initiator	Action taken
Cold-rolled carbon steel sheet and strip (731–TA–74)	11 Jan 1982	France	US Steel, Bethlehem Steel, and other steel corporations	Affirmative preliminary injury determination (3 Mar 1982); petition withdrawn, case terminated (29 Oct 1982)
Galvanized carbon steel sheet (731–TA–75)	11 Jan 1982	Belgium	US Steel, Bethlehem Steel, and other steel corporations	Affirmative preliminary injury determination (3 Mar 1982); petition withdrawn, case terminated (29 Oct 1982)
Galvanized carbon steel sheet (731–TA–76)	11 Jan 1982	France	US Steel, Bethlehem Steel, and other steel corporations	Affirmative preliminary injury determination (3 Mar 1982); petition withdrawn, case terminated (29 Oct 1982)
Galvanized carbon steel sheet (731–TA–77)	11 Jan 1982	Italy	US Steel, Bethlehem Steel, and other steel corporations	Affirmative preliminary injury determination (3 Mar 1982); petition withdrawn, case terminated (29 Oct 1982)
Galvanized carbon steel sheet (731–TA–78)	11 Jan 1982	Luxembourg	US Steel, Bethlehem Steel, and other steel corporations	Affirmative preliminary injury determination (3 Mar 1982); petition withdrawn, case terminated (29 Oct 1982)
Galvanized carbon steel sheet (731–TA–79)	11 Jan 1982	Netherlands	US Steel, Bethlehem Steel, and other steel corporations	Affirmative preliminary injury determination (3 Mar 1982); petition withdrawn, case terminated (29 Oct 1982)
Galvanized carbon steel sheet (731–TA–80)	11 Jan 1982	United Kingdom	US Steel, Bethlehem Steel, and other steel corporations	Affirmative preliminary injury determination (3 Mar 1982); petition withdrawn, case terminated (29 Oct 1982)

Product	Date	Country	Petitioner	Determination
Galvanized carbon steel sheet (731–TA–81)	11 Jan 1982	Germany (FR)	US Steel, Bethlehem Steel, and other steel corporations	Affirmative preliminary injury determination (3 Mar 1982); petition withdrawn, case terminated (29 Oct 1982)
Carbon steel structural shapes (731–TA–82)	11 Jan 1982	Belgium	US Steel, Bethlehem Steel, and other steel corporations	Affirmative preliminary injury determination (3 Mar 1982); petition withdrawn, case terminated (29 Oct 1982)
Carbon steel structural shapes (731–TA–83)	11 Jan 1982	France	US Steel, Bethlehem Steel, and other steel corporations	Affirmative preliminary injury determination (3 Mar 1982); petition withdrawn, case terminated (29 Oct 1982)
Carbon steel structural shapes (731–TA–84)	11 Jan 1982	Luxembourg	US Steel, Bethlehem Steel, and other steel corporations	Affirmative preliminary injury determination (3 Mar 1982); petition withdrawn, case terminated (29 Oct 1982)
Carbon steel structural shapes (731–TA–85)	11 Jan 1982	United Kingdom	US Steel, Bethlehem Steel, and other steel corporations	Affirmative preliminary injury determination (3 Mar 1982); petition withdrawn, case terminated (29 Oct 1982)
Carbon steel structural shapes (731–TA–86)	11 Jan 1982	Germany (FR)	US Steel, Bethlehem Steel, and other steel corporations	Affirmative preliminary injury determination (3 Mar 1982); petition withdrawn, case terminated (29 Oct 1982)
Certain seamless steel or certain pipes and tubes (731–TA–87)	20 Jan 1982	Japan	Babcock and Wilcox Company	Affirmative final SLFV and injury determinations, cash deposit of 23 percent (1 Mar 1983); waiver of deposit (8 Jun 1983)
Carbon steel wire rod (731–TA–88)	10 Feb 1982	Venezuela	Seven US producers of carbon steel wire rod	Negative final injury determination, case terminated (24 Feb 1983)

B-3 ANTIDUMPING INVESTIGATIONS, 1979–85 *(continued)*

Product	Date initiated	Country involved	Initiator	Action taken
Prestressed concrete steel wire strand (731–TA–89)	4 Mar 1982	United Kingdom	Six domestic manufacturers of prestressed concrete strand	Affirmative final SLFV determination (20 Dec 1982); negative final injury determination, case terminated (9 Feb 1983)
Chlorine (731–TA–90)	28 Apr 1982	Canada	US industry producing chlorine	Negative preliminary injury determination, case terminated (20 May 1982)
Industrial sodium nitrate (731–TA–91)	12 Apr 1982	Chile	Olin Corp.	Affirmative final SLFV and injury determinations, cash deposit $39 a short ton (25 Mar 1983); security deposit in lieu of duty (6 May 1983); cash deposit 1.4 percent ad valorem (26 Sep 1983); cash deposit 0.07 percent (4 Mar 1986)
Certain stainless steel sheet and strip products (731–TA–92)	26 Apr 1982	Germany (FR)	Tool and Stainless Steel Industry Committee; United Steelworkers of America	Affirmative final SLFV and injury determinations, cash deposit on case-by-case basis (23 Jun 1983)
Frozen french fried potatoes (731–TA–93)	12 May 1982	Canada	McCain, Inc.	Negative preliminary injury determination, case terminated (23 Jun 1982)
Bicycle tires and tubes (731–TA–94)	12 May 1982	Taiwan	Carlisle Tire and Rubber Co.	Affirmative preliminary injury and SLFV determinations (7 Dec 1982); negative final SLFV determination, case terminated (17 May 1983)

Product	Date	Country	Petitioner	Determination
Certain stainless steel sheet and strip products (731–TA–95)	13 May 1982	France	Tool and Stainless Steel Industry Committee	Affirmative final SLFV and injury determinations, duty of 4 percent to 7 percent ad valorem (29 Apr 1983); amended to cash deposit on case-by-case basis (6 Jun 1983); cash deposit of 1 percent to 10 percent ad valorem (8 Mar 1984)
Industrial nitrocellulose (731–TA–96)	7 Jul 1982	France	Hercules, Inc.	Affirmative final SLFV and injury determinations, average duty of 1.4 percent ad valorem (3 Aug 1983)
Steel rails (731–TA–97)	28 Jul 1982	Germany (FR)	CP&I Steel Corp.	Petition withdrawn, case terminated (13 Aug 1982)
Steel rails (731–TA–98)	28 Jul 1982	France	CP&I Steel Corp.	Petition withdrawn, case terminated (13 Aug 1982)
Steel rails (731–TA–99)	28 Jul 1982	United Kingdom	CP&I Steel Corp.	Petition withdrawn, case terminated (13 Aug 1982)
Certain tool steels (731–TA–100)	30 Jul 1982	Germany (FR)	Nine US producers of tool steel bars and rod; United Steelworkers of America	Affirmative final SLFV and injury determinations, cash deposit on case-by-case basis (25 Jul 1984); security deposit in lieu of duty (6 Sep 1983)
Greige polyester/cotton printcloth (731–TA–101)	5 Aug 1982	People's Republic of China	American Textile Manufacturers Institute, Inc.	Affirmative final SLFV and injury determinations, suspension of liquidation continued (6 Sep 1983); average duty of 22 percent (12 Feb 1985)
Certain radio paging and alerting receiving devices (731–TA–102)	20 Aug 1982	Japan	Motorola, Inc.	Affirmative final SLFV and injury determinations, cash deposit on case-by-case basis (16 Aug 1983)
Shop towels of cotton (731–TA–103)	26 Aug 1982	People's Republic of China	Milliken Industries, Inc.	Affirmative final SLFV and injury determinations, cash deposit on case-by-case basis (5 Oct 1983); final review: cash deposit on case-by-case basis (24 Jun 1985)

B-3 ANTIDUMPING INVESTIGATIONS, 1979–85 (continued)

Product	Date initiated	Country involved	Initiator	Action taken
High-capacity pagers	15 Sep 1982	Japan	Motorola, Inc.	Affirmative final SLFV and injury determinations, cash deposit on case-by-case basis (23 Jun 1983)
Steel rails (731–TA–104)	29 Sep 1982	Germany (FR)	CP&I Steel Corp.	Affirmative preliminary injury determination (18 Oct 1982); petition withdrawn, case terminated (10 Feb 1983)
Steel rails (731–TA–105)	29 Sep 1982	France	CP&I Steel Corp.	Affirmative preliminary injury determination (18 Oct 1982); petition withdrawn, case terminated (10 Feb 1983)
Steel rails (731–TA–106)	29 Sep 1982	United Kingdom	CP&I Steel Corp.	Affirmative preliminary injury determination (18 Oct 1982); petition withdrawn, case terminated (10 Feb 1983)
Melamine (731–TA–107)	13 Oct 1982	Brazil	Melamine Chemicals, Inc.	Negative preliminary injury determination, case terminated (10 Nov 1982)
Portland hydraulic cement (731–TA–108)	19 Oct 1982	Australia	AFL/CIO, and others	Affirmative final SLFV determination, suspension of liquidation (13 Sep 1983); negative final injury determination, case terminated (2 Nov 1983)
Portland hydraulic cement (731–TA–109)	19 Oct 1982	Japan	AFL/CIO, and others	Affirmative final SLFV determination, suspension of liquidation (13 Sep 1983); negative final injury determination, case terminated (2 Nov 1983)

Product	Date	Country	Petitioner	Determination
Bicycles (731–TA–110)	19 Oct 1982	Republic of Korea	The Bicycle Manufacturers Assn. of America, Inc.	Affirmative final SLFV determination, suspension of liquidation (11 Jul 1983); negative final injury determination (8 Sep 1983)
Bicycles (731–TA–111)	21 Oct 1982	Taiwan	The Bicycle Manufacturers Assn. of America, Inc.	Affirmative final SLFV determination, suspension of liquidation (11 Jul 1983); negative final injury determination (8 Sep 1983)
Steel wire rope (731–TA–112)	28 Sep 1982	Republic of Korea	The Committee of Domestic Steel Wire Rope and Specialty Cable Manufacturers	Negative final SLFV determination, case terminated (16 Sep 1983)
Carbon steel wire rod (731–TA–113)	30 Sep 1982	Brazil	US producers of carbon steel wire rod	Affirmative final SLFV and injury determinations, suspension of liquidation continued (7 Nov 1983); security deposit in lieu of duty (19 Dec 1983)
Carbon steel wire rod (731–TA–114)	30 Sep 1982	Trinidad and Tobago	US producers of carbon steel wire rod	Affirmative final SLFV and injury determinations, suspension of liquidation continued, cash deposit 10 percent ad valorem (16 Nov 1983)
Canned mushrooms (731–TA–115)	29 Oct 1982	People's Republic of China	Four "H" Corp.	Affirmative preliminary injury and SLFV determinations, duty 7 percent ad valorem (20 May 1983); negative final injury and SLFV determinations, case terminated (5 Oct 1983)
Certain carton-closing staples (731–TA–116)	17 Dec 1982	Sweden	International Staple and Machine Co.	Affirmative final SLFV and injury determinations, cash deposit on case-by-case basis (20 Dec 1983)
Nonautomatic carton-closing staples or staple machines (731–TA–117)	17 Dec 1982	Sweden	International Staple and Machine Co.	Affirmative final SLFV and injury determinations, cash deposit of 123 percent (20 Dec 1983); cash deposit on case-by-case basis (25 Jan 1985)

B-3 ANTIDUMPING INVESTIGATIONS, 1979–85 (*continued*)

Product	Date initiated	Country involved	Initiator	Action taken
Certain lightweight polyester filament fabric (731–TA–118)	6 Jan 1983	Japan	American Textile Manufacturers Institute	Affirmative preliminary injury and SLFV determinations (8 Aug 1983); duties of 2 percent to 11 percent ad valorem (21 Dec 1983); petition withdrawn, case terminated (1 Feb 1984)
Certain lightweight polyester filament fabric (731–TA–119)	6 Jan 1983	Republic of Korea	American Textile Manufacturers Institute	Affirmative preliminary injury and SLFV determinations, duty of 0.5 percent ad valorem (8 Aug 1983); negative final injury determination, case terminated (14 Dec 1983)
Certain tapered (journal) roller bearings and parts thereof (used for freight cars) (731–TA–120)	26 Jan 1983	Italy	Brenco, Inc.	Affirmative final SLFV determination, duty 25 percent ad valorem (19 Jan 1984); negative final injury determination (7 Mar 1984)
Certain tapered (journal) roller bearings and parts thereof (used for freight cars) (731–TA–121)	26 Jan 1983	Germany (FR)	Brenco, Inc.	Affirmative preliminary injury and SLFV determinations, duty of 12 percent ad valorem (30 Aug 1983); negative final SLFV determination, case terminated (19 Jan 1984)
Certain tapered (journal) roller bearings and parts thereof (used for freight cars) (731–TA–122)	26 Jan 1983	Japan	Brenco, Inc.	Affirmative preliminary injury and SLFV determinations, average duty of 4 percent ad valorem (30 Aug 1983); affirmative final SLFV determination, duty of 12.5 percent ad valorem (19 Jan 1984); negative final injury determination (7 Mar 1984)

Product	Date	Country	Petitioner	Determination
Certain flat-rolled carbon steel products (731–TA–123)	31 Jan 1983	Brazil	Bethlehem Steel Corp.	Affirmative final SLFV and injury determinations, suspension of liquidation, cash deposit on case-by-case basis (22 Mar 1984); order revoked (21 Aug 1985)
Fall-harvested round white potatoes, or fresh/chilled potatoes (731–TA–124)	17 Feb 1983	Canada	Maine Potato Council	Affirmative preliminary injury and SLFV determinations, average duty of 17 percent (2 Aug 1983); negative final injury determination, case terminated (29 Dec 1983)
Potassium permanganate (731–TA–125)	22 Feb 1983	People's Republic of China	Carus Chemical Company	Affirmative final SLFV and injury determinations, average duty of 40 percent ad valorem (25 Jan 1984)
Potassium permanganate (731–TA–126)	22 Feb 1983	Spain	Carus Chemical Company	Affirmative final injury determination, cash deposit of 5 percent ad valorem (19 Jan 1984); negative final SLFV determination (30 Apr 1984)
Hot-rolled carbon steel sheet (no investigation number)	22 Feb 1983	Brazil	Bethlehem Steel Corp.	Affirmative preliminary injury and SLFV determinations, suspension of liquidation (7 Sep 1983); cash deposit on case-by-case basis (22 Mar 1984)
Carbon steel plate (no investigation number)	22 Feb 1983	Brazil	Bethlehem Steel Corp.	Affirmative preliminary injury and SLFV determinations, suspension of liquidation (7 Sep 1983); cash deposit on case-by-case basis (22 Mar 1984)
Regular and high quality thin sheet glass (731–TA–127)	16 Mar 1983	Germany (FR)	Jeanette Sheet Glass Corp.	Negative preliminary injury determination, case terminated (11 May 1983)

B-3 ANTIDUMPING INVESTIGATIONS, 1979–85 (continued)

Product	Date initiated	Country involved	Initiator	Action taken
Regular and high quality thin sheet glass (731–TA–128)	16 Mar 1983	Belgium	Jeanette Sheet Glass Corp.	Negative preliminary injury determination, case terminated (11 May 1983)
Regular quality thin sheet glass (731–TA–129)	16 Mar 1983	Switzerland	Jeanette Sheet Glass Corp.	Negative preliminary injury determination, case terminated (11 May 1983)
Chloropicrin (731–TA–130)	6 Apr 1983	People's Republic of China	LCP Chemicals and Plastics; Niklor Chemical Co., Inc.	Affirmative final injury and SLFV determinations, suspension of liquidation, average duty of 58 percent ad valorem (22 Mar 1984); cash deposit of 58 percent (22 Jan 1985)
Certain circular welded carbon steel pipes and tubes (731–TA–131)	25 Apr 1983	Republic of Korea	The Committee on Pipes and Tubes	Affirmative final SLFV and injury determinations, suspension of liquidation continued, average duty 1 percent (7 May 1984); order revoked (21 Oct 1985)
Certain circular welded carbon steel pipes and tubes (731–TA–132)	25 Apr 1983	Taiwan	The Committee on Pipes and Tubes	Affirmative preliminary injury and SLFV determinations, suspension of liquidation continued, average duty of 61 percent (28 Oct 1983); affirmative final SLFV and injury determinations (7 May 1984)
Forged undercarriage components (731–TA–133)	29 Apr 1983	Italy	Seven American producers	Affirmative preliminary injury determination (22 Jun 1983); negative preliminary and final SLFV determinations, case terminated (27 Feb 1984)

Product (investigation number)	Date	Country	Petitioner	Determination
Color television receivers (731–TA–134)	2 May 1983	Taiwan	Six American producers	Affirmative final SLFV and injury determinations, average duty of 6 percent (30 Apr 1984)
Color television receivers (731–TA–135)	2 May 1983	Republic of Korea	Six American producers	Affirmative final SLFV and injury determinations, average duty of 15 percent ad valorem, (30 Apr 1984); cash deposit of 15 percent (28 Dec 1984)
Cyanuric acid and its chlorinated derivatives (731–TA–136)	3 Jun 1983	Japan	Monsato Industrial Chemicals Company	Affirmative final SLFV and injury determinations, cash deposit on case-by-case basis (27 Apr 1984)
Tubes for tires, other than for bicycle tires (731–TA–137)	11 Jul 1983	Republic of Korea	Seven US tire and rubber manufacturers	Affirmative preliminary injury determination (31 Aug 1983); negative final SLFV determination, case terminated (29 Jun 1984)
Certain rectangular welded carbon steel pipes and tubes (731–TA–138)	14 Jul 1983	Republic of Korea	Committee on Pipe and Tube Imports	Affirmative final SLFV and injury determinations, average duty 2 percent (11 May 1984); order revoked (21 Oct 1985)
Acrylic film, strips and sheets at least 0.03 inches in thickness (731–TA–139)	17 Aug 1983	Taiwan	E.I. du Pont de Nemours and Co.	Affirmative final SLFV determination, suspension of liquidation, average duty of 5 percent (23 Mar 1984); negative final injury determination (1 Jun 1984)
Certain spindle belting (731–TA–140)	9 Sep 1983	Germany (FR)	Barber Manufacturing Co.	Negative preliminary injury determination, case terminated (28 Sep 1983)
Certain spindle belting (731–TA–141)	9 Sep 1983	Italy	Barber Manufacturing Co.	Negative preliminary injury determination, case terminated (28 Sep 1983)

B-3 ANTIDUMPING INVESTIGATIONS, 1979–85 (continued)

Product	Date initiated	Country involved	Initiator	Action taken
Certain spindle belting (731–TA–142)	9 Sep 1983	Japan	Barber Manufacturing Co.	Negative preliminary injury determination, case terminated (28 Sep 1983)
Certain spindle belting (731–TA–143)	9 Sep 1983	Netherlands	Barber Manufacturing Co.	Negative preliminary injury determination, case terminated (28 Sep 1983)
Certain spindle belting (731–TA–144)	9 Sep 1983	Switzerland	Barber Manufacturing Co.	Negative preliminary injury determination, case terminated (28 Sep 1983)
Certain steel valves and certain parts thereof (731–TA–145)	22 Sep 1983	Japan	The Valve Manufacturers Assn.	Affirmative final SLFV determination, average duty of 13 percent (20 Jun 1984); negative final injury determination (8 Aug 1984)
Certain flat-rolled carbon steel products (731–TA–146)	29 Sep 1983	Belgium	Gilmore Steel Corp.	Petition withdrawn, case terminated (22 Nov 1983)
Hot-rolled carbon steel plate (731–TA–147)	29 Sep 1983	Germany (FR)	Gilmore Steel Corp.	Petition withdrawn, case terminated (22 Nov 1983)
Fresh cut roses (731–TA–148)	30 Sep 1983	Colombia	Roses, Inc.	Affirmative final SLFV determination, suspension of liquidation, cash deposit on case-by-case basis (1 Aug 1984); negative final injury determination (10 Sep 1984)
Barium chloride (731–TA–149)	25 Oct 1983	People's Republic of China	Chemical Products Corp.	Affirmative final SLFV and injury determinations, cash deposit 15 percent (17 Oct 1984)

Barium carbonate (731–TA–150)	25 Oct 1983	People's Republic of China	Chemical Products Corp.	Negative final SLFV determination, case terminated (27 Aug 1984)
Certain hot-rolled carbon steel plate (731–TA–151)	31 Oct 1983	Republic of Korea	Gilmore Steel Corp.	Affirmative final SLFV and injury determinations, cash deposit of 5 percent f.o.b. value (22 Aug 1984)
Pads for woodwind instrument keys (731–TA–152)	7 Nov 1983	Italy	Prestini Musical Instruments Corp.	Affirmative final SLFV and injury determinations, cash deposit on case-by-case basis (11 Jul 1984)
Hot-rolled carbon steel sheet (731–TA–153)	10 Nov 1983	Brazil	US Steel Corp.	Affirmative final SLFV and injury determinations, suspension of liquidation continued (11 Jul 1984); cash deposit on case-by-case basis (10 Sep 1984)
Cold-rolled carbon steel sheet (731–TA–154)	10 Nov 1983	Brazil	US Steel Corp.	Affirmative final injury determination, suspension of liquidation continued (11 Jul 1984); cash deposit on case-by-case basis (10 Sep 1984); negative final injury determination (3 Oct 1984)
Choline chloride (731–TA–155)	15 Nov 1983	Canada	Syntax Agribusiness, Inc.	Affirmative final SLFV and injury determinations, average duty 10 percent (16 Nov 1984)
Choline chloride (731–TA–156)	15 Nov 1983	United Kingdom	Syntax Agribusiness, Inc.	Affirmative preliminary injury determination (11 Jan 1984); negative final SLFV determination (18 Sep 1984)
Carbon steel wire rod (731–TA–157)	23 Nov 1983	Argentina	Six domestic steel producers	Affirmative final SLFV and injury determinations, average duty of percent (23 Nov 1984)

B-3 ANTIDUMPING INVESTIGATIONS, 1979–85 (continued)

Product	Date initiated	Country involved	Initiator	Action taken
Carbon steel wire rod (731–TA–158)	23 Nov 1983	Mexico	Six domestic steel producers	Affirmative preliminary injury determination (18 Jan 1984); negative preliminary SLFV determination (8 May 84); petition withdrawn, case terminated (6 Jul 1984)
Carbon steel wire rod (731–TA–159)	23 Nov 1983	Poland	Six domestic steel producers	Affirmative final SLFV determination, average duty of 36 percent f.o.b. value (20 Jul 1984); negative final injury determination (12 Sep 1984)
Carbon steel wire rod (731–TA–160)	23 Nov 1983	Spain	Six domestic steel producers	Affirmative final SLFV and injury determinations, average duty of 36 percent (15 Nov 1984)
Titanium sponge (731–TA–161)	1 Dec 1983	Japan	RMI Co.	Affirmative final SLFV and injury determinations, cash deposit on case-by-case basis (30 Nov 1984)
Titanium sponge (731–TA–162)	1 Dec 1983	United Kingdom	RMI Co.	Affirmative final SLFV determination, average duty of 109 percent (1 Oct 1984); negative final injury determination (15 Nov 1984)
Certain cell-site radio apparatus (transceivers) and related subassemblies thereof (731–TA–163)	30 Dec 1983	Japan	E.F. Johnson Co.	Affirmative preliminary injury and SLFV determinations, average duty of 41 percent (12 Jun 1984); affirmative final SLFV and injury determinations, average duty of 60 percent ad valorem (12 Dec 1984)

Product	Date	Country	Petitioner	Determination
Certain stainless steel sheet and strip products (751–TA–164)	20 Jan 1984	Spain	Specialty steel industry of the United States; United Steelworkers of America	Affirmative final SLFV determination, average duty of 40 percent ad valorem (10 Sep 1984); negative final injury determination (31 Oct 1984)
Acrylic sheet (751–TA–8)	26 Jan 1984	Japan	USITC	Petition dismissed on grounds that it is moot (5 Jul 1984)
Certain valves, nozzles and connectors of brass for use in fire protection systems (731–TA–165)	27 Jan 1984	Italy	Badger-Powhatan, Inc.	Affirmative preliminary injury and SLFV determinations (10 Jul 1984); affirmative final SLFV and injury determinations, average duty 1.2 percent ad valorem (27 Feb 1985)
Bicycle tires and tubes (pneumatic), redetermined from 1977 investigation (731–TA–166)	27 Jan 1984	Taiwan	Carlisle Tire and Rubber Company	Affirmative final SLFV determination, cash deposit on case-by-case basis (15 Feb 1984)
Certain table wine (731–TA–167)	27 Jan 1984	France	American Grape Growers Alliance for Fair Trade	Negative preliminary injury determination (21 Mar 1984); decision reversed to affirmative (12 Dec 1985)
Certain table wine (731–TA–168)	27 Jan 1984	Italy	American Grape Growers Alliance for Fair Trade	Negative preliminary injury determination (21 Mar 1984); decision reversed to affirmative (12 Dec 1985)
Carbon steel plate (not in coils) (731–TA–169)	10 Feb 1984	Finland	US Steel Corp.	Affirmative preliminary injury and SLFV determinations, suspension of liquidation, average duty of 23 percent ad valorem (25 Jul 1984); petition withdrawn, case terminated (29 Jan 1985)

B-3 ANTIDUMPING INVESTIGATIONS, 1979–85 (continued)

Product	Date initiated	Country involved	Initiator	Action taken
Carbon steel plate (not in coils) (731–TA–170)	10 Feb 1984	South Africa	US Steel Corp.	Affirmative preliminary injury determination, cash deposit on case-by-case basis (4 Apr 1984); petition withdrawn, case terminated (7 Jun 1984)
Carbon steel plate (not in coils) (731)–TA–171	10 Feb 1984	Spain	US Steel Corp.	Affirmative preliminary injury and SLFV determinations, cash deposit on case-by-case basis (25 Jul 1984); petition withdrawn, case terminated (29 Jan 1985)
Carbon steel plate (in coils) (731–TA–172)	10 Feb 1984	South Africa	US Steel Corp.	Affirmative preliminary injury determination, cash deposit on case-by-case basis (4 Apr 1984); petition withdrawn, case terminated (7 Jun 1984)
Carbon steel plate (in coils) (731–TA–173)	10 Feb 1984	Spain	US Steel Corp.	Affirmative preliminary injury and SLFV determinations, cash deposit on case-by-case basis (25 Jul 1984); petition withdrawn, case terminated (29 Jan 1985)
Hot-rolled carbon steel sheet (731–TA–174)	10 Feb 1984	South Africa	US Steel Corp.	Affirmative preliminary injury determination, case deposit on case-by-case basis (4 Apr 1984); petition withdrawn, case terminated (7 Jun 1984)

Product	Date	Country	Petitioner	Determination
Cold-rolled carbon steel sheet (731–TA–175)	10 Feb 1984	Argentina	US Steel Corp.	Affirmative preliminary injury and SLFV determinations, cash deposit on case-by-case basis (25 Jul 1984); affirmative final SLFV determination, average duty 30 percent (13 Dec 1984); negative final injury determination (6 Feb 1985)
Cold-rolled carbon steel sheet (731–TA–176)	10 Feb 1984	South Africa	US Steel Corp.	Affirmative preliminary injury determination, cash deposit on case-by-case basis (4 Apr 1984); petition withdrawn, case terminated (7 Jun 1984)
Cold-rolled carbon steel sheet (731–TA–177)	10 Feb 1984	Spain	US Steel Corp.	Affirmative preliminary injury and SLFV determinations, cash deposit on case-by-case basis (25 Jul 1984); petition withdrawn, case terminated (29 Jan 1985)
Galvanized carbon steel sheet (731–TA–178)	10 Feb 1984	Australia	US Steel Corp.	Affirmative preliminary injury and SLFV determinations, average duty of 36 percent (25 Jul 1984); petition withdrawn, case terminated (29 Jan 1985)
Galvanized carbon steel sheet (731–TA–179)	10 Feb 1984	South Africa	US Steel Corp.	Affirmative preliminary injury determination, cash deposit on case-by-case basis (4 Apr 1984); petition withdrawn, case terminated (7 Jun 1984)
Galvanized carbon steel sheet (731–TA–180)	10 Feb 1984	Spain	US Steel Corp.	Affirmative preliminary injury and SLFV determinations, cash deposit on case-by-case basis (25 Jul 1984); petition withdrawn, case terminated (29 Jan 1985)

B-3 ANTIDUMPING INVESTIGATIONS, 1979–85 (continued)

Product	Date initiated	Country involved	Initiator	Action taken
Carbon steel angles, shapes and sections (731–TA–181)	10 Feb 1984	South Africa	US Steel Corp.	Affirmative preliminary injury determination, cash deposit on case-by-case basis (4 Apr 1984); petition withdrawn, case terminated (7 Jun 1984)
Carbon steel angles, shapes and sections (731–TA–182)	10 Feb 1984	Spain	US Steel Corp.	Affirmative preliminary injury and SLFV determinations, cash deposit on case-by-case basis (25 Jul 1984); petition withdrawn, case terminated (29 Jan 1985)
Certain large diameter carbon steel welded pipes (731–TA–183)	21 Mar 1984	Brazil	Berg Steel Pipe Corp.	Affirmative final SLFV determination, average duty 24 percent (28 Jan 1985); petition withdrawn, case terminated (11 Mar 1985)
Potassium chloride (731–TA–184)	30 Mar 1984	Germany (DR)	Amax Chemical, Inc.; Ken McGee Chemical Corp.	Affirmative preliminary injury determination (23 May 1984); negative final SLFV determination, case terminated (31 Jan 1985)
Potassium chloride (731–TA–185)	30 Mar 1984	Israel	Amax Chemical, Inc.; Ken McGee Chemical Corp.	Affirmative preliminary injury determination (23 May 1984); negative final SLFV determination, case terminated (31 Jan 1985)
Potassium chloride (731–TA–186)	30 Mar 1984	Spain	Amax Chemical, Inc.; Ken McGee Chemical Corp.	Affirmative preliminary injury and SLFV determinations (12 Sep 1984); petition withdrawn, case terminated (26 Nov 1984)

Product	Date	Country	Petitioner	Determination
Potassium chloride (731–TA–187)	30 Mar 1984	USSR	Amax Chemical, Inc.; Ken McGee Chemical Corp.	Affirmative final SLFV determination, average duty 2 percent (31 Jan 1985); negative final injury determination (20 Mar 1985)
Lamb meat (731–TA–188)	18 Apr 1984	New Zealand	American Lamb Co.	Negative preliminary injury determination, case terminated (13 Jun 1984)
Calcium hypochlorite (731–TA–189)	25 Apr 1984	Japan	Olin Corp.	Affirmative final SLFV and injury determinations, average duty 12 percent (17 Apr 1985)
Stainless steel wire cloth (731–TA–190)	1 Jun 1984	Japan	American wire cloth industry	Affirmative final SLFV determination, average duty 3 percent (15 Mar 1985); petition withdrawn, case terminated (27 Mar 1985)
Oil country tubular goods (731–TA–191)	13 Jun 1984	Argentina	Lone Star Steel Co.	Affirmative final SLFV determination, average duty 62 percent (29 Mar 1985), negative final injury determination (22 May 1985)
Oil country tubular goods (731–TA–192)	13 Jun 1984	Brazil	Lone Star Steel Co.	Affirmative preliminary injury and SLFV determinations, average duty of 33 percent (16 Jan 1985); petition withdrawn, case terminated (11 Jun 1985)
Oil country tubular goods (731–TA–193)	13 Jun 1984	Republic of Korea	Lone Star Steel Co.	Negative preliminary SLFV determination (16 Jan 1985); petition withdrawn, case terminated (7 Jun 1985)
Oil country tubular goods (731–TA–194)	13 Jun 1984	Mexico	Lone Star Steel Co.	Affirmative preliminary injury and SLFV determinations, average duty of 21 percent (15 Jan 1985); petition withdrawn, case terminated (10 Jun 1985)

B-3 ANTIDUMPING INVESTIGATIONS, 1979–85 (continued)

Product	Date initiated	Country involved	Initiator	Action taken
Oil country tubular goods (731–TA–195)	13 Jun 1984	Spain	Lone Star Steel Co.	Affirmative final injury and SLFV determinations, cash deposit on case-by-case basis (24 May 1985); order revoked (30 Jul 1985)
Certain red raspberries (731–TA–196)	5 Jul 1984	Canada	Washington Raspberry Commission	Affirmative final injury and SLFV determinations, suspension of liquidation, cash deposit on case-by-case basis (24 Jun 1985)
Certain welded carbon steel pipes and tubes (731–TA–197)	17 Jul 1984	Brazil	Committee on Pipe and Tube Imports	Affirmative preliminary injury and SLFV determinations, cash deposit on case-by-case basis (31 Dec 1984); petition withdrawn, case terminated (27 Mar 1985)
Certain welded carbon steel pipes and tubes (731–TA–198)	17 Jul 1984	Brazil	Committee on Pipe and Tube Imports	Affirmative preliminary injury and SLFV determinations, cash deposit on case-by-case basis (31 Dec 1984); petition withdrawn, case terminated (8 Feb 1985)
Certain salted codfish (731–TA–199)	1 Aug 1984	Canada	Codfish Corp.	Affirmative final injury and SLFV determinations, suspension of liquidation, cash deposit on case-by-case basis (8 Jul 1985)
Radial ply tires for passenger cars (731–TA–200)	1 Aug 1984	Republic of Korea	Armstrong Rubber Co., and others	Negative preliminary injury determination (19 Sep 1984)
Egg filler flats (731–TA–201)	15 Aug 1984	Canada	Keyes-Fibre Co.	Affirmative final SLFV determination, average duty of 15 percent (7 Jun 1985); negative final injury determination (24 Jul 1985)

Date	Product	Country	Petitioner	Status
15 Aug 1984	Dry-cleaning machinery (751–TA–9)	Germany (FR)	USITC	Administrative review results: finding of dumping, cash deposit on case-by-case basis (11 Mar 1985)
17 Aug 1984	Tubular metal framed stacking chairs (731–TA–202)	Italy	Frazier Engineering, Inc.	Affirmative final SLFV determination, cash deposit on case-by-case basis (29 May 1985); negative final injury determination (17 Jul 1985)
17 Aug 1984	Tubular metal framed stacking chairs (731–TA–203)	Taiwan	Frazier Engineering, Inc.	Negative preliminary and final SLFV determinations, case terminated (29 May 1985)
21 Sep 1984	Grand and upright pianos (731–TA–204)	Republic of Korea	Aeolian Pianos, Inc., and others	Affirmative preliminary injury determination (15 Nov 1984); negative preliminary and final SLFV determinations (16 Sep 1985)
3 Oct 1984	Carbon steel wire rod (731–TA–205)	Germany (DR)	Atlantic Steel Co., and others	Affirmative preliminary injury and SLFV determinations, average duty of 26 percent ad valorem (12 Mar 1985); petition withdrawn, case terminated (1 Aug 1985)
11 Oct 1984	Fabric and expanded neoprene laminate (731–TA–206)	Japan	Rubatex Corp.	Affirmative final injury and SLFV determinations, suspension of liquidation, average duty of 3 percent, cash deposit on case-by-case basis (24 Jul 1985)
15 Nov 1984	Cellular mobile telephones and subassemblies thereof (731–TA–207)	Japan	Motorola, Inc.	Affirmative final injury and SLFV determinations, cash deposit on case-by-case basis (19 Dec 1985)
28 Nov 1984	Barbed wire and barbless wire strand (731–TA–208)	Argentina	Forbes Steel and Wire Corp.	Affirmative final injury and SLFV determinations, cash deposit of 6... percent ad valorem (13 Nov...)

B-3 ANTIDUMPING INVESTIGATIONS, 1979–85 (*continued*)

Product	Date initiated	Country involved	Initiator	Action taken
Barbed wire and barbless wire strand (731–TA–209)	28 Nov 1984	Brazil	Forbes Steel and Wire Corp.	Affirmative preliminary injury and SLFV determinations, duty of 48 percent (3 May 1985); petition withdrawn, case terminated (14 Aug 1985)
Barbed wire and barbless wire strand (731–TA–210)	28 Nov 1984	Poland	Forbes Steel and Wire Corp.	Affirmative preliminary injury and SLFV determinations, duty of 57 percent (3 May 1985); petition withdrawn, case terminated (22 Jul 1985)
Certain welded carbon steel pipes and tubes (731–TA–211)	18 Dec 1984	Taiwan	Committee on Pipe and Tube Imports	Affirmative final SLFV determination, cash deposit of 7 percent ad valorem (12 Dec 1985); negative final injury determination (24 Jan 1986)
Certain welded carbon steel pipes and tubes (731–TA–212)	18 Dec 1984	Venezuela	Committee on Pipe and Tube Imports	Affirmative preliminary injury and SLFV determinations, duty of 26 percent (3 Jun 1985); petition withdrawn, case terminated (19 Jul 1985)
Carbon steel plates (731–TA–213)	19 Dec 1984	Czechoslovakia	US Steel Corp.	Affirmative preliminary injury and SLFV determinations (13 Feb 1985); petition withdrawn, case terminated (4 Jun 1985)
Carbon steel plates (731–TA–214)	19 Dec 1984	Germany (DR)	US Steel Corp.	Affirmative preliminary injury and SLFV determinations, cash deposit on case-by-case basis (3 Jun 1985); petition withdrawn, case terminated (19 Aug 1985)

Product	Date	Country	Petitioner	Determination
Carbon steel plates (731–TA–215)	19 Dec 1984	Hungary	US Steel Corp.	Affirmative preliminary injury determination (13 Feb 1985); petition withdrawn, case terminated (4 Jun 1985)
Carbon steel plates (731–TA–216)	19 Dec 1984	Poland	US Steel Corp.	Affirmative preliminary injury and SLFV determinations, average duty of 15 percent ad valorem (3 Jun 1985); petition withdrawn, case terminated (19 Aug 1985)
Carbon steel plates (731–TA–217)	19 Dec 1984	Venezuela	US Steel Corp.	Affirmative preliminary injury and SLFV determinations, average duty of 5 percent ad valorem (3 Jun 1985); petition withdrawn, case terminated (17 Jul 1985)
Carbon steel plates (in coils) (731–TA–218)	19 Dec 1984	Finland	US Steel Corp.	Petition withdrawn, case terminated (7 Feb 1985)
Hot-rolled carbon steel sheet (731–TA–219)	19 Dec 1984	Austria	US Steel Corp.	Affirmative preliminary injury and SLFV determinations (3 Jun 1985); affirmative final SLFV determination, duty of 2.2 percent ad valorem (19 Aug 1985); negative final injury determination (12 Dec 1985)
Hot-rolled carbon steel sheet (731–TA–220)	19 Dec 1984	Finland	US Steel Corp.	Petition withdrawn, case terminated (31 Jan 1985)
Hot-rolled carbon steel sheet (731–TA–221)	19 Dec 1984	Hungary	US Steel Corp.	Affirmative preliminary injury determination (13 Feb 1985); petition withdrawn, case terminated (4 Jun 1985)
Hot-rolled carbon steel sheet (731–TA–222)	19 Dec 1984	Romania	US Steel Corp.	Affirmative preliminary injury and SLFV determinations, average duty of 50 percent ad valorem (3 Jun 1985); petition withdrawn, case terminated (11 Jul 1985)

B-3 ANTIDUMPING INVESTIGATIONS, 1979–85 (continued)

Product	Date initiated	Country involved	Initiator	Action taken
Hot-rolled carbon steel sheet (731–TA–223)	19 Dec 1984	Venezuela	US Steel Corp.	Affirmative preliminary injury and SLFV determinations, average duty of 5 percent ad valorem (3 Jun 1985); petition withdrawn, case terminated (19 Jul 1985)
Cold-rolled carbon steel sheets and plates (731–TA–224)	19 Dec 1984	Austria	US Steel Corp.	Affirmative preliminary injury and SLFV determinations, average duty of 33 percent ad valorem (3 Jun 1985); negative final SLFV determination (19 Aug 1985); case terminated (12 Sep 1985)
Cold-rolled carbon steel sheets and plates (731–TA–225)	19 Dec 1984	Czechoslovakia	US Steel Corp.	Affirmative preliminary injury determination (13 Feb 1985); petition withdrawn, case terminated (4 Jun 1985)
Cold-rolled carbon steel sheets and plates (731–TA–226)	19 Dec 1984	Germany (DR)	US Steel Corp.	Affirmative preliminary injury and SLFV determinations, cash deposit on case-by-case basis (3 Jun 1985); petition withdrawn, case terminated (19 Aug 1985)
Cold-rolled carbon steel sheets and plates (731–TA–227)	19 Dec 1984	Finland	US Steel Corp.	Petition withdrawn, case terminated (31 Jan 1985)
Cold-rolled carbon steel sheets and plates (731–TA–228)	19 Dec 1984	Romania	US Steel Corp.	Affirmative preliminary injury and SLFV determinations, average duty of 63 percent ad valorem (3 Jun 1985); petition withdrawn, case terminated (19 Jul 1985)

Product	Date	Country	Petitioner	Determination
Cold-rolled carbon steel sheets and plates (731–TA–229)	19 Dec 1984	Venezuela	US Steel Corp.	Affirmative preliminary injury and SLFV determinations, average duty of 4.8 percent ad valorem (3 Jun 1985); petition withdrawn, case terminated (19 Jul 1985)
Galvanized carbon steel sheets (731–TA–230)	19 Dec 1984	Austria	US Steel Corp.	Negative preliminary injury determination (13 Feb 1985)
Galvanized carbon steel sheets (731–TA–231)	19 Dec 1984	Germany (DR)	US Steel Corp.	Negative preliminary injury determination (13 Feb 1985)
Galvanized carbon steel sheets (731–TA–232)	19 Dec 1984	Romania	US Steel Corp.	Negative preliminary injury determination (13 Feb 1985)
Galvanized carbon steel sheets (731–TA–233)	19 Dec 1984	Venezuela	US Steel Corp.	Negative preliminary injury determination (13 Feb 1985)
Carbon steel angles and shapes (731–TA–234)	19 Dec 1984	Norway	US Steel Corp.	Affirmative preliminary injury and SLFV determinations, average duty of 0.9 percent ad valorem (3 Jun 1985); affirmative final SLFV determination, duty of 14 percent ad valorem (23 Oct 1985); negative final injury determination (12 Dec 1985)
Carbon steel angles and shapes (731–TA–235)	19 Dec 1984	Poland	US Steel Corp.	Affirmative preliminary injury and SLFV determinations, average duty of 33 percent ad valorem (3 Jun 1985); negative final SLFV determination (19 Aug 1985); case terminated (12 Sep 1985)
Certain castor oil products (731–TA–236)	27 Dec 1984	Brazil	American Manufacturers of Castor Oil Products	Affirmative preliminary injury and SLFV determinations, cash deposit on case-by-case basis (1 Aug 1985); affirmative final SLFV determination, cash deposit on case-by-case basis (19 Dec 1985); negative final injury determination (6 Feb '

B-3 ANTIDUMPING INVESTIGATIONS, 1979–85 (continued)

Product	Date initiated	Country involved	Initiator	Action taken
Hydrogenated castor oil (731–TA–237)	27 Dec 1984	Brazil	American Manufacturers of Castor Oil Products	Affirmative preliminary injury and SLFV determinations, cash deposit on case-by-case basis (1 Aug 1985); negative final SLFV determination (19 Dec 1985); case terminated (15 Jan 1986)
12 volt motorcycle batteries (731–TA–238)	11 Jan 1985	Taiwan	General Battery Corp.	Negative preliminary injury determination (25 Feb 1985)
Rock salt (731–TA–239)	25 Jan 1985	Canada	International Salt Company	Affirmative preliminary injury and SLFV determinations, suspension of liquidation, cash deposit on case-by-case basis (15 Jul 1985); affirmative final SLFV determination (4 Dec 1985); negative final injury determination (24 Jan 1986)
Photo albums and photo album fillers (731–TA–240)	30 Jan 1985	Hong Kong	Esselte Pendaflex Inc., and others	Affirmative final injury and SLFV determinations, cash deposit of 3.7 percent ad valorem (29 Oct 1985)
Photo albums and photo album fillers (731–TA–241)	30 Jan 1985	Republic of Korea	Esselte Pendaflex Inc., and others	Affirmative final injury and SLFV determinations, suspension of liquidation, average duty of 65 percent (29 Oct 1985)
Tapered tubular steel transmission structures (731–TA–242)	11 Feb 1985	Republic of Korea	Not available	Petition withdrawn, case terminated (7 Mar 1985)
Certain expansion tanks (731–TA–243)	14 Feb 1985	Netherlands	Amtrol, Inc.	Negative preliminary injury determination (10 Apr 1985)

Product	Date	Country	Petitioner	Determinations
Natural bristle paint brushes (731–TA–244)	19 Feb 1985	People's Republic of China	US paint brush manufacturers and suppliers	Affirmative preliminary injury and SLFV determinations, weighted average margin 211 percent (2 Aug 1985); affirmative final injury and SLFV determinations, weighted average margin 127 percent (14 Feb 1986)
Low-fuming brazing copper wire and rod (731–TA–245)	19 Feb 1985	France	American Brass Co.	Negative preliminary injury determination (10 Apr 1985)
Low-fuming brazing copper wire and rod (731–TA–246)	19 Feb 1985	New Zealand	American Brass Co.	Affirmative final injury and SLFV determinations, average duty of 27 percent ad valorem (21 Oct 1985)
Low-fuming brazing copper wire and rod (731–TA–247)	19 Feb 1985	South Africa	American Brass Co.	Affirmative final injury and SLFV determinations, averaged duty of 3.3 percent ad valorem (29 Jan 1986)
Certain ethyl alcohol (fuel ethanol) (731–TA–248)	25 Feb 1985	Brazil	Ad Hoc Committee of Domestic Fuel Ethanol Producers	Affirmative preliminary injury and SLFV determinations, cash deposit on case-by-case basis (25 Sep 1985); affirmative final injury and SLFV determinations, cash deposit on case-by-case basis (11 Mar 1986)
Oil country tubular goods (731–TA–249)	28 Feb 1985	Austria	US Steel Corp.	Affirmative preliminary injury and SLFV determinations, average duty of 2.9 percent ad valorem (14 Aug 1985); petition withdrawn, case terminated (7 Jan 1986)
Oil country tubular goods (731–TA–250)	28 Feb 1985	Romania	US Steel Corp.	Affirmative preliminary injury determination (24 Apr 1985); petition withdrawn, case terminated (9 Aug 1985)

B-3 ANTIDUMPING INVESTIGATIONS, 1979–85 (continued)

Product	Date initiated	Country involved	Initiator	Action taken
Oil country tubular goods (731–TA–251)	28 Feb 1985	Venezuela	US Steel Corp.	Affirmative preliminary injury determination (24 Apr 1985); petition withdrawn, case terminated (19 Aug 1985)
Certain welded carbon steel pipes and tubes (731–TA–252)	28 Feb 1985	Thailand	Committee on Pipe and Tube Imports	Affirmative preliminary injury and SLFV determinations, 1.8 percent ad valorem subtracted for deposit (3 Oct 1985); affirmative final injury and SLFV determinations, suspension of liquidation, average cash deposit of 15.6 percent on case-by-case basis (11 Mar 1986)
Certain welded carbon steel pipes and tubes (731–TA–253)	28 Feb 1985	Venezuela	Committee on Pipe and Tube Imports	Affirmative preliminary injury and SLFV determinations, average duty of 55.7 percent f.o.b. port value (13 Aug 1985); petition withdrawn, case terminated (27 Nov 1985)
Heavy walled rectangular welded carbon steel pipes and tubes (731–TA–254)	25 Mar 1985	Canada	Several steel companies	Affirmative final SLFV determination, cash deposit on case-by-case basis (22 Nov 1985); negative final injury determination (12 Feb 1986)
Animal feed grade DL-methionine (731–TA–255)	3 Apr 1985	France	Degussa Corp.	Negative preliminary injury determination (30 May 1985)
Carbon steel wire rod (731–TA–256)	8 Apr 1985	Poland	Several steel companies	Affirmative preliminary injury determination (30 May 1985); negative preliminary SLFV determination (19 Sep 1985)

Product (case number)	Date	Country	Petitioner	Determination
Carbon steel wire rod (731–TA–257)	8 Apr 1985	Portugal	Several steel companies	Affirmative preliminary injury and SLFV determinations, average duty of 24.6 percent ad valorem (23 Sep 1985); petition withdrawn, case terminated (20 Nov 1985)
Carbon steel wire rod (731–TA–258)	8 Apr 1985	Venezuela	Several steel companies	Affirmative preliminary injury determination (30 May 1985); petition withdrawn, case terminated (30 Aug 1985)
Offshore platform jackets and piles (731–TA–259)	18 Apr 1985	Republic of Korea	Kaiser Steel Corp.	Affirmative preliminary injury and SLFV determinations, average duty of 25 percent ad valorem (25 Nov 1985)
Offshore platform jackets and piles (731–TA–260)	18 Apr 1985	Japan	Kaiser Steel Corp.	Affirmative preliminary injury and SLFV determinations, cash deposit on case-by-case basis (25 Nov 1985)
12-volt lead-acid type automotive storage batteries (731–TA–261)	8 May 1985	Republic of Korea	General Battery International Corp.	Negative preliminary injury determination (3 Jul 1985)
Iron construction castings (731–TA–262)	13 May 1985	Brazil	Municipal Castings Fair Trade Council	Affirmative preliminary injury and SLFV determinations, suspension of liquidation, cash deposit of 68.3 percent (28 Oct 1985); affirmative final SLFV determination, cash deposit on case-by-case basis (19 Mar 1986)
Iron construction castings (731–TA–263)	13 May 1985	Canada	Municipal Castings Fair Trade Council	Affirmative final injury and SLFV determinations, suspension of liquidation, cash deposit on case-by-case basis (16 Jan 1986)

B-3 ANTIDUMPING INVESTIGATIONS, 1979–85 *(continued)*

Product	Date initiated	Country involved	Initiator	Action taken
Iron construction castings (731–TA–264)	13 May 1985	India	Municipal Castings Fair Trade Council	Affirmative preliminary injury and SLFV determinations, suspension of liquidation, cash deposit on case-by-case basis (28 Oct 1985); affirmative final SLFV determination (19 Mar 1986)
Iron construction castings (731–TA–265)	13 May 1985	People's Republic of China	Municipal Castings Fair Trade Council	Affirmative preliminary injury and SLFV determinations, suspension of liquidation, average duty of 25.5 percent (28 Oct 1985); affirmative final SLFV determination, duty of 11.7 percent ad valorem (19 Mar 1986)
Certain steel wire nails (731–TA–266)	5 Jun 1985	People's Republic of China	Several steel companies	Affirmative preliminary injury and SLFV determinations, suspension of liquidation, average duty of 8 percent ad valorem (9 Jan 1986); affirmative final SLFV determination, average duty of 6.3 percent (25 Mar 1986)
Certain steel wire nails (731–TA–267)	5 Jun 1985	Poland	Several steel companies	Affirmative preliminary injury determination (31 Jul 1985); petition withdrawn, case terminated (30 Aug 1985)
Certain steel wire nails (731–TA–268)	5 Jun 1985	Yugoslavia	Several steel companies	Affirmative preliminary injury and SLFV determinations (31 Jul 1985); suspension of liquidation, cash deposit of 84.76 percent (20 Nov 1985); petition withdrawn, case terminated (3 Feb 1986)

Product (case number)	Date	Country	Petitioner	Determination
Nylon impression fabric (731–TA–269)	10 Jun 1985	Japan	Bomont Industries	Affirmative preliminary injury determination (31 Jul 1985); negative preliminary SLFV determination (6 Dec 1985)
64K Dynamic random access memory components (731–TA–270)	24 Jun 1985	Japan	Micron Technology, Inc.	Affirmative preliminary injury and SLFV determinations, suspension of liquidation, cash deposit on case-by-case basis (11 Dec 1985)
Certain carbon steel welded pipes and tubes (731–TA–271)	16 Jul 1985	India	Committee on Pipe and Tube Imports	Affirmative preliminary injury and SLFV determinations, suspension of liquidation, cash deposit on case-by-case basis (31 Dec 1985); affirmative final SLFV determination, duty 7 percent ad valorem (17 Mar 1986)
Certain carbon steel welded pipes and tubes (731–TA–272)	16 Jul 1985	Turkey	Committee on Pipe and Tube Imports	Affirmative preliminary injury and SLFV determinations, cash deposit 12.78 percent for standard pipe and 32.55 percent for line pipe (3 Jan 1986)
Certain carbon steel welded pipes and tubes (731–TA–273)	16 Jul 1985	Taiwan	Committee on Pipe and Tube Imports	Affirmative preliminary injury and SLFV determinations, cash deposit 27.9 percent (31 Dec 1985); affirmative final SLFV determination, duty of 28 percent ad valorem (14 Mar 1986)
Certain carbon steel welded pipes and tubes (731–TA–274)	16 Jul 1985	Yugoslavia	Committee on Pipe and Tube Imports	Affirmative preliminary injury and SLFV determinations, cash deposit 31.2 percent (31 Dec 1985); affirmative final SLFV determination, duty of 32.3 percent ad valorem (14 Mar 1986)
Oil country tubular goods (731–TA–275)	22 Jul 1985	Argentina	Lone Star Steel Co.	Affirmative preliminary injury and SLFV determinations, average duty 18.1 percent (27 Jan 1986)

B-3 ANTIDUMPING INVESTIGATIONS, 1979–85 (continued)

Product	Date initiated	Country involved	Initiator	Action taken
Oil country tubular goods (731–TA–276)	22 Jul 1985	Canada	Lone Star Steel Co.	Affirmative preliminary injury and SLFV determinations, cash deposit on case-by-case basis (7 Jan 1986)
Oil country tubular goods (731–TA–277)	22 Jul 1985	Taiwan	Lone Star Steel Co.	Affirmative preliminary injury and SLFV determinations, average duty of 5.81 percent ad valorem (7 Jan 1986)
Cast iron pipe fittings (731–TA–278)	31 Jul 1985	Brazil	Cast Iron Pipe Fittings Committee	Affirmative preliminary injury and SLFV determinations, suspension of liquidation, average duty of 4.59 percent, cash deposit on case-by-case basis (14 Jan 1986); affirmative final SLFV determination, duty of 5.6 percent ad valorem (31 Mar 1986)
Cast iron pipe fittings (731–TA–279)	31 Jul 1985	Republic of Korea	Cast Iron Pipe Fittings Committee	Affirmative preliminary injury and SLFV determinations, suspension of liquidation, average duty of 13.3 percent, cash deposit on case-by-case basis (14 Jan 1986); affirmative final SLFV determination, average duty 12.5 percent ad valorem (31 Mar 1986)
Cast iron pipe fittings (731–TA–280)	31 Jul 1985	Taiwan	Cast Iron Pipe Fittings Committee	Affirmative preliminary injury and SLFV determinations, cash deposit on case-by-case basis (14 Jan 1986); affirmative final SLFV determination, cash deposit on case-by-case basis (31 Mar 1986)

Product (case number)	Date	Country	Petitioner	Determination/status
Non-malleable cast iron pipe fittings (731–TA–281)	31 Jul 1985	Taiwan	Cast Iron Pipe Fittings Committee	Affirmative preliminary injury determination (25 Sep 1985); negative preliminary SLFV determination (14 Jan 1986); petition withdrawn, case terminated (28 Mar 1986)
Petroleum wax candles (731–TA–282)	4 Sep 1985	People's Republic of China	National Candle Assn.	Affirmative preliminary injury and SLFV determinations, average duty of 135 percent ad valorem (7 Mar 1986)
Certain table wine (731–TA–283)	10 Sep 1985	Italy	American Grape Growers Alliance for Fair Trade	Negative preliminary injury determination (30 Oct 1985)
Certain table wine (731–TA–284)	10 Sep 1985	France	American Grape Growers Alliance for Fair Trade	Negative preliminary injury determination (30 Oct 1985)
Certain table wine (731–TA–285)	10 Sep 1985	Germany (FR)	American Grape Growers Alliance for Fair Trade	Negative preliminary injury determination (30 Oct 1985)
Anhydrous sodium metasilicate (731–TA–286)	16 Sep 1985	United Kingdom	PQ Corp.	Affirmative preliminary injury and SLFV determinations, average duty of 3.9 percent ad valorem (3 Mar 1986)
In-shell pistachio nuts (731–TA–287)	26 Sep 1985	Iran	California Pistachio Commission	Affirmative preliminary injury and SLFV determinations, average duty of 192 percent (11 Mar 1986)
Erasable programmable read only memories (EPROMS) (731–TA–288)	30 Sep 1985	Japan	Intel Corp.	Affirmative preliminary injury and SLFV determinations, cash deposit on case-by-case basis (17 Mar 1986)
Welded steel wire fabric for concrete reinforcement (731–TA–289)	24 Oct 1985	Italy	Wire Reinforcement Institute	Petition withdrawn, case terminated (14 Nov 1985)

B-3 ANTIDUMPING INVESTIGATIONS, 1979–85 (continued)

Product	Date initiated	Country involved	Initiator	Action taken
Welded steel wire fabric for concrete reinforcement (731–TA–290)	24 Oct 1985	Mexico	Wire Reinforcement Institute	Petition withdrawn, case terminated (14 Nov 1985)
Welded steel wire fabric for concrete reinforcement (731–TA–291)	24 Oct 1985	Venezuela	Wire Reinforcement Institute	Petition withdrawn, case terminated (14 Nov 1985)
Certain welded carbon steel pipes and tubes (731–TA–292)	13 Nov 1985	People's Republic of China	Committee on Pipe and Tube Imports	Affirmative preliminary injury determination (8 Jan 1986)
Certain welded carbon steel pipes and tubes (731–TA–293)	13 Nov 1985	Philippines	Committee on Pipe and Tube Imports	Affirmative preliminary injury determination (8 Jan 1986)
Standard welded carbon steel pipes and tubes (731–TA–294)	13 Nov 1985	Singapore	Committee on Pipe and Tube Imports	Affirmative preliminary injury determination (8 Jan 1986)
Heavy-walled rectangular pipes and tubes (731–TA–295)	13 Nov 1985	Singapore	Committee on Pipe and Tube Imports	Negative preliminary injury determination (8 Jan 1986)
Light-walled rectangular pipes and tubes (731–TA–296)	13 Nov 1985	Singapore	Committee on Pipe and Tube Imports	Affirmative preliminary injury determination (8 Jan 1986)
Welded steel wire fabric for concrete reinforcement (731–TA–289A)	20 Nov 1985	Italy	Wire Reinforcement Institute	Negative preliminary injury determination (15 Jan 1986)

Product	Date	Country	Petitioner	Determination
Welded steel wire fabric for concrete reinforcement (731–TA–290A)	20 Nov 1985	Mexico	Wire Reinforcement Institute	Negative preliminary injury determination (15 Jan 1986)
Welded steel wire fabric for concrete reinforcement (731–TA–291A)	20 Nov 1985	Venezuela	Wire Reinforcement Institute	Negative preliminary injury determination (15 Jan 1986)
Porcelain on steel cooking ware (731–TA–297)	4 Dec 1985	Mexico	General Housewares Corp.	Affirmative preliminary injury determination (30 Jan 1986)
Porcelain on steel cooking ware (731–TA–298)	4 Dec 1985	People's Republic of China	General Housewares Corp.	Affirmative preliminary injury determination (30 Jan 1986)
Porcelain on steel cooking ware (731–TA–299)	4 Dec 1985	Taiwan	General Housewares Corp.	Affirmative preliminary injury determination (30 Jan 1986)
Dynamic random access memory semiconductors of 256 kilobits and above (731–TA–300)	17 Dec 1985	Japan	US Department of Commerce	Affirmative preliminary injury and SLFV determinations, cash deposit on case-by-case basis (19 Mar 1986)

, Francis M., 90
er, Raymond A., 5n, 13n, 23n, 24n, 140n, 145n, 150n
ayard, Thomas O., 140n
Beef quotas, 32, 93, 202
Belgium, 21
Bello, Judith H., 127n, 137n, 138n
Bentsen, Lloyd, 75, 83, 139n, 148, 180, 205n, 200, 226, 236
Benzenoid chemicals, 63, 95n
Bergsten, C. Fred, 25n, 38n, 52n, 78, 158, 169n, 171n, 175n, 179n, 181n, 186n, 191n, 210n, 218n, 233n
Berkeley Roundtable on the International Economy (BRIE), 155
Berliner, Diane T., 23n, 125n
Bethlehem Steel Corp., 133
"Bicycle theory," 15
Bingaman, Jeff, 102n
Blumenthal, W. Michael, 18, 68, 89, 203n
Board of Trade, 203n
Bolling Committee, 59
Bolts, nuts, and screws, 119
Bonker, Don, 206
Bradley, Bill, 148
Branson, William H., 42
Brazil, 47, 83, 106, 126, 128n, 130, 236
Bressand, Albert, 158
Bretton Woods system, 38
Britain, 46, 51, 91, 106, 128, 129, 186n, 237
British Steel Corp., 128
Brock, William E., 71–72, 78–81, 85, 86, 88, 100–104, 106–8, 134–35, 207, 209, 214, 224, 226, 229–32, 234, 237
Bromine, 79, 227, 230
Budget deficit, 107, 157, 170, 177, 185, 210, 233–34
    European Community, 182
Bureau of the Budget, 97
Burke-Hartke quota bill, 75, 114, 160
Burns, Arthur, 170
Business Roundtable, 77, 138, 158, 161, 184
Byrd, Harry F., Sr., 17
Byrd, Robert C., 225

Cabinet Council on Commerce and Trade, 101
Cabinet Council on Economic Affairs, 190–91
Calhoun, John C., 10
Camps, Miriam, 48n
Canada, 51, 128n, 189
Canned foods, 113
Cannon, Joe, 26
Capital flows, 52–54, 157, 181, 185
Carbon steel. See Steel industry
Carter administration, 30, 61–62, 66–68, 70, 95, 118–19
    export politics, 93
    steel TPM, 25, 120
    TAA support, 141, 217
    USTR relationship, 87, 99–100, 108
Cassidy, Robert C., Jr., 63n, 64n, 65, 66n
Caterpillar, Inc., 178
Caves, Richard E., 220n
Chafee, John H., 147, 220, 234
Chamber of Commerce, 138, 151, 161
Chamberlain, Neville, 4
Cheese import quotas, 32, 67
China, People's Republic of, 5, 129–30, 132, 162
Chrysler Corp., 70, 194
Cigarettes, 179
Citrus fruit quotas, 93, 202
Clark, Timothy B., 128n
Clayton, Will L., 17
Cline, William R., 76n, 167n, 169n, 171n, 179n, 181n, 215, 233n
Coelho, Tony, 148
Cohen, Stephen D., 70n, 98n
Cohen, William S., 69
Commerce Department, 17, 44, 88, 89, 94, 102, 106, 179, 202, 205, 234
    conflict with USTR, 88, 101, 201, 203
    proposal to abolish, 203
    trade relief authority, 99, 100, 123, 125, 128, 129
Commercial attachés, 99
Committee on. See specific committee names
Common Market. See European Community
Communism, 5
Comparative advantage, 42

Garten, Jeffrey E., 53n
General Agreement on Tariffs and
    Trade (GATT), 4, 5, 10, 24, 34, 88,
    99
  agricultural import quotas, 32
  Article VI, antidumping and
    countervailing duty measures,
    20, 63, 111
  Article XIX, escape clause, 20, 48–
    49, 111
  diminished effectiveness, 37, 48–49,
    55
  ministerial talks, 102, 103, 107, 209
General Motors Corp., 70
Generalized system of preferences
    (GSP), 78–81, 160, 224, 227–31
Gephardt, Richard A., 74, 80, 83, 148,
    236
Germany, 4, 46, 51, 84, 92, 106, 129,
    186n, 237
Gibbons bill, 136–39
Gibbons, Sam M., 71, 73, 80, 83, 107,
    135–38, 155, 193, 228–30
Glennon, Michael J., 63n, 64n, 65n,
    66n
Gloves, 63
Goldstein, Judith, 4–5, 149
Government Operations Committee,
    House, 68
Government procurement, 11, 48, 62,
    69, 93, 95, 215
Governmental Affairs Committee,
    Senate, 102
Gowa, Joanne, 38n
Graham, Thomas R., 66n
Gramm-Rudman-Hollings law, 186,
    217
Green, Carl J., 131n
"Green tube" controversy, 231
Greenwald, John C., 132
Grossman, Gene M., 155n
Group of Five, 52, 106, 158, 186, 210
Grubel, Herbert G., 113n

Hall, H. Keith, 112n
Hart, Gary, 148, 155
Hartke, Vance, 75, 146
Hathaway, William D., 92–93
Havana Charter, 32
Hayes, Philip, 128n

Heinz, John, 68, 76, 121, 129, 218,
    225
Helms, Jesse, 130
Herter, Christian A., 18, 89, 108
Heston, Alan, 42n
High-technology industries, 41–42,
    216
  sectoral reciprocity, 214–15
  see also specific industries
Hitler, Adolf, 4
Hodin, Michael W., 25n, 120n
Hollings, Ernest F., 27, 61, 83, 236
Holmer, Alan F., 127n, 137n, 138n
Holmes, Oliver Wendell, Jr., 141
Hong Kong, 7, 24, 78, 181n, 224
Hoover, Herbert C., 88, 145
Horlick, Gary, 126n
Houdaille case, 132, 137
House committees. See specific
    committee names
Hufbauer, Gary Clyde, 23n, 115, 116n,
    117n, 120n, 128n, 140n, 209n,
    218
Hull, Cordell, 1, 4, 10, 12, 13, 15, 16,
    29, 101

IBM Corp., 162
Import ratio, 169–70, 212
Import relief. See Trade remedies
Import surcharge, proposed, 188–89,
    236
Import valuation, as political issue,
    44–45, 179n
Income per capita, 42, 46, 47n
Industrial policy, 144, 152–58, 192–96
Industrial targeting, 136–39, 154–55,
    159
Industries Assistance Commission of
    Australia, 220
Industry-specific protection, 75–78,
    83–86, 232–33
Inflation, 49–50, 171
Intellectual property rights, 231
Interest equalization tax, 39
Interest-group politics, 143, 158–63
International Trade Administration,
    Department of Commerce, 100,
    203

McCulloch, Rachel, 198n
McDonald, Alonzo L., 91
McDonald, David J., 21
Machine tools industry, 35, 132, 137, 159, 160, 166
McIntyre, Thomas J., 115
McKinley Tariff of 1890, 10, 14n
McKinnon, Ronald I., 190n
Macroeconomic policy, impact on trade balance, 177–92
Malmgren, Harald B., 18, 64n, 90, 130n
Managed trade, 166, 172
Management and Budget, Office of, 108
Manley, John F., 28n
Mann, Thomas E., 26n, 66n
Market-Oriented Sector-Specific (MOSS) talks, 215, 233, 234
Marks, Matthew J., 64n
Marris, Stephen, 157n, 170n, 181n, 212n
Mathias, Charles McC., 190
Mayhew, David R., 58n
Meany, George, 146
Meat import quotas, 62
Meese, Edwin, 101, 102, 107, 201
Merchandise trade deficit. See Trade deficit
Metzenbaum, Howard M., 226
Metzger, Ronald I., 70n
Mexico, 20, 46, 47, 130, 137
Middle East, 49
"Mills bill," 28, 60
Mills, Wilbur D., 17, 27–28, 58–61, 85, 90
Ministry of International Trade and Industry (MITI), Japan, 19, 71, 167, 202, 235
Moffett, A. Toby, 67, 73
Mondale, Walter F., 81, 146–48, 155, 165, 227, 228
"Most favored nation" (MFN) principle, 15, 224
Motorcycles, 148, 159, 166
Motorola Co., 159, 160
Moynihan, Daniel P., 218
MTN codes, 11, 48, 68, 215
Multi-Fiber Arrangement (MFA), 24, 68, 83–84, 235
Multilateral Trade Negotiation (MTN), 11, 48. See also Tokyo Round

Nader, Ralph, 161
Nakasone, Yasuhiro, 83, 104, 179, 233
National Association of Manufacturers, 161
National Bureau of Economic Research (NBER), 154–55
National Security Council, 18, 97, 108, 202, 204
National security import relief, 23, 166
Natural resource subsidies, 137–39, 230
Nelson, Douglas R., 112n
Neustadt, Richard E., 107–8
Newly industrializing countries (NICs), 7, 47, 49, 55, 81, 224, 227, 230, 231
Nippon Telephone and Telegraph (NTT), 93, 202, 234
Nissan Motor Co., 71, 72
Nixon administration, 30, 45, 49
dollar devaluation, 1971, 37–40
NTB procedures, 63–64
STR relationship, 18, 87, 90, 107
textile protection, 24, 27, 28, 30, 33, 90, 144
Nontariff barriers (NTBs), 34–35, 48, 51, 62, 82, 95, 115, 121, 139, 141, 232
"fast-track" procedures, 63–69, 209

Odell, John S., 38n, 162n, 201n
Offsets. See Antidumping measures; Countervailing duty measures
Oil industry, 23, 37, 40, 41, 49, 69, 137
Oleszek, Walter J., 59n
Olmer, Lionel H., 101
Olson, Mancur, 2n, 157n
Omnibus trade bill of 1986, House, 74, 139–40, 148, 149, 174, 206–7, 210, 214, 218
O'Neill, Thomas P. (Tip), 74, 78, 148, 236
Opinion polls, 5, 143, 149–52
Opinion Research Corp. (ORC), 152
Oppenheimer, Bruce I., 206n
Orderly marketing agreements (OMAs), 49, 71, 92, 118
Organization for Economic Cooperation and Development (OECD), 116

Organization of Petroleum Exporting
Countries (OPEC), 49
Ornstein, Norman J., 26n, 66n
Ottinger, Richard L., 72, 73

Packard, David, 159–60
Packwood, Bob, 180, 235
Paper products, 179
Partisan politics, 29–30, 143–49, 163,
165
Pastor, Robert A., 9n, 16n, 21n
Patrick, Hugh, 154n
Patterson, Gardner, 46n
Pauly, Peter, 189n
Pearce, William R., 3n, 18
Pease, Donald J., 230
"Peril point," 20–21
Petersen, Christian E., 189n
Petersen, Howard C., 17
Peterson, Peter G., 90
Pharmaceuticals, 233
Policy Development, Office of, 204n
Policy entrepreneurship, 74–76
Political party alignments, 29–30,
143–49
Pool, Ithiel de Sola, 5n, 13n, 23n, 24n,
140n, 145n, 150n
Porter, Roger, 118n
Preeg, Ernest H., 47n
Private-sector advisory committees,
94–96, 216
Process protectionism, 85, 139–40,
142, 174, 210
Procurement codes, 11, 48, 62, 69, 93,
95, 215
Product standards codes, 11, 34, 48,
62, 68, 95
Productivity, 195–96
Public opinion, 5, 143, 150–52

Quasi-judicial procedures. See Trade
remedies

Randall, Clarence B., 17
Randall Commission, 17, 21, 22
Rashish, Myer N., 17

Rayburn, Sam, 23
Reagan administration, 50, 74, 79, 84,
103–7, 206, 208, 214, 216, 233,
236–37
auto industry protection, 70, 83,
166, 167, 179–80, 234, 235
steel protection, 77–78, 134–35
TAA curtailment, 141, 217
textile protection, 130, 162, 174
trade policy position, 147–48, 163,
173
USTR relationship, 100–107
Reciprocal Trade Agreements Act of
1934, 1, 10, 14, 16, 62, 144
Reciprocity. See Sectoral reciprocity
Regan, Donald T., 104, 109, 234
Reich, Robert, 155 , 195n
Reifman, Alfred, 76
Retaliation, Sec. 301 authority, 117,
120, 122, 125, 135, 139, 173, 208
Ribicoff, Abraham A., 61, 98, 99
Richardson, J. David, 76n, 116n,
141n, 155n, 198n
Rightor-Thornton, Anne H., 89n
Rivers, Richard R., 65, 66, 92
Roderick, David M., 130
Rohatyn, Felix G., 156
Roosevelt administration, 16, 29, 107
Rosen, Howard F., 128n, 140n, 218
Rosovsky, Henry, 154n
Rostenkowski, Dan, 74, 80–83, 85,
148, 207, 228–33, 232, 236
Roth, William M., 18, 89, 108
Roth, William V., Jr., 92, 98, 198n,
201, 202, 204n, 218
Rowen, Hobart, 104, 183n
Rubber footwear, 95n
Ruggie, John Gerard, 34n
"Rules, The." See Trade remedies

Safeguards. See Escape clause
Sato, Hideo, 24n, 25n, 28n, 47n, 70n,
90n, 93n, 120n, 198n, 215n
Saxonhouse, Gary R., 154n
Schattschneider, E. E., 1, 11, 16n, 29,
159n, 222
Schneider, William, 151–52, 184n
Schott, Jeffrey J., 209n, 218n
Schultze, Charles L., 155–56, 196

Chinese exports, 129–30, 162
export restraints, 22–24, 27–28, 31–
33, 49, 61–62, 68, 69, 103, 166
GSP exclusion, 78, 224
import statistics, 167, 171
interest-group politics, 158–60
Jenkins bill, 174, 200
1984 Act, 80, 226, 227, 230
quota bill, 27–28, 39, 82–84, 90,
105, 200
Thurmond, Strom, 83, 130
Thurow, Lester, 183n
Tokyo Round, 40, 48, 51, 62n, 67,
114, 116, 126, 166
Toyota Motor Corp., 71, 72
Trade Act of 1974, 15, 62n, 121, 160
"fast-track" procedures
authorization, 64, 67, 68
generalized system of preferences,
78, 224
private-sector advisory committees,
94
remedies available under, 114–17,
140
Section 201, 114. *See also* Escape
clause
Section 301, retaliation authority,
117, 120, 122, 125, 135, 139,
173, 208
STR provision, 18, 87, 91
Trade adjustment assistance (TAA),
36, 70, 82, 146, 160, 232
demise of, 140–41
eligibility criteria, 115
funding, 218
reform proposals, 216–20
relief provided, 21–22, 111, 140
relief record, 113, 118
Trade Agreements Act of 1979, 66–68,
114, 121–23, 219
Trade and Tariff Act of 1984, 87, 148,
163, 166, 167, 173
enactment and provisions, 78–82,
223–32
Trade balance
imbalance, political consequences
of, 43–45, 171–72, 209–14
macroeconomic policies affecting,
181–92, 197
1980s imbalance, 7, 157–58, 169–71,
178

postwar figures, 11, 35
Smoot-Hawley effects, 9
with Japan, 41, 178–81
Trade Barrier Assessment Agency,
proposed, 220
Trade deficit
evolution and effects, 43–45, 54
1980s rise, 7, 78, 104, 169–70, 223–
24
1984, 82, 178, 233
1985, 169, 237
1986, 210
recommended threshold for new
legislation, 188, 211–12
with Japan, 44, 76, 83, 104, 178–79,
233, 237
Trade department proposal, 87, 98–99,
102, 104, 156, 198, 201
Trade Expansion Act of 1962, 29, 62,
67, 144
escape clause relief, 113, 114
STR establishment, 17–18, 87, 89
TAA authorization, 21–22, 111, 146
Trade, proposed House Ad Hoc
Committee on, 206
Trade law reform, 68, 225
Trade Policy Council, proposed, 203n
Trade reconciliation procedure,
proposed, 207
Trade remedies, 19–22, 29, 57, 82, 99,
109, 111–42, 158, 166, 199, 208,
236
dilemma and limits of, 35–36, 141–
42
early relief denial, 112–14
Gibbons bill, 135–39, 229
as import harassment, 131–33
1974 Act provisions, 114–20
1979 Act provisions, 121–23
1980s relief record, 123–27
1986 bill, process protectionism,
84–85, 139–40, 174
political pressure exerted by
petitioners employing, 127–30,
133–35, 140, 165, 174, 200, 219
political role of, 19–22, 35–36, 111–
12
reform attempts, 135–40, 229
types available, 19–22, 111
see also specific industries and
remedies